Charles Dickens and Georgina Hogarth

Manchester University Press

Charles Dickens and Georgina Hogarth

A curious and enduring relationship

Christine Skelton

MANCHESTER UNIVERSITY PRESS

The right of Christine Skelton to be identified as the author of this work has been asserted in accordance with the Copyright, Designs and Patents Act 1988.

Published by Manchester University Press
Oxford Road, Manchester M13 9PL

www.manchesteruniversitypress.co.uk

British Library Cataloguing-in-Publication Data
A catalogue record for this book is available from the British Library

ISBN   978 1 5261 6608 1   hardback

First published 2023

Typeset
by New Best-set Typesetters Ltd
Printed in Great Britain
by Bell & Bain Ltd, Glasgow

For my goddaughter, Kate Aston.

Contents

Illustrations

Figure 1 is taken from Alan S. Downer, *The Eminent Tragedian: William Charles Macready* (London: Oxford University Press, 1966). Every effort has been made to trace copyright holders. Figures 2, 4, 5, 8, 10, 14, 16, 17, 19, 23, 25, 26, 27, 28 and 29 are reproduced by courtesy of the Charles Dickens Museum, London. Figure 3 is reproduced by courtesy of the Meynell Archive. Figure 7 is reproduced by permission of Alamy. Figures 15, 18 and 22 are reproduced by permission of the National Portrait Gallery, London. Figure 21 is reproduced by courtesy of the Metropolitan Museum of Art. Figure 30 is reproduced by permission of the E. O. Hoppé Estate Collection. All other images are from Wikimedia Commons.

Acknowledgements

I am especially grateful to the people I have met through the Dickens Fellowship; the renowned Dickens scholar, Professor Michael Slater, gave me his time and expertise in helping shape the narrative; Paul Graham sent me a copy of Georgina's will when I was just starting my investigation; and Professor Jenny Hartley has shared her vast knowledge and wisdom with me on several occasions. Lunch with Catherine Dickens's biographer, Lillian Nayder, whose exhaustive and detailed research I have drawn on extensively, offered an opportunity to hear about her insights into the Hogarth sisters. The staff of the Charles Dickens Museum have offered support and taken an interest in my project, especially the Director, Cindy Sughrue, and I am particularly grateful for the tremendous assistance given by the senior curators of the Charles Dickens Museum, Louisa Price and her successor Emily Dunbar, as well as Frankie Kubicki. Gail David-Tellis has generously shared her own research on Georgina Hogarth with me.

I am indebted to all the librarians and museum archivists who have searched their collections seeking out material relating to Georgina Hogarth, especially Dr John Boneham, Reference Specialist (Rare Books and Music) at the British Library; staff at the Henry E. Huntington Library, Hertfordshire Archives and Local Studies, and those at Senate House Library, University of London. I am grateful to Mark Dickens for his permission to search Georgina's

Acknowledgements

bank accounts and to Tracey Earl, Coutts Bank Archivist, for authorisation to cite from these ledgers. Thanks also to Jon Burroughs for sending me a copy of a letter from Georgina that is in his possession; Catherine Wynne, author of *Lady Butler: War Artist and Traveller, 1846–1933* for providing me with information about Lady Butler's mother, Christiana Weller; and Oliver Meynell at the Meynell Archive who not only granted permission for the reproduction of Christiana Weller's image, but reminded me of an incident concerning Dickens and a particularly eye-catching waistcoat.

At Manchester University Press, Emma Brennan has been exceptional in her encouragement and support for this project, from my initial approach through to publication. Lucy Burns was another brilliant editor from whom I learned a great deal.

Members of the University of the Third Age, History's People group, kindly read and commented on early drafts of the introduction, and special thanks to Stephen, Tricia, Ann, Barbara and Carolyn.

Friends and family have been unendingly patient and supportive. Many of them appear to have inadvertently found themselves acting as unpaid staff. My sister, Tricia, provided help with the technology, and my friend of more years than we care to remember, Jane, found herself taking on the role of research assistant (she is no doubt still recovering from the many hours spent in the archives of RBS taking down notes as I searched through forty years of Georgina's bank statements). Both Jane and David have listened endlessly as I tried out different titles and chapter headings, uncomplainingly tolerated my recounting sections of the manuscript, and accompanied me on walks around the streets of London and Higham, tracing Dickens and Georgina's footsteps. My dear friend, Kathryn Ecclestone, is another star in my eyes. She used her journalistic skills to edit early drafts and has read through the book on several occasions, while all the time engaging with the story of Dickens and Georgina's complex relationship.

A note on language

There are several women with the name of 'Catherine' in this book. To avoid confusion, Catherine Dickens is referred to as Catherine throughout although there are quotations from Dickens's letters where he calls her 'Kate'. Their second daughter was also Kate, but usually called 'Katey' (sometimes spelled Katie or Katy) by her family and friends; I have referred to her as Katey. Catherine's best friend, Catherine Macready, was always known by her full first name after marriage but as Kitty before then; I have retained use of the shortened version for clarity. The appearance of any other 'Catherine' or 'Kate' in the text is accompanied by a surname.

In keeping with the language of the day, I have used gender-specific nouns e.g. actress/actor and Henry Mayhew's categorisation and use of the term 'prostitutes' in *London Labour and the London Poor* (1851), referring to women who exchanged sexual services for economic benefit.

The Dickens family tree

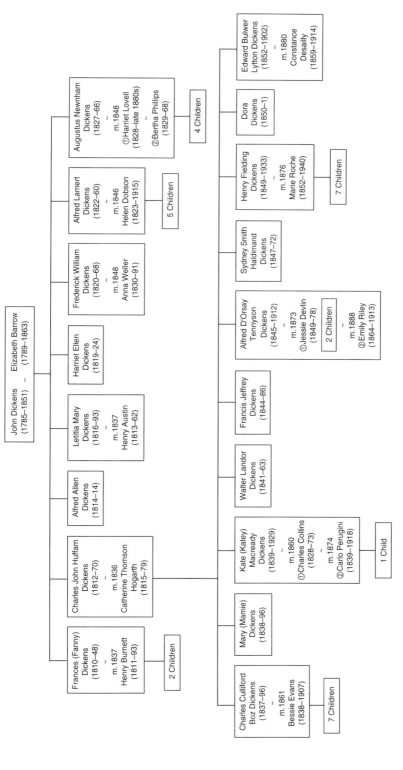

Please see the Who's who on p. 233 for biographical information on the Dickens and Hogarth families, and other people mentioned in the book.

The Hogarth family tree

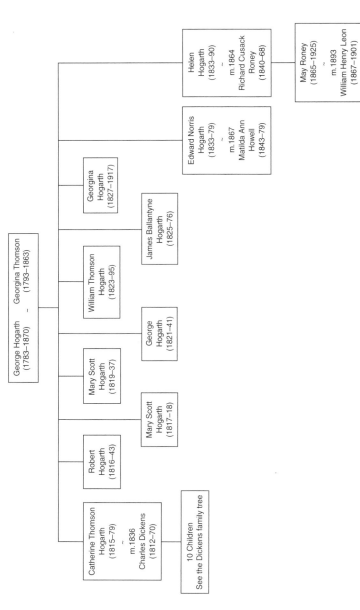

George Hogarth (1783–1870) ~ Georgina Thomson (1793–1863)

- Catherine Thomson Hogarth (1815–79)
  ~
  m.1836
  Charles Dickens (1812–70)
  - 10 Children
    See the Dickens family tree
- Robert Hogarth (1816–43)
- Mary Scott Hogarth (1817–18)
- Mary Scott Hogarth (1819–37)
- George Hogarth (1821–41)
- James Ballantyne Hogarth (1825–76)
- William Thomson Hogarth (1823–95)
- Georgina Hogarth (1827–1917)
- Edward Norris Hogarth (1833–79)
  ~
  m.1867
  Matilda Ann Howell (1843–79)
- Helen Hogarth (1833–90)
  ~
  m.1864
  Richard Cusack Roney (1840–68)
  - May Roney (1865–1925)
    ~
    m.1893
    William Henry Leon (1867–1901)

Introduction

Charles Dickens's personal life was as fascinating as his novels. Discovering that such a pillar of Victorian respectability reputedly kept a mistress the same age as his younger daughter, was rumoured to have fathered children with his sister-in-law and, according to a neighbour, tried to have his wife committed to a mental asylum when he grew tired of her, is irresistibly compelling. In the first fifty or so years after Dickens's death, his family attempted to suppress conjecture and to maintain his image as a sincere and honourable man. They were largely successful, thanks mainly to his sister-in-law, Georgina Hogarth. A younger sister of Dickens's wife, Catherine, Georgina moved into the Dickens household when she was fifteen. She was one of the women rumoured to be the cause of the Dickenses' marital separation, gossip that was fuelled further by Georgina staying on after Dickens banished Catherine from the family residence. For twenty-eight years Georgina shared his home and was with him when he had a fatal stroke at their Gad's Hill house in 1870. Knowing only too well that speculation in England and America about his relationships with women had attracted substantial newspaper interest, it was either a mischievous or mocking Dickens who provoked further gossip in his last will and testament. In it, Dickens dealt Catherine a final punishing blow for not being the wife he had wanted by referring to his alleged mistress, Ellen Ternan, while praising Georgina fulsomely as his 'best and truest friend'. Dickens made Georgina guardian of his youngest child, left her all his private papers and the treasured personal objects from his study, as well as the vast sum of £8,000 (£1 million today).[1] Unfounded accusations of an affair between Dickens and his sister-in-law have persisted into the twenty-first century, and yet, regardless of his evident admiration for Georgina, there have been few attempts to examine their very close attachment.

Dickens and Georgina's profound, enduring affection for one another and their central place in each other's life are both noteworthy and curious. The fact that their deep bond was forged in a period when power and prestige lay in the hands of men is significant given the disparities between the older, successful Dickens and the younger, dependent Georgina. Furthermore, there was little consistency in their relationship as, throughout their years together, they played a range of different roles at different times. When Georgina joined the Dickens household, she was a child and Dickens was *in loco parentis*, but their father–daughter relationship was soon replaced by a teenage Georgina developing a crush on her celebrity brother-in-law. It was when Georgina reached adulthood that they entered a new stage as she and Dickens forged a genuine friendship. Along with Catherine, the three of them were affectionate and convivial company for one another. Everything changed again when Dickens instigated a separation from Catherine and rumours spread about Georgina being the cause of the marital split. By remaining with Dickens after Catherine was forced to move out, Georgina scandalised middle-class Victorian society. As a means of presenting an acceptable face to the public, they embarked upon another new chapter when Dickens designated Georgina as assistant housekeeper to his eldest daughter, effectively making them employer and employee. In Dickens's own words, Georgina remained family (his 'wife's sister'), but he also referred to her as his 'servant housekeeper'.[2]

Four years after they had settled into this new arrangement, Dickens's intimacy with Ellen Ternan took a turn that devastated

Georgina and shifted relations between her and Dickens once again. On learning that Dickens had lied and that his association with Ellen Ternan was more than that of a guardian, Georgina had a mental and physical breakdown. The crisis brought Dickens and Georgina closer together as her illness shook him out of his, by now, somewhat complacent attitude towards his sister-in-law. A final stage was reached in Dickens's remaining years, whereby they maintained a deeply affectionate and mutually reliant, if unequal, alliance. He was the centre point in her life; she was a constant, low-key but essential, presence in his. What is curious – and the question this book attempts to answer – is how their affection for one another survived given the different phases and often difficult changes their relationship went through.

Without acknowledging Catherine's presence in the life of her sister and husband, it is impossible to understand how the alliance between Georgina and Dickens developed. Although Georgina came to define herself so closely to Dickens that '[t]o a large extent her life was his life', this cannot be fully explained without considering the role her relationship with Catherine played in bringing this about.[3] Catherine helped to raise her younger sister and acted as a guide as Georgina learned to negotiate Victorian social protocols in making the transition from girl to young woman. They did everything together, from visiting friends, attending the same social events, being with the children, to carrying out domestic duties. For many years the sisters apparently enjoyed a harmonious relationship, but, as her later comments showed, the negative opinions Georgina expressed about Catherine were formed during these years. At the time of the collapse of the Dickenses' marriage, Georgina's admiration for Dickens, combined with his flattery, saw her adding her voice to Dickens's in listing all the aspects of Catherine she disliked. Dickens spoke about Georgina's role in his family as a corrective to Catherine: the loving aunty in comparison to the alleged unloving mother; the woman cherished by himself and the children as opposed to Catherine who, according to Dickens, was distant and impossible to become attached to. The two women aligned themselves differently to Dickens. Where Catherine saw herself as a mother, friend and sister, as well as 'Mrs Dickens', Georgina clung to her identity as 'sister-in-law of Charles Dickens', to the point that the descriptor appears on her gravestone.

Given the pressure of Victorian expectations on middle-class women, the ties between Georgina and Catherine were always bound to come under strain as the younger sister reached adulthood. There had been nothing unusual about Georgina moving in with the Dickenses, as children were often sent to live temporarily with another family member because of parental ill health or financial difficulties. The problems started when Georgina was still there in her twenties. While Catherine and Georgina were from the same privileged middle class, they were divided by age and status. Joining the household as a younger sister came with its own obligations; Georgina was, after all, closer in age to the Dickenses' eldest daughter than to Catherine and was required to defer to her sister. Expectations of behaviour were laid down in popular household-management and etiquette books. Every aspect of social behaviour, from how to act and dress, who was allowed to speak and when, what to do and say, and even how to say it, were set out. For example, when carrying out the daily ritual of calling at the homes of friends and acquaintances, Georgina, as the younger woman, was obliged to follow in the steps of Catherine and never assert herself. Young women were told that, when visiting, they needed to wait to catch the eye of the mistress of the house before speaking and then only to express interest in her home and family. Georgina was expected to dress more modestly than Catherine, according to her station as a family member living on the charity of her relations. One imagines the frustrations caused by these social rules to a teenage girl expected always to show subservience to her elder sister.

In terms of status, as the unmarried sister-in-law to the master of the house, Georgina was less significant than the married Catherine. The discovery in the 1851 census that there were 500,000 'excess' (i.e. unmarried) women gave rise to concerns about how these so-called 'surplus' females should be dealt with.[4] Emigration was considered as a possible solution, but whether it was to include middle-class as well as working-class women was not specified. Only around 10 to 15 per cent of the 500,000 'surplus' women were middle class, and by 1851 Georgina was one of these. Georgina's unmarried condition may have been a social problem, but in other ways she was in a stronger position than Catherine. As a married woman, Catherine was subject to the law of coverture, where a woman's legal rights and obligations were subsumed by those of her husband. In other words, a woman could only retain a legal identity if single or widowed. Yet for most women the anticipation of loving companionship, long-term financial security and status meant marriage was both a desirable and expected goal. Georgina's refusal of two proposals has been interpreted as a 'choice'. While the concept of choice is debatable, what is certain is that by remaining in the Dickens home, her lingering presence as a stand-in for her sister meant Catherine had to share the limited authority she had in managing the household.

For Catherine, being mistress of a household allowed her to possess a small amount of power. Although this power was largely symbolic, women were able to wield a degree of influence within the home by being in charge of household organisation and the management of servants.[5] As Kay Boardman writes, the title, mistress of the house, 'had meaning because of what it represented rather than because of what she actually did'.[6] As Georgina stepped in to cover for Catherine during her frequent pregnancies and confinements, this symbolic representation continued, but their shared role diluted their individual power. Catherine's biographer, Lillian Nayder, rightly criticises those who present 'the Hogarth sisters as natural antagonists and competitors vying for primacy at Dickens's side', emphasising instead their situations as 'a product of social circumstances and expectations'.[7] Nevertheless, accepting this as a dilemma does not detract from the reality of Georgina's difficult balancing act of trying to claim some authority for herself within the household without invading Catherine's territory.

Exacerbating these tensions was Dickens himself. Victorian domesticity may have been regarded as a woman's domain, but it was still the master of the house who maintained control. The expectation that men worked outside the home, while women managed the private, domestic sphere, did not apply to the Dickenses.[8] Not only was their home also Dickens's workplace until 1850, but Catherine struggled to maintain control of the domestic organisation because of her husband's insistence on managing his surroundings. His constant watchful eye hampered Catherine's opportunities to exercise the small degree of authority she had as mistress of the house. John Forster, Dickens's biographer and close friend, had to admit that Dickens was 'personally interested in every detail … of the four walls within which [he] live[d]' and exhibited the 'kind of interest in a house which is commonly confined to women'.[9] His involvement in how the house looked and was run went far beyond 'interest', however, and Catherine (and later Georgina) were relegated to a position where they had no jurisdiction and were simply left to follow his instructions. Dickens's meticulous supervision of his household helps to explain why later generations of the family questioned Dickens's much-lauded praise of Georgina's housekeeping skills. In 1946, Dickens's grandson defended Georgina from the allegations of an affair between her and his grandfather, describing how '[t]he story that she was a wicked conspirator is a myth', adding, 'as is, I fear, the story, that is accepted as a fact, that she was a perfect housekeeper and wonderful manager of his affairs and upbringer of his children. In fact, she was nothing of the sort.'[10]

Dickens's celebrity status was another significant factor in his relationships with not only Georgina, but Catherine and the rest of his family. He was considered to be a 'man of genius'; it was a phrase often used in the Victorian period to single out those who possessed rare abilities in their chosen field. Being labelled as a 'man of genius' afforded this group even greater social privileges. Given that power resided solely in the hands of men, especially those who were white and middle or upper class, we might wonder what added benefits these 'men of genius' could expect. Dickens's friend John Forster explained that everyone outside this exalted group should be prepared to expect and tolerate behaviour that would be criticised in other men: 'Men of genius are different from what we suppose them to be. They have greater pleasures and greater pains, greater affections and greater temptations, than the generality of mankind, and they can never altogether be understood by their fellow men.'[11]

When it came to the aspect of celebrity that involved female admirers, Dickens did not need any encouragement to believe he could do whatever he liked. He enjoyed female attention and was a terrific flirt, but it was far less fun for Catherine and Georgina, who would often find themselves pushed aside as the fans tried to attract Dickens's eye. When Catherine, who was generally sympathetic to his young fans, complained of his over-familiarity with them, he accused her of jealousy. Georgina's biographer mistakenly claimed that she never felt any jealousy towards other women. She later confessed to feelings of jealousy but dealt with it by befriending any woman whom Dickens approved of. Regardless of how accepting Georgina and Catherine were, Dickens's celebrity profile added another level of scrutiny to their reputations as respectable, middle-class women.

A problem for Georgina and Catherine was Dickens's tendency to flout social rules without recognising the impact this had on them. His mercurial temperament meant he could be both the austere master of the house and the relaxed author who described his domestic environment as reflecting that of a casual 'artist kind of life'.[12] It was the easy-going Dickens who told friends and acquaintances to ignore social etiquette ('pray do me the favour to have no ceremony with me') and was publicly affectionate with his children (he always 'kissed his boys, just as he did Mamie and

Katie').[13] Nonetheless, as Nancy Weston reminds us about Dickens, 'When we step away from the world of the novels to the world of his life, not surprisingly, we find an Englishman of his time and place.'[14] Weston is right in that respectability mattered to him, and while he could ignore Victorian etiquette rules, he expected his wife and sister-in-law to be seen to conform to social conventions. At literary salons, Dickens mixed freely with, and befriended, the Countess of Blessington and Mrs Caroline Norton, who were both regarded as having dubious reputations. This left Catherine and Georgina to negotiate if, and how, they could invite or call on these women deemed socially unacceptable without risking their own good names. The contradiction between what was publicly tolerated from a male celebrity, while his middle-class female friends and family could be condemned by association, was illustrated at the time of the Dickenses' marital breakdown. When newspapers reported on Dickens's decision to separate from Catherine, eyes turned to the other woman in the house, Georgina, as the culprit.

Dickens scholars have never given any credence to rumours of an affair between Dickens and Georgina or the suggestion they had children together, but it is a scandal that refuses to go away and continues to attract media interest. A by-product of this rumour mill is that Georgina's reputation and significance in Dickens's life has been subject to constant speculation. At best, she has been described as a 'fly in the ointment' of the Dickenses' marriage and, at worst, she stands accused of being either a 'yes-woman' who stayed with Dickens at his insistence, or a manipulator who usurped Catherine because she wanted to be mistress of the house.[15] Most recently, she has been implicated in a plot to transfer a dying Dickens from Ellen Ternan's house back to Gad's Hill.[16] In telling the story of the lifelong relationship between Dickens and Georgina, this book not only unpicks the usual descriptors associated with her role – 'confidante', 'housekeeper', 'adviser' – but puts into context the events underpinning the scandalous rumours.

Dickens and Georgina's complex and shifting relationship raises many questions about Georgina herself. What happened to propel Georgina from a confident, happy young woman to a quasi-religious acolyte? What were the events that shaped the fifteen-year-old girl, regarded by her sister and brother-in-law as a delight to have around, into the often sharp-tongued and somewhat self-righteous woman who emerged after Dickens's death? How did she progress from being an admirer of her brother-in-law to displaying an almost religious devotion, 'fervent to the point of obsession', where her every action and word were informed by what she thought Dickens would do and say?[17] And why did Georgina turn against her sister Catherine? As the Dickenses' marriage began to collapse, Georgina not only backed Dickens's claims that Catherine was unloving and an unfit mother, but repeated them when she must have known they were untrue. Why was Georgina prepared to fall out with her family and risk her reputation to remain with Dickens after he exiled Catherine from the family home? Why did the Dickenses' daughter Katey say it was 'the greatest mistake ever' to invite a sister to live with a husband and wife?[18]

Dickens was a prolific letter writer and, such was his fame and popularity, anyone receiving mail from him preserved it. The vast archive that exists on Dickens means we have extensive insight into his views of his family, friends and colleagues, as well as a range of other subjects. Unfortunately, he destroyed all the letters he received, including those from Georgina. Although she could not bring herself to go as far as her brother-in-law, Georgina admitted to their solicitor, Frederic Ouvry, that she had burned many of his letters and from others had cut out numerous passages that she felt were too personal for publication.[19] While, like Dickens, Georgina also wrote copious letters to friends, she was not famous, and many of her missives were not kept. The majority of those that have survived were penned after Dickens's death. As one of his executors, she exercised her rights to both defend and promote his reputation, resulting in an abundance of letters to solicitors and biographers as well as close friends. However, Georgina was determined to preserve Dickens's privacy and was generally very cautious in what she said in the interviews she gave to Dickens's biographers. What is largely absent from the archive of material on Georgina are letters she wrote during Dickens's lifetime. She often acted as his secretary in corresponding with friends, but she was delivering Dickens's words, not her own opinions.

Arthur Adrian devoted two-thirds of his biography of Georgina to the years following Dickens's death, when her voice can clearly be heard. It is, though, still possible to get a sense of Georgina during Dickens's lifetime from various sources. Her brief correspondence with Edward Bulwer-Lytton at the beginning and end of the 1850s, reveals her as a passionate young woman but one who was under strain by the end of the decade. Georgina occasionally made personal observations in the letters she sent on Dickens's behalf to friends. There are, too, contemporary references to Georgina to be found in the letters, journals and articles of the friends and acquaintances of Dickens and his family.

In the letters Georgina wrote to their most intimate friends after Dickens's death there are occasions when she refers to the years between 1842, when she joined the Dickens household, and 1870. Particularly revealing are the letters written over the course of more than forty years to Annie Adams Fields, with whom she was more openly reflective about her time with Dickens than with any of her other correspondents. The fifty-two letters to Percy Fitzgerald, although he was regarded as a close family friend, indicate she was not prepared to give away too much information about family matters.[20]

While on first reading, Georgina's letters to Fitzgerald, Annie Fields, Frederic Ouvry and the children and their spouses appear to reveal a great deal – and there are many examples of when she became so exasperated with a person or something that happened that she made her feelings and opinions known – this is not wholly accurate.[21] A second reading indicates she rarely disclosed anything about Dickens or close family that might hint at a scandal. For example, Georgina never mentioned Ellen Ternan, even to those people who knew of her, although she spoke of other friends, and hid from family members the fact that Mamie died of alcoholism. With people Georgina reconnected with many years after Dickens's death, or met when she was in her seventies, such as the youngest daughter of Harrison Ainsworth and new friends Horace and Jane Pym, she said little about Dickens or her sister and their children, perhaps because these people did not know the family well enough.

Further sources of information are the insights gained from Georgina's bank accounts as to how she lived her life after Dickens's death. Arthur Adrian's handwritten notes of an interview he conducted with William Macready's granddaughter present interesting insights into Georgina as a spirited elderly woman, with opinions on current affairs and a fund of entertaining – but never contentious – stories about Dickens and his friends. There are too the observations Georgina made about Dickens's working patterns, his wife and their friends, which she made in interviews and letters to authors writing biographies of Dickens or his literary colleagues. She was not always completely honest, though; for example, she provided misleading observations about Catherine in A. Ward's *Dickens* (1882).

There are many instances in this book where Dickens's actions towards women are questionable, to say the least. His own daughter, Katey, described how her father 'did not understand women', and in recent times he has been regarded by some as a 'cruel misogynist' who had a problem with women.[22] It is not my intention to condone or excuse Dickens's behaviour, rather we must acknowledge it within its context. As the historian Margaret MacMillan reminds us:

> To understand the people of the past we must start by respecting the fact ... they were shaped by different social structures and their ideas came from different sources than our own ... and also remind ourselves that we cannot expect them to think things that hadn't yet been discovered or articulated.[23]

Wherever and whenever possible the book employs women's views on Dickens and other 'men of genius'. These voices explain how they experienced being attracted to, pursued by, or simply observed encounters with, these powerful male figures.

Chapter 1

The Hogarths and Dickens become in-laws

One thing Dickens and Georgina had in common was fathers who spent more than they earned. Despite John Dickens earning a reasonable wage as a navy pay clerk and George Hogarth practising as a solicitor, both men were frequently in debt and pursued by creditors. It was an attempt to make a fresh start that prompted George Hogarth to move his family from Edinburgh to England in 1831. Three years later, when employed in the offices of the *Morning Chronicle*, George Hogarth met the young parliamentary reporter and up-and-coming writer Charles Dickens. In the autumn of 1834, Mr Hogarth took the young man home to meet his family. Three of George Hogarth's daughters were to have a profound impact on Dickens's life. Less than a year after meeting the eldest daughter, twenty-year-old Catherine, Dickens proposed. Catherine and her sister, Mary, aged sixteen, were strong friends as well as siblings, and it was not long before Dickens developed a deep affection for this sister-in-law.[1] At the time Catherine and Dickens became engaged, the third Hogarth girl, the one who was to become his closest and most trusted female friend and confidante, was just eight years old.[2] Georgina was the eighth of the Hogarths' ten children and she, together with her younger twin brother and sister, spent her childhood years in England. As a result, Georgina grew up with a less pronounced Scottish accent than her older siblings.

Initially, Dickens embraced the Scottish roots of his in-laws. Walter Scott had been a hero of his since childhood and shortly after his marriage Dickens declared to an audience of Edinburgh dignitaries, 'I shall love while I have life her people, her hills, and her houses, even the very stones of her streets'.[3] This passionate commitment did not last. When he was irritated by Catherine or her family, Dickens complained he could not bear to hear the Scottish accent and hated 'Scotch stories and everything else Scotch'.[4] Yet, his antipathy towards everything Scottish never included Georgina.

Named after her mother, Georgina Hogarth was born in Edinburgh on 22 January 1827 and her first year was spent at 2 Nelson Street in Edinburgh's New Town. Her father's career as a solicitor seemed to be going well enough to allow the family's move to an elegant townhouse with a grand entrance hall at 19 Albany Street. However, far from experiencing professional success and financial security, George Hogarth was struggling. By the autumn of 1830, his debts were so great that he had to 'submit himself and his family to the publicly humbling experience of bankruptcy'.[5] With his legal practice having collapsed and being declared a bankrupt, George made the decision to seek work in the field of journalism.

In the same month Georgina was four, the family moved to London, where her father expected to be offered the job of editor of the *Courier*. The job never materialised. Instead, in July 1831, George became editor of an Exeter newspaper, the *Western Luminary*, but this did not work out and after a year they returned to London. A few months later, in November 1832, the Hogarths were on the move again when George was appointed editor of a new paper, the *Halifax Guardian*. Although this post lasted longer, he fell out with the owners and, in June 1834, brought his family back once more to London, where he took on the role of music and drama critic at the *Morning Chronicle*. Within a short space of time he was made co-editor of the sister paper, the *Evening Chronicle*, alongside John Powell.

Meeting George Hogarth and his family could not have come at a better time for Dickens. George was an amateur cellist and composer and wrote articles on a variety of musical topics. It was this cultured, intellectual background that impressed the aspiring author. At the age of twenty-three, Dickens was not only keen to become part of literary circles but he was also in the market for a wife. Catherine was pretty, blue-eyed, curvaceous and refined, and her father's links to cultural and literary intelligentsia, particularly Walter Scott, made an association especially appealing. In terms of social class, the Hogarths were a cut above Dickens's own family. Dickens's paternal grandparents met when they were in service, as a manservant and housemaid, whereas Catherine's maternal grandparents were both wealthy and educated. Unlike his experiences with the family of his first love, Maria Beadnell, Dickens's lower social status did not prevent the Hogarths from welcoming him into their home.

The Hogarth's address in London was 18 York Place, Queen's Elm, Brompton. Mr and Mrs Hogarth's grandson, Charles Dickens junior, described the area as 'at one time almost exclusively the artist quarter'.[6] It was a pleasant enough house, one of a terraced row with a small front garden, overlooking orchards and fields. Given the family's straitened financial circumstances, they could only afford a maid-of-all-work, meaning that the eldest girls, Catherine and Mary, had to help with domestic duties and look after their youngest siblings, Georgina and the one-year-old twins. All the girls were educated at home. Mr Hogarth, who supplemented his income by offering lessons in Classics, mathematics and English composition, was on hand to tutor them. The Hogarth boys were sent away to school. Robert, the second eldest, was educated at Edinburgh Academy, and when William and James reached the ages of thirteen and eleven, they were sent to Hamburg to learn French and German.

Being so young, Georgina's first memories of Dickens are hazy, but she often repeated an incident told to her by her mother. In

July 1835, the family were sitting in the drawing room with eight-year-old Georgina and the two-year-old twins, Edward and Helen, who were convalescing from a bout of measles,

> when suddenly a young man, dressed as a sailor, jumped in at the window, danced a hornpipe, whistling the tune, jumped out again, and a few minutes afterwards Charles Dickens walked gravely in at the door, as if nothing had happened, shook hands all round, and then, at the sight of their puzzled faces, burst into a roar of laughter.[7]

Dickens and Catherine's engagement should have been a happy time for the Hogarths, but it was marred by the news that George Hogarth had once again lost his job. The proprietors of the *Evening Chronicle* had decided to make John Powell sole editor and take away Mr Hogarth's sub-editorship of the *Morning Chronicle*. Someone who knew George Hogarth said he was 'the most simple of all men. He was a gentleman in feeling and education, and a man that would not have made any show, if he had possessed the means. He did not.'[8] George's reticence and mild manner were not the characteristics needed to become a successful newspaper manager. The family were left relying solely on the income he could derive from writing pieces for the music and drama pages.[9]

Georgina was too young to attend the modest wedding ceremony of Catherine and Dickens on 2 April 1836 at St Luke's Church, Chelsea, but she was allowed to take part in the wedding breakfast at York Place.

Once Catherine married and moved away, Mary took over the care of her younger siblings, but their strong sisterly bond, and Dickens's affection for his sister-in-law, meant she was regularly with the newly-weds. The devoted friendship between Catherine and Mary fascinated Dickens. As Dickens's biographer Michael Slater observed, '[t]he actual sister–sister relationship always seems to have charmed him', adding, '[i]t is indeed an absolute hallmark of a good womanly woman in Dickens that she should form emotional attachments to other women'.[10] Mary gave the impression of being a convivial, intelligent, attractive young woman. A visitor to the Hogarth home spoke of her as 'a beautiful and light hearted girl' and a 'fine young woman', while one of Dickens's publishers asked, 'How does [Boz's] pretty little sister-in-law get on. She is a sweet interesting creature.'[11] After the Dickenses' return from honeymoon, Mary often slept over at their three room flat in Furnival's Inn. On the first anniversary of the Dickenses' marriage, Georgina accompanied Mary on a return visit to the couple's honeymoon cottage in Chalk, Kent, but, other than this, Georgina had few memories of Mary, writing to a friend over sixty years later, 'I can scarcely remember Mary. I was a very little girl when she died – but I know she was very lovely – in mind and body'.[12]

In January 1837, nine months after the Dickenses' wedding, Charley was born and Mary wrote to their cousin that Catherine was greatly upset when she found she was unable to feed her new baby.[13] Two months later the young family moved to 48 Doughty Street, a genteel area of Bloomsbury. The move represented Dickens's increasing success. The house had five storeys, with the kitchen, scullery and wine cellar in the basement and the morning and dining rooms on the ground floor. The drawing room and Dickens's study were on the first floor; on the second floor, the master bedroom and adjoining dressing room were at the front of the house. Although Mary continued to live with her parents, she also had her own bedroom just along the short corridor from her sister and brother-in-law's room. Up another flight of stairs was the nursery and servants' sleeping quarters. A gated lodge at either end of the street, where a uniformed porter closed the gates at night, was intended to advertise the area's respectability and provide security. Unfortunately, these symbols also attracted criminals, and seven months after the move to Doughty Street, Dickens wrote to Catherine's aunt about a break-in while they were on holiday in Broadstairs.

Despite having a new-born child and a second on the way, Dickens and Catherine threw themselves into entertaining family and friends. Georgina, together with Mary and Dickens's sisters, Fanny and Letitia, was a frequent guest at Doughty Street. The parties would often go on late into the night and Dickens had no compunction in exploiting Mary's attractions to encourage guests to stay longer. Richard Bentley, Dickens's publisher, recorded that when he tried to leave one such boisterous evening event, Dickens waylaid him:

> Towards midnight ... I rose to leave, but D stopped [me] & pressed me to take another glass of Brandy & water. This I wd gladly have avoided, but he begged Miss Hogarth to give it to me. At the hand of the fair Hebe I did not decline it.[14]

Just a week later the entrancing, vibrant, Mary was dead.

On Saturday 6 May 1837, Catherine, Mary and Dickens went to St James's Theatre for a performance of *Is She His Wife?*, a farce penned by Dickens. Returning home, all appeared perfectly normal and at one o'clock they retired to bed. Catherine and Dickens were undressing when they heard Mary call out and, rushing to her bedroom, found her on the floor. She was extremely unwell and a doctor was called but he was completely unable to say what was afflicting her. Dickens explained what happened next:

> [A]lthough every effort was made to save her, and no danger apprehended until nearly the very last, she sank under the attack and died – died in such a calm and gentle sleep, that although I had held her in my arms for some time before, when she was certainly living (for she swallowed a little brandy from my hand) I continued to support her lifeless form, long after her soul had fled to Heaven. This was about three o'clock on the Sunday afternoon.[15]

The cause of death was given as undiagnosed heart disease but current medical knowledge suggests that she had a stroke.[16]

The death of Mary was a terrible shock. Catherine miscarried and Mrs Hogarth was distraught. Dickens had known Mary for less than three years, but her loss provoked intense, and rather odd, reactions in him. He took a ring Mary was wearing when she died and wore it on his little finger for the rest of his life. He kept the dresses she had in her bedroom at Doughty Street and purchased a double grave plot so that he could be buried alongside her.[17] It has to be imagined how Catherine felt when she heard him telling people that Mary was the 'grace and life' of his home, that he had 'lost the dearest friend I have ever had' and that he loved her, after his wife, 'more deeply and fervently than anyone on earth'.[18] An indication of his devastation was that, for the first and only time in his writing career, he failed to meet a publication deadline – for the June issues of *Pickwick* and *Oliver Twist*.

Dickens's emotions were undeniably intense but do not necessarily indicate he was harbouring a sexual desire for Mary. Although, for Dickens, she possessed 'every attraction of youth and beauty', this might simply mean that he was not oblivious to her appeal as a young woman.[19] Nevertheless, he was haunted by her in his dreams for months and these only stopped after talking to Catherine about them. He had the words 'dear Sister' inscribed on a mourning locket containing a strand of her hair.[20] While he was later to claim Georgina as a 'dear Sister', his feelings were never of the same depth, nor was he to grieve so deeply over the deaths of his own sisters. The way he talked about Mary implied that she too felt an intimate bond between them, but Catherine's biographer points out: '[Mary] did not center her affections on her brother-in-law, despite Dickens's wishful imaginings … In the months before her death, Mary concerned herself with her sister and infant nephew; their needs, not her brother-in-law's, were primary.'[21]

The emotions Dickens experienced at the time of Mary's death never left him and he returned to them over and again in his writing, lingering over the attractions of young women on the brink of womanhood. Commentators on Dickens's work have observed how the appeal of youth and female beauty to older men is a recurring theme in his novels, for example, *Bleak House*, *Hard Times*, and *Little Dorrit*.[22] Despite the fact that it took him a long time to recover from Mary's death, Dickens was less understanding of the intense grief Mrs Hogarth displayed, urging her to distract herself: 'I wish I could hear that you had been out to walk. You cannot think how much it would please me. It is really time you made the effort.'[23]

Georgina was ten years old when Mary died. While tragic, it created a space in Dickens and Catherine's life which would be taken up by Georgina five years later. Her sister's death was just one of several losses within a short space of time. Five of her siblings left the family home. Catherine married and, in the same year, her brothers William and James were sent to school in Hamburg. Soon after, the eldest boy, Robert, left London to take up a position in Mexico. Georgina's domestic world shrank to just her parents, elder brother George, and the twins. The following year, 1838, George Hogarth proposed moving what remained of the family back to Scotland and made an unsuccessful attempt to be appointed as Chair of Music at the University of Edinburgh.

Constant house moves indicated that money, or the lack of it, was an ongoing problem. The Hogarths gave up their well-to-do middle-class home in York Place, renting houses in streets inhabited by the less comfortably off (first, 10 Powis Place, Great Ormond Street, Bloomsbury, and then 35 Frederick Street, Gray's Inn Road). A few months after failing to secure the Chair of Music, it became clear that the reason George Hogarth was trying to get away from London was because he owed a large amount to his creditors. Soon after Georgina's twelfth birthday, Mr Hogarth was jailed for debt at Whitecross Street Prison, Islington. There is no evidence of him gambling or spending extravagantly. One possible explanation for his debts is that he, like so many others during the 1830s, fell victim to 'railway mania', investing heavily only to see his shares collapse and his money disappear.[24]

Two years after George Hogarth's incarceration in prison, the family emerge again in the 1841 census, where they can be found renting 20 Chester Terrace. He still had his job on the *Morning*

Chronicle. George Jr (aged twenty) was also employed but his job is not stated in the census, nor does it indicate how William (aged eighteen) and James (aged sixteen) were occupied since their return from school in Hamburg. Also listed are Mrs Hogarth, Georgina (fourteen years), the eight-year-old twins, Helen and Edward, and a seventeen-year-old female servant. Given the size of the family, it is likely that space was limited and Georgina would have shared a room with the twins in the attic.

Regardless of the impression given in household-management journals that all domestic work in middle-class homes was carried out by servants, the reality was very different. The demand for servants exceeded the supply, and the number of people stating they worked in domestic service in the London area failed to match the number of middle-class homes.[25] Those families who employed only a maid-of-all work, as the Hogarths did, found that the sheer number of tasks needing to be done required the ladies of the house to assist. With Catherine married, Mary deceased and Mrs Hogarth unavailable through ill health, the responsibility for helping the servant fell to Georgina. Some household journals recognised that, where there was only one maid, the mistress and daughters might have to undertake some of the domestic chores. However, the suggestion that they dust ornaments and help make the beds fell far short of what many middle-class women found themselves doing. Laundry day alone was extremely time consuming, starting early in the morning and requiring at least two pairs of hands. The range, as well as the copper, was employed to heat water, meaning that family meals had to be cold and light on those days. The account left by one middle-class Victorian woman living a few streets away from the Hogarths revealed that she worked alongside her servant in making the breakfast, sweeping the parlour, blackleading the grate, cleaning lamps, washing windows, cooking, sewing, upholstering, laundrywork and, on the occasions when the maid was busy, answering the front door herself.[26] Undoubtedly, the domestic skills Georgina possessed and which so pleased Dickens, were forged while learning to manage her time so that she could look after the twins, order from and deal with tradesmen, help the maid to cook, clean and sew – in short, keep house for eight people.

With most of the family in Scotland, there were few relatives on hand to offer support. Georgina's maternal grandmother and grandfather, Katherine and George Thomson, relocated to London in spring 1841, but tragedy struck once again. In October that year, Katherine Thomson died suddenly. Just eleven days later, twenty-year-old George Hogarth was drinking in the Horse Shoe pub in Southwark when he collapsed and died.[27] Mrs Hogarth was devastated. Not only had she lost her mother, but a second child had died in young adulthood. Mrs Hogarth's grief was exacerbated by anxiety; she had five children yet to reach their late teens. Contemporary investigation into the deaths of brother and sister – Mary's from a brain haemorrhage and George's from a ruptured intestine – challenges any claim that the two had an inherited condition.[28]

In the space of four years, the family experienced several deaths, suffered financial hardship and prison, and struggled to maintain a stable home. In November 1841, Mrs Hogarth's fragile emotional state was further strained by the departure of her eldest daughter, Catherine, who was due to set sail with Dickens for America at the start of the new year. It was a difficult period for Catherine too. She had lost a beloved grandmother and brother and was now anticipating having to say goodbye to her, by now, four children for six months. When Dickens had first talked to Catherine about going to America to gather ideas for a travel book and as a respite from an intense period of writing, he had intended the children to accompany them. Catherine found herself in a dilemma. Realistically, travelling for six months around the east coast of America with four infants was foolhardy, but the alternatives were either to leave them behind or to abandon Dickens to make the long journey alone. Catherine cried every time she contemplated what to do.

After the intervention of Dickens's friend, the actor William Macready, who reminded Catherine that her first duty was to her husband, she agreed to leave the children behind. In September, when Catherine reluctantly decided to travel without her children, she assumed that Mrs Hogarth would be seeing her grandchildren often and could update her about how they were. Her somewhat unreliable brother-in-law, twenty-two-year-old Fred Dickens, was given the main responsibility for looking after them, with William and Kitty Macready keeping a watchful eye. By November, it was evident to Catherine that her ill, grieving mother was not able to look after herself, let alone the four young children. The one person Catherine could turn to was the practical Georgina.

We have no idea how Georgina coped with all the emotional turmoil of the previous few months. She too was suffering the loss of a grandmother and brother, but also had a sick, inconsolable mother and a worried sister. In years to come, Georgina proved over and again that her way of coping was to put emotions to the side and get on with what needed doing. Her character was a mixture of both parents. Just as people warmed to George Hogarth's unassuming and reserved nature, speaking of him as a pleasant, courteous man, these same attributes were often remarked on in Georgina. She was frequently described as 'amiable', and a great-nephew remembered her as 'a really delightful person, plain, unassuming'.[29] Mrs Hogarth was the dominant force in the family, a confident woman, said to be a 'frank and forthright character'.[30] Mrs Hogarth's willingness to voice her opinions has resulted in her being denounced as 'excitable, not to say somewhat hysterical'.[31] Certainly, the even-tempered George got on much better with his son-in-law than did Mrs Hogarth, who was not afraid of letting Dickens know what she thought of him. Georgina could be as forthright as her mother, but the difference was that she avoided offering anything more than a mild rebuke to her brother-in-law. In later years, when a close friend expressed her shock at hearing a clergyman in Boston declaring from the pulpit that drink had killed Dickens, Georgina admitted she had long been annoyed by the accusations of intemperance and had chided him about his celebration of good food and drink. She lightened her admonishment saying she 'sometimes laughingly begged him not to speak about his dinner – in a joking way he had [as] certain stupid people … did *not* understand him'.[32]

Given the age-gap between Catherine and Georgina, the sisters had not forged the kind of closeness that Catherine had experienced with Mary. Recognising that Georgina was growing up and proving she could be relied upon, Catherine began to cultivate a stronger bond with her younger sister. Georgina was invited frequently to the Dickenses' new home in Devonshire Terrace and for weekends away. Dickens, too, encouraged his sister-in-law and, following his painful fistula operation in November 1841, took Catherine and Georgina with him to recuperate for four days at the White Hart Hotel at Windsor.

Yet, however dependable Georgina appeared to be, she was only about to turn fifteen when the Dickenses left for America, too young to do more than assist. The children ranged in age from eleven-month-old Walter to five-year-old Charley, with Mamie and Katey in between. After their parents departed, Georgina called daily at their rented home at 25 Osnaburgh Street and took the children across Regent's Park to the Macready home at 5 Clarence Terrace. Sometimes Georgina accompanied Fred Dickens in taking the children to see their grandparents. Catherine's letters reveal mixed emotions of concern, relief and reliance on Georgina and Fred: 'I am so glad to hear Mama has been out and that she has seen the children. I have written a long letter to Georgina by this Packet' and she was pleased to hear 'you go out sometimes to see them at Kensington as I am sure it must do Mama good'.[33] In June 1842, when Catherine and Dickens returned from America, the impression of the Hogarths was a family struggling emotionally and financially. Even more changes were to take place in the coming months. Within a year, the eldest son Robert, who had made his way from Mexico to take up government service in Jamaica, died. Georgina's two remaining elder brothers, William and James, left England to start a new life in Australia. The only people left in the Hogarth home were Mr and Mrs Hogarth, the twins and Georgina – and Georgina was reaching the age when she would be expected to start looking for a husband.

Chapter 2

Friends and flirting (1836–42)

Dickens and Catherine had been married for six years before Georgina joined their household. By this time, the dynamics of the couple's relationship had been established. As the only people who really know what goes on inside a marriage are the couple themselves, then Dickens jokingly signing a letter to friends from 'Bully and Meek' tells us a lot about their relationship.[1] Exploring the workings of the Dickenses' marriage offers interesting insights into the couple, but readers may wonder why a book on Dickens and Georgina includes this chapter, in which she does not appear. The reason is that there are certain matters that come up later on, at the time of the Dickenses' marital breakdown, which Georgina was a party to and which need a background context. For example, Dickens complained that Catherine was a jealous wife, unloving mother and emotionally unstable. Georgina added weight to his accusations by alluding to Catherine's 'constitutional misfortune and incapacity', implying that her sister possessed these negative temperamental characteristics long before her marriage.[2] Yet, according to the reports of the young women Dickens trifled with, Catherine was quite the opposite of jealous. She was loving and compassionate towards them and tolerant of her husband. Reading accounts of Dickens's flirtations with young women, when he would cajole and flatter – whether he was gently mocking or genuinely attracted – gives an insight into how the teenage Georgina may have come to hero-worship her brother-in-law. He frequently teased, praised and complimented her, and Georgina's aunt believed it was Dickens's extravagant eulogising of her niece that turned her head, saying she became 'delusional' after having Dickens stoke her 'vanity ... no doubt flattered by his praise'.[3]

Being emboldened by Dickens's lauding of her importance to him was not the only reason for Georgina making scathing observations about Catherine. From the comments Georgina made after the Dickenses' marital separation, she objected to the attitudes of many of the women in Catherine's social network. With the exception of one long-time servant, Anne Cornelius, who remained close to both sisters, Catherine and Georgina had established very different friendship groups. Georgina had begun distancing herself some years earlier, long before Dickens made it known that anyone who continued to see Catherine would not be welcome in his home. Georgina disliked those of her sister's friends who talked openly about the constraints of married life in general, and who used humour as a means of dealing with their difficult, famous, husbands. Their letters, diaries and reminiscences, written in the years before Georgina joined the Dickens household, illustrate the kinds of conversations and observations Georgina later criticised.

What do we know about the early years of the Dickenses' marriage? Temperamentally very different, the couple were far from an ideal match. After having had his heart broken by his first love, Maria Beadnell, Dickens was not prepared to put up with feminine guile from any woman. He had a clear idea of what he wanted from his domestic life: a loving, calm wife who was careful with money, intuitive of his needs, and who maintained a well-run, comfortable home. He did not want a wife who challenged him. The amenable and attractive Catherine fell in love with Dickens and wanted to please him, but he discovered during their engagement that she was no doormat. If she was unhappy when he put work before her, she showed it by withdrawing emotionally. Such tactics might have worked with other suitors but Dickens would have none of it: 'I shall not forget you lightly, but you will need no second warning.'[4] In an era when single women were regarded as 'redundant', remaining unmarried was not an attractive option.[5] Dickens's threat to end their engagement had the desired effect. When confronted by Dickens's annoyance Catherine often backed down, but she was not a meek, subservient woman, choosing instead to pick her battles.

The year 1836 marked the Dickenses' wedding day and the time when his career took off. Catherine married an unknown parliamentary reporter, but within two years he was one of the most famous authors of the day. Alongside his day job, Dickens started writing, mainly comical, sketches based on his observations of life around London. It was when Dickens was editing these sketches into a single volume (*Sketches by Boz*) that his publishers asked him to write the text for a series of comic plates made by the famous illustrator, Robert Seymour. Dickens agreed but had no intention of writing a story for someone else's pictures, however famous they were, insisting instead that he would write his own story and Seymour should illustrate his text. This venture was to turn into *The Pickwick Papers* and the first issue was published in March 1836, less than a month before the wedding. During this year Dickens determinedly set about doing all he could to become a full-time writer. By November that year, after agreeing to various writing projects, including a libretto, dramatising one of his comic tales for the stage, taking on the editorship of a new journal (*Bentley's Miscellany*) and penning his first social crusading report on the potential impact on working people of the Sunday observance bill, Dickens felt able to resign from his job.

As word spread of the talented young writer, Dickens was sought out by the most popular novelists of the day and found himself invited to the prestigious literary salon of the Countess of Blessington. Within a short space of time his name was included in that group styled 'men of genius'. Dickens was particularly fond of two other 'men of genius', the acclaimed dramatic actor William

Macready and the historian and biographer Thomas Carlyle. These three men shared certain personal characteristics; they were all hypersensitive, finicky and tended to be dictatorial. Of the three, Dickens was by far the most outwardly cordial and sociable. William Macready was caring and generous but appeared so serious and humourless that his friends nicknamed him 'Grim'.[6] Of Thomas Carlyle, Dickens's son, Henry, wrote that, while he was 'one of my father's dearest friends', he appeared 'a bit dogmatic and domineering in his manner … but he was really a kind-hearted man, and whatever faults he had were always held in check by a very small wife – so far as her stature was concerned – but with a singularly sensible mind'.[7]

The woman with the 'singularly sensible mind' was Jane Carlyle and she, Kitty Macready and Catherine Dickens shared a common bond in being married to temperamental and often dictatorial 'men of genius'. Kitty and Jane were chivvied along as much by their husbands as Catherine was by Dickens. While Dickens showed Catherine exactly where every item of furnishing should be placed in the house and took her shopping to teach her how to get the best deals on food, William Macready issued written instructions to his wife. Macready reminded Kitty how to store the wood and to keep accounts of her spending, told her she must get up at 7 a.m. every morning, but 6.30 a.m. in the summer months, and urged her to ask questions only if necessary, but otherwise remain silent. He criticised her when he felt her letters were too chatty and recommended she study philosophy in order to improve herself.

In Jane Carlyle's case, where Dickens churlishly reminded Catherine that being married to him raised her status and gave her great privileges, Thomas Carlyle was forthright in telling his wife what he expected in return.[8] He was emphatic that '*The Man should bear rule in the house and not the Woman*. This is an eternal axiom … I must not and I cannot live in a house of which I am not the head.'[9] If Jane complained of something Thomas had done, he 'let her know … that he did not like her fits of pique'.[10]

1 Catherine (Kitty) Macready by Daniel Maclise, 1845

Despite having much in common, Jane Carlyle and Catherine Dickens were never more than social acquaintances. In contrast, a deep friendship existed between Catherine and Kitty Macready, and the same can be said of Jane Carlyle and Kitty. Catherine and Kitty became close in 1837. Both women were to have ten children and, when they met, Kitty was pregnant with her fifth child while Catherine was expecting her first. Two years later Kitty was introduced to Jane Carlyle at a lunch at the Carlyles' home. Writing to her mother, Jane reported that, over the meal, Kitty had asked her what she thought of Harriet Martineau's latest novel *Deerbrook*. Jane, wary of saying something that might spark dissent with someone she had just met, politely turned the question back to Kitty, asking 'how do *you* like it?', to which Kitty 'made wide eyes at me and drew her little mouth together into a button', at which '[w]e both burst out a-laughing, and that is the way to get fast friends'.[11] Although Jane and Catherine were never especially intimate, having a shared friend in Kitty meant they probably knew as much about each other's lives as if they had been close.

Catherine, Kitty and Jane were intelligent women, respectful of their husbands' talents but not prepared to subordinate themselves or lose a sense of their own self-worth. In the case of Catherine and Jane, both had been raised by fathers who recognised women's abilities. Mr Hogarth wrote that the paucity of education was the reason why '[t]he mind of women has … occasionally asserted its claims to the highest intellectual power', and Jane's father went against the wishes of her mother by employing a tutor to teach his daughter Latin.[12] Kitty Macready's background was quite different in that she came from an acting family and was appearing on the stage from an early age. However, starting her career when so young and in the tough world of the theatre required Kitty to develop the self-assurance that she later showed in dealing with Helen Faucit, the actress alleged to be having an affair with her husband. Although Victorian etiquette books warned, '[a] wife should never allow a word about any faults of her husband to pass her lips', Catherine, Kitty and Jane were capable and opinionated Scotswomen.[13] Jane ridiculed the obligation for women to be unobtrusive, quiet and submissive, calling it the 'Mrs. Ellis-code' after the leading writer on social propriety, Sarah Stickney Ellis.[14] While deriding Victorian conduct books, all three women respected tradition and were careful to exhibit conventional wifely behaviour in public, but Jane's letters reveal how humour was often employed as a means of making light of the difficulties of married life. After reading in the newspapers of the case of a Frenchwoman being imprisoned for life after murdering her husband who had tricked her into marriage, Jane wrote to a friend:

> Ah poor Marie Capelle! I mean to propose to dear Mrs. Macready that we married women shall by round robin or otherwise make some public demonstration of our sympathy towards her and our approbation of her strenuous and well meant tho' ill-fated exertions in the condition of the married woman question.[15]

In other words, the only way women had of ending a marriage was murder or death.

Poking fun at 'men of genius' acted as an antidote to the deferential treatment the wives often witnessed their famous husbands enjoying. On one occasion Kitty Macready turned the tables on the frugal William by getting him to wear a coat he had had made for a stage production. The couple had arrived at the Carlyles' house for an 'at home' gathering and Jane was taken aback to see William wearing the magnificent coat with a fur collar and elaborate button and loop fastenings. Several visitors had congregated in the drawing room and, although William was accustomed to appearing before large audiences, he blushed at finding himself in company.

Kitty abandoned William, forcing him to mingle while she joined Jane on the sofa, laughingly confessing that she was the cause of his embarrassment:

> Do you know poor William is in a perfect agony today at having been brought here in that great-coat? It is a stage great-coat, but was only worn by him twice; the piece it was made for did not succeed, but it was such an expensive coat, I would not let him give it away, and doesn't he look well in it?[16]

Amusing though it was for Kitty to get the better of her husband, she would not have wanted to upset him. Jane was also fond of William, so the women made sure that the ever-sensitive Macready was oblivious to their making fun of him. Unfortunately, the one time Catherine jokingly teased Dickens failed spectacularly. Instead of restricting her witty observations on Dickens to the ears of her women friends, she made the mistake of making a playful comment in front of her husband.

The incident occurred one evening when Catherine and Dickens were at a dinner party at the house of Judge Talfourd, a politician, author and friend. At some point the conversation turned to Dickens's last book, and one of the female guests asked him when and how the strange thoughts that appeared in the story came into his head. 'Oh', replied Dickens, 'I don't know. They come at odd times, sometimes in the night, when I jump out of bed, and dot them down, for fear I should have lost them by the morning.'[17] Catherine's immediate riposte was, 'That is true. I have reason to know it, jumping out of bed, and getting in again, with his feet as cold as a stone.'[18] The guests fell silent as Dickens stood up and left the table and it was some time before he could be induced to return. Talking later about what happened, several of the male guests said they felt that Catherine had been publicly complaining about her husband and thought her tactless and insensitive to Dickens's highly strung nature. Catherine made no more light-hearted observations about her husband in public.

Being married to a 'man of genius' meant wives having to deal with their admiring fans. Success, fame and, in Dickens's case, charisma, are powerful aphrodisiacs and all three wives watched as women vied for the attention of their menfolk. Initially, it was not a problem for Jane Carlyle. She told her cousin there was no cause for her to fear as Thomas's 'indifference to *all* women *as* women … secure me against jealousy'.[19] However, around the same time that Georgina moved in with the Dickenses, Jane complained of a young girl staying with them who came down before lunch displaying '*a bare neck*' and '*gazing*' at Thomas, trying 'all sorts of *seductions* on him … stretching herself on the hearth rug at his feet and sleeping there'.[20]

Female fans were more of a problem for Kitty Macready, who had to contend with numerous young actresses pursuing her husband. Macready was known to be highly moral but was evidently quite taken with some of these attractive young women. There was one who caused Kitty particular problems. The beautiful and accomplished Helen Faucit, aged twenty-two, spent three years chasing the much older Macready (he was forty-three). When she withdrew from a play, there were rumours that she was pregnant by him. Macready protested his innocence and, for some reason, thought the best way of confounding any gossip was for Kitty to befriend Helen, inviting her to their home on a regular basis. Kitty was put in a difficult position. Even though William was himself an actor, social mores dictated that it was inappropriate for a respectable woman like Kitty to associate with actresses, let alone one who was the subject of newspaper speculation and rumoured to be having an affair with her husband. Nevertheless, Kitty did as she was asked, but Helen interpreted the gesture as a sign that William wanted a closer relationship. This went on for several years, with Macready refusing her advances at the same time as insisting she remain his leading lady on stage and inviting her to family occasions. Macready's tactic of trying to protect his reputation using the smokescreen of a friendship between his wife and the 'other woman'

2 Jane Welsh Carlyle, 1854

was a strategy Dickens was to attempt with Catherine when he fell in love with the actress Ellen Ternan.

Long before Ellen Ternan came into their lives, Catherine had become familiar with the sight of Dickens's admirers trying to obtain his attention – and her husband's, sometimes rather enthusiastic, reaction to them. In his twenties, Dickens was undeniably attractive both in looks and charm. On seeing him for the first time in 1839, Mary Cowden-Clarke gushed that he was 'superlatively handsome, with his rich, wavy locks of hair, and his magnificent eyes'.[21] At five feet nine inches tall (1.75 metres), with a slim, slight build, he was a man very aware of his appearance and went to great pains to make the best of himself. He had come to adulthood when the Byronic hero was the model for young gentlemen – a dandy, dashing in his vivid clothes, extravagantly complimentary yet smoulderingly romantic. Dickens embraced the image wholeheartedly. Perhaps too wholeheartedly, as some of Dickens's friends regarded his fashion taste as 'generally somewhat "loud" and he always prided himself upon his daring to wear vests of a pattern and colour so resplendent … that his friends wondered at the courage he thus displayed at a period when a more sober form of attire became general'.[22] He wore his light brown hair fashionably long. Unhappily for him, though, he began to lose his hair in his twenties. To hide this, he contrived an elaborate comb-over, which explains the apparent abundance of hair evident in images made of him after 1842.[23] Irrespective of what was happening to his hair, and later his looks, Dickens could always use his charm to make an impression. His brother-in-law, Henry Burnett, observed him escorting a lady into the dining room at Devonshire Terrace 'whom no doubt he was making happy'.[24]

Catherine was well aware that her husband enjoyed flirting. Less than a year after their wedding, Dickens was making a play of swooning over a Miss Harrison, a nineteen-year-old relative of his new friend, the author William Harrison Ainsworth. Asking to be remembered to the young woman, Dickens sent, 'My best to the Ladies. I hope Miss Harrison is married – if I were a single man I should hate her husband mortally.'[25] A week later he had dinner at Ainsworth's house and sang the praises of the absent Miss Harrison. Later that evening, Miss Harrison's aunt wrote to her niece, 'there can be no doubt that you would have the option of being Mrs. Dickens, had that title not already been disposed of'.[26] There is no way of knowing whether or not Miss Harrison's aunt was joking.

When nineteen-year-old Eleanor Emma Picken met the Dickenses at a dinner party in 1840 she soon found herself included in their social circle. In her later years, Emma (as she was known) wrote two articles about her involvement with Dickens and his family. On that first evening, when the women were in the bedroom tidying their hair and clothes before going down to dinner, Emma was introduced to Catherine. Emma thought Catherine looked tired, which was not surprising as she had given birth to three children in quick succession and recently suffered a miscarriage. Emma found Catherine to be friendly and, in looks, 'a pretty little woman, plump and fresh coloured; with the large heavy-lidded, blue eyes so much admired by men. The nose was slightly retroussé, the forehead good, mouth small, round and red-lipped with a genial smiling expression of countenance.'[27] Although nervous at being introduced to Dickens, Emma was immediately captivated, observing how his eyes lit up his face and mesmerised her. He said little at the dinner, but he did notice Emma and she was thrilled: 'How proud I used to feel whenever I had said a better thing than usual to get an approving smile or word from our *maestro!*'[28]

Emma's romantic dalliance with Dickens started in the summer of 1840 in Broadstairs. It had only been a few months since she had met the Dickenses at the dinner party given by their widowed friend, T. J. Thompson. Emma was an orphan who had been taken under the wing of T. J. Thompson's sisters, Elizabeth (Smithson) and Millie. Shortly after the dinner party, Dickens encouraged Elizabeth Smithson and her husband to rent a house next to his in Broadstairs for the holiday season. He must have realised that Emma was very likely to be with them. Emma's memories of that summer describe how Dickens behaved when he was sexually attracted. She explains, too, what it was like for her, as an admirer of Dickens, to be on the receiving end of his ardent interest. Emma was not the only woman to leave a record of that time, as Catherine's friend Eliza Franklin added another perspective. Eliza was among the guests staying with the Dickenses in Broadstairs. She was twenty-seven years old and had become friends with Catherine when they were teenagers. Eliza was also charmed by Dickens and, according to Emma, jealousy soon raised its head.

Emma was golden-haired, young, very pretty, vivacious and slim. If Dickens had a 'type' then she was the archetypal version of it.[29] He was drawn to the purity and virginal qualities of slender girls on the cusp of sexual awakening. On the night of Emma's arrival in Broadstairs, she was terribly excited at the prospect of meeting the celebrated author again and describes how her heart was fluttering in anticipation. The Dickens and Smithson/Thompson families spent most of their time together, playing games, dancing, walking and visiting local attractions. Dickens flirted openly with all the women, including thirty-one-year-old Millie Thompson. He pretended to be in love with both Millie and Emma, calling them in turn '"My charmer", "Beloved of my soul", Fair enslaver" and "Queen of my heart"'.[30] Emma confessed to entering enthusiastically into the play-acting. Dickens singled Emma out for particular attention by writing a poem on the white shutters of a window, praising her beauty and carving her name on a rock. At least three times during the holiday his manhandling ruined her clothes; twice he jostled her into a waterfall and, on another occasion, wrecked her silk dress by holding her at the water's edge long enough for the tide to come in, making the fabric cling to her legs. Emma described the scene and the reactions of those observing what happened.

> Dickens seemed suddenly to be possessed with the demon of mischief; he threw his arm around me and ran me down the inclined plane to the end of the jetty till we reached a tall post. He put his other arm round this, and exclaimed in theatrical tones that he intended to hold me there till 'sad waves' should submerge us.
>
> 'Think of the emotion we shall create! Think of the road to celebrity which you are about to tread! No, not exactly to *tread*, but to flounder into!'
>
> Here I implored him to let me go, and struggled to release myself.
>
> 'Let your mind dwell on the column in *The Times* wherein will be vividly described the pathetic fate of the lovely E. P., drowned

by Dickens in a fit of dementia! Don't struggle, poor little bird; you are powerless in the claws of such a kite as this, child!'

The tide was coming up rapidly and surged over my feet. I gave a loud shriek and tried to bring him back to common sense by reminding him that 'My dress, my best dress, my *only* silk dress, would be ruined'. Even this climax did not soften him: he still went on with his serio-comic nonsense, shaking with laughter all the time, and panting with his struggles to hold me.

'Mrs. Dickens!' a frantic shriek this time, for now the waves rushed up to my knees; 'help me! Make Mr. Dickens let me go – the waves are up to my knees!'

The rest of the party had now arrived, and Mrs. Dickens says 'You will both be carried off by the tide … and you'll spoil the poor girl's silk dress!' 'Dress!' cried Dickens … 'talk not to me of *dress*! When the pall of night is enshrouding us … when we already stand on the brink of the great mystery, shall our thoughts be of fleshly vanities?'[31]

After escaping from Dickens's grasp, Emma ran back to the others only to find '[m]y chaperone, Mrs. S_, received me with unjust severity evidently thinking I could have got away if I had chosen'.[32] Unlike Catherine, Elizabeth Smithson had no sympathy for the young woman's predicament. She told Emma to run home at once and take off her wet things, adding in a severe tone that she was '*surprised*' at her. Elizabeth evidently blamed what happened on Emma for playing up to Dickens. Catherine could see whose fault it actually was and remonstrated with Dickens, saying, 'It was too bad of you, Charles; remember poor Emma cannot afford to have her dress destroyed. Of course you'll give her another?' To which came the reply, 'Never! I have sacrificed her finery and my boots to the infernal gods. Kismet!'[33] Elizabeth Smithson was not the only one unhappy with the obvious sexual chemistry displayed between Dickens and Emma. Eliza Franklin appeared to be jealous of the attention Emma was receiving and attempted to put a spoke in the wheel by insinuating to Dickens that Emma had been mocking him to others.

According to Emma, Eliza had taken her opportunity to cause ill feeling after noticing Emma sitting on the beach making a sketch of Dickens standing motionless, watching the waves coming in. Emma had real artistic skill and went on to have ten portraits exhibited at the Royal Academy of Arts. When, later that afternoon, the families returned to their respective houses, Eliza told Dickens she had seen Emma secretively making a 'horrid caricature' of him.[34] Dickens was incensed. When the families met again Dickens was visibly annoyed with Emma. Confused, Emma asked Catherine what she had done. Catherine, who had heard the full story from both Eliza and Dickens, and who must have been aware of the chemistry between her husband and Emma, nevertheless, took pity on her. When Emma produced the sketch to show that it really was not a caricature, Catherine reassured her: 'Let me show it to Charles at once. He will see that she was completely mistaken. Don't look so tearful, poor little girl! such nonsense to make a false report about this pretty sketch. Will you give it to me dear? I shall value it very much!'[35]

When Emma next saw Dickens his eyes were twinkling and geniality was restored. Taking courage, and with tears in her eyes, Emma murmured, 'Mr. Dickens, how could you think I would presume to caricature you! That odious girl put that into your head because she can't bear you to be amiable to any one but herself. Horrid, red-haired thing! I can't think why you like her!'[36] Dickens soothed Emma, saying, 'I always loved ginger-bread even after childhood's hours had vanished into the dim past; and her ruddy tresses awaken fond memories of my lollipop days; but I don't like her ginger as I do your gold.'[37]

As far as Emma was concerned, the disagreeable episode was over and their romance could resume. When the families parted at the end of the holidays, Emma was in tears until Catherine 'in her sweet caressing way' said, '[n]ever mind dear, we shall all meet again in London'.[38] However, as Emma went on to observe: 'Alas! We never met again in the same kindly way. Everything was changed.'[39] Although Emma saw Catherine quite often at Elizabeth Smithson's house, invitations to spend time with the Dickenses were infrequent. When Emma did go to the Dickenses' home at Devonshire Terrace, she found Dickens preoccupied and cold towards her. The final quashing of Emma's hopes of regaining Dickens's interest occurred after she called at Devonshire Terrace with a portrait she had painted of Catherine. Catherine had commissioned the painting as a gift for Dickens's birthday. If he liked it then he might be willing to sit for one of himself, which would enhance Emma's reputation as an artist. Emma and Catherine arranged for her to call at Devonshire Terrace to hear Dickens's opinion of the portrait. When Emma arrived, the Dickenses were out, so she was shown into the dining room which was set for lunch. It was over an hour before Catherine and Dickens arrived home. On being told Emma was waiting to see them, Dickens went straight to his study. Catherine's manner was as amiable as ever and she was most apologetic for having kept Emma waiting. She loved the likeness of herself and took it straightaway to Dickens.

Notwithstanding the closed door, and that I sat far from it at the fire, I could hear the tones of their voices. Mrs. Dickens's expostulatory, Mr. Dickens's imperatively; at last she returned, looking flurried, but trying to put the best face on the matter. She made apologies for him, 'That he was not very well, and tired. She hoped I would excuse him not being able to see me.'

I faltered out, 'Does he not like the portrait?'

'He has not had time to look at it properly. Of course he will think it like. You mustn't mind dear, but to tell the truth he is a little grumpy just now, but it will be all right presently. You know a man is always cross when he has been kept without his dinner. Won't you stay?' she added, hesitatingly, and in such a tone that I knew she was *afraid* I might.

I was thoroughly cut up, and wanted to have a 'good cry'. I broke from her even while she was kissing me, and telling me she would write and let me know how he liked it; she slid into my hand a folded piece of green paper which I knew was a cheque, and which

I purposely dropped as I passed into the hall. She came after me looking very vexed, and put it into my reticule saying 'For my sake!' Glad to get out of the house … I almost ran into the rain. Round the corner I found an empty cab, and in it I cried to my heart's content all the way home. I never crossed his threshold again.[40]

An explanation of why Dickens was cool to the point of being cruel to the smitten young girl may lie in the behaviour of the equally besotted Eliza Franklin. As Catherine's friend, Eliza had returned to London with the Dickenses following the Broadstairs holiday and stayed with them for a week. She wrote excitedly to her brother, talking far more about Dickens than about her friend. Eliza was flattered by his consideration, how he gave her his stories to read before they were published, and included her in social jaunts with other friends: 'I cannot sufficiently describe how much I feel Mr. Dickens [sic] kindness & credit to show me about, for as you may suppose he is much engaged, & no mistake about his being courted, & thought enough of here.'[41] Dickens and Eliza took breakfast alone as Catherine, five months pregnant, felt unable to join them, 'so Mr. D & I sip our coffee together'.[42] It is conceivable that Eliza used her time alone with Dickens to take revenge on her rival, reminding him of the sketch Emma had made behind his back. Emma admitted in her 1880s articles that she and Millie Thompson talked about the mercurial temperament of their celebrity neighbour. After his experiences with his first love, Maria Beadnell, and her friend making fun of him, Dickens was deeply suspicious of women's motives. Any hint he was being ridiculed would have caused him to turn against Emma. While Emma seemed to have fallen in love and was desperately hurt by Dickens, he did not appear to be emotionally or intellectually attracted to her; her appeal for him lay in her youth and prettiness.

Catherine's attitudes and behaviour to her husband, Emma and her somewhat disloyal friend Eliza was admirable. Emma shows Catherine to be tolerant, kind and doing her best to maintain warm relationships. Catherine was, though, also prepared to remind female interlopers that she was not to be ignored. During the Broadstairs holiday, she had been pregnant with their fourth child, Walter. After Walter's birth in February 1841, she abandoned the three-week period of confinement in order to resume her hostess responsibilities. It was a confident Catherine who met up with Emma Picken, just one year after the summer romance, and she took the opportunity to put the young woman in her place. When T. J. Thompson held a dance at the Willis Rooms in London for 200 guests, Emma espied Dickens across the room and made a beeline for him. She still harboured feelings for Dickens and was upset to find he had no interest in her: 'Mr. Dickens looked very handsome and seemed to enjoy himself immensely; but he never danced once with me, and was only coldly polite, which did not increase my enjoyment.'[43] Emma thought she might distract herself with Dickens's great friend, the eligible, handsome and renowned artist, Daniel Maclise. Maclise signed Emma's dance card but, to her surprise, when the dashing artist came to claim her, Catherine intervened and insisted he dance with her instead: 'He told her he was engaged to me, but she would take no denial, and laughing at my discomfiture she whirled off with him.'[44] This was one of Emma's last encounters with the Dickenses.

It was the American tour in 1842 when Dickens experienced, and Catherine was a party to, unprecedented fan intrusion. 'Bozmania' (a reference to Dickens's pen-name 'Boz') was pervasive across England. People would name their pets after Dickens's characters, disreputable publishers would pirate his latest work, and children would learn the latest serial by heart to play-act at home. The couple's reception in January 1842 proved that Bozmania had crossed the Atlantic and was more difficult to cope with than the Dickenses anticipated. From New York, Dickens wrote to John Forster:

> If I turn into a street, I am followed by a multitude. If I stay
> at home, the house becomes, with callers, like a fair. If I visit a
> public institution, with only one friend, the directors come down

incontinently, waylay me in the yard and address me in a long speech. I go to a party in the evening, and am so enclosed and hemmed about by people, stand where I will, I am exhausted for lack of air. I dine out and have to talk about everything to everybody. I go to church for quiet and there is a violent rush to the neighbourhood of the pew I sit in and the clergyman preaches *at* me. I take my seat in the railroad car, and the conductor won't leave me alone. I get out at a station, and can't drink a glass of water without having a hundred people looking down my throat when I open my mouth to swallow.[45]

Levels of female idolisation exceeded anything Dickens had experienced so far. During the painting of his portrait in Boston, women besieged the artist's studio and the door had to be locked, only for them to scream excitedly at Dickens and mob him when he tried to leave. Even women from well-to-do backgrounds were not above cutting off bits of his seal-skin overcoat as souvenirs. When a woman at a dinner party asked for the red flower he wore in his buttonhole, Dickens refused, saying that the others would be jealous. But the other female dinner guests insisted and so he took the flower from his coat, at which point petals fell off, followed by an unseemly scramble on the floor to pick them up. Young women pestered him constantly for locks of hair and his New York barber collected the clippings to offer as incentives to encourage female clients.

Dickens appreciated Catherine's capacity to cope with the stresses and strains of the tour. He told John Forster that he thought her '*most admirable*' and praised her for never 'express[ing] alarm under circumstances that would have fully justified her in doing so, … has never given way to despondence or fatigue, … has always accommodated herself, well and cheerfully, to everything; and has pleased me very much'.[46] Yet, for all she supported him, it never seemed to occur to Dickens that he owed it to Catherine to show her some respect in front of others.

Catherine's embarrassment can be imagined when Dickens made clear his sexual appreciation of certain women in front of people they had only just met. At a dinner party in Boston, the guests were discussing which, out of the Duchess of Sutherland and Mrs Caroline Norton, was the more beautiful. '"Well, I don't know", said Dickens, expanding himself in his green velvet waistcoat: "Mrs Norton perhaps is the most beautiful; but the duchess, to my mind, is the more kissable person."'[47] Recalling the incident many years later, one of the young female guests, Elizabeth Wormeley, described how Catherine and the other members of the party were stunned. Elizabeth thought Dickens uncouth while 'Mrs. Dickens … showed signs of having been born and bred her husband's social superior'.[48] Less embarrassing, but still potentially awkward, was Dickens making up to Frances Wilkes Colden, the wife of his host in New York. He called her 'my better angel' and wrote in a playfully anguished tone of the need to prevent her husband reading his letter: 'if this should meet HIS eye, I trust you to throw dust in the same. HIS suspicions must not be aroused. HE says that I have applied tender epithets to a certain Mrs. D.'[49] While this was clearly written tongue-in-cheek, the fact that he also openly complained to Frances about Catherine – 'It is more clear to me than ever, that Kate is as near being a Donkey, as one of that sex … can be' – shows a lack of consideration or loyalty towards his wife.[50]

Another woman Dickens was introduced to during the American tour was Emma Mordecai, from a prominent, wealthy family. After attending one of his readings, Emma sent flowers to Dickens's hotel, to which he responded:

> My Dear Dreamer,
>   I have received the flowers most joyfully – though I need nothing to remind me of *you*, believe me. I shall place them on my pillow tonight, and trust to their influence for some sweet visions in which you may be the chief actor.[51]

There is no suggestion that Dickens was even remotely interested, sexually or emotionally, in Frances Wilkes Colden, Emma Mordecai or any of the other females he flattered. He simply enjoyed being admired and actively encouraged the attention but, equally, it would be understandable if Catherine was made uncomfortable by her husband's flirting. Despite his behaviour, Dickens never mentioned that his wife complained or even commented on these dalliances.

It was not until many years later that Catherine was talked about as a jealous woman. Their daughter Katey told a friend that her mother was jealous of her father, and a neighbour commented that it was 'pretty generally conceded that Mrs. Dickens was needlessly jealous'.[52] An alternative view came from one of Catherine's neighbours, who described her as a 'shrewd, sensible, practical Scotswoman', with an 'incapacity for unlimited idolatry' and who was not 'blind to specks and foibles' in her husband.[53] It would have been surprising if, after twenty-two years living with this 'man of genius' who 'had a curious, almost objective, appreciation of his own uniqueness, [r]egarding himself as the phenomenon that he indeed was', had not changed Catherine in some ways.[54] Yet, pointing to Dickens as the sole cause of Catherine's transformation from a tolerant, compassionate woman to a jealous wife is too simplistic. Victorian gender and social codes of conduct limited the lives of even privileged women. The Dickenses' marriage was similar to that of the Macreadys and Carlyles, where the 'men of genius' made every effort to mould their wives. When women's well-being was tied to the men they had to rely on, there were only a few outlets in which they could subvert the compliance expected of them; joking about their dictatorial husbands and the married state was one of them.

Regardless of what Dickens and Georgina were to say in later years, there was nothing to suggest that Catherine was an inherently careless wife and neglectful mother. Those who saw the Dickenses together in the early years of the marriage spoke of Catherine as kind, capable and supportive. Rather than showing signs of jealousy, she was generally tolerant of her husband's enthusiastic encouragement of pretty young women. Dickens may have found reasons to be irritated with Catherine, but if anyone had cause to grumble, it was her. Seeing her husband flirting and professing undying love to women, however playfully it was done, must have been tiresome. Did Georgina fail, or simply refuse, to acknowledge the difficulties caused for her sister of living with a flirtatious man who was also often openly critical of her? It is fair to say that if Georgina had visited the holiday home in Broadstairs in 1840, she would have been too young to have made sense of Dickens's flirtation with Emma. However, similar incidents occurred when she was older, when she could see for herself how Dickens could and did intimidate Catherine. Georgina only began to regard her sister in a negative light after she herself reached her twenties and then over the course of several years.

At the start of 1842 the Dickens family consisted of a husband, wife and their four children, all aged under six. By the end of the year they had been joined by a teenager whose presence, although welcome, introduced a new element into family relations.

Chapter 3

Dickens and his 'little Pet'
(1842–7)

Six months after the Dickenses returned from America, Georgina moved into 1 Devonshire Terrace.[1] The children were fond of 'Aunty Georgy' and she could help take care of them, but that is only part of the reason why she was invited to join the family. The Dickenses already employed a nursemaid, plus three other female servants, making Georgina's assistance useful rather than necessary. A more pressing reason for the Dickenses to take Georgina into their home was to alleviate some of the demands on Mr and Mrs Hogarth. At nearly sixteen years of age, it would not be long before Georgina needed to find a husband, and mixing in the Dickenses wide social circle would increase her opportunities of meeting a suitor with good prospects. More importantly, Georgina's removal to the Dickens home saved Mr Hogarth money. His sons were also of an age when they were leaving home and a smaller family meant he was able to rent cheaper accommodation. Georgina had been needed to help with domestic chores and look after the twins but, once the boys had left, the family could manage with just a maid-of-all-work.

Georgina said that life only really began for her when she became part of Dickens's family.[2] After reading the volume of John Forster's biography of Dickens which covers the years when she first joined the household, Georgina declared, 'it is so true and real that to read it, *to me*, was like living over my whole life again– and I seemed

47

to awaken from a dream to the reality of present things – and to a great *blank* when I close the book'. The move was a new start in many ways. The house at 1 Devonshire Terrace had been home to the Dickens family since 1839 and was far grander than her parents' current residence. The Dickenses lived in the first of three upper-middle-class terraced houses in the street. There were thirteen rooms in all over five storeys, including the basement and two small attics. Visitors talked of finding a warm and welcoming atmosphere as soon as they entered the large, square entrance hall. Two doors led off, one to the library, a room Georgina rarely ventured into, and then only with permission, because it served as Dickens's study. Adjoining Dickens's study was the dining room; this was where Emma Picken had nervously hovered as she heard Catherine arguing with Dickens, imploring him to look at the portrait Emma had painted. While she waited, Emma might have cast her eye over the large dining table surrounded by twelve green leather-covered chairs, which indicated a family that liked to entertain. Over the mantelpiece was the famous 'Nickleby' portrait of Dickens, aged twenty-seven, by Daniel Maclise.[3] An imposing staircase curved along the back wall, leading to the first floor where an impressively large drawing room that overlooked the gardens was to be found. Dickens insisted Georgina be given the second-best bedroom, which was also located on the first floor, alongside the Dickenses' own bedroom, and that most modern of conveniences, a water closet. On the top floor were two attic storeys housing the day and night nurseries and the servants' bedrooms.

What was daily life like for Georgina in the Dickens household? It was certainly different to living with her parents. For one thing, Dickens's home was also his workplace. Whereas Mr Hogarth left the house each morning around 10 a.m. for his work at the offices of the *Morning Chronicle*, Dickens went to his study at 9 a.m. His writing routines took priority over everything else. The day began at around 7 a.m. with Dickens taking a cold bath, while in the attic nursery the children were woken, placed on chamber pots, then washed and dressed ready to go downstairs.[4] The family gathered for breakfast at 7.30 a.m. when Dickens would forgo the hot rolls, preferring a rasher of bacon with an egg and a cup of tea. Everyone, including the children, were expected to be punctual. Following breakfast, household-management books advised the mistress of the house to make her rounds to check that all was as it should be and give her orders for the day to the servants. However, Victorian expectations of a separation between a 'man's place' of work and a 'woman's place' in the domestic sphere were almost impossible to achieve at Devonshire Terrace. It was Dickens, not Catherine, who toured the house; his eldest daughter recalled how, '[h]e made a point of visiting every room in the house once each morning, and if a chair was out of its place, or a blind not quite straight, or a crumb left on the floor, woe betide the offender'.[5] In the girls' bedroom he opened drawers and left notes on their pincushions to reprimand or praise them. If the contents were not ordered to his satisfaction, they had to set to and tidy them immediately.

Dickens's hours of work were between 9 a.m. and 2 p.m., during which time he required absolute silence. Georgina would be in the nursery with Charlotte, the nursemaid, helping to teach the children the basics of reading and writing and keeping an eye out for any toddler likely to dash out of the nursery and down the stairs. Dickens had installed a barred gate at the bottom of the staircase to stop the youngest children from bursting in on him and tried to minimise noise by fitting an extra baize door to the existing study door. According to Mamie, '[h]is study, to us children, was a rather mysterious and awe-inspiring chamber, and while he was at work no one was allowed to enter it. We little ones had to pass the door as quietly as possible'.[6] Despite her nervousness about entering the study, Mamie described it as a cheerful, pleasant room, with a vase of bright, fresh flowers ever present. Over 2,000 books lined the walls. There was a mirror, in front of which Dickens performed his characters, contorting himself to acquire the physical attributes he would transfer to the page. On the only wall space not covered with bookshelves hung a portrait of Catherine in her mid-twenties by Dickens's friend Daniel Maclise. One visitor to the house recalled looking at 'a fine portrait of ... the domestic Madonna of this chaste household', when he noticed 'the door opened discreetly and a naively curious youngster came in to tiptoe around us with the charming confidence of the *enfant gâté* – head to one side, finger on lips – I could take note at leisure of the likeness of mother to son'.[7]

Dickens took a short break from his work at 1 p.m., at which time his son Harry recalled how the rest of the family were expected to avoid engaging him in conversation: '[H]e would occasionally stroll into the dining-room to take a biscuit and a glass of sherry. But at such times his mind was far away; walking about the room in deep thought he would speak but little.'[8]

At the time Georgina moved in, Dickens was writing at a prodigious rate. Since the publication of *The Pickwick Papers* in 1836–7, he had written in rapid succession, *Oliver Twist* (1837–9), *Nicholas Nickleby* (1838–9) and *The Old Curiosity Shop* (1840–1). He had completed *Barnaby Rudge* before sailing for America, produced *American Notes* shortly after arriving back in London and, at the beginning of 1843, the first numbers of *Martin Chuzzlewit* appeared. Everyone in the household was wary of encountering Dickens on the days when, struggling to create a storyline, he admitted he was likely 'to be so horribly cross and surly, that the boldest fly at my approach'.[9]

With Dickens engrossed in his work, Catherine and Georgina followed a routine similar to that of other middle-class women. The Dickenses' younger daughter, Katey, observed:

> Their mornings were occupied with the usual small domestic worries and more often than not, in looking after the interests of their poorer neighbours. Business disposed of, they managed to get through a large amount of letter-writing, embroidery and reading ... for many of them were thoughtful in those days and greatly given to introspection, a fault no doubt of too much leisure.[10]

On the days when the writing did not flow and Dickens required distraction, his physical restlessness quashed any plans Catherine and Georgina might have to take part in the Victorian social ritual of calling or going out on visits. Instead, Dickens would whisk them off for a jaunt in the countryside: 'In a kind of despair, I started off at half past two with my pair of petticoats to Richmond and dined there!!'[11]

In Georgina's first few years in the Dickens household, her place was dictated by her age. No longer a child but still not an adult, the twelve-year age-gap between Georgina and Catherine meant the Dickenses were a second father and mother. Georgina had very different relationships with her actual and substitute parents. In the Hogarth family, she was a useful younger daughter but, as the eighth child, she was one of many.[12] In the Dickens home she quickly became the spoiled darling of a charismatic man and loving sister. Dickens embraced the role of an indulgent father figure, treating his 'little Pet' as a 'favourite young daughter', and giving her a quarterly allowance when she reached the age of nineteen.[13] He told Mrs Hogarth how much Georgina reminded him of Mary Hogarth and the comfort this gave him:

> I trace in many respects a strong resemblance between her mental features and Georgina's – so strange a one, at times, that when she and Kate and I are sitting together, I seem to think that what has happened is a melancholy dream from which I am just awakening. The perfect like of what she was, will never be again, but so much of her spirit shines out in this sister, that the old time comes back again at some seasons, and I can hardly separate it from the present.[14]

When Dickens and Catherine received invitations to social events, he always requested that Georgina be included. If Catherine was indisposed because of pregnancy and unable to make her usual round of calls, Dickens made sure Georgina's social life continued by taking the unusual step of accompanying her. His escorting of Georgina certainly surprised the author William Thackeray, when he returned home to hear he had missed a visit by Dickens 'with Miss Hogarth on his arm'.[15] Dickens bought presents for Catherine and the children whenever he went away and Georgina was not only included, but indulged. One wonders what Catherine made of a disgruntled letter sent by her husband after a disappointing shopping expedition:

> I bought you a shawl at Norwich – I don't think much of it. It's Norwich manufacture. That's all I can say … Tell Georgy with my love that I should have bought her one but I thought she would prefer a muff. She shall have which she likes, in town.[16]

Dickens flattered the young Georgina by showing he valued her opinion, once implying he would only purchase paintings he had commissioned of Dolly Varden and Kate Nickleby from the artist William Powell Frith if Georgina liked them. Georgina was reaching the age Dickens found appealing and he called her 'the Virgin' or 'small virgin', drawing attention to Georgina's budding sexuality.[17] However, there is nothing to suggest that Dickens meant this as anything more than a teasing comment.

Did Georgina see Dickens simply as an kindly father figure? Georgina's biographer insisted she harboured no romantic or sexual feelings for Dickens, yet this seems implausible given her teenage adoration of her brother-in-law.[18] We can only guess what the adolescent Georgina made of Dickens's gift giving, his endearments and his teasing. However, the tendency for schoolgirls to develop crushes on celebrity figures were acknowledged by the author Sarah Stickney Ellis writing in *The Daughters of England* (1842) about:

> the popular tendency amongst the young and inexperienced, to attach undue importance to the casual notice of distinguished men; such as popular speakers, eloquent ministers of religion, or any who hold conspicuous situations in society … The most objectionable feature which this tendency assumes is an extravagant and enthusiastic attachment.[19]

What was it about Dickens that would have attracted teenage adulation? Fame, youth, talent, handsome looks and charm all contributed, but Dickens also had an air of devil-may-care about him which might have enhanced his appeal to young ladies brought up to conform. He was not afraid to ruffle feathers and flaunt his masculinity. Emma Picken appears to have been both shocked and titillated to hear Dickens singing ribald songs in front of ladies, and, at another time, to discover him swimming in the nude next to her bathing machine.[20] He flouted social rules, astonishing his fellow author Elizabeth Gaskell when she found him knocking on her door one morning, writing to her daughter that '[o]n Wednesday morning Mr. and Mrs. Dickens and Miss Hogarth came to call *before 10*' instead of during the designated 'at home' hours between 3 and 5 p.m.[21]

Added to this, Dickens's multiple talents fascinated even the far from easily impressed, such as Jane Carlyle. At a Boxing Day celebration, Jane declared Dickens 'the best conjuror I ever saw' when he produced a plum pudding from an empty saucepan.[22] Just days later, Georgina watched Dickens entertaining guests at Charley's birthday party by turning watches into tea caddies, making coins fly across the room and setting light to pocket handkerchiefs, which emerged unscorched. The Dickenses' family doctor, John Elliotson, taught Dickens mesmerism, which he used to entertain guests, as well as a means of healing. While Georgina may have admired Dickens's skill, it was not always pleasant. There was one incident when Dickens hypnotised her in front of a group of people during which she became violently hysterical.[23]

For her part, Georgina wanted to impress Dickens. She amused him with her impersonations of people they knew, rendering him 'weak with laughter', and gave him an extraordinarily generous gift of a pair of ivory binoculars.[24] This was before she was given a quarterly allowance and it would have taken her a considerable amount of time to save the money. Dickens repaid her by treasuring the binoculars all his life.

Georgina and Catherine were constant companions and appeared to share a loving, sisterly bond. Those who met them used similar terms to describe the two sisters as affable, kind and unassuming. The motherless daughters of William Thackeray loved to visit the

Dickens home and remembered how kind Catherine and Georgina were to them: 'We were a little shy coming in alone but Mrs. Dickens called us to sit beside her till the long sweeping dance was over and talked to us as if we were grown up, which is always flattering to little girls. Then Miss Hogarth found us partners.'[25] Georgina and Catherine had a similar sense of humour, often finding themselves having to stifle their laughter in company when a guest said or did something unintentionally that they found amusing. One such occasion was at a dinner party when the opera singer Catherine Hayes complimented Catherine 'on her having had for her father so clever a painter as Mr. Hogarth', mistaking Catherine's very much alive papa for the long-dead artist William Hogarth.[26]

The loving and supportive amity between the sisters was broken when the Dickenses' marriage disintegrated, but Georgina's criticisms suggest that her animosity towards Catherine had been building for some time. Were there any warning signals of possible tension points even during the period when the sisters were getting on well together? Bearing in mind that Georgina was fifteen years old when she arrived at Devonshire Terrace, some antipathy towards Catherine might be expected. The adolescent phase was as tricky to negotiate for Victorian teenagers and their guardians as for any other generation, and Catherine was in the unenviable position of being both elder sister and substitute mother to Georgina. With Mrs Hogarth living several streets away, still grieving and with ongoing money worries, Catherine was left to guide Georgina through the difficult years from adolescence to respectable young lady.

Catherine, as mistress of the house, was responsible for introducing the then taboo subject of menstruation with Georgina, and how it was dealt with in the Dickens household. The Dickenses' doctor, John Elliotson, was one of the few with medical knowledge who wrote about the subject. Urging women to keep themselves away from others, he suggested that '[t]o regard women during menstruation as unclean is certainly very useful'.[27] Servants and wives involved in food preparation were advised that 'it is firmly believed by many that meat will not take salt if the process is conducted by a menstruating woman'.[28] Regarded as an illness and used as evidence of their mental and physical inferiority, the message to women was to withdraw from society during their periods. Women were told to avoid travelling on trains, read novels, or practise the piano. Nor should they eat 'indigestible food', imperil themselves by 'dancing in warm rooms' or experience 'sudden exposure to cold or wet (or) mental agitations'.[29] There is no information as to how Catherine and Georgina, or indeed the four young female servants at Devonshire Terrace, dealt with menstruation or how it affected their daily lives, nor whether they followed any of their family doctor's advice. Quite evidently, Dr Elliotson's instructions were aimed at middle-class women, as female servants would have been expected to continue working.[30]

There was scope for a teenage Georgina to be irritated by her elder sister's more privileged position. Catherine could be the bossy older sister, asking Dickens to send a message to Georgina with the instructions, 'Kate says will you bring her a box of toothpowder'.[31] Catherine arranged for four-year-old Katey, who was suffering with nightmares, to be moved into 'Aunty's' bedroom, making it Georgina's responsibility to soothe the distraught little girl and get her back to sleep. It was Georgina that Catherine asked to take the children home early when they were invited to social events, leaving the Dickenses free to carry on enjoying themselves and spoiling Georgina's fun. Besides suffering the indignities of being the younger sister, Georgina experienced the constraints imposed by Victorian etiquette on young women which were almost designed to stir up teenage umbrage and envy.

Victorian social codes dictated that young, single girls dressed in a particular way – one that demonstrated their different, and inferior, position to married women. Dickens was a prominent figure in Victorian society and was expected to display his prosperity through his family and, as such, dress and appearance were an important means of exhibiting his status. Catherine and Georgina needed a substantial number of outfits as they would change their clothes several times a day, but as a single girl, Georgina had to wear more modest outfits than her married sister and never dress above her (unmarried) station for fear of appearing unrefined. A neat and simple dress worn for undertaking domestic duties would be exchanged for one of an acceptably restrained colour, such as navy blue, grey or dark green, and accessorised with minimum jewellery for morning calls and visits (which confusingly took place in the afternoon). Catherine and Georgina might also have changed out of the good dresses they wore to dinner into elaborate evening gowns if they were accompanying Dickens to the theatre or a party.

When Georgina moved to Devonshire Terrace she would not have owned the extensive wardrobe of clothes she needed for socialising in her brother-in-law's celebrity circles. To mark Georgina's approaching sixteenth birthday, she had been allowed to start dressing as an adult woman. The hems on her skirts had been dropped and her light brown hair was put up in the latest fashion of a centre parting, side coils and a bun at the back. Georgina was particularly fond of accessories, and when she was in her later years would wear rings on every finger, something not encouraged in young women, who were expected to wear minimum jewellery. The sisters experimented with new styles and Georgina helped embellish her sister's hair for Catherine's first appearance in the drawing room a week after giving birth to Sydney. Dickens did not approve of the result. The sight of Catherine's false fringe caused him to dash off a letter to Kitty Macready saying, 'My young "ooman" … has come out with an amount of curl on the temples, that stupefies me. I was horribly alarmed last Sunday!'[32] Whatever Dickens thought, the new hairstyle shows that both Georgina and Catherine were innovative and interested in the latest fads. Yet a solution needed to be found that would allow Georgina to increase her wardrobe at minimum cost and within social conventions.

Dickens had enough financial responsibilities with his own growing family, as well as perpetual requests for money from his relatives, without funding new dresses for his sister-in-law. Nor could the Hogarths afford to buy the clothes Georgina needed. According to the artist William Powell Frith's daughter, a middle-class woman in the mid-Victorian period could manage on a clothes allowance of £50 (£7,200), but she noted that a silk brocade gown could cost between £10 and £50 (£1,400 and £7,200).[33]

The most likely way in which Georgina added to her wardrobe was by Catherine passing on her unwanted gowns. Georgina was an excellent seamstress and there is a sketch showing her stitching a garment. This portrait is unusual in itself as ladies from affluent households would usually be depicted doing needlecraft, but seeing Georgina engaged in her sewing does indicate the important role played by women in making clothes.[34] When Dickens married Catherine in 1836, it was expected that she would make her husband's shirts, nightshirts and drawers, and repair his trousers and coats. Georgina could easily refit Catherine's dresses for herself but, nevertheless, these were still second-hand clothes and would probably have required the removal of ornamentation so that she might appear simply dressed. Georgina would also have had to avoid dresses made of expensive materials as Victorian moral codes deemed that only by dressing demurely would a girl attract a husband.[35] It can only be imagined how the adolescent Georgina felt at having to make-do with her sister's cast-off clothes and altering them in ways that showed her subordinate status.

The rituals around calling and visiting cards provided another opportunity for Georgina to experience youthful anguish. As a symbol of entry to adulthood and status, these cards were a rite of passage for all young women and were therefore highly prized. Because Georgina was only just sixteen when she started to accompany Catherine in making calls, she did not need her own visiting card. When carrying out social visits, Catherine would present her own card, turning down the right-hand corner to indicate to the hostess she was accompanied by a female family member. After being in society for a year, and around the age of seventeen to eighteen, young ladies were given their own cards. Although it was Catherine's responsibility, as mistress of the house, to organise a visiting card for Georgina, she did not do so. The reason is not clear. In Catherine's defence, she was preoccupied throughout Georgina's seventeenth year, starting with the birth of her fifth child, packing and moving to Italy for twelve months, and coping with Dickens becoming fascinated by two women. On the other hand, Catherine did make social gaffes around visiting card conventions. The first year the Dickenses stayed at their summer home, Gad's Hill in Kent, Catherine relied on the protocol of London society, where the wife of a newly arrived family would call and leave her husband's visiting card. Unfortunately for Catherine, the opposite was the accepted protocol in the countryside. Etiquette dictated that local residents would call first on the newcomers and leave their cards. By taking the initiative, Catherine insulted the neighbours by implying that Dickens did not want to extend the acquaintance beyond alerting them to his presence in the area.[36] After Catherine and Dickens separated in 1858, the fact that Georgina had not been given her own calling card had embarrassing repercussions.

How did the Dickenses chaperone Georgina through her adolescent years? Although before his marriage Dickens had had his thirteen-year-old brother, Fred, living with him at Furnival's Inn, he and Catherine had no experience of acting *in loco parentis* to a teenage girl. There were occasions when the Dickenses appeared to forget Georgina was young and socially inexperienced. One consequence of treating her as more mature than her years was allowing her to meet people her Hogarth parents might not have approved of, such as the scandalous Mrs Caroline Norton and the actress, Helen Faucit.[37] Georgina accompanied the Dickenses to parties at Kensal Lodge, where William Harrison Ainsworth lived with Eliza Touchet, the widow of his cousin. Even though Eliza was a member of Ainsworth's family, any single woman living alongside a man separated from his wife, provoked gossip. Ainsworth's three daughters, who had been living with his estranged wife, moved in with him after their mother's death. As an elderly woman of eighty-four, Georgina recalled the parties at the home of the famous author:

> The guests were generally all the best known people in literature and art, and the evenings were most social and informal. There were always dinner parties – succeeded by games and music, and very often winding up with a dance, in which the three young daughters joined. Mr. Ainsworth was a most kind friend of mine and I was very fond of his three daughters.[38]

Many of these 'best known people' also had rakish reputations. Georgina evidently saw herself, at the age of sixteen, as a sophisticated, mature young woman, but the idea that the celebrated, thirty-eight-year-old Ainsworth was a friend of hers illustrates a touch of adolescent arrogance. One of Ainsworth's daughters pricked Georgina's memory of her youthful self-importance when, after reading these comments in a book about her father, she wrote to remind her that 'the three young daughters' were of a similar age to Georgina; in fact her sister Fanny Ainsworth was Georgina's exact contemporary. Georgina could not resist having the final word, insisting that as she was born in January, 'I was older than your sister Fanny – not by much – but still *older*'.[39]

While the teenage Georgina enjoyed the frisson of being allowed to mix with famous people, because many of them were regarded in non-celebrity circles as risqué, her association threatened her reputation. Dickens's friendships with the Countess of Blessington and Mrs Caroline Norton placed his wife and sister-in-law in a socially difficult position. Both Blessington and Norton were regarded as outside 'respectable' society because the Countess lived with her son-in-law, Count D'Orsay, and Caroline Norton left her abusive husband and had an affair with the prime minister, Lord Melbourne. The kind-hearted side of Dickens was happy for Catherine and

Georgina to associate with both women, but how were they to do so while also maintaining their own social respectability? At least with Caroline Norton, Catherine seems to have achieved a compromise, with the women dining at each other's homes but not participating in 'at homes' where their intimacy would be on public display. On one occasion Caroline asked Catherine, 'if agreeable', to bring 'your pretty sister' to dinner, although the invitation had to be declined.[40]

At sixteen, Georgina was too young for marriage, as the average age for women to marry in the 1840s was between eighteen and twenty-three. Nevertheless, she was not too young to be aware of prospective suitors, especially as engagements typically lasted between six months to two years. Two of Dickens's single friends were regularly to be found at Devonshire Terrace. John Forster and the artist Daniel Maclise were both eligible prospective husbands but were really too old for Georgina. Forster was the same age as Dickens (thirty) and Maclise claimed to be the same, but was actually thirty-six. Georgina would say later that she did not agree with large age-gaps in marriage, yet she was clearly attracted to men much older than herself. Of the sixty-four-year-old writer Sydney Smith, Georgina gushed that he was 'a very handsome man – and I remember always being impressed with the massive beauty of his face'.[41] She also had a huge crush on the renowned author Edward Bulwer-Lytton, twenty-four years her senior, and flirted with him by letting him know how 'deeply impressed' she was with his knowledge of the occult.[42] In middle-age, she was enthralled by Dickens's friend, the handsome actor Charles Fechter (a mere three years her senior), saying he was 'a most *magnetic* man – it is impossible to help being attracted by him'.[43] Fechter, Bulwer-Lytton and Maclise were similar in being good looking, dark haired, with a slim build, and all were significant figures in London's elite social circles. John Forster was certainly not Georgina's type, being square jawed, broad shouldered and of medium height, with a tendency to be pompous and overbearing. Forster's positive qualities of personal loyalty and great kindness made him a dependable friend, but nothing more. Daniel Maclise was an altogether much more attractive option.

Daniel Maclise, or 'Mac' as he was known, was every bit as charming, talented and popular as Dickens. Men and women found him physically attractive with an endearing personality. Thackeray described him as 'Byronic and ambitious'.[44] Unlike Dickens, Maclise was modest and oblivious to his effect on people: 'His fine genius and his handsome person, of neither of which at any time he seemed himself to be in the slightest degree conscious, completed the charm.'[45] Eliza Franklin, Catherine's friend, was as fascinated with Daniel Maclise as she had been with Dickens, and so too was her rival, Emma Picken: 'I was impressed with his striking appearance the first time I saw him. Tall, well built, and artistic-looking, he wore his dark hair very long, in heavy waves; and his countenance was attractive … His manners … were, like his face, agreeable and inclining to the humorous.'[46] Maclise had an affair with Lady Henrietta Sykes that was much publicised in the newspapers after her husband discovered them *in flagrante*. In keeping with Victorian notions of morality, it was Lady Sykes who was blamed for the affair. Queen Victoria, who had a soft spot for Maclise, commissioning him to paint surprise gifts for Prince Albert, wrote in her diary that Henrietta was from 'a bad set'.[47] Being attractive had its drawbacks for Maclise. He had the embarrassment of having to tell his friend John Forster that Forster's then fiancée, Letitia Landon, twice propositioned him when he was painting her portrait.

If Georgina needed to find a husband in the coming years, the successful, handsome and kind Maclise would be ideal. They had things in common, from a talent with languages to musical abilities. Both were able to speak French and Italian, although Georgina was the more fluent. Georgina was a competent piano player, while Maclise was adept on the flute and Spanish guitar. At the time Georgina was moving her bags into Devonshire Terrace, the friendship between Dickens and Mac was at its height. Dickens had good reason to encourage Mac to take an interest in his pretty relative; it would seal their already devoted friendship. Dickens took every opportunity to encourage a romance. He responded to an invitation to dinner by asking leave 'to bring Mrs. D.'s sister' and also 'a very dear friend of mine and a very famous fellow; to wit, Maclise, the painter'.[48] Dickens involved both Georgina and Maclise in birthday celebrations, anniversaries, theatre visits and holidays, as well as evenings at Devonshire Terrace. He contrived games for Georgina and Maclise to spark off against each other. Knowing both Maclise and Georgina were exceptionally longsighted, a favourite amusement on excursions to the countryside was for Dickens to offer a small prize for which of them could see the furthest. Maclise usually won. Dickens only changed to a gentle nudging of Georgina in Maclise's direction after a shocking start to his matchmaking efforts. It was all to do with Maclise's painting *Waterfall at St. Nighton's Kieve, near Tintagel.*[49]

A few months after returning from America, Dickens, accompanied by Mac, John Forster and another artist, Clarkson Stanfield, went on a short holiday to Cornwall where the painters took the opportunity to sketch local scenes. On their return, Maclise was keen to work up one of his sketches for a larger painting. He needed a model to pose on the rocks, carrying a water jug on her shoulder, and Dickens suggested Georgina could pose for the painting. It was not unusual for Maclise to make images of the Dickens family, notably the 'Nickleby' portrait, as well as two paintings of Catherine, a sketch of the four youngest Dickens children, and one with Dickens, Catherine and Georgina in profile.[50] However, for Dickens to suggest Georgina pose for *Waterfall at St. Nighton's Kieve* was astonishing and inappropriate. Artists did use female members of their own family as models, but this was more likely when the painter was unknown and could not afford to pay for professionals. Maclise could easily have afforded a professional model. Most often drawn from the working class, 'the general public believed that artists' models were used for sexual purposes as well as sittings' and, in fact, many did earn money through prostitution.[51] Charles Collins, a painter who was to marry Katey Dickens, referred to artists' models as 'sluts'.[52] The very act of Georgina posing was scandalous enough, but the way in which Maclise dressed her for the sitting should have rung warning bells.

Catherine or Mrs Hogarth, possibly both, would have chaperoned Georgina in the artist's studio. Etiquette books warned women against raising their skirts to show too much ankle as this was not only vulgar, but provocative. Yet Georgina was put in a dress that clung to her, revealing a curvaceous figure and exposing the outline of her leg.[53] Questions have to be asked about why Dickens, Catherine or Mrs Hogarth did not protest at Georgina being asked to pose in such a sexually suggestive way. One can imagine Dickens declaring it an honour for Georgina to appear in a painting by so skilful and prominent an artist as Maclise. At the same time, he was well aware of Maclise's reputation with women. In fact, Maclise's biographer argues that one reason their friendship was so intimate was because they felt able to speak openly about their desires for women. Maclise wrote to Dickens about an actress, 'the small waist, the neatly turned leg … You will like her, love her, doat [sic] upon her.'[54] In return, Dickens enticed Maclise to join him in seeking out prostitutes: 'there are conveniences of *all kinds* at Margate (do you take me?) and I know where they live'.[55] Dickens was worldly wise enough to know what might happen if the semi-clad, pretty, sexually burgeoning Georgina was closeted for hours on end with the sensual, attractive, Maclise.

Dickens no doubt trusted Maclise enough to hope he would not seduce Georgina, but failed to consider the harm it could do to her good name when the painting was put on sale and viewed publicly. Perhaps it was to limit the damage that, after the painting was finished, Dickens contrived to buy *Waterfall at St. Nighton's Kieve* without Maclise knowing he was the purchaser. The ruse was successfully accomplished and Dickens paid 100 guineas (£12,200) in late December 1842. However, Maclise discovered he had been tricked, and an argument ensued. This must have been resolved by March 1843, as Maclise asked for *Waterfall at St. Nighton's Kïeve* to be loaned to him for submission to a Royal Academy of Arts exhibition. Aspects of the painting have been described as 'a lesson in Victorian subtle-erotica'.[56] One can only wonder how Georgina felt, knowing the general public were filing past her image, staring at her naked ankles and the shapely contour of her figure through her clinging dress. She later tried to distance herself from the painting, but in some ways made matters worse, by admitting she was 'barely out of the schoolroom' when she posed.[57] She could justifiably have been upset with Dickens as the idea of her modelling was his, but her mother and sister let her down by failing to defend her modesty.

The disagreement behind them, Dickens continued to encourage Maclise to take a romantic interest in Georgina. As soon as the family moved to Italy for a year's stay, Dickens immediately wrote to persuade his friend to visit, sending a drawing of the Villa di Bella Vista, with a mischievous note saying, 'The (-) window in shadow, young sir, is the bower of Miss H'.[58] As far as Georgina's feelings were concerned, she never gave any indication she was ever in love with Maclise but she certainly appreciated his looks, remarked on his 'true boyish enthusiasm and ardour' and held him in deep affection.[59] By the time Georgina reached her eighteenth birthday, it was clear that nothing romantic was going to happen. A letter to Augusta de la Rue, a woman both Dickens and Georgina had become very friendly with, suggests that any hopes there might have been of an engagement were over. Writing after a performance of a play Dickens had produced, *Every Man in His Humour*, for which Maclise designed the costumes, he described his friend's anxious behaviour as the orchestra struck up the overture. Speaking of Maclise prompted a link to Georgina and he went on to add, 'Georgy is very well, and takes long country walks with me. – She is quite happy, I think. And I have left that matter where it was;

trusting to its wearing itself out, on her part, in due course.'[60] The editors of Dickens's letters infer that he is alluding to something that had occurred between Georgina and Maclise.

From this point on, Dickens, although still close to Maclise, started to mock his friend's appearance to Georgina. It may have been an attempt to comfort Georgina that he wrote how Maclise was losing his looks, '[he is] exceedingly bald on the crown of his head', and on a trip to Paris Dickens disparaged Maclise's clothes: 'I don't know what he may have, in a portmanteau like a Bible; but he certainly don't put it on, whatever it is. His shirt in front is very like a pillow-case.'[61] When Georgina was asked by an early biographer of Dickens what had caused the rupture in her brother-in-law's friendship with Maclise, she offered the unconvincing explanation that the widening of the Dickens circle made the earlier familiarity no longer possible. This was nonsense as their friendship had begun and thrived within a wide and busy social scene. More likely was the fact that the small irritations between the men, including Maclise's failure to propose to Georgina, grew into greater differences which, together, contributed to the breakdown in their friendship. Besides, Georgina was an unlikely choice of wife for Maclise. He was more than twenty years older than her and, unlike Dickens, he did not find young girls captivating. Maclise once said to Forster about Dickens, 'I'm never up to his young girls – he is so very fond of the age of "Nell", when they are most insipid'.[62]

As Georgina moved through her teenage years, she found herself increasingly enmeshed in the domestic running of Devonshire Terrace. In January 1844 Catherine gave birth to her fifth child, Francis Jeffrey (known as Frank). Prior to his arrival, a tetchy Dickens gloomily told a friend, 'Our domestic news is slight, but portentous. Coming events cast their shadows before. I have visions of a fifth child.'[63] Georgina's help was not required for the birth itself as Mrs Hogarth, Mrs Dickens senior, a wet nurse for the baby and a monthly nurse were in situ to oversee the arrival of the latest addition to the family.[64]

At first, Catherine seemed to regain her strength quickly and Georgina sent out invitations to Dickens's birthday dinner with the news that Catherine had cut short her confinement and 'is in the drawing room, and both she and Baby ... are getting on capitally', but post-natal depression descended shortly after.[65] Georgina stepped in, taking on some of her sister's domestic responsibilities and the secretarial work Catherine usually did for Dickens. As she got older, Georgina also deputised for Catherine as Dickens's social companion. Lamenting Catherine's lack of stamina after Frank's birth to Jane Carlyle ('Your countrywoman is going on very favourably – though with Northern caution and slowness'), there was always Georgina to join him on his brisk, lengthy walks around London.[66]

In early 1844, Dickens met Christiana Weller, a talented eighteen-year-old pianist. His attraction to Christiana is especially interesting in that, looked at alongside Emma Picken's account, a pattern in Dickens's romantic courting emerges that was to be repeated with Ellen Ternan. Later in 1844, he became close to Augusta de la Rue, the attractive thirty-four-year-old wife of a Swiss banker. It was Dickens's relationships with these two women that created a fissure in Georgina and Catherine's sisterly accord.

Dickens met Christiana Weller at a benefit at the Liverpool Mechanics' Institute in February 1844. He had left home in a despondent mood. Unnerved by having recently heard from his publishers that the success of *A Christmas Carol* had not generated the revenue he had anticipated, and with the arrival of his fifth child, his money worries were piling up. It was a completely different, more animated, Dickens who returned from Liverpool a few days later. He had met and become besotted by the young Christiana, whom he had heard play at the concert. The morning after the benefit and accompanied by his friend T. J. Thompson, Dickens rode over to see Christiana at her brother-in-law's house. In the same way that he had written a poem for Emma about Emma, Dickens composed a piece of doggerel which he insisted in writing in Christiana's album. Referring to the character of Sam Weller,

3 Christiana Weller

from *The Pickwick Papers*, the verse ended with the lines 'I love her name which has won me some fame/But Great Heaven how gladly I'd change it!' Arriving back in London, he despatched his own treasured copies of Tennyson, which the poet himself had given him, marking up the pages he wanted Christiana to read. After meeting Emma Picken, Dickens had contrived to see her again by encouraging the Smithsons to rent a holiday home next to his; using the same strategy again, Dickens urged Mr Weller to move his family from Liverpool to London. Promising to help promote her career, Dickens offered to introduce Christiana to the best musical professors in London. Christiana was constantly on Dickens's mind and he talked about her at every opportunity. Writing to his elder sister, Fanny Burnett, after a particularly demanding week, he wistfully declared: 'but for the recollection of Miss Weller (which has its tortures too), I don't know but I would as soon be comfortably suffocated, as continue to live in this wearing, tearing, mad, unhinged, and [m]ost extraordinary world'.[67] Dickens sent Maclise a copy of the verse he had written for 'that most wonderful girl, Miss Weller', while to T. J. Thompson he wrote, 'Good God what a madman I should seem, if the incredible feeling I have conceived for that girl could be made plain to anyone!'[68]

A part of his attraction to Christiana was, according to Michael Slater, that she 'seemed to him to be Mary come alive again', which ignited a fear in him that her fragility meant she was destined for an early death.[69] There is no consensus amongst biographers on how to construe Dickens's emotions. Some have interpreted Dickens's response to Christiana as more spiritual than carnal because she provoked memories of Mary.[70] Others have claimed there was a jocular element in his behaviour, while there are those who refer to him as being infatuated or having fallen in love.[71] Dickens was open with Christiana about how attracted he was to her; he told her in a letter that had he not been married he would have wooed her and went onto say that if he had encountered a rival for her love, it would be 'the greatest happiness and pleasure of my life to have run him through the body. In no poetical or tender sense, I assure you, but with good sharp Steel.'[72] Assessing how seriously Dickens was being, Edgar Johnson argued that 'it does not sound like pure fooling, nor would the circumstances be altogether appropriate for joking'.[73] Johnson wrote this in 1952, which hints at how twentieth-century attitudes to male privilege would slowly begin to change; a powerful man who was sending letters, giving presents, and finding ways of inveigling a much younger woman to spend time with him, all within twenty-four hours of meeting her, has uncomfortable undertones of control.

Dickens's friend T. J. Thompson had also fallen in love with Christiana and, as a widower, was free to pursue her. Thompson proposed to Christiana almost immediately, which she accepted but then called it off, confessing there were 'other footprints in the field'.[74] While the identity of Thompson's rival is, as David Paroissien remarks, 'an intriguing problem', he goes onto say that Dickens may have suspected that he was the one who had 'made an impression on Christiana Weller's heart'.[75] Dickens intimated he enjoyed the rivalry with T. J. Thompson in finding ways to win Christiana's attention. When Christiana finally agreed to marry Thompson and the date of the wedding was set, Dickens ordered a copy of an elaborate waistcoat with 'broad stripes of blue or purple' that Count D'Orsay designed for Macready's role in a play. Finding his tailor unable to envisage the garment, he wrote to Macready:

[L]end me that waistcoat for five minutes. I am bidden to a wedding … and my artist cannot, I find … imagine such a waistcoat. Let me show it to him as a sample of my tastes and wishes … and *eclipse* the bridegroom.'[76]

In his analysis of Christiana's letters and diaries, David Paroissien argues it would have been understandable if the inexperienced young girl had taken Dickens's conduct more seriously than he might have intended. Christiana recorded one episode in her diary that gives a clue to her emotions. Mr Weller had accepted Dickens's offer of mentoring his daughter and moved his family to London. The Dickenses were in Italy when Christiana and her sister, Anna, were walking around the streets near to their Chelsea home.[77] They came across Mrs Hogarth and her youngest daughter and Christiana invited the Hogarth women back to their house for tea, where the conversation turned to the Italian travels of the Dickens family. After tea, Christiana and Anna walked Mrs Hogarth and her daughter to their omnibus stop. As soon as the Hogarths had departed, Christiana and Anna abandoned their dignified behaviour, so thrilled had they been by something Mrs Hogarth had said. Christiana wrote in her diary that night that the two sisters had made 'shows of ourselves afterward from excitement' upon hearing 'about Boz and her daughter who died' (Dickens's beloved Mary Hogarth). Christiana was 'in ecstasies' when Mrs Hogarth revealed that her family thought how like Mary she was, 'a charming compliment for she must have been an angel'.[78] There are two ways of interpreting Christiana's response. Either she was flattered because she was likened to a long-dead girl who had had many good qualities, or her 'ecstatic' reaction was because Dickens was known to have idolised the deceased Mary, and if she reminded him of her, then some of that admiration might be deflected onto Christiana.

How did Georgina and Catherine respond when they met Christiana? Catherine could not have failed to realise Christiana was yet another young woman her husband was attracted to. Once again, Catherine showed no signs of jealousy, acting as kindly to

Christiana as she had towards Emma Picken. She played a part in helping Dickens fulfil his offer of furthering Christiana's musical career. Catherine arranged for Christiana to meet Mr Hogarth, who in turn introduced her to his own musical connections, and lent a hand in organising the young pianist's debut performances in London. When the Dickens family moved to Italy for a year, Catherine and Georgina maintained a friendly correspondence with her. After Christiana agreed for her engagement to T. J. Thompson to go ahead and, on the Dickenses' return to London, a party comprising the Dickens and Thompson families went for an outing on the Thames, with everyone staying over that night at Devonshire Terrace. The following morning Christiana said she 'talked confidentially' with Catherine, while Georgina accompanied Dickens to church.[79] The wedding was set for October and Christiana asked Georgina to be a bridesmaid. Georgina's reply to Christiana showed how keen she was to forge an intimacy: 'My dear Christie (I will not say *Miss Weller* – tho' *you* are so ceremonious)'.[80] What was to become a notable feature of Georgina's friendships was that she only chose women of whom Dickens approved, and her most intimate friendships were with females who had a deep regard and admiration for him.

When Dickens changed his opinion of Christiana, so, it seems, did Georgina. The year after Christiana and Thompson had married, they were reunited with the Dickenses in Lausanne. At this point Dickens made it clear that there was a lot he did not like about the new Mrs Thompson, saying she 'disappoints me very much. She is a mere spoiled child, I think, and doesn't turn out half as well as I expected. Matrimony has improved him, and certainly has not improved her.'[81] To his long-time friend Thomas Mitton he derided Christiana, writing she 'seems … to have a devil of a whimpering, pouting temper – but she is large in the family way, and that may have something to do with it'.[82] Regardless of Dickens's opinions, Catherine chose to continue her friendship with Christiana and the two women visited, went shopping, walking and driving together. After the holiday was over, Christiana and Catherine wrote to one another, albeit briefly. Fred Dickens's ill-fated marriage to Christiana's sister, Anna, put strains on relations between the families but, in *The Other Dickens*, Lillian Nayder places the blame for the disruption of Christiana and Catherine's friendship on the bickering between Dickens and Mr Weller. Where was Georgina in all this? It seems that once Dickens started to complain about Christiana, Georgina trod warily, careful to be seen to be neither friendly or unfriendly. In Lausanne, she occasionally joined Catherine in visiting Christiana, but chose to stay in the background playing the piano rather than chatting. If Catherine's continuing warmth could be interpreted as a refusal to countenance Dickens's condemnation of Christiana, then Georgina's distancing was a sign that she agreed with him.

It was in Genoa in September 1844 that the Dickenses and Georgina met Augusta de la Rue and her Swiss banker husband, Emile. Dickens's fascination with Augusta was very different to his attraction to Christiana. Augusta was a similar age to Catherine, petite, vivacious and suffered from facial spasms. Hearing her describe how she was also afflicted with headaches, experienced convulsions and was haunted by an apparition in her dreams, intrigued Dickens. Having tried mesmerism with some success back in England, Dickens suggested to Emile de la Rue that he use this method to treat his wife. Before long Dickens was mesmerising Augusta every day, occasionally in the early hours when she was in her night clothes. Although Augusta appeared to have genuine mental and physical health problems, these were not disabling enough to prevent her from socialising and travelling around Italy. She certainly seems to have been well enough to have enjoyed attracting the attention of their famous literary neighbour. Why Emile de la Rue allowed an enthusiastic amateur, however skilled, to become so intimate with his wife has to be wondered at.

Catherine was less gullible. Well aware of the possibility for sexual chemistry in the intimacy of the sessions, it seems that she may have made her unhappiness known early on at an event in Genoa attended by the two women because Augusta suddenly ended her treatment sessions with Dickens.[83] Despite her efforts, anything Catherine said had little lasting impact; Dickens soon resumed his daily mesmerising appointments with Augusta. Three months into her sixth pregnancy, Catherine lost patience, refusing to speak to either of the de la Rues or to travel in the same coach. This was exceptional behaviour by Catherine since she hardly ever had the courage to stand up to Dickens. Dickens deeply resented what he regarded as her jealousy, although others might see it as justifiable anger on Catherine's part, but he agreed to terminate his treatment of Augusta. Nevertheless, Augusta continued to try to make him see her.

Georgina must have seen how distraught Catherine was by the increasing familiarity between Dickens and Augusta. It was clear too how angry Catherine was, as much with the manipulative Augusta as with Dickens. Even so, Georgina was more than cordial with Augusta, in fact she befriended her. What could have made her prioritise a friendship with a woman she barely knew above supporting her upset sister? A possible reason is that Georgina was already in Dickens's bad books and she did not want to make matters worse by taking Catherine's side against him.

Georgina had angered Dickens by complaining to one of his friends about the female relative of another of their close friends. Displaying an adolescent arrogance, Georgina wrote to John Forster from Italy making snide comments about a visitor, Susan Atkins, the sister of Kitty Macready. Dickens was back in London for the publication of *The Chimes* and Georgina and Catherine were alone with Susan at the villa. Behind Susan's back the sisters talked and made fun of her, regarding her as stupid and boring. Georgina passed on their views of the unfortunate Susan to Forster. When Forster told Dickens how Catherine and Georgina had hatched a plan to get rid of Susan by urging her to go on a sightseeing tour to Rome on her own or, if she could not be persuaded to do that, they would leave her at the house while they travelled, he was furious. Dickens singled Georgina out for particular criticism because she had recorded her sarcastic observations in a letter to Forster. Dickens wrote to Catherine:

> I was pained to see (as I should have told Georgy before I left if I had had an opportunity) that in such a case as the Messages to Forster (she will know what I mean) she does a glaringly foolish and unnecessary silliness, and places huge means of misrepresentation in very willing hands. I should never forgive myself or you; if the smallest drop of coldness or misunderstanding were created between me and Macready. It will be created – I see it very clearly.[84]

Georgina had been warned. Dickens rarely reprimanded Georgina, so it was a salutary lesson for the seventeen-year-old girl. Choosing to take Catherine's side in the dispute over Augusta would run the risk of offending Dickens both because it suggested he was wrong in the way he was conducting himself and because it would imply that Georgina thought more highly of her sister than of him.

Apart from Georgina wanting to please Dickens, it seems that Augusta was both kind and interested in her. Whether it was youthful insecurity or a character trait, Georgina was impressed and grateful when she was taken notice of. Even in later life, Georgina expressed surprise and delight if someone appeared fond of her. She once wrote to a friend, thanking them for inviting a Miss Walter, 'I hope you will like her – I do very much. She is a little brusque – and a little eccentric but she is *most* intelligent – and energetic – and very warm hearted and sympathetic. And I believe she likes *me*!'[85] Augusta took Georgina under her wing when Dickens and Catherine went travelling around Italy and she treated her as Dickens did, as a treasured elder daughter. It would have been during this time that Georgina confided in Augusta any interest she had in the eligible Daniel Maclise. The de la Rues arranged for Georgina to be escorted from Genoa to Naples to join her sister and brother-in-law, from where a relieved Dickens wrote to say, 'My little Pet just arrived and safely.'[86]

As Georgina's teenage years drew to an end Dickens gave her another nickname to add to 'little Pet'. Calling her the 'Marchioness' after the character in *The Old Curiosity Shop*, Dickens summons up an image of a Georgina who was candid, loyal, full of common sense, timid and yet brave, someone with 'sharp, little worldly and also kindly ways'.[87] Catherine and Dickens regarded Georgina as mature and reliable enough to be left in Paris with five of the children when, in February 1847, they had to dash back across the Channel. Charley, who was at the King's School in London, had contracted scarlet fever. By May, Charley had recovered enough to recuperate in Brighton and be reunited with his brothers and sisters, only for them all to get whooping cough. In August, as Georgina and Catherine nursed the sick Dickens brood, more devastating news reached them, this time of their father, who was to be imprisoned for debt for a second time. Dickens had helped his in-laws three years earlier when George Hogarth owed money, but he was not in a position to bail him out this time. At the end of December 1847, Catherine miscarried when she and Dickens were in Scotland. Charley's birthday party on Twelfth Night was cancelled, with Georgina reporting Catherine's miscarriage as an 'unfortunate illness'.[88]

However useful Georgina was to the Dickenses, she was at an age when she needed to take stock of the possibilities for her future, and Dickens moved from teasing to urging her to consider her options. When Dickens organised a tour of his amateur theatrical group to the provinces, Georgina and Catherine went with them. It was while on tour that Dickens introduced her to one of the players, the artist Augustus Egg, who was to figure largely in the decisions Georgina was to make in the near future.

As she approached her twenties, Georgina's relationship with Catherine was far less complicated than her relationship with Dickens. Georgina and Catherine got on well together, even assuming an occasional bout of adolescent flouncing in the younger sister. Together, Dickens and Catherine accorded Georgina much attention and made her integral to their social and domestic life. Dickens acted as a caring father figure, but also flirted with her. At a time when the most thrilling men young Victorian women were likely to meet were the clergymen they encountered at Sunday worship, readers will have to decide for themselves the effects on a teenager of attention from a famous celebrity. Kindly words from the 'men of genius' Dickens or William Macready earned her trust and respect, and as far as Dickens was concerned, Georgina always accepted what he said. If he claimed that his only interest in Christiana Weller was mentoring her career or insisted his sole reason for spending time with Augusta de la Rue was to help her heal, then, as far as Georgina was concerned, there was nothing more to say; Dickens's word was enough. There was another side to Dickens that could be intimidating in ways that made men, as well as women, fearful of crossing him. The Dickens daughters, Mamie and Katey, discovered that when Catherine either upset or annoyed their father, Dickens expected them to side with him. Undoubtedly, the young Georgina would have felt herself under the same pressure. As she blossomed into young adulthood, Georgina's relationships with her sister and brother-in-law were set to change irrevocably.

Chapter 4

A 'lively young damsel' (1848–51)

Dickens and the twenty-one-year-old Georgina were great friends. The differences created by the age-gap between them had diminished, making their relationship less parental and more adult, and their mutual interests resulted in a genuine rapport. Georgina was an avid newspaper reader with a keen interest in current affairs and Dickens enjoyed their conversations, saying of her that, intellectually, 'she has one of the most remarkable capacities I have ever known'.[1] Both Dickens and Georgina shared a need for brisk daily walks, whether they were in the city or countryside. Keeping up with Dickens was no mean accomplishment. A young friend, Edmund Yates, joked that if any of Dickens's country house guests made the mistake of offering to 'face the ordeal' of a walk with their host, 'they seldom [asked] twice'.[2] Georgina was one of the few people with the enthusiasm and stamina to hike for seven to twelve miles at Dickens's rate of four miles per hour. The two bonded over their sense of humour, and Georgina would play pranks on friends to entertain Dickens.

A talented Georgina was an asset to the Dickenses' social and domestic life. Having inherited her father's musical skills, she could entertain their guests by playing the piano. Already fluent in French before joining the Dickens household, she learned Italian alongside Catherine and Dickens prior to their year in Genoa. As she was multilingual, Dickens enlisted her help in seeking out accommodation abroad for family holidays. Privately, she kept the family amused with impressions of people they knew. Georgina spoke of the years of her late teens and early twenties as 'my young and *happiest* days', 'my youthful days of carelessness and happiness'.[3] Meeting her for the first time, visitors found her cheerful and friendly and she received many compliments: 'Miss Hogarth, a very lovely person, with charming manners', and men commented on how attractive she was, describing her as 'a lively young damsel of twenty or twenty-four, rather good-looking' with a 'winning smile'.[4]

While Georgina was enjoying herself, the late 1840s were a busy and more stressful period for both Dickens and Catherine. Between January 1844 and August 1850, Catherine gave birth to five more children and had a miscarriage.[5] She was also fulfilling all the demands that came with Dickens's active social life, such as giving dinner parties, accompanying her husband to the theatre and visiting friends outside London. Dickens had all the pressures of earning enough money to support his ever-growing family and maintaining his reputation as a popular author. Having completed *Dombey and Son* in March 1848, he started working on ideas for what was to be one of his most popular books, *David Copperfield*. In December 1848 he produced the last of his Christmas books, *The Haunted Man*, and began sounding out John Forster about starting a weekly periodical. On top of his writing, Dickens was involved on a daily basis with Urania Cottage, the Home for Homeless Women he founded with Angela Burdett-Coutts in 1847.[6]

Catherine's frequent pregnancies and confinements meant Georgina regularly stepped in to support her sister, in terms of domestic duties, and Dickens, in acting as his social companion. Was Georgina the inspiration for the character of Agnes Wickfield, the competent, loyal, supportive housekeeper who more or less ran the family's domestic affairs in *David Copperfield*? When he was writing the book, Dickens stopped referring to Georgina as 'my little Pet' and started calling her 'my little housekeeper'.[7] However, the scholar Michael Slater argues that while Georgina may have been 'responsible for a touch or two in Dickens's portrayal of Agnes's "little housekeeper" ways', the principal inspiration for 'David's "good angel" was ... surely Mary Hogarth'.[8] Besides, Georgina adamantly denied she was the model for Agnes: 'No, no, no, ... not Agnes. Possibly there is something of me in Esther Summerson, but certainly not Agnes.'[9]

This situation, where Georgina took over when Catherine was in the late stages of pregnancy and confined, was not ideal for the Dickenses' marriage. As Catherine's biographer, Lillian Nayder, points out, it created an impression of Georgina in charge of the house while Catherine was the 'specialist in childbearing'.[10] Nayder argues Georgina was in a better position than Catherine to achieve a more equivalent, although not equal, relationship with Dickens because she was single. While Georgina's unmarried status and the fact she was a younger sister made her subordinate to Catherine, she was not confined by childbearing nor subject to the law of coverture (which made Catherine's identity subservient, and regarded both legally and socially as an extension of Dickens). Certainly, Dickens encouraged Georgina's wit – witticisms he may not have found acceptable coming from Catherine. We can only imagine Dickens's reactions if it were Catherine, rather than Georgina, making jokes at his friends' expense. Writing to a friend suffering from a minor illness, Dickens remarked, 'Mrs Dickens sends you her best regards, and Miss Hogarth says she thinks you are shamming'.[11] On another occasion, during a holiday on the Isle of Wight, Georgina, Dickens and family friend John Leech visited an infant school. They sat in the classroom watching the children take an examination. Leech described his horror when a child came up to him with:

> a sum in arithmetic of the most terrific nature to look over, and see if it was correct. I looked at it for some time, went through pantomime expressions of decided approval and passed it on to Dickens who immediately (to my confusion) found no end of blunders ... Miss Hogarth I have found out sent this fiend in childish shape to me.[12]

Just days after Georgina set Leech up, she acted as Dickens's sidekick to produce a piece of theatre he could later regale his friends with. It involved the owner of a hotel they were staying in who simultaneously amused and frustrated Dickens. Dickens complained that, '[h]e won't let me have an opinion of my own, and bruises me (as Maclise would say) and dances on my body every day at dinner. Here is a specimen.' Dickens went on to recount what happened when he asked after a local woman who looked after the bathing machines. The hotel owner, Ballard, contradicted everything Dickens said:[13]

> *Inimitable* (taking Punch) And how's Miss Collin going on, Ballard?[14]
>
> *Ballard.* Oh, well Sir, she ain't going on at all – not what can be called going on Sir, you know.

After more back and forth Georgina interjected, giving Dickens an opportunity to turn the episode into an entertainment:

> *Georgina* (here you must suppose the imitation) But she drinks, don't she Mr. Ballard.
>
> *Ballard.* Oh dear no Miss!
>
> *Inimitable* (to Georgina fiercely). What the Devil are you so fond of disparaging people for? Drinks! Who ever heard of her drinking! What a damned extraordinary thing it is, that you can't hold your tongue! – *I* never heard of her drinking (*to Ballard*) nor anybody else.
>
> *Ballard* (with a smile of pity) Oh everybody *here*, has heard of it Sir – and knows it well – but we don't see these things in Broadstairs, Sir, and make it a rule among ourselves never to mention 'em you know Sir. It's best not.[15]

It seems that although Victorian codes of conduct were restrictive for all women, unmarried women had greater freedom to publicly tease men than their married counterparts did.

Although Georgina was regarded as an asset to his household, Dickens hoped to see her married off. The first sign that Georgina might shortly be settled and start her own family came in 1849. She was twenty-two when she received a proposal of marriage. The suitor's name is unknown, but John Forster seems a likely contender as he had watched Georgina grow into an attractive, intelligent woman. Whoever it was had their offer refused. As Dickens observed dolefully in an end-of-year letter to a friend, 'We have had no marriages or giving in marriage here. We might have had, but a certain young lady, whom you know, is hard to please.'[16] There was, though, another admirer waiting to pay court to Georgina: the artist Augustus Egg.

Dickens was quick to spot a possible match in Augustus Egg. A formally trained painter, Egg made his debut at the Royal Academy in 1838. Egg was well liked by his fellow artists and had many friends. In terms of looks, the artist William Holman Hunt described Augustus Egg as handsome, broad chested, with wide shoulders, an aquiline nose, thin lips, large chin and a sallow complexion. At five feet seven inches (1.70 metres) in height, he was significantly shorter than Daniel Maclise, nor as tall as Dickens. While there was a twenty-one-year age-gap between Georgina and Maclise, and a fifteen-year age difference between her and Forster, Egg was eleven years older than Georgina. Egg joined Dickens's amateur theatrical group in 1848 and Dickens soon grew fond of the kind-hearted artist. Egg was hard working, generous and always willing to lend others a helping hand; Dickens described him as a 'dear gentle little fellow', 'always sweet-tempered, humorous, conscientious, thoroughly good, and thoroughly beloved'.[17] After Dickens had completed *Dombey and Son*, he threw himself into at least five different stage productions in which Egg played a full part. When Georgina met Egg, Dickens noticed how well the two got on together. Seizing the chance to matchmake, he took them on a scouting trip to find suitable locations for a tour of the acting company. The party were in the West Midlands in May 1848, when Dickens made a detour to Shakespeare's birthplace at Stratford-upon-Avon, where he, Georgina and Egg, with four others, signed the visitors' book.

Augustus Egg had weaknesses that Georgina would have found difficult to tolerate given her admiration for self-possessed 'men of genius'. A kind description of Egg was that he was modest but, in contrast to Maclise's attractive humility, Egg displayed a severe lack of confidence. One of his best friends, Wilkie Collins, spoke of 'his readiness to be convinced that he was wrong on any question'.[18] There was also the matter of Egg's poor health. If they married, Georgina would have to go on the long walks she so enjoyed alone because Egg was a severe asthmatic. He also possessed an idiosyncrasy that amused and occasionally discomfited his friends. According to fellow artist William Frith, Egg, 'either from a defective ear or from Cockney surroundings … had some peculiarities in his pronunciation which were embarrassing and sometimes ludicrous'.[19] When Egg played the part of a poet in one of the amateur theatrical productions, his opening line was 'Years ago when patrons were' which, despite constant reminders, he persisted in saying 'Here's a go! when patrons were'.[20] His romantic feelings for Georgina are clearly evident in an affectionate sketch he made of her, head gracefully bowed over her sewing. Georgina liked Egg, and her brother-in-law's fondness for the talented, kindly artist would have endeared him to her. What Egg did not possess was charisma and, sadly for him, he was trying to woo Georgina when she had so many other exciting things going on in her life.

Georgina had started to appear on stage as a member of Dickens's amateur theatrical group. Dickens usually allocated backstage jobs to her, asking her to notify the actors of the times and places for rehearsals, numbering the seats and sending out invitations and tickets for the performances. In October 1850, he offered her an opportunity to share some of the limelight she had only ever before enjoyed as a spectator. An old acquaintance, but only recently a friend, Sir Edward Bulwer-Lytton, asked Dickens to bring his acting company to perform *Every Man in His Humour* at his home, Knebworth House. Eleven years older than Dickens, Bulwer-Lytton was already a famous writer when the younger author took up his pen.

Bulwer-Lytton, described as 'handsomely aquiline, auburn-curled, beringed and ornate of dress, had been, together with D'Orsay and Disraeli, one of the flamboyant dandies emulated by the youthful Boz'.[21] On the occasion of the Knebworth performances, the main female character was played by another new friend of Dickens's, Mary Boyle, with Georgina taking the part of Mistress Bridget. Dickens announced this event to Maclise, exclaiming, 'Miss Boyle – Amateur, who plays one part – Georgina t'other(!)'.[22] Georgina also appeared in two farces, as Miss Knibbs in *Turning the Tables* and as Constance in *Animal Magnetism*.

For Georgina, the Knebworth House visit was a high point in her life, but less so for her sister, who had given birth to a baby just three months earlier and was also due to perform in the play. Catherine sprained her foot falling through a trap door at rehearsal and had to be replaced. From 19 November 1850, the play ran for three nights. On Georgina's first public appearance the *Hertford Mercury* reported that she and Catherine's replacement, Nelly Lemon, played with 'such charming *naivete*' that 'we regretted the scenes in which they did not appear'.[23] Dickens was very pleased with her, reporting to friends that she had 'covered herself in glory'.[24] As well as basking in the accolades, Georgina found their host, Sir Edward Bulwer-Lytton, fascinating.

It was becoming clear what type of man she was attracted to. Edward Bulwer-Lytton possessed considerable creative talent. Not only a popular author of novels, plays and verse, he was also the editor of two magazines, had an interest in mysticism and enjoyed a successful political career. Alongside his tall, athletically proportioned, handsome appearance, Bulwer-Lytton displayed a languid, aristocratic, self-assured presence. Women found Bulwer-Lytton very attractive and he received many letters from besotted young women from all walks of life. Servant girls and milliners were as likely as the highest-born ladies in society to send him gushing messages. He was a married man, but he and his wife had separated acrimoniously fourteen years earlier, partly because of his adulterous behaviour. Like Dickens, he had the power to charm but, unlike Dickens, Bulwer-Lytton had no compunction about responding fulsomely to women who showed an ardent interest in him. After his death, it was discovered he had fathered many children besides his legitimate son and daughter. When Georgina met Bulwer-Lytton and was as bowled over by him as other young women had been, she would have known only that he was married, but living separately from his wife.

On the final night of the performances and buzzing with excitement, Georgina plucked up courage to ask Bulwer-Lytton for a sample of his writing – the equivalent of a fan asking for an autograph. The day after returning to Devonshire Terrace, Georgina received a letter from Bulwer-Lytton, addressed to her. This was a thrill in itself as it was more common for any notes for her to be included in correspondence addressed to Dickens. The fact that this 'man of genius' had not only noticed her but taken the trouble to write, seemed almost overwhelming, and one can almost hear the quiver of pleasure in her voice as she wrote back:

> Dear Sir Edward
>
> How can I thank you enough for the delightful manner in which you have complied with my request. When I asked for a line of your writing I did not venture to hope for a long kind letter, and I assure you I never was more gratified in my life, than I was by receiving it this morning. Believe me it will be preserved among my most precious possessions as much as the memory of the happy week at Knebworth will be treasured among the dearest and most delightful recollections of my life.[25]

Bulwer-Lytton had an interest in the occult, and Georgina asked Dickens to pass on a message saying how deeply impressed she was by his knowledge of the magical and mystical. She asked Dickens to tell him that she agreed with the man who had called Bulwer-Lytton 'a Wizard'.[26] It may have been these supernatural skills she was referring to when she talks in her letter about his prediction for her marriage prospects:

> Once more, dear Sir Edward, let me assure you how sensible I am of, and how grateful to you for, all your great kindness to me. I have such confidence in your predictions that I feel sure no King of Hearts will interfere with the visit to Knebworth in the Summer, which we are already looking forward to ... I hope it will not be long before we see you in London.
> Believe me
> Yours affectionately (if I may say so?)
> Georgina Hogarth[27]

An experienced man like Bulwer-Lytton would have recognised Georgina's attempts to flirt with him. Georgina's letter shows she was gripped by the allure of Bulwer-Lytton in a way she had not been since her first adolescent crush on Dickens; later she said, 'I sincerely loved [him] ... for he showed a never failing regard for me from the time I first knew him'.[28] In comparison, Augustus Egg was not an attractive option. Wisely, Egg decided to say nothing about marriage that year. Instead he bided his time, waiting until the debonair Bulwer-Lytton was not around, when Georgina might be amenable to his proposal. The offer of marriage came a year later, in autumn 1851.

Given the amount of attention Egg was paying her, Georgina must surely have realised that he was going to propose at some point. As a level-headed, twenty-four-year-old woman, she knew that Dickens's nickname for her as 'the Virgin' was wearing thin.[29] The older she got, the harder marriage proposals would be to come by. How long it took Georgina to decide is not clear, but she eventually refused Egg. Dickens believed a marriage to Egg would have been a good match for Georgina, telling a friend that in marrying him 'she would still have the Artist kind of life she is used to, about her'.[30] He admitted encouraging her to accept, as '[i]t would have been a good thing for her, as he is an excellent fellow, and is well off, over and above his professional reputation which stands high. But she said No, though they are very good friends.'[31]

While several biographers have asserted that Georgina 'chose' not to marry, it is not the same thing as acknowledging she did not get married. Georgina probably hoped to marry a man she had fallen in love with, but she was also well aware that marriage for a woman was about much more than romance. Aside from societal expectations which regarded single females as inferior to wives, it was imperative for women to seek financial security. Georgina was a relation by marriage and could not assume that Dickens would continue to provide for her. She also gave the impression that she wanted her own children, treating her eldest niece Mamie as a substitute daughter, referring to her in later years as '*my* girl' and envied those who were able to have a 'Daughter living with you' as it 'gives so much more happiness to your life!'[32] Her brother-in-law's enthusiasm for the match might also have been expected to have influenced Georgina to look favourably upon the suitor.

After Egg's initial proposal was rejected, he kept his offer open. Two years later, when on holiday in Italy with Wilkie Collins and Egg, Dickens continued to advocate on Egg's behalf, writing to Catherine, 'A general sentiment expressed this morning, that Georgina ought to be married. Perhaps you'll mention it to her!'[33] With spinsterhood beckoning, and the idea of her own home and family disappearing into the mist, there had to be more to Georgina's refusal to accept Egg's proposal than because she saw him as a friend.

Setting to one side the fact that Georgina did not love Egg, there are two corresponding explanations for her decision to turn him down. The first was that Dickens's opinion of a man mattered to Georgina and it was evident to her that he did not respect Egg as he did Maclise or Bulwer-Lytton. Dickens urged Georgina to accept Egg while at the same time showing that he regarded him as something of a joke. There were occasions when Dickens, albeit affectionately, mocked the hapless painter in public. When the amateur theatrical group was on tour, Dickens would shout out during supper, 'Augustus!' When the hard of hearing Egg eventually heard his name and looked up, Dickens declaimed in a serio-comic voice, 'God bless you, Augustus!'[34] The company collapsed in mirth, leaving Egg at a loss for words.[35] There were other slights and put downs. He told Georgina and others that Egg was not bright enough for her. Dickens wrote disparagingly to Angela Burdett-Coutts that Egg was 'very far her inferior intellectually', and was only slightly less direct with Georgina, saying, 'Egg is an excellent fellow and full of good qualities – I am sure a generous and staunch man at heart. He is not above the average, intellectually; but I believe he is, in a good and honorable nature.'[36] Dickens made fun too of Egg's faltering attempts to get to grips with the Italian language, telling Georgina: 'He understands much more than you would suppose of what is said, but it is such a painful effort to him to acquire anything, although I have really taken pains to explain it with the greatest clearness and patience, that I doubt if he understands now.'[37] Whatever Dickens said to support Egg's offer of marriage, Georgina was hardly likely to be impressed by a suitor regarded as inferior by her esteemed brother-in-law. The idea of becoming 'Mrs Egg' when she had probably hoped for 'Mrs Maclise' was not appealing; overall, Augustus Egg was simply in a lower league.

There was also the matter of what Georgina would lose if she swapped her place in the Dickens household for a home with Augustus Egg. As Mrs Dickens's sister, she was included on the guest lists of London's elite, invited to stay in grand country houses, and she could meet the most important people of the day in the drawing room at Devonshire Terrace. At the times when Catherine was incapacitated and Georgina was promoted to acting mistress of the house, she got to display her wide range of skills. It was Georgina whom Dickens asked to scribe for him as he walked about the study composing chapters for *A Child's History of England*.

Not only did Georgina demonstrate she was an effective secretarial assistant and domestic manager of a large and busy household, she also possessed the social graces required to be the hostess and companion of a famous man. What was to be gained in exchanging the highs and occasional lows of being a sister in the large household of a prominent member of society for the life of a wife in the small establishment of a minor artist? Did she ever think that if Catherine could get herself a talented, charismatic husband, then surely she, who had proved herself more than able, was worthy of an equivalent match? Dickens was to say that Georgina 'sacrificed the best part of her youth and life' to look after his children, but whether she regarded it as a sacrifice is another matter.[38] Georgina's motivation for rejecting Egg's proposal might, in part, have been a refusal to accept a husband and home inferior to the one Catherine had achieved. It did not mean, though, that she had given up on marriage, rather that she was prepared to wait for a better offer.

Tragedy haunted the Dickenses in the latter part of the 1840s. Dickens's sister, Fanny, died of consumption in 1848, then his father, John Dickens, died following an operation in 1851 and, most upsetting of all, baby Dora died of a seizure two weeks later. Moving into Tavistock House in November 1851 was to be a new start for the family. Within two months of losing Dora, Catherine was pregnant again. The new house was familiar territory for the Dickenses, being just streets away from their first home in Doughty Street. Dickens and Catherine's good friends Mark and Nelly Lemon, with their ten children, were nearby at Gordon Street. When Dickens first looked round Tavistock House it was far less impressive than Devonshire Terrace, but it had potential. He signed a forty-five-year lease on 25 July 1851, paying £1,542 (£229,000) and set about having major renovations done. It was one of three houses, set back from the main road behind iron railings and sharing a common carriage area. There were eighteen rooms spread over the ground floor, two upper floors, an attic with bedrooms for the servants and the basement. The most striking feature was the new bathroom.

Although there had been a water closet at Devonshire Terrace, bathing still took place in dressing rooms. At Tavistock House a shower, surrounded by brightly coloured waterproof curtains, was installed, with the lavatory partitioned off. Dickens's study was on the first floor and had a door which was designed to catch the visitor's eye. When inside the study, the closed door appeared to be an extension of the library. Fake bookshelves displaying the spines of dummy books gave observers the impression that they were looking at an extension of the actual bookshelves lining the walls. The simulated book-spines carried amusing titles: *The Life of a Cat – in Nine Volumes*, *Hansard's Guide to Refreshing Sleep* and the *History of a Short Chancery Suit* in twenty-one volumes.

With more bedrooms than at Devonshire Terrace, Mamie and Katey were given one on a lower floor decorated with wallpaper covered in wildflowers and chintzy floral-patterned bedspreads. Dickens wanted Catherine, who had been left in charge of the decorations while he was on tour with the theatrical group, to give special attention to his sister-in-law's accommodation: 'See that Georgina's room is made as comfortable as possible, with any little garniture that can be ingeniously got into it – a larger washing stand – table with ample writing materials – the books upon it, the Scarlet letter and Sydney Smith's lectures on Moral Philosophy.'[39] Exhibiting his usual need to control his surroundings, Dickens left instructions for the paintings in the dining room to be hung in exactly the same order they had been in Devonshire Terrace. The children were allocated their own pegs in the hall and Dickens would be after them if they left hats on the seat or wrong peg. Alfred recalls that he once risked brushing his coat in the dining room, rather than outside, but his father caught him and the telling-off he received guaranteed 'I never by any chance committed that particular offence afterwards'.[40]

The relationships between Georgina, Catherine and Dickens were shifting. The close bond between the sisters had loosened as Georgina reached adulthood. One illustration of this was that

Georgina started to make her own friends, independent of Catherine and her friendship group. She had always gravitated towards those women Dickens showed a particular liking for, such as Christiana Weller and Augusta de la Rue, and immediately took to one woman who revered Dickens as much as she did, Mary Louisa Boyle.

The two women met in 1849 on a rail journey to stay with Dickens's friends Richard and Lavinia Watson at Rockingham Castle. Mary, a cousin of Lavinia, was sitting alone in her carriage when Dickens threw open the door and insisted she return with him to his compartment to meet Georgina and Catherine. That weekend, Dickens and Mary entertained their Watson hosts and the other guests by performing a scene from *Nicholas Nickleby* and became fast friends thereafter. They conducted an exaggerated flirtation in which he addressed her as his 'Dearest Meery'. With Mary having Dickens's seal of approval, Georgina was motivated to forge her own friendship with 'Dearest Meery'. Both women adored Dickens and shared a love of amateur theatricals. They remained single and childless, yet both disapproved of the growing women's movement for greater equality. Georgina's position on women was that 'Woman's Disability' was not due to her legal status, but 'consists in her own constitution and temperament'.[41] For her part, Mary wrote regretfully in 1902 of the time when 'the gentler sex [had not] the ambition of their sisters of the present day who demand a right to sit at the official board with the lords of creation'.[42]

Less is known about another woman who became a lifelong friend, Rosa White, the wife of the Reverend James White of Bonchurch, Isle of Wight. Dickens always liked Rosa much more than he liked James, whom he found a bit of a bore. Whatever Rosa thought of Dickens is unrecorded but, judging from an argument she had with Catherine in 1854, she was not particularly fond of her. Both Mary Boyle and Rosa White were older than Georgina by several years, as indeed was Augusta de la Rue, all being around the same age as Dickens.

It was predictable too that the relationship between the sisters changed once Georgina reached adulthood and took on more responsibility. When the Dickenses had to make a hasty retreat from Paris to care for Charley when he caught scarlet fever, Georgina was given £80 (£11,900) to spend as she deemed appropriate on housekeeping. As she entered her twenties, Dickens increased her quarterly allowance to £7.10 (£1,000). It was not unusual to find two adult female family members living under one roof. Kitty Macready experienced a similar 'job share' with Letitia Macready, but the difference was that Letitia, as the sister of the master of the house, occupied a different, higher, status to that of Georgina as a wife's sister. While the adult Georgina could exercise more authority than previously, she remained subordinate to Catherine. Any upgrade to acting mistress of the house was always short-lived and Georgina had to readjust to the occasional indignity that went with being lower down the family hierarchy. When the Macreadys held a celebratory dinner party to commemorate their twenty-third wedding anniversary and the christening of their daughter, Catherine, Georgina and Dickens were invited. Dickens told Georgina she could not go as this would have meant thirteen at table.

Relations between Dickens and Catherine were also changing. In November 1850, Dickens started his weekly magazine, *Household Words*, recruiting a colleague from his newspaper days, William Henry Wills, to be secretary and sub-editor. He set up a permanent office for the magazine at 16 Wellington Street, thus establishing a separate workspace. His study at Tavistock House was where Dickens continued to write but, from now on, a considerable part of each week involved visits to the office. Dickens's biographer Claire Tomalin pointed out that 'from the start he used Wellington Street as much more than an office … it became a means to escape into bachelor life'.[43] He had two rooms made comfortable and tastefully furnished, using it as overnight accommodation and a place to entertain his male friends.

At home, Dickens's unmarried, childless, sister-in-law had freedoms his wife and mother of his children did not have. Lillian Nayder comments, '[e]ven as she deferred to his authority, Georgina could identify with Dickens and participate in a number of his masculine activities'.[44] He did not need to experience a loss of a social companion when Catherine was in the latter stages of pregnancy and during her confinement, as Georgina could step in. After Dora's birth on 16 August 1850, Dickens did not adhere to his previous practice of remaining close at hand in the days following the arrival. Within hours of Catherine giving birth, Dickens left London in time to join Georgina and the children for dinner in Broadstairs. Although Dickens wrote Catherine loving letters, telling her how missed she was, he did not return to London for seven days and, when he was due, told Catherine he would arrive home:

> between 11 and 12. This is not for your information (as you will have shut up shop then), but for Annes, that she may make my bed in the night-nursery where I can have air. If I can't come tomorrow, I shall come on Friday, when I have a good deal before me at the H. W. office.[45]

Dickens then spent all day at the office and returned to Broadstairs the following morning. The reason for his swift departure and prolonged period away from home was that he was rushing to finish *David Copperfield* and needed quiet. However, at Tavistock House Catherine was attended by Mrs Hogarth, youngest sister Helen and a monthly nurse, all looking after one baby, and it must surely have offered a more peaceful environment than Broadstairs, where there were guests staying and children running around. Catherine remained at home for three weeks while Georgina kept house for Dickens, looked after the children as well as several visitors, and organised dinner parties for eight or more guests.

Between 1852 and 1857 events took a turn that would destroy the Dickenses' marriage and undermine Georgina's privileged place within their household.

Chapter 5

Dickens's mid-life crisis (1852–7)

Dickens was in his early forties when he had a mid-life crisis. It caused almost as much devastation to Georgina as it did to Catherine. Not only did it change Georgina's relationship with Dickens, but it also brought her and Catherine's sisterly union to breaking point. If Dickens had not made it obvious that he valued his sister-in-law's company and her domestic skills over those of his wife, then Georgina and Catherine's relationship might have survived the Dickenses' separation. Although biographers cite 1854–5 as the period in which the Dickenses' marriage was under pressure, indications of an increasingly unhappy Dickens were there some time earlier.

The year 1852 began in a familiar way. Georgina took over her sister's duties as Catherine prepared for the birth of her last child, Edward (known as Plorn), who arrived on 13 March. Dickens did not welcome the arrival of his tenth child, telling Angela Burdett-Coutts that his son was blooming, but 'I cannot afford to receive [him] with perfect cordiality, as on the whole I could have dispensed with him'.[1] He immersed himself in his work, seemingly unable to rest and expending his energies through writing *Bleak House* (1852), then *Hard Times* (1854), followed by *Little Dorrit* (1855) and editing *Household Words*. He also kept up a regular involvement with Urania Cottage, gave innumerable talks to raise money for charity and was busy planning tours for his amateur theatrical group.

Dickens increasingly called on Georgina to act as his personal assistant. She copied out the manuscript he had written for his own youngsters, *The Life of Our Lord*, and she was still doing Catherine's job of writing letters for Dickens a year after Plorn's birth. He handed over responsibility for scouting out properties abroad for their summer vacation to Georgina, which meant her making a trip across to Boulogne, accompanied only by a servant. At least, for the most part, these assignments gave Georgina a distinct role which did not encroach on Catherine's territory. However, as Dickens's mid-life crisis began to take hold and he blurred the appropriate boundaries between wife and sister-in-law, his behaviour provoked a disastrous reaction from Georgina.

What were the signs that Dickens was having a mid-life crisis? For one thing, he sought out new experiences and people. He developed a keen interest in 'table-turning', a fashionable American parlour trick that is known today as a séance. It involved people attempting to communicate with spirits by sitting around a table, placing their hands on it and slowly speaking the alphabet aloud. The table would tilt at the appropriate letter to spell out words. Dickens described an evening at his home when '[w]e spun a table in the most extraordinary manner last night. Mamey, Katey, their governess, I, Catherine, Georgina … The Pembroke table in my study gambolled like an insane elephant.'[2] Dickens started drinking more than usual, telling a friend, 'I think you may like to know … that I am … working, walking, eating, and drinking – my bottle of wine a day – at tenpence'.[3] He was able to find some distraction from his restlessness through the company of a new friend, the author Wilkie Collins. Collins was twelve years his junior and leading a more adventurous life than that of Dickens; he held bohemian and unconventional attitudes, was a frequent laudanum user and was conducting a relationship with a woman he referred to as his housekeeper. As Robert Douglas-Fairhurst argues, 'Dickens quickly recognised [Collins] as another potential rival self, even if he liked to pretend they were attracted to each other purely as opposites.'[4]

Collins soon became his chosen companion for jaunts around Britain and Europe.

Classic signs of a male mid-life crisis are efforts to change appearance and act in a more youthful way. Aged forty-three, Dickens re-grew a moustache and found a new young woman to flirt with.[5] Kate Horne was the comely, auburn-haired wife of a writer for *Household Words*. Dickens clearly found her attractive. Kate wrote to her husband how 'Dickens has teazed me more than ever', saying, 'he and I must some day go to Italy together' and telling her she looked 'provokingly well'.[6] Kate, though, was an astute woman and when she joined Dickens and his family on holiday, she saw through the façade. Finding the constant excursions, games and attempts to generate a sense of fun being had by all both frenetic and wearing, she observed, 'I think with the Dickens's [sic] almost more than anyone else you require to have some room to breathe alone'.[7]

Dickens was drawn to slim, young girls and a photograph of a thirty-seven-year-old Catherine, taken shortly after the birth of Plorn and while she was suffering from ill health, illustrates how much she had aged. Dickens was quick to criticise any woman carrying weight, joking about a once-beautiful, but now exceedingly corpulent, opera singer, saying, 'I live in terror of asking Adelaide Kemble to dinner (she lives near at hand), lest she should not be able to get in at the dining room door'.[8] He began commenting on Catherine's changing figure: 'Mrs. Dickens is stouter, though not quite so well in health as she used to be'.[9] Georgina was put in the difficult position of repeating to her overweight sister that Dickens and others were commenting publicly on her size. Writing to Georgina, Dickens added a postscript: 'Oh! – Something else for Catherine! – She is described in Mrs. Stowe's book which Forster … informed me [of] yesterday … Mrs. Stowe is of the opinion that she is "large", I believe.'[10] Dickens became more and more critical as the decade wore on, seeing Catherine's increased weight as a sign of her lack of self-control, rather than the effect of constant childbearing: 'Last Friday I took Mrs. Dickens, Georgina and Mary and Katey to dine at the Trois frères. Mrs. Dickens nearly killed herself, but the others hardly did that justice to the dinner that I had expected.'[11]

Replying to an invitation to eat with friends, Dickens wrote sardonically: 'Mrs. Dickens would be glad to kill the Dragon – as glad, let us say, as Miss Saint Georges – and would triumph in the act'.[12] He could not have said any more clearly that Catherine was a glutton and, like the once-slim actress Marguerite Saint Georges, had become exceedingly fat.

Catherine's appearance reflected on Dickens at a time when, as Kathryn Hughes says, 'the lady of the house [was] a walking billboard for her husband's material success'.[13] Although Catherine dressed-up to her station as Dickens's wife, her physical appearance was scrutinised in the same way that Dickens commented on the wives of other men. He observed that the French dramatist Augustin Eugène Scribe had a wife with 'the figure of five and twenty, and is strikingly handsome', and he reported that he was relieved to discover that a friend's wife, whom he thought 'the most disagreeable-looking woman … I ever saw in my life', was not in fact 'his wife; [as] she is ill, [but] was her sister'.[14] Observations on Catherine's appearance by acquaintances of the Dickenses were mostly unkind. The author Eliza Lynn Linton remarked caustically, 'Dickens had no eye for beauty per se. He could love a comparatively plain woman – and did.'[15] Charles Kingsley, the writer, wrote nastily to his wife, 'Mrs. Dickens! Oh the fat vulgar vacancy!'[16] One imagines how irritated Dickens would have been to hear about such comments and not because they insulted Catherine.

As Dickens's disinclination for Catherine grew, he turned towards his sister-in-law. Dickens had always teased and flattered Georgina, encouraging a certain level of intimacy, although there is nothing to suggest he ever meant anything serious by it. Aged twenty-five, Georgina was past the late-adolescent bloom he found so physically appealing. The fact he was not sexually attracted could explain how he failed to realise that, by showing his increased need for her, he risked deepening her feelings for him. His demands on Georgina were both physical and emotional. Dickens was seemingly oblivious to how a married man should not be invading the privacy of an unmarried woman's bedroom. The holiday homes they leased in Broadstairs or Boulogne often required rearrangements to the accommodation, and while it was one thing for Georgina to give up her bedroom to a visitor or to share it with a female guest, it was quite another to find Dickens had moved in with her. He would use her bedroom to wash and undress, and although this did not happen when she was in bed, it was, nevertheless, encroaching on her private space. If he was unable to concentrate in a house full of family and guests, he tried to recreate the sanctity of his study by having his writing materials brought into her bedroom.

When he needed emotional support, Dickens sought Georgina out for solace and companionship. He did not think twice about going to her when she was in bed and waking her up. After one argument with his friend John Forster, he was 'so disordered ... that by no process I could possibly try, could I get to sleep afterwards. At last, I gave it up as a bad job, and walked about the house 'til 5 – paying Georgina a visit and getting her up for company.'[17] On another occasion, he turned to Georgina to help him expend his pent-up energy after receiving news that the courts were failing to put an end to the persecution of Angela Burdett-Coutts by her stalker. He wrote to a friend that he only prevented himself from 'explod[ing] ... like a shell, on the subject of the English law in general' by 'going out to refresh myself with a walk, and shattering the peace of my sister-in-law instead'.[18] It would hardly be surprising if Georgina found her adolescent romantic and sexual feelings for Dickens were rekindled as he singled her out and acted in a rather too intimate manner towards her.

Dickens made it obvious to the rest of his family that he felt greater affection for Georgina than Catherine. When he went on a tour of Italy in 1853 with Augustus Egg and Wilkie Collins, the sisters remained in London with the children. Since his letters home were intended to be passed around or read aloud, one wonders what the two women made of the much warmer tone in those addressed to Georgina.

To Georgina Hogarth, 29 October 1853 from Genoa

I wish you were here to take some of the old walks. It is quite strange to walk about alone. Good-bye, my dear Georgy … I was charmed with your account of the Plornishghenter and everything and everybody else. Kiss them all for me.

To Catherine Dickens, 30 October 1853 from Genoa

This is merely a business letter containing the sketch of our movements that I have at last been able to make … It is not very important but you may naturally like to know where we are … My heartiest love to dear Macready, and to Miss Macready … With love to Georgy.

On the day the party left for the next stage of the journey, Dickens, unusually, wrote to his wife and sister-in-law simultaneously.

To Georgina Hogarth, 4 November 1853 from Naples

I look forward with joy to coming home again, to my old room, and the old walks, and all the old pleasant things … I am afraid this is a dull letter, for I am tired. You must take the will for the deed, my dear, and good night.

To Catherine Dickens, 4 November 1853 from Naples

My best love to Mamey and Katey, and Sydney the King of the Nursery, and Harry, and the dear little Plornishghenter … I hope to hear nothing but good news from you, and to find nothing but good spirits in your expected letter, when I come to Rome. I already begin to look homeward, being now at the remotest point of the journey, and to anticipate the pleasure of return.

It was around this time that Georgina appeared to fall in love with Dickens. Since her flirtation with Edward Bulwer-Lytton, no other man had caught her eye. While she could never have expected anything to develop with Bulwer-Lytton, he had provided a thrill and someone to look forward to seeing. Augustus Egg had never stirred any passion in her, but he at least offered some romantic interest. Once Georgina refused Egg's proposal, despite the offer of marriage remaining open, any excitement offered by the romance was gone. If Georgina hoped to keep her feelings for Dickens undetected, she did not do a good job. It was not long before a fifteen-year-old Katey and her best friend, seventeen-year-old Anny Thackeray, noticed that 'Aunty' had formed a passionate attachment to Dickens. Anny was to tell her own daughter that Georgina 'was in love with C.D. and was always charming and well and beautifully dressed, while Mrs. C.D. was a weak overwhelmed woman never out of having a child'.[19] Katey too could see her aunt had fallen for her father, describing how Georgina was 'without doubt in love with C.D.'.[20]

For the most part, the sisters were still getting on well, but Georgina's emotional state in 1853 led her to commit at least one decidedly unsisterly action by deliberately stirring up trouble between Catherine and Dickens. With Dickens, Egg and Collins still in Italy, Georgina and Catherine made a trip to Bonchurch on the Isle of Wight, to stay with the Reverend James and Rosa White. The visit did not go well. Something happened to make Catherine feel unwelcome and, whether she feared a lecture or was embarrassed by what occurred, Catherine decided not to tell Dickens. Knowing the tensions between the husband and wife, Georgina must have realised what she might unleash when she took it upon herself to make sure Dickens found out about the incident. Predictably, he was cross with his wife for not informing him directly and, indeed, for going to the Whites' in the first place:

> From what Georgina says, and from what Forster indicates that he supposes you to have told me, I infer that your stay at Bonchurch was sufficiently disagreeable. But you know my old principle; that there are very few people indeed, in whose house it will ever do to stay … and I wonder you ever went there.[21]

Georgina's interference was particularly ill-timed. Dickens was, at that moment, planning to visit the de la Rues. Not only was Catherine's outburst over his relationship with Augusta a festering sore, the news she had fallen out with another set of friends added to his aggravation. Somewhat pompously, Dickens reminded Catherine that whatever aspects of his character she had complained about over the Augusta incident in Genoa, these were the same traits that 'made you proud and honored in your married life, and given you station better than rank, and surrounded you with many enviable things. That is the plain truth, and here I leave it.'[22] However, Dickens refused to leave the matter, proceeding to add how, in complete contrast to Catherine, both the de la Rues had always asked affectionately about her and the children. Implausibly claiming that he was not asking her to write, but noting it was in her 'power' to make things better, he advised her to contact Augusta to ask for forgiveness. Meanwhile, Georgina had remained on good terms with Augusta. Imploring Dickens to tell Augusta she was 'making all kinds of enquiries after her' put Georgina at odds with Catherine, and implied she believed Dickens was in the right in accusing Catherine of jealousy.[23]

In her letters to Dickens, Georgina tried gently flirting with him. One attempt was so subtle that it completely mystified him. Dickens was away when a long-time friend of the family, Charles Knight, called at Tavistock House. The sixty-one-year-old grandfather took tea with Catherine and Georgina, telling them about his daughter's problems in finding a governess for her children. Catherine offered to introduce him to Mamie and Katey's governess, who happened to be looking for additional work. It may have been that Knight complimented or flirted mildly with the lively, good-looking Georgina. Dickens and many of his friends behaved in this way towards young ladies without a second thought, and she would have witnessed it on innumerable occasions. After the visit, Georgina wrote to Dickens with an account of Knight's social call. Bewildered, Dickens wrote to W. H. Wills, his right-hand man at the office of *Household*

Words, that 'Georgina complains that he "philanders" – I don't know what that involves, or where it ends – and also that he is "an old Donkey". He didn't present himself in that light to me.'[24]

Catherine's biographer, Lillian Nayder, interprets Georgina's remarks as her condemning Charles Knight for his inappropriate interest in governesses. However, Georgina was living in a house where the master was involved in a home for 'fallen women', so she could hardly be shocked by a father wanting to help his daughter find a suitable teacher for her children. Rather, Georgina's observations can be understood as her way of telling Dickens that Knight had been flirting with her. Knight obviously said something in the drawing room of Tavistock House to draw the accusation 'he philanders' and was 'an old Donkey' either in relation to Georgina, Catherine or the (absent and unknown) governess. The implicit message to Dickens was that a man (men) found her attractive. In another letter, Dickens responded to a lengthy and teasing missive from Georgina by putting her in her place:

> I am afraid you must have been fishing for a compliment when you talk about the postage of your letters; so I shall punish you by saying that indeed it does come heavy and that I would propose, if you see no objections, to make your mind easy on that score by stopping it out of your quarter.[25]

Although Dickens never saw Georgina in any romantic light, he puzzled over what he did want from her, admitting to one friend, 'Whether it is, or is not a pity that she is all she is to me and mine instead of brightening up a good little man's house ... is a knotty point I never can settle to my satisfaction.'[26]

It was a question he was pondering in 1852, while working out the plot of *Bleak House*, and at the same time that Georgina's emotions began to get the better of her common sense. The narrative structure of *Bleak House* was completely different to anything he had tried before, as the authorial voice is that of a woman, Esther Summerson, who tells her story in the past tense alongside a narrator and observer who comment in the present tense. Esther's personality and situation resonate strongly with Georgina's in the Dickens household, and she later agreed that she was indeed the model for this character.

> Esther is presented as a modest, sensible, cheerful, attractive young woman with a great aptitude for housekeeping and a passionate desire to devote herself lovingly to the service of others. She is taken into the family of the benevolent old bachelor, Mr. Jarndyce, whom she comes to venerate as almost a saint and becomes his 'little housekeeper' and the loving companion of his two young wards.[27]

Dickens's characters draw on aspects of people he knew, but they were never exact replicas. This was certainly the case with Esther, as Georgina was much sharper than her fictional counterpart. The authentic Georgina appears in one episode in which the otherwise flawless Esther makes a sarcastic comment, giving readers a surprising jolt. Speaking on the British Honours system, Esther remarks: 'I said it was not the custom in England to confer titles on men distinguished by peaceful services, however good and great; unless occasionally, when they consisted of the accumulation of some very large amount of money.'[28]

There is an odd plot twist in which Mr Jarndyce, Esther's guardian, proposes to her and is accepted. Writing of this proposal, Michael Slater poses the question, 'Why introduce the crisis of his improbable offer of marriage to Esther? Is this not an attempt to dramatise what Dickens felt was now happening in Georgina's life?'[29] Slater argues that Dickens was probably concerned that Georgina was putting herself in a position where she would be seen as sacrificing any possibility of a married life in order to devote herself to Dickens: 'In his story Dickens can present this dedication as a consciously made decision at a particular moment by the dramatic device of having Jarndyce propose marriage to her.'[30] Following Slater's analysis, perhaps Dickens was also asking himself difficult questions about Esther/Georgina's feelings for their hero. Dickens has Esther respond to Jarndyce's proposal with a mixture of happiness, gratitude and unease – an unease caused by the misinterpretation of grateful feelings towards a kind beneficiary. Esther observes that the written proposal from Jarndyce is 'not a love letter', thereby acknowledging the absence of passionate feelings. In the novel, Dickens positioned Esther's love as rooted in higher emotions, far removed from sexual desires. If Dickens was wondering whether Georgina's love for him was more than that of a sister for her brother-in-law, then he may have reassured himself, through his characterisation of Esther, that Georgina was too intelligent to harbour improper emotions.

Dickens's dissatisfaction with his marriage began in earnest in 1855–6 when he started opening up to Forster:

> Am altogether in a dishevelled state of mind … miseries of older growth threatening to close upon me. Why is it, … that a sense comes always crushing on me now, when I fall into low spirits, as of one happiness I have missed in life, and one friend and companion I have never made?[31]

When his old flame Maria Beadnell (now Mrs Winter) reappeared in his life in 1855, he grasped at the opportunity to start a new romance. Imagining her to be a slightly older version of the pretty, slim, seventeen-year-old he had been in love with as a young man, Dickens arranged a rendezvous at Tavistock House. 'It is almost a positive certainty that there will be no one here but I, between 3 and 4', he wrote to Maria.[32] When they did meet, he was horrified to discover Maria's warnings that she was now 'toothless, fat, old and ugly' were true.[33] Having wooed her so ardently, Dickens was suddenly keen to avoid her and insisted that Georgina respond to any requests from Maria to him. In her dealings with Maria, Georgina was always warm, referring to her as 'dearest Mrs. Winter', expressing gratitude for her 'kind recollection', saying how her 'suggestions were *most valuable*' and describing her as 'a very dear friend' but, when the letters between Dickens and his first love were published many years later, the editor provided a foreword based on a memorandum Georgina had written.[34] In it, she made critical, nasty observations on Maria's 'common' personality and increased weight.

Dickens's dissatisfaction with his marriage spread to include the entire Hogarth family, with the exception of Georgina. With some justification, Dickens thought they abused his generosity. The precarious state of the Hogarth finances, which had twice put George Hogarth into a debtors' prison, were a constant problem. Dickens covered their medical expenses and let them live rent free at Tavistock House while his family were in France. Mrs Hogarth was not the most assiduous of housekeepers and when, on a flying return visit to London, Dickens discovered she had allowed his home to become dirty and untidy, he was furious. When the family returned to Tavistock House with the Hogarth family still in situ, he declared exasperatedly to Wills: 'The Hogarth family don't leave Tavistock House till next Saturday. And I cannot in the meantime bear the contemplation of their imbecility any more. (I think my constitution is already undermined by the sight of Hogarth at breakfast).'[35] He wrote wearily to Wilkie Collins, 'I am dead sick of the Scottish tongue in all its moods and tenses'.[36] Mrs Hogarth had always been unperturbed by her son-in-law's displays of anger, which only served to annoy Dickens even more. At a time when Dickens was making it plain that he did not want Catherine as his wife any longer, Mrs Hogarth was not making matters any better.

Although Georgina avoided much of Dickens's criticism, she could still get on his nerves. She was soon told when she had done something to annoy him, as on one occasion raising his ire by sharing Catherine's fascination with a neighbour's wedding day: 'All the women and girls in my house, stark mad on the subject. Despotic conjugal influence exerted to keep Mrs. Dickens out of the church. Caught putting bonnet on for that purpose and sternly commanded to renounce idiotic intentions.'[37] Undoubtedly, the same instruction was given to Georgina. Following the reprimand she had been given over the comments about Susan Atkins in Genoa, Georgina took care to keep her sharp tongue in check.

She was not careful enough, though, it seems. After giving her opinion on Wilkie Collins's new novel, *Hide and Seek*, Dickens responded harshly, 'Neither you nor Catherine did justice to Collins's book. I think it far away the cleverest Novel I have ever seen written by a new hand.'[38]

When it came to Mrs Hogarth, Dickens either knew or simply assumed that Georgina shared his opinion. On the occasion when Mrs Hogarth decided to take out a life insurance policy, Dickens had no qualms about showing Georgina his contempt for her mother and, in the same letter, manages to be short-tempered with her as well:

> [I]t appears to me that unless your mother positively renounces the idea you had better come, whether or no, and the thing disposed of … What you are wanted for is merely your signature. I never in my days beheld anything like your mother's letter, for the desperation of its imbecility. What she imagines would be done – might, could or should be done – by her insuring her life, I cannot conceive.[39]

Where Dickens had once praised Georgina for her efficiency, he was now complaining that she was tawdry. He blamed her for mismanaging a hotel booking when, in actuality, the fault lay with the postal service for not delivering the letter quickly enough. Writing testily to Catherine, he grumbled:

> I have been perplexed by the non-arrival of any letter from Georgy who was to have written to tell me what arrangement she had made for Collins. This failure rendered it impossible for me to tell him last night what had been done for him in the way of quarters and made me look rather foolish. I write in the middle of the day (the middle of my birthday bye the bye) and even yesterday's foreign post is in, and yet I have no letter. I cannot conceive what she had been about.[40]

Stress, probably brought about by Dickens's irritation with her and the rest of the Hogarths, resulted in Georgina developing a nervous tic in the head.[41]

It was Catherine, though, who took the brunt of Dickens's disappointment and frustration with his personal life. Those who knew the Dickenses observed that Catherine was struggling to cope with her husband's unforgiving attitude. She was perpetually nervous and worried about upsetting him. Harriet Martineau, the social theorist and writer, who had a public spat with Dickens, had no compunction in telling acquaintances of something she heard from Dickens's one-time publisher, Fred Evans:

> Even Mr. Wills, his worshipper, and Mr. Evans … declined their annual visit to the D.s country house because they 'could not stand his cruelty to his wife'. I asked what 'cruelty' meant; and he said 'swearing at her, in the presence of guests, children and servants;' – swearing often and fiercely.[42]

Even if we recognise that Harriet's dislike of Dickens probably meant she was exaggerating and distorting the gossip, this letter still suggests that he was being openly short-tempered with his wife. Kate Horne, who had experienced Dickens's charm, also saw this other side to him and noted how subservient Catherine was. She wrote to her husband about one incident she witnessed, regarding it as indicative of the relationship between the couple. Kate had called on Catherine at Tavistock House to explain that she had a visitor staying on the day she had been invited to dinner at their home:

> Mrs. Dickens said she was very sorry but I knew how strange & shy 'Charles' was and that he could not endure any stranger when they dined quietly alone, as they intended to do on Sunday. Presently, however, he came in and Mrs. Dickens told him I could not dine there, and why. He said 'I shall be most happy to see any friend of Mrs. Horne's; she sanctifies the stranger &c['].[43]

Lillian Nayder points out that, given Dickens's contradictory nature and how he would often reverse a previous instruction to his wife, Catherine was understandably wary. When Dickens encouraged her to decide for herself, she was right to be suspicious, 'knowing her word was not the last in most matters'.[44]

Dickens's mid-life crisis coincided with a period when Catherine had been through a lot. Within a relatively short space of time Catherine had to deal with the deaths of her father-in-law, her baby daughter and her dearest friend, Kitty Macready. Katey Dickens spoke of her mother's constant anxiety, giving the example, 'If one of [us] tumbled downstairs and set up a howl in consequence, she would immediately fly to the conclusion that he or she had broken an arm or a leg.'[45] Many people commented on Catherine's 'sleepy look' and 'slow-moving eyes' and how she sometimes appeared 'heavy and unregardful'.[46] Harriet Martineau, who liked Catherine, blamed Dickens: '[he] … terrified and depressed her into a dull condition', adding less sympathetically, 'and she never was very clever'.[47]

It seems that Georgina attempted to broker some kind of peace between her sister and Dickens. Catherine later spoke of her gratitude to Georgina during this period and Dickens praised Georgina for having 'remonstrated, reasoned, suffered, and toiled, … to prevent a separation between Mrs. Dickens and me'.[48] We do not know exactly how Georgina was advising Catherine at this point, but what is important to remember is that they were different women with different attitudes. Looking at their quite distinct friendship groups tells us something about the kinds of women they had things in common with. The women in Catherine's social set would, and did, express very different opinions to those in Georgina's group.

Georgina preferred to be with women who honoured 'men of genius', such as Mary Boyle. As Lillian Nayder has observed, 'Georgina characterises herself as a woman who knows her place'.[49] Georgina acknowledged when writing to a male friend of Dickens's, 'I think it safer to keep within my depth'.[50] In contrast, Catherine's group of intelligent, feisty women friends sound as if they had much in common with the outspoken Mrs Hogarth. If Catherine disclosed anything about how harshly Dickens was treating her, then the advice of her friends such as Nelly Lemon and Isabella Frith would have reflected their own spirited attitudes. Nelly was happily married to Mark Lemon, editor of *Punch*, but she was certainly not a meek, submissive wife. As Lemon once explained: 'I never argue with my wife: I say "no" twice, and then hold my tongue'.[51] Similarly, Isabella Frith, wife of the painter William Powell Frith, was another sharp-witted and resilient woman. After giving birth to twelve children, she discovered her husband had another home with his mistress and their seven children, just streets away. She refused to separate, and her husband chose not to cross her; he had witnessed his wife's temper and knew better. After a woman stole Isabella's cloak at a Royal Academy ball, she confronted the thief and drew a crowd of onlookers by loudly declaring the theft. The result was that the cloakless female robber and her shamefaced husband sloped off home, never to attend a Royal Academy soirée again.[52]

Georgina did not take to many of Catherine's friends and especially objected to wives of the 'men of genius' who voiced an opinion that was either critical of, or dissented from, the views of their husbands. She would not have approved of hearing Jane Carlyle jokingly advising Katey Dickens and Anny Thackeray, 'If you wish for a quiet life ... never marry a dyspeptic man of genius.'[53] Not that Georgina voiced her views of Catherine and her friends at the time, as it could only have added to the already fraught relations in the Dickens home. It was after Catherine's death that Georgina made disparaging comments of Kitty Macready, describing her as 'very pretty, but stupid', adding that Kitty 'demanded too much attention – as though more attention should be paid her than Macready'. Catherine did not escape reproach either: 'Mrs. Dickens wasn't the right sort of wife for the genius of Dickens. She was a whiney sort of woman who wanted attention.'[54]

Wisely, whenever possible, Georgina kept herself busy outside the tense domestic atmosphere in the house. She took part in several amateur theatrical productions, including *The Lighthouse*, and began rehearsing for one of Wilkie Collins's plays, *The Frozen Deep*. Dickens gave her the job of sending out over 200 handwritten invitations, adding to her workload by dictating personal notes to be included with each one. Performances of *The Frozen Deep* were mainly held in private at Tavistock House, but there were several public presentations which were reviewed by the newspapers. Georgina and her nieces were singled out for praise in the *Leader*, which reported that the male actors were 'delightfully aided by the refined vivacity of Miss Hogarth, the dramatic instinct of Miss Mary and the fascinating simplicity of Miss Kate'.[55] Dickens received a request from Queen Victoria to put on a private performance of the play but, on the night, he denied the Queen's request to meet the actors on the basis that it would be inappropriate to present himself wearing theatrical costume. It meant Georgina and the other cast members missed out on being introduced to the Queen and Prince Albert. Georgina was, though, able to tell Maria Beadnell Winter that they 'made a most excellent audience; so far from being cold, as was expected, they cried and laughed and applauded and made as much demonstration as so small a party could do'.[56]

Georgina's approach to her agitated, often irritable, brother-in-law was to try and keep him happy. When the Danish author Hans Christian Andersen came to visit, but outstayed his welcome, Georgina made it clear to him that it was time for him to leave. He had arrived at the Dickenses' summer home at Gad's Hill in June 1857.[57] Andersen did not enjoy his visit as much as he had hoped. To his disappointment, Dickens did not have the time he had promised to devote to his guest. The sudden death of a friend, Douglas Jerrold, galvanised Dickens into raising money for the Jerrold family. He was in London for much of June and July, enlisting the help of fellow authors and organising various benefit events. Unbeknownst to Andersen and everyone else,

Jerrold's death was the spark that lit the end of the Dickenses' marriage.

Left in the company of the family at Gad's Hill, Andersen initially thought there was a tight-knit bond between the sisters and that Georgina, whom he saw teaching music to Mamie and Katey, was a 'most kind and cultured lady'.[58] He found Catherine to be welcoming and charming but reported to a friend how he had seen her, eyes full of tears, leaving a room and being consoled by Mrs Hogarth. When Andersen failed to depart at the end of the two weeks he had been invited for, the children started to be rude towards him. Harry Dickens recalled how 'the small boys in the family rather laughed at him behind his back; but, so far as the members of the family were concerned, he was treated with the utmost consideration and courtesy'.[59]

Andersen was not of the same opinion. When the family was together, he felt that they maintained cordial relations; however, outside of these instances, he repeatedly encountered a displeased Georgina: 'Miss Hogarth is not at all attentive'… 'Today … Mrs. Dickens tired, the daughters without thought for me, the aunt even less' … 'To dinner here with Mrs. Dickens' mother and sister; little Kate sarcastic; the aunt is certainly weary of me'.[60]

When Andersen finally left, Dickens pinned up a card above the mirror in his room, reading, 'Hans [Christian] Andersen slept in this room for five weeks – which seemed to the family AGES!'[61] There is no record of Georgina ever behaving this way with any other visitor, but she knew her brother-in-law was getting increasingly annoyed by Andersen's presence at Gad's Hill. As Dickens confessed, the family were 'suffering a good deal from Andersen', and so it seemed Georgina took it upon herself to relieve them of the burden.[62]

Although no one could know it at the time, the Dickenses were about to embark upon the last year of their marriage. The tension in the home caused by Dickens's unhappiness with Catherine, his anger towards his in-laws, and his inconsistent attitude to Georgina

– sometimes overly intimate, other times castigating – destabilised relationships. Catherine and Georgina were united in their adoration for Dickens and desire for the marriage to survive. Dickens wavered between resignation to an unhappy marriage and frustration at having to endure it. However, the Manchester production of *The Frozen Deep* set him on a path that resulted in the destruction of his existing family life.

Chapter 6

Loyalty and disloyalty (1857–8)

In his efforts to raise money for the Douglas Jerrold fund, Dickens arranged for two benefit performances of *The Frozen Deep* to be held at Manchester's Free Trade Hall.[1] So great was the demand for tickets that he was easily persuaded to include a third night. Although Georgina and the Dickens girls had won much praise for their acting in the play, there was no possibility of them appearing in the Manchester production. Not only did their lack of vocal training mean their voices would be lost in the cavernous hall, but 'ladies' did not appear as actresses in public. On the advice of theatre manager, Alfred Wigan, Dickens approached the widowed, fifty-one-year-old actress Mrs Frances Ternan and two of her three daughters, Maria and Ellen. Dickens's decision to employ this respectable acting family resulted in a domestic crisis which shattered the lives of Catherine and Georgina.

The Dickenses' marriage collapsed within ten months of the Manchester performances of *The Frozen Deep*. At the end of this time, Dickens, Georgina and the children went off to Gad's Hill, while Catherine was banished to a new home at Gloucester Crescent. It was a shocking state of affairs. A wife sent away from her own house while her sister stayed with the husband was bound to cause gossip. Adding to the scandal was confusion as to whether Dickens was having an affair and, if so, with whom? Was it an actress or his sister-in-law or both? As a respectable Victorian woman,

Georgina was expected to show allegiance to her sister, but instead she opted to take the side of her brother-in-law. Georgina's great-great-great-great niece, Lucinda Hawksley, has pointed out that: 'Why she chose to be shunned by her parents, grandparents and siblings in order to stay with her sister's husband has never been satisfactorily explained; nor how she could be so deliberately cruel to Catherine.'[2]

Was Georgina blinded by such great love for Dickens that she was prepared to sacrifice her reputation for him? Did her disloyalty to Catherine and her family stem from what she perceived as their disrespect for Dickens's genius and generosity? Setting Georgina's emotions to one side, there are practical considerations. How much free will did she have in choosing whether to stay with Dickens or leave with Catherine? Georgina was, after all, financially dependent on Dickens. How much pressure did Dickens place on Georgina to stay with him? Did he consider or care what remaining in his household would do to Georgina's reputation? Answering these questions is complicated because much depends on what the protagonists knew or believed at each point. For example, a key factor in understanding Georgina's motivations in turning against her family involves trust: whether she trusted Dickens's honesty above that of her parents. Was she to believe Dickens's protestations that his intentions towards the Ternan girls were simply that of mentor or guardian? Or were the Hogarths right to claim that Dickens was lying and his romantic involvement with Ellen Ternan was the reason why he wanted to be rid of Catherine?

Dickens's association with the Ternan family began on 17 August 1857, after telling a friend he was returning to London for 'three days drill of the professional ladies who are to succeed our Tavistock girls' in *The Frozen Deep*.[3] Maria he already knew, as she had appeared in one of his other plays. Ellen (always known as Nelly) was by far the weakest actress in the family, but Dickens regarded her as competent enough to take on Georgina's minor role as Lucy Crayford. During the rehearsals, one biographer claims that both

Maria and Nelly fluttered around Dickens, 'but only one [Nelly] sat on the arm of the manager's chair, sang duets with him at the schoolroom piano and seemed, to the family, to take possession of the house'.[4]

Wanting to see the professional actresses recreate their parts, Georgina and the girls begged Dickens to be allowed to accompany the theatrical troupe to Manchester. In the days prior to departure Catherine became quite unwell, but she rallied sufficiently to make the journey. The troupe played to packed houses and enthusiastic crowds and the newspapers raved over Dickens's portrayal of his character, Richard Wardour.

On the return rail journey from Manchester, Dickens enquired of Mrs Ternan where their next acting engagements would take them. She informed him they were to join Charles Kean's Princess's Theatre Company for a booking at the Theatre Royal in Doncaster. Dickens at first appeared to be enthralled by Maria Ternan, writing effusively to Angela Burdett-Coutts:

> Mentioning Richard Wardour, – perhaps Mr. Wills has not told you how much impressed I was at Manchester by the womanly tenderness of a very gentle and good little girl who acted Mary's part … At night when she came out of the cave and Wardour recognised her, I never saw any thing like the distress and agitation of her face – a very good little pale face, with large black eyes; – it had a natural emotion in it (though it was turned away from the audience) which was quite a study of expression … By the time the Curtain fell, we were all crying together, and then her mother and sister used to come and put her in a chair and comfort her, before taking her away to be dressed for the Farce. I told her on the last night that I was sure she had one of the most genuine and feeling hearts in the world; and I don't think I ever saw any thing more prettily simple and unaffected.[5]

Dickens experienced a sense of anti-climax following the Manchester performances and his mood of 'grim despair and restlessness' prevented him from writing.[6] He had not produced anything for *Household Words* for a couple of months; consequently, only a few days after returning to London, an unsettled Dickens wrote begging Wilkie Collins to go 'anywhere – take any tour – see anything'.[7] He suggested to Collins they write a travelogue based on a short tour; it would be a fictionalised version of their adventures, in the guise of two characters, the intense Francis Goodchild and easy-going Thomas Idle. Dickens told a friend, '[w]e have not the least idea where we are going', although Collins had made it clear where he wanted to visit as '*he* says "let's look at the Norfolk Coast"'.[8] Dickens's subterfuge began when they agreed on Cumberland, but he booked rooms at the Angel Hotel in Doncaster, 158 miles away from their chosen destination of Maryport. What explanation did he give Collins and his family for this lengthy diversion which would take up a week of their fourteen-day tour? It was Doncaster Race Week, but he had never been an enthusiastic racegoer. The truth was that their visit would coincide with the dates when Mrs Ternan and her daughters were appearing at Doncaster Theatre Royal.

Dickens might not have confessed to Wilkie Collins why he wanted to visit Doncaster, but he told Georgina that he intended to seek out the Ternans. When Collins sprained his ankle climbing Carrick Fell in Cumberland, it looked as if the rest of the tour would have to be cancelled. Yet Dickens wrote to Georgina, '[o]f course I shall go to Doncaster, whether or no (please God)'.[9] Collins recovered and they went on together. Shortly after arriving at the Angel Hotel, Dickens sent word to Georgina: 'We breakfast at half past eight, and fall to work for H. W. [*Household Words*] afterwards. Then I go out, and – hem! look for subjects'; the 'subjects' being the Ternans.[10] Although Georgina knew of her sister and brother-in-law's fraught marital relations, there was no particular reason why she should have been alarmed about Dickens's pursuit of the Ternans. Dickens seeking out 'subjects' was not unusual in that his book characters were often composites of people he knew or had observed in the street. He was always attracted to the seedier side of life and, as the Ternan family were evidently respectable, but

4 Charles Dickens by Margaret Gillies, 1843

5 Catherine Dickens, engraving after Daniel Maclise, 1847

7 1 Devonshire Terrace

6 Catherine Dickens between 1852
and 1855, daguerreotype by John
Jabez Edwin Mayall

8 Drawing of entrance hall of Devonshire Terrace by
Percy Home

9 Charles Dickens, 1850

10 John Forster by Herbert Watkins

11 Charles Dickens by Herbert Watkins, 29 April 1858

12 Ellen Ternan, 1858

13 Maria, Ellen and Fanny Ternan, 1858

14 Daniel Maclise by E. M. Ward, 1846

16 Augustus Egg, circa 1855

15 Edward Bulwer-Lytton by Mayer
Brothers, carte de visite, 18 April 1861
(1840s)

17 Tavistock House

18 Georgina Hogarth by Herbert Watkins, 1860s

19 Gad's Hill

20 Dickens on the porch at Gad's Hill, 1866, with, left to right: Henry Chorley, Katey and Mamie. Seated: Charley Collins and Georgina

21 Annie Adams Fields, 1861

22 Mary Louisa Boyle, carte de visite, 1860s

23 Georgina Hogarth, 1866

24 Charles Dickens by Jeremiah Gurney, 1867

25 Georgina Hogarth, 1870s

26 Catherine Dickens, 1879

28 Ellen (Ternan) Robinson with her husband, George, and their son, 1883

27 Mamie Dickens

working in a disreputable profession, they would have been interesting 'subjects' to study. Whatever explanation, if any, Dickens gave Georgina about why he followed the Ternans to Doncaster, we can be fairly certain none of them declared his interest in trying to entrance a girl young enough to be his daughter.[11]

During the time Dickens was away, between 7 and 21 September, he neither wrote nor sent word to Catherine. His letters to Gad's Hill were addressed to Georgina and, when he signed off, he sent messages only to his children Charley, Mamie, Katey, Harry and Plorn. This has been interpreted as a deliberate slight to Catherine and, given the state of relations between them, that is plausible. However, Catherine and the other children might not have been at Gad's Hill. She could have returned to Tavistock House in London in order to get Frank, Alfred and Sydney ready for their return to boarding school in Boulogne that month.

When Catherine and Georgina were reunited with Dickens on his return to London, he made it clear he was besotted with Nelly Ternan. Until Doncaster his emotions were not settled on either Maria or Nelly as, 'given his lifelong fascination with sisters and sisterly feelings, it could well have been both'.[12] Seeing Nelly being heckled by lewd, boorish men in the audience at the Theatre Royal may have brought out his protective instincts. Once back in London, his daughter Katey recalled how '"all was open" regarding the affair – he concealed nothing', even though there was, as yet, no sexual affair.[13] She implies that her father confessed to having fallen in love. This might not have been the thunderbolt that it sounds, given Dickens's propensity for making wild and grand proclamations about his adoration of young, attractive women. Both Catherine and Georgina had seen him besotted (with Christiana Weller) and intrigued (by Augusta de la Rue), and his fascination for Nelly would have seemed to be no different. In the past, Dickens's sexual/ emotional interest in other women had been intense, only to fade quickly. Also, Dickens argued he was not sexually motivated, claiming he regarded all the Ternan girls as virtuous and honourable and told their male cousin that, as far as his own intentions were concerned, 'there could not live upon this earth a man more blamelessly and openly [a] friend than I am'.[14] He also accused Catherine 'of not having the character to appreciate his platonic attachment to Nelly'.[15] In other words, he contended that all he was guilty of was caring and offering support to these admirable women working in the tough environment of the theatre.

Georgina and Catherine took different positions on Dickens's obsession with Nelly and her family. While Georgina accepted Dickens was innocent because he said he was, Catherine did not believe him. Katey recalled one afternoon when she heard her mother crying in the bedroom and went in to find Catherine 'seated at the dressing table in the act of putting on her bonnet, with tears rolling down her cheeks … "Your father has asked me to go and see Ellen Ternan." "You shall not go!" exclaimed [Katey] angrily stamping her foot. But she went.'[16] Catherine's biographer has argued that Dickens's reason for getting his wife to visit the Ternans was 'to sanction and make proper his relations with them'.[17] Dickens put Catherine's initial refusal to visit the Ternans down to her irrational jealousy which he insisted she overcome. There is no mention of Georgina accompanying Catherine but they always visited together, and one imagines Dickens would want Georgina to report back so he could make sure Catherine had behaved in a manner he approved of.

When the serialisation of Dickens's travels with Collins appeared in *Household Words*, under the title of *The Lazy Tour of Two Idle Apprentices*, Catherine and Georgina could read how Dickens had fallen in love. A scene early on captures Dickens's excitement at escorting a pretty young girl to a day's racing. His retaining of the actual name of the Angel Hotel where they were staying adds to the impression that this is a report of events rather than a fictionalised account. Dickens appears as Francis Goodchild and Wilkie Collins as Thomas Idle:

Mr. Goodchild would appear to have been by no means free from lunacy himself at 't'races', though not of the prevalent kind. He is suspected by Mr. Idle to have fallen into a dreadful state concerning a pair of little lilac gloves and a little bonnet that he saw there. Mr. Idle asserts, that he did afterwards repeat at the Angel, with an appearance of being lunatically seized, some rhapsody to the following effect: 'O little lilac gloves! And O winning little bonnet, making in conjunction with her golden hair quite a Glory in the sunlight round the pretty head, why anything in the world but you and me! Why may not this day's running … be prolonged through an everlasting autumn sunshine, without a sunset!'[18]

The third episode makes chilling reading. Within the main narrative is a short story of a man who terrorised his despised, pathetic wife to death. Oddly, the wife is given the name Ellen. *The Bride's Chamber* tells of a young man, Dickens himself as a romantic youth, whose love is destroyed on getting married. As the wife apologises over and again for herself, begging for forgiveness, standing before him, 'nervously plaiting and folding her white skirts' and promising to do anything he asks of her, the husband's detestation increases.[19] His embitterment and loathing is unmistakable:

> She was … a weak, credulous, incapable, helpless nothing.
> … She was not worth hating; he felt nothing but contempt for her. But she had long been in the way, and he had long been weary.
> … When she fell upon her old entreaty to be pardoned, she was answered 'Die!'… When … the rising sun flamed into the sombre room, she heard it hailed with, 'Another day and not dead? Die!'[20]

Every complaint the fictional husband made about his wife, Dickens had said of Catherine.

Catherine did not allow Dickens simply to ride roughshod over her. In the month *The Lazy Tour of Two Idle Apprentices* appeared, Dickens told their servant Anne Cornelius to change the sleeping arrangements, sealing up the door between the dressing room and the bedroom. When Catherine discovered Dickens had decided to abandon the marital bedroom, informing their servant but not discussing it with her, there was a heated argument. Catherine spoke out against his flirtations with other women. Dickens told Emile de la Rue about the argument: 'She has been excruciatingly jealous of, and has obtained positive proofs of my being on the most confidential terms with, at least Fifteen Thousand Women of various conditions in life, every condition in life, since we left Genoa.'[21]

Yet Catherine's kindliness to Emma Picken and Christiana Weller is proof that, at least in the early years of their marriage, she rarely, if ever, displayed sexual jealousy. Dickens did not provide any more information about what the couple argued about, but as a mother of daughters the same age as Nelly, Catherine could have reminded her husband that if a young girl, the same age as his own daughters, became entangled with a married man it would destroy her reputation and chances of a respectable family life. There was too the matter of Dickens's reputation. Would he not be seen as a hypocrite if he, famous for his writing on the virtues of family, hearth and home, abandoned his own? Whatever Catherine said during their heated argument, it was enough for a distraught Dickens to get out of bed at 2 a.m. and walk thirty miles from Tavistock House to Gad's Hill. Dickens was to recall his anguish in *Great Expectations* where Pip, distressed and restless after learning of Estella's coming marriage and discovering that Miss Havisham had denied them a potential love match, walks through the night from Rochester to London.

Dickens went to extreme lengths to put an end to his marriage. Catherine was later to tell a neighbour that Dickens had tried to persuade the doctor attending her for a physical illness to certify her as insane.[22] Had he been successful, Dickens could have arranged for Catherine to be committed to a mental asylum. Forster would have told Dickens, as he had Bulwer-Lytton, that when it came to husbands trying to rid themselves of unwanted wives by having them declared insane, it was 'a case belonging exactly to the class which it is most difficult to get medical men to certify'.[23] Fortunately for Catherine, even the forceful Dickens was unable to persuade the doctors to compromise their medical integrity and wrongfully declare her insane. When Dickens failed to remove Catherine from the house by having her certified, he suggested she go and live abroad, alone. Catherine turned this idea down flat. He then proposed that she have a set of rooms at Tavistock House to which she was confined, but continue to act as his hostess when he requested. She was also to agree to visit friends with him and thereby keep up appearances. Again, she refused. Finally, Dickens suggested she have one servant and live at Gad's Hill while he, the family and the main servants lived at Tavistock House, exchanging abodes when he chose. Catherine was not prepared to accept any of these suggestions.

While Dickens raged and Catherine refused to acquiesce to his wishes, Georgina appeared to be neutral. Her aunt said that the family thought Georgina merely 'affectionate and disinterested'.[24] Katey Dickens had a different opinion, later deploring Georgina and Forster's efforts:

> There came a day when, out of the combined efforts of her sister, Miss Georgina Hogarth, and Mr. John Forster, to facilitate matters for the supposed comfort of Charles, a triangle evolved, in which Mrs. Dickens formed no part. So that incidents connected with the children and the home requiring consideration and adjustment were frequently settled by one or other of these two, in conference with the master of the house, without any reference to the mistress of it, who, in the natural sensitiveness of her refined nature, suffered exquisitely under this treatment; this led to many misunderstandings and muddles; and later to the accusation, by Miss Hogarth, that she threw the responsibility of her children upon others. An accusation as unkind as it was untrue.[25]

Why did Georgina and Forster make decisions without consulting Catherine? Was it that Dickens did not want her to be included or because Georgina and Forster believed she was not able to make any decisions?

Catherine was under a lot of pressure. Less than a year earlier, she had had the agony of saying goodbye to her son, Walter, who having obtained a cadetship with the East India Company, set sail for Calcutta (Kolkata) in July 1857. Of course, Catherine did not then know she would never see him again but, given that the Indian Rebellion was headline news in 1857, there was always that possibility. Then there was the constant stress of Dickens's irritation making her wary and nervous. Katey said that her mother 'could not be herself – she was (as it were) in prison not allowed to say what she felt'.[26] Harriet Martineau had an explanation for Dickens's accusation that Catherine had a 'mental disorder', saying: 'she is subject to that *fretfulness* & *jealousy* which are the *specific results* of such a life as he has chosen that her's shd be'.[27] In other words, any man who exercised stringent control over his wife by 'regard[ing] his wife as "*his* woman"', will reduce her to a needy, anxious, shell'.[28] Others were less understanding; Hans Christian Andersen described Catherine as 'rather indolent', and Edmund Yates said that she displayed 'a little love of indolence and ease'.[29] In an era before mental health was recognised, Andersen and Yates did not connect Catherine's 'indolence' to the sadness and exhaustion she was going through at being sidelined in her own home. It may well have been that a combination of Dickens's disregard for his wife and an already stressed Catherine encouraged Georgina and Forster to avoid involving or seeking her opinion.

On 9 May 1858 Dickens wrote his first letter signalling the coming separation. It is a querulous and self-pitying letter that did Dickens no favours in the eyes of the recipient, Angela Burdett-Coutts; the woman whose friendship he hoped to retain. In it he blamed Catherine, claiming, 'she has never attached one of [the children] to herself', accusing her of having 'fallen into the most miserable weaknesses and jealousies' while portraying himself as a stoical husband and Georgina as a saintly presence ('the best, the most unselfish and the most devoted of human Creatures').[30]

As the negotiations for an official separation began in earnest, Mr and Mrs Hogarth assumed that Georgina would leave Tavistock House when Catherine did. They were shocked to discover Georgina intended to remain with Dickens and the children. When her parents insisted she leave, Georgina dug her heels in and refused. Mr and Mrs Hogarth were only too aware of the difficulties this would cause Catherine. In staying on, Georgina gave credibility to Dickens's claims that Catherine was an unloving and unfit mother. A letter written by Helen Thomson, Mrs Hogarth's sister, reveals that the family regarded Georgina's behaviour as 'strange' and a consequence of her being 'blinded by the sophistry of her brother-in-law'.[31] Dickens made it very evident that he wanted to keep Georgina with him. He wrote to Emile de la Rue, 'What we should do, or what the Girls would be, without Georgy, I cannot imagine. She is the active spirit of the house, and the children dote upon her.'[32]

Once it was known that Georgina would continue in the Dickens household, the gossip started. One version of a story that was said to be the catalyst for the Dickenses' separation involved Georgina. An American friend, John Bigelow, was having dinner at Thackeray's house when he heard that Georgina had mistakenly received a package from a jeweller containing a bracelet intended as a gift from Dickens to Nelly. According to Bigelow, 'Mrs. Dickens's sister, who had always been in love with him and was jealous of Miss Teman [sic] told Mrs. Dickens of the brooch'.[33] Thackeray himself inadvertently found himself implicated in spreading rumours. He was entering the Garrick Club when he overheard fellow clubmen chattering about the affair Dickens was having. Thackeray tried to quash the gossip that Dickens was getting Catherine to move out because of a liaison with Georgina, by leaping to her defence: 'No says I no such thing – it's with an actress.'[34] Dickens stopped speaking to him, assuming that Thackeray was deliberately spreading gossip about Nelly.

Dickens himself was largely to blame for the gossip. In February 1858, concerned that news of his marital difficulties might deter audiences from buying tickets for a planned reading tour, Dickens had drafted a statement. Dickens gave this statement, known as the 'Violated' letter, to his manager, Arthur Smith, telling him to show it 'to any one who wishes to do me right, or to any one who may have been misled into doing me wrong'.[35] The letter began by saying that the separation was because of differences in personality and temperament, but moved swiftly on to accuse Catherine of having a 'mental disorder', a 'peculiarity of character' and failing to mother their children.[36] In case anyone reading the statement had not got Dickens's message, that the marital breakdown was all Catherine's fault, he asserted: 'Mrs. Dickens has been in the habit of representing to me that it would be better for her to go away and live apart, ... that she felt herself unfit for the life she had to lead as my wife, and that she would be better far away.'[37] In the letter, Georgina was lauded for 'her affectionate care and devotion'.[38] If Dickens intended his extravagant praise of Georgina to serve as a justification for her remaining in his household after Catherine left, it backfired. Instead, rumours began that they were having an affair.

As relations between Georgina and the Hogarths deteriorated, she added her voice to Dickens's in vilifying Catherine. Like Dickens, she would twist events to put Catherine in the wrong. Where Catherine may, in a fit of anger, have declared she might as well move out, in Georgina's report this became: 'My sister has often expressed a desire to go and live away, but Charles never agreed to it on the girls' account; but latterly he thought it must be to their advantage as well as to his own and Catherine's to consent to this and remodel their unhappy home.'[39]

Georgina's aunt expressed the anger the Hogarths felt, saying, '[she] is an enthusiast, and worships him as a man of genius, and has quarrelled with all her relatives because they dare to find fault with him'.[40] Mrs Hogarth and younger sister Helen spoke openly against Georgina. They were pressing Catherine to go to court to apply for a divorce under the new Divorce and Matrimonial Causes Act. This would make public how Dickens was not the blameless soul he was portraying himself as and that the separation was not a mutual decision. Catherine resisted, and if she would not defend herself, then Mrs Hogarth and Helen would. Dickens heard from Edmund Yates that his mother had been told by Mrs Hogarth and Helen of Dickens's supposed indiscretions with Nelly and/or Georgina. He had a similar testimony from his reading manager, Arthur Smith, who had met the two women at a concert. It seems inconceivable that Mrs Hogarth spread rumours that her own daughter was having an affair with Dickens, even if the thought had crossed her mind. A more likely scenario is that Mrs Hogarth repeated her belief about a liaison between Dickens and Nelly and, annoyed as she was with Georgina for taking Dickens's part, criticised her too. She was certainly angry enough to intimate that amongst the many disservices Dickens had done his wife was the deliberate enthralling of Georgina and, as often happens when gossip is passed on, this had become embellished into an affair.

This was incendiary news. Firstly, it came from Dickens's mother-and sister-in-law, who would be expected to have direct knowledge of what had been going on; secondly, a sexual relationship with an in-law was deemed incestuous and, as such, illegal. This perceived betrayal by the Hogarth women, and Georgina's defence of Dickens, resulted in an irretrievable breakdown between Mrs Hogarth and her daughter. Georgina's aunt had no doubt that, as far as the family were concerned, Georgina had burned her bridges, saying of the situation: '[H]e has proved a spoiled child of fortune, dazzled by his popularity and given up to selfish egotism … she must bitterly repent, when she recovers from her delusion, her folly; … she has disappointed us all.'[41] Dickens was beside himself, furious with the 'wicked' Mrs Hogarth and her 'little serpent' of a daughter, Helen, for openly making accusations of an affair, not least because it contradicted his account of 'mutual incompatibility' which was caused by Catherine's personality defects.[42]

Dickens's reaction to hearing that Mrs Hogarth and Helen were accusing him of having an affair was to put a hold on the deed of separation that had been drawn up and agreed. Catherine was to have her own household, near enough to the family home to allow her to see the children, and £600 (£79,400) a year plus a carriage. Dickens insisted that only after the Hogarths had signed a statement saying that they not only withdrew their accusations of adultery, but they had never believed him to have been unfaithful in the first place, would he go ahead and sign the deed. Mrs Hogarth refused to sign any such statement. Mr Hogarth, though, was willing to comply and had a statement drafted by his solicitor:

> I can have no difficulty or hesitation in assuring you that the report that I or my wife or daughter have at any time stated or insinuated that any impropriety of conduct had taken place between my Daughter Georgiana [sic] and her Brother-in-Law Mr. Charles Dickens is totally unfounded.
>
> It is of course a matter of grief to us that after the unfortunate differences which have arisen between my daughter Mrs. Chas Dickens and her husband, my daughter Georgiana [sic] should remain with his family[,] but while we regret what we regard as a mistaken sense of duty[,] we have never for one instant imputed to her any improper motive for so doing.[43]

Dickens knew very well that in the Hogarth marriage, Mrs Hogarth ruled. Whatever the statement said, Mr Hogarth's signature was no guarantee that his wife agreed with its contents. Nor could Helen Hogarth's agreement be assured as she had her mother's outspoken temperament and was equally as suspicious of Dickens. An alternative declaration was drafted by Dickens's solicitor, Frederic Ouvry, which was phrased as if written by Mrs Hogarth and Helen, shrewdly drawing attention to their guilt in supposedly lying about his behaviour. Dickens's amendments are in italics.

It having been stated to us that in reference to the differences which have resulted in the separation of Mr. and Mrs. Charles Dickens, certain statements have been circulated that such differences were occasioned by circumstances deeply affecting the moral character of Mr. Dickens. We solemnly declare that such statements did not originate with, and have not been circulated by us or either of us. *(We solemnly declare that we now disbelieve such statements.)* We know that the statements are wholly repudiated by Mrs. Dickens and we believe them to be entirely destitute of foundation. We pledge ourselves on all occasions to contradict them. *(We know that these are not believed by Mrs. Dickens and we pledge ourselves on all occasions to contradict them as entirely destitute of foundation.)*[44]

The deed of separation was finally agreed, with Catherine's signature dated 4 June and Dickens signing on 10 June.

Gossip about the Dickenses became even more intense after the signing of the deed of separation, largely due to Dickens's mishandling of his private business. As the dates of the reading tour grew closer, Dickens was keen for the general public to hear his account of the marital breakdown. John Forster and Mark Lemon warned him of the likely consequences but, nevertheless, his 'Personal' statement appeared on 7 June 1858 and was picked up by local newspapers in the days that followed. Dickens made it the frontpage of *Household Words* on 12 June, referring to how he had been the subject of misrepresentation and falsity, as have 'innocent persons dear to my heart'.[45] When the 'Violated' letter was reproduced in newspapers in August, the public were able to read Dickens's anger about '[t]wo wicked persons, who should have spoken very differently of me, in consideration of earnest respect and gratitude, have … coupled with this separation the name of a young lady for whom I have a great attachment and regard'.[46] Making references in the letter to 'grossly false' rumours, 'innocent persons' and 'slanders' served only to stoke speculation about whether he was having an affair and who with.

Dickens failed to heed his own advice, given only months earlier to the artist William Holman Hunt, not to speak out as it would be telling 'the public what they have not the faintest idea of, and that its effect would be exactly the reverse of your desire'.[47] Days after the appearance of the 'Personal' statement, *Reynolds's Weekly Newspaper* told its readers that the references Dickens was making to 'innocent persons' were a 'female relative and a professional young lady'.[48] Even more pointedly, the gossipy *Court Circular* reported Dickens's preference for 'his wife's sister over his wife'.[49] Georgina was remarkably unruffled about being the subject of this gossip. When, at Dickens's behest, she had written to Maria Beadnell Winter, telling her of the impending separation of Catherine and Dickens, Georgina added her own observation: 'Charles is too public a man to take such a step as this without exciting a more than usual nine days' wonder – and we have heard of the most wonderful rumours and wicked slanders which have been flying about the town.'[50]

Within the Dickenses' social circle there was a great deal of support for Catherine from the women, little for Dickens, and Georgina was rarely mentioned. The majority of women who knew the couple were sceptical about Dickens's protestations of a mutually agreed separation. Helen Tagart, the wife of Dickens's friend, the Rev. Edward Tagart, wrote to her daughter:[51]

> I am going up to Hampstead with the carriage … to call on Mrs. Stanfield … [who] can tell me more about the Dickenses than anyone – I don't give any credit to the multitude of gossiping stories that are in circulation – Mrs. Dickens puts a brave face on it (but I can't think how she can leave her children) & says neither party are to blame but they think they shall be happier separated & he makes her a very handsome allowance £600 & therefore he is giving these readings to help out his income.[52]

When she heard Dickens's explanation, Elizabeth Barrett Browning exclaimed, 'Incompatible of temper after twenty-three years of married life? What a plea! … Poor woman! She must suffer bitterly

– that is sure.'[53] The daughter of Catherine's good friend Isabella Frith wrote about an evening when the three of them went to the theatre and saw Dickens in the opposite box with a party of friends, possibly including Nelly: 'She could not bear it. My mother took her back to her house ... I heard her tell Papa about it, and add, "I thought I should never be able to leave her; that man is a brute".'[54] The woman Dickens hoped to win over, Angela Burdett-Coutts, was not persuaded by his excuses for the separation because '[t]o her marriage was sacrosanct, and not to be broken for any mere incompatibility of nature. Besides which, having lived with his wife for twenty-two years, she considered that he might well continue to do so'.[55] Catherine's fellow Scots-woman, Jane Carlyle, wrote a riddle in one of her notebooks: 'When does a man really ill-use his wife? Ans. – When he plays the Dickens with her!'[56] More than anyone else, Jane could empathise with Catherine as her husband, Thomas Carlyle, was carrying on a romantic entanglement with another woman.[57]

There is only one record of what Catherine's friends thought of Georgina continuing to live in the Dickens household. Ironically, the report came via Catherine, who was defending her sister. After she had left Tavistock House, Catherine complained to Isabella Frith and her daughter, Jane, that she was tired of hearing suggestions that Georgina had taken her family from her. Jane recalled, 'I have ... often heard Mrs. Dickens say that her presence among "the children" was her one comfort and consolation, and that she wished people who did not know all would not talk'.[58]

Catherine's goodwill towards Georgina did not last. Although the sisters had not broken off contact with one another immediately following the separation, Georgina did something which angered Catherine. Visiting Gloucester Crescent in February 1859, William Thackeray came away with the impression that there had been a recent argument for which Catherine held Georgina responsible: 'The row appears to be [about] not the actress, but the sister-in-law.' Thackeray reported that, while Catherine did not suspect any sexual impropriety (she had 'nothing against Miss H.'), her caustic comments displayed outrage with Georgina. Sarcastically, Catherine repeated what Dickens implied in the 'Violated' letter and his 'Personal' statement, that Georgina was 'the cleverer and better woman of the two' and had 'got the affections of the children and the father'.[59] A few days after Thackeray's visit, Dickens's old publisher, Richard Bentley, recorded Catherine's opinion of Georgina in his diary. Catherine blamed 'her sister, who had not only behaved badly toward her herself, but had been the means of estranging her children from her. Dickens at Boulogne was frequently out with her.'[60]

Georgina's friends Rosa White and Mary Boyle appear not to have kept in contact with Catherine after the separation. Janet Wills, the wife of Dickens's sub-editor, W. H. Wills, who had regularly spent time with Catherine and Georgina, developed a close friendship with Georgina after the Dickenses split up. Once Catherine left, Janet let it be known that she had no time for Mrs Dickens. Janet's niece, Nina Lehmann, was taken aback to receive a letter from her aunt condemning Catherine's behaviour, just weeks after she had been banished from Tavistock House. W. H. Wills had gone down to visit Catherine in Brighton, where she was staying with Mrs Hogarth, and found her reading a novel on the pier. Janet was shocked by her seemingly careless attitude. Sympathising with Catherine, Nina observed, 'I don't see the harm … Is she to bury herself within four walls and weep her lost lord all day? She must live and … she must read something, having nothing else to do.'[61]

What explanations are there for Georgina's loyalty to Dickens and disloyalty to Catherine? Her strong affection for Dickens was a factor. He had, after all, been a father figure, the focus of an adolescent crush, someone she had fallen in love with, as well as a generous, caring and fascinating friend. However, Georgina's feelings for Dickens were not the only reason why she was prepared to abandon Catherine. Georgina had been growing apart from her sister since reaching adulthood, as shown by her choice of a very different set of friends to Catherine's. It appears Georgina's disapproval of Catherine and her friends stemmed from what she saw as a lack of respect for the 'men of genius'. Some mid-twentieth-century biographers argued that Georgina's disloyalty was a result of her envy and a desire to outshine Catherine.[62] Put in a wider social context, there may be something in this deprecatory view of Georgina. In the Victorian world, 'relationships between women [were] central to femininity, marriage and family life'.[63] As an unmarried woman, Georgina had greater freedoms and privileges than Catherine because she was not subject to the authority of a husband, but this did not free her from societal and cultural constraints. Where women's opportunities to assert themselves were confined to the domestic sphere, and where there were two women under the same roof claiming the role of housekeeper, Georgina measured her own capabilities against those of Catherine, and found those of her sister to fall short.

In her later years, Georgina described the reasons for her low opinion of her sister. Catherine's apparent failure in Georgina's eyes to be 'the right sort of wife for the genius of Dickens' included her sister's preparedness to argue.[64] Georgina said she thought that when women shouted, they 'mak[e] themselves odious and intolerable' and 'destroy the influence which they have'.[65] Georgina's comment to her parents about Dickens, that 'a man of genius ought not to be judged with the common herd of men', implies that Catherine should have been more acceptant of whatever Dickens said or chose to do.[66] After the deaths of Dickens and Catherine, Georgina was to claim that if people had known more about her sister's 'peculiarities', Dickens would have received more sympathy when they split up.[67]

Georgina's aunt suggested that Dickens's 'exaggerated praises of her to the depreciation of his wife' might have been a factor in Georgina's desire to remain with him.[68] Both Dickens and the Hogarths wanted Georgina on their side, but there was a crucial difference between how they tried to persuade her. Dickens heaped plaudits on her publicly: 'she has devoted herself to our house and our children' and 'has a higher claim … upon my affection, respect, and gratitude than anybody in this world'.[69] In contrast, the Hogarth family and, later on, Katey Dickens, were dismissive of the part Georgina played in the family, claiming she was merely 'useful'. Aunt Helen reported to her friend, 'all … Georgina did was to teach the little boys to read and write until they went to school … [and] made herself occasionally useful, I believe, as a sort of amanuensis to Dickens'.[70] Katey said of Georgina, 'she was useful to my mother, of course, but that was all'.[71] Nor did Mr and Mrs Hogarth appear to consider Georgina's feelings, assuming that loyalty to Catherine would take precedence. Did they talk to Georgina about what was best for her or consider that they were asking her to give up the home and family she had lived with for half her life and all her adult years? Dickens was being equally self-centred in wanting Georgina to stay, but where the Hogarths were commanding her to leave, he was flattering her into remaining in his household.

There were practical matters too that an unmarried, financially dependent woman like Georgina would have taken into consideration. What would have been the situation if she had wanted to leave Dickens's household to be with her sister? It would have put a strain on Catherine's income if it had to cover Georgina's living costs which, in turn, would have put pressure on Georgina to earn her own living by taking on a teaching or governess role. Besides, although 'many women chose to remain single for political reasons', Georgina had no more desire than Catherine to be independent.[72] As Katey Dickens suggested, Catherine and Georgina were content with their domesticated lives and 'shrank modestly from encroaching upon man's domain'.[73]

It was also the case that Georgina trusted Dickens; she trusted that what he told her was the truth. While he was open with Georgina at the very start of his dealings with the Ternan family, he soon started to use subterfuge and misdirection. He had been honest with Georgina about wanting to pursue the family to Doncaster, but it was to W. H. Wills that he confessed he had something more on his mind than acting as a mentor and guardian.[74] Georgina was to pay a price for her loyalty to Dickens. Her respectable reputation was damaged, she was to be humiliated, experience a diminution in her status, and face the loss of a once 'more equitable and frank relation with a non-kinsman'.[75]

On 18 June 1858, the Dickens family departed for Gad's Hill. The move out of London for the summer months could not have come at a better time. The city was experiencing an unprecedented heatwave, hitting thirty-four degrees in the shade at Hyde Park. The combination of the unremitting heat and lack of a sewage system increased the threat of typhoid and cholera epidemics. The smell from the River Thames was so great that Parliament had to close down for a time. As the middle classes escaped from London, there were fewer opportunities for gossip to be spread and appear in the press. The peace and fresh air of the Kent countryside brought Georgina some much-needed respite and, for a few short weeks, she was able to pick up a newspaper and not read something about herself and the Dickenses' marriage.

Chapter 7
'Poor Miss Hogarth' (1858–63)

Following the separation, Dickens and Georgina focused on how best to protect Dickens. A priority for him was to make a success of the forthcoming reading tour, which to a large extent involved holding onto his popularity and reputation. A second priority was his relationship with Nelly Ternan. Family matters featured some way down the list. Georgina's concerns were with Dickens's happiness, health, and his work. Meanwhile, the atmosphere inside the Dickens household was tense. Comments made by Katey Dickens and their friend Annie Fields give an impression of what it was like for Georgina and the family. According to Katey, Dickens was 'acting like a madman … He did not care a damn what happened to any of us.'[1] Reflecting on 'poor Miss Hogarth' and her attempts at trying to maintain a sense of normality, Annie Fields said: 'It is not an easy service in this world to live near such a man, to love him, to desire to do for him.'[2] Any influence or control Georgina had within their relationship reached its lowest point. Whether knowingly or unthinkingly, Dickens took advantage of Georgina's loyalty to him by using it for his own ends.

Had Catherine died, rather than been dismissed, the Dickens's domestic set-up would have appeared much more acceptable. Sympathy for the Dickens family might, at least temporarily, have overlooked the fact that the unmarried Georgina was keeping house for her brother-in-law and providing comfort to the children. That

Catherine was still very much alive and had been ousted from her home meant that not only were many people ill at ease with the new living arrangements, but so were Dickens and Georgina. If Georgina had hoped that the summer of 1858 would provide a chance for normal family life to resume at Gad's Hill, she was disappointed. Dickens was as unhappy and unsettled as he had been before Catherine was packed off to Gloucester Crescent. He remained irritable, only wanting to see those who were sympathetic to the changes he had made to his family circumstances. When Georgina enquired which of his oldest friends he wanted to invite for a weekend, Thomas Beard or T. J. Thompson and his wife, Christiana, Dickens exclaimed, 'take Thompson! There is no comparison between them. He is not wearisome – really has tact – and is far more formable and mouldable altogether.'[3]

Eager to avoid stoking the gossip mill with any suggestion that she would be replacing her sister, Georgina made it known that Mamie was taking over as mistress of the house. She told Maria Beadnell Winter, '[Mamie] and Katy and I will divide the *work* amongst us, but all the dignity will be [Mamie's] and she will do the honours modestly, gracefully and prettily, I know'.[4] Annie Fields learned from Dickens that Mamie had the job of managing the servants, while Georgina oversaw the wine cellar and provisions. In reality, Georgina had to take overall charge. At just twenty years old when her parents separated, Mamie had no experience of acting as manager of a large, busy household. She and Katey were used only to fitting into the domestic set-up of Tavistock House organised by their mother and aunt. Once friends started to arrive for visits at Gad's Hill, it would be apparent it was actually Georgina running Dickens's household. He prepared guests accordingly, emphasising that he had a '[t]riumvirate of housekeepers' and while Mamie 'is a capital housekeeper', she 'delegates certain appointed duties to her sister and her aunt'.[5]

In his returns for the 1861 census, Dickens listed Georgina as 'servant housekeeper' and, in the stroke of a pen, reduced her status to below stairs. The census had a column for 'Rank, Profession or Occupation', but Dickens could have chosen to have left this blank, as he did when entering Mamie's details. Georgina was now officially designated as an employee and he certainly treated her as a housekeeper. Two days after the family arrived at Gad's Hill in June 1858, the water pump broke down again and the local man refused to try and fix it. Dickens begged his brother-in-law, Henry Austin, to come and sort it out and, after briefing Georgina, left her in charge while he escaped to Tavistock House. Later, when Gad's Hill was in a state of upheaval due to the renovations, he advised an absent Mamie not to 'come back too soon. There is no hurry, the house is not near to-rights yet.'[6] Tackling the relentless mud and dust created by twenty-seven workmen as they tunnelled, knocked down and rebuilt walls and roofs was left to Georgina and the servants. When the Christmas of 1860 saw such low temperatures that even the water in the bedroom jugs froze, cracking the crockery, and the thaw caused burst pipes, sending water everywhere, it was too much for Dickens. He took himself off to London the day after Boxing Day, leaving Georgina to clear up. Dickens wrote to her from the office of *All the Year Round* (the journal that replaced *Household Words*): 'It is certainly less cold here than at Gad's Hill, and the pipes are *not* frozen – which is a great comfort.'[7] She must have received this while wading through water and trying to dry out rugs.

There were instances when Dickens castigated Georgina as if she was a servant:

> You can scarcely imagine what a ridiculous amount of small distress has been caused me by a peculiar and detestable shirt button you have put at the throat of my coloured shirts … This very day, I went through this process *three times*. From *three* clean shirts, one after another, the button burst, when I had at last got the collar on to it![8]

It was one thing to reduce her official status to that of below stairs, but Dickens went much further. In the past he had never seen anything wrong in invading Georgina's privacy, so opening letters addressed to her may have been just another step. Attaching a note to one letter, Dickens told Georgina, '[k]nowing that the enclosed from Mrs. Watson would refer to me, I opened it, to see if there were anything that I could answer. Discovering nothing of that kind, I send it on to you to answer for yourself'.[9]

When Dickens chastised Georgina, he generated a nervous response in her. Dickens was away on the Scottish leg of his reading tour in 1858 when Georgina wrote to her old flame Edward Bulwer-Lytton, asking whether he knew of any job opportunities for her younger brother. There was a brief exchange of letters when Bulwer-Lytton intimated the possibility of Edward Hogarth securing a writership. Regrettably, he directed his last reply to Dickens, asking him to inform Georgina of his advice and, judging by the profuse apology she sent, Georgina had found herself in trouble. Her letter to Bulwer-Lytton reads like a summary of the reprimand she received, presumably for approaching Bulwer-Lytton without Dickens's knowledge and consent. After offering an anxious apology for being imprecise, dilatory in replying and bothering Bulwer-Lytton with the matter in the first place, she said she had abandoned any notion of assisting her brother further. Georgina ended the letter with a plea: 'I should be very glad to hear one line – one *word* from you – to say that you understand that this unfortunate mistake does not arise from any negligence on my part.'[10]

Dickens appeared wary of being seen too often in public accompanied by Georgina. At a family dinner party at Tavistock House, Annie Fields wrote in her diary about meeting 'the family' at this intimate dinner, but only Mamie and Katey were there, and most unusually, Georgina was absent. Annie had the feeling that Dickens was deeply unhappy: 'A shadow has fallen on that house, making Dickens seem rather the man of labor and of sorrowful thought than the soul of gaiety we find in all he writes.'[11] This was far from the only occasion when Georgina found her presence was not wanted. When a friend issued an invitation to her home, Dickens informed Georgina, 'Laura wants us to dine there on Sunday at 6 ½. Family dinner, she expressly says. No one there', asking, 'Shall we go? Perhaps it might be well to take the opportunity.'[12] But even with trusted people like Laura Olliffe, Dickens erred on the side of caution and, without waiting for a reply from Georgina, sent a note in the same post declining the invitation.

Yet Dickens also wanted Georgina to be more than a housekeeper. He left responsibility for the children in her hands. The older boys were now young men. Charley was living with his mother, Walter was in India and Frank in Germany, furthering his plans to join the medical profession. In the summer of 1858 the rest of the boys were home from school in Boulogne. The loss of a mother to death would have been something the children could have understood. Instead, they were expected simply to accept the new living arrangements. Alfred, who was aged twelve when his parents separated, said, 'not one word on the subject *ever* passed the lips of either father or mother. Of the causes which led to the unfortunate event … we know no more than the rest of the world.'[13] Dickens often emphasised the deep affection the children had for Georgina, implying they regarded her as a mother figure, yet with the exception of Harry, the brothers never mentioned her. It was Catherine they remembered tenderly; Alfred said of his parents he 'loved them both equally' and Harry wrote fondly of 'my dear mother' and recalled jokes she told them.[14]

Unlike today, Victorian society did not consider the effect of divorce on children and, on that basis, a generous reader might excuse Dickens's attempts to get his offspring to side with him against Catherine. Reminding them that the Dickens name was their best asset, he refused to hear them speak of their mother and forbade them from seeing her if she was accompanied by their Hogarth relatives, the Lemons or the family of Charley's fiancée, Bessie (the daughter of his ex-publisher, Fred Evans).[15] It fell to Georgina to make sure everyone complied with Dickens's orders, checking to see there were no unapproved visitors at Catherine's house when she dropped the boys off at Gloucester Crescent. She would, of course, be expected to report back to Dickens had there been any defiance of his instructions.

Initially the older boys appeared to be coping, as they were used to being away at school and not seeing their parents for long stretches of time. The cracks soon started to show. Frank was only in Germany for six months before asking his father if he could return home and abandon his plans of becoming a doctor, giving the excuse that his stammer would handicap any professional career. Six-year-old Plorn was the one most shaken by the changes. He lost his mother overnight when she moved out and, within a month, the family had removed to Gad's Hill, a house he was barely familiar with. Adding to his loss was Dickens's absence on a reading tour in late summer and autumn 1858, which took him away for months with only short visits home. Plorn was talked about in the family as being a rather shy and sensitive boy, but this had not always been the case. Dickens recalled him as a lively infant, on one occasion overbalancing and hurting himself as he tried to kick his nursemaid. It was only after the separation of his parents that Plorn became increasingly nervous, hating to be amongst large groups of people and getting upset at even the thought of being away from home.

Mamie and Katey supposedly adored 'Aunty'. According to Dickens: 'Miss Hogarth, always Miss Hogarth, is the guide, philosopher and friend of all the party, and a very close affection exists between her and the girls'.[16] The Dickens girls were very close, despite having different interests and different attitudes to their parents' separation. Mamie unreservedly took her father's side and never visited her mother. Katey saw Catherine occasionally, but was reluctant to annoy or upset Dickens, and guiltily avoided calling on her, even though she and her sister took music lessons in a house opposite their mother's in Gloucester Crescent. Up until their parents' separation, they had enjoyed considerable freedom. Some years earlier, Katey had persuaded her father to allow her to take art lessons with a view to becoming a professional artist. Mamie loved to indulge in vigorous physical activities outdoors. She was one of the first women to ride a bicycle at Gad's Hill and was also a skilled horse rider and coach driver, often getting hurt when she tested her sporting skills to the limit. On more than one occasion she turned over the brougham with her sister and aunt on board because she was driving so fast.

In the summer and autumn of 1858, Aunt Georgy chaperoned the girls as they socialised at military balls and events in the surrounding Kent countryside. Once they returned to London for 'the season' in February 1859, all three women had to suffer the social fallout from Dickens's actions at the time of the separation. His behaviour, from banishing Catherine to arguing with anyone and everyone who dared disagree, alienated many people. Added to which, according to Elizabeth Gaskell, his misjudgement in assuming the public wanted to know his personal business resulted in further disapproval: 'Mr. Dickens happens to be extremely unpopular just now, – (owing to the well-grounded feeling of dislike to the publicity he has given to his domestic affairs)'.[17] The repercussions were felt by Georgina, Mamie and Katey, who were exposed to social shaming by people once considered friends. Eneas Sweetland Dallas, a young author whom Dickens had gone out of his way to help, showed himself to be particularly ungrateful, writing gleefully to the publisher John Blackwood:

> With the exception of a few toadies there is not a soul to take his part. They cut him at the clubs. His daughters – now under the benign wing of their aunt, Miss Hogarth – are not received into society. You would be excessively amused if you heard all the gigantic efforts the family make to keep their foot in the world – how they call upon people that they never called on before & that they have treated with the most dire contempt. Fancy Dickens & his family going to call on that worthy couple – Mr. & Mrs. Pecksniff

[i.e. S. C. Hall, the original of that character], & informing these people upon whom they never called before that they would be happy to see them at Tavistock House. But still better – fancy Pecksniff & his wife in a high moral transport and religious spite informing Miss Hogarth & the Miss Dickenses, that it was with Mrs. Dickens they were acquainted, that if Mrs. Dickens were at Tavistock House they should be happy to call, but otherwise – afraid – very sorry – but etc., etc. It is a wretched business altogether.[18]

As Dallas suggested, there were people who seized the opportunity to punish Dickens by making Georgina and the girls a target. Their visiting card presented one such opportunity. Following an incident at the Lord Mayor's dinner, when William Thackeray had tried to talk to Mamie but she walked away, causing him to call after her, 'Let fathers hate like hell but why should children quarrel?', he took his revenge.[19] After being presented with the visiting card the women were using, Thackeray wrote sneeringly to a fellow clubman at finding 'the 2 Misses Dickens & Miss Hogarth (on one card)'.[20] The offending visiting card listed three names; in descending order: Miss Dickens, Miss Kate Dickens and, lastly, Miss Hogarth. It was a social *faux pas*. Catherine's failure to follow etiquette rules by ensuring that her daughters had their own calling cards when they reached eighteen might be excused by her preoccupation with her disintegrating marriage. Georgina had also experienced this oversight and it made her and the Dickens girls a laughing stock. It can only be that Dickens was in no mood to be bothered about the social protocols of calling cards, illustrating Katey's claim that his mood was such that he showed little care for his family. If this unorthodox calling card was to be used, Georgina's name should have been first, as the senior female relative in the house, but Catherine was alive and the girls' mother and it would have looked as if Georgina was replacing Catherine. There had been enough scandal already without fuelling that fire, and as Mamie was ostensibly mistress of the house, her name had to come first. There was, though, no precedent for having a younger woman's name before an older

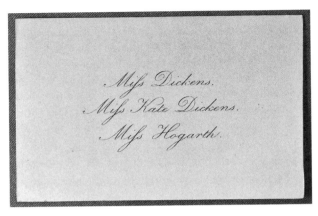

29 Mamie Dickens, Katey Dickens and Georgina Hogarth's visiting card, 1858

relative's, and being the third name on her nieces' visiting card put Georgina in a demeaning position.

At home, Georgina did what she could to relieve them of their household duties, but Mamie and Katey were neither settled nor happy. The girls found different ways of dealing with their unhappiness, Mamie into alcohol and Katey into marriage. Determined to get away from home, Katey became engaged to the artist Charles Collins, the brother of Wilkie. Charles was thirty-one years of age, good looking and, according to Katey, the kindest and most sweet-tempered of men, but she was not in love with him.[21]

Aside from looking after his children, 'it was Georgina who regularly coped with ... the tribe of troublesome relatives that swarmed after Dickens'.[22] One of these 'troublesome relatives' was another of Dickens's sisters-in-law, Helen Dobson Dickens. Helen lived in Manchester with Dickens's engineer brother, Alfred. On Alfred's sudden death in 1860, Helen was left penniless with five children to feed. Dickens moved the family to London, leasing a house for her and his mother, Elizabeth Dickens. Elizabeth was showing signs of dementia. At first, Dickens thought highly of

Helen, calling her a 'patient, uncomplaining, self denying, and quietly practical' person.[23] When the struggle to bring up five young children and look after Dickens's increasingly confused mother became overwhelming, Helen took to writing desperate letters to him, and he started referring to her as 'that disagreeable woman'.[24] After receiving one of Helen's letters detailing his mother's difficult and eccentric behaviour, Dickens wrote to Georgina, 'I must consult you when I come back touching the best means of making known to her that I wish her in future to communicate personally with you, or with you and Mary'.[25] He reasoned, 'I really can not bear the irritation she causes me, and the strife she gets up in my uneasy mind about the whole business. I was completely disgusted and worn out by her on this last occasion.'[26] Georgina must have smoothed things over as there were no more complaints about Helen until four years after the death of his mother.

The next time Dickens instructed Georgina to intervene was far more sensitive. Although Georgina and Catherine were not on speaking terms, both sisters maintained friendly relations with the other women in the Dickens family. When Dickens suspected Helen and his estranged wife of colluding in a plot to trap him into seeing Catherine, he was furious. He believed a request from Helen to call at her home with regard to a housekeeping matter was a cover, and that he would arrive to find that, coincidentally, Catherine had dropped in for a visit. The task of delivering his angry tirade was handed over to Georgina:

> I wish you would reply … and that you think it well to tell her at once that you are absolutely certain that I never will go to her house, and that it is my fixed purpose to hold as little personal communication with her [Helen] as I possibly can.[27]

Georgina's role as a mouthpiece for Dickens was unlikely to foster friendly relations with Helen; there is no evidence of any contact between her, her children and Georgina ever again after this particular episode.

After the turmoil of the spring and summer of 1858, Dickens and Georgina preferred to make their main home Gad's Hill rather than Tavistock House. At Gad's Hill, Georgina created the sense of domestic calm and order that Dickens required in order to work. After a two-year hiatus in novel writing, in February 1859 Dickens began *A Tale of Two Cities*. In December the following year, the first numbers of *Great Expectations* were published. Removing themselves from London to Gad's Hill did not provide any relief from the ongoing rumours, however. Gossip of an affair was followed by speculation they had children together.

In October 1858 Dickens was contacted by a journalist telling him of a shocking conversation he had had with Colin Rae Brown, the editor of a prominent Scottish newspaper. Brown had asked the journalist whether he knew that 'Mr. Dickens's sister in law had had three children by him'.[28] An apoplectic and horrified Dickens immediately had his solicitor draft a letter demanding that Colin Rae Brown admit misconduct and declare that the accusations were bogus. Brown sent a grovellingly apologetic letter, but made matters more worrying for Dickens by telling him that he was only repeating gossip from informants in London. Dickens accepted the apology, reluctant for any such case to come to court as it could easily backfire. Should the Hogarths ever persuade Catherine to divorce Dickens, they might use this evidence to issue a claim of incest between Dickens and Georgina. If there is any truth in the story that Georgina was asked to undergo a virginity test to prove her sexual innocence, this would have been the time.[29] Proof of Georgina's virginity would certainly have been useful should Dickens have found himself having to instigate a libel case against any newspaper printing this particular snippet of scurrilous gossip.

Asking women to take a virginity test was not that unusual in the 1850s. Effie Millais took a virginity test to prove that her marriage to John Ruskin had not been consummated; Emily Faithfull, publisher of *English Woman's Journal*, was questioned about her virginity in court when in fact she was a completely innocent bystander in the divorce case of Codrington *versus* Codrington. If Georgina did undergo such a medical examination to prove her virtue, it would undoubtedly have been mortifying to have a male doctor inspecting intimate parts of her body; besides which, using a woman's body to prove the sexual morality of a man was exploitative even in Victorian times.

Georgina's faith in Dickens's honesty about his virtuous intentions towards Nelly was confirmed when he acquired a sexually transmitted disease (STD), probably gonorrhoea.[30] He was hardly likely to have caught the STD from Nelly or to risk passing it on to her. Whether Georgina knew about his condition is another matter. The first mention of having caught an STD came in a note to his doctor, Frank Beard: 'My bachelor state has engendered a small malady on which I want to see you.'[31] Beard prescribed silver nitrate, then used in the treatment of gonorrhoea, which itself caused problems – a week later Dickens was asking, 'What I principally want to know is, whether your medicine irritates my skin. In other respects, I hope I am certainly better.'[32] He was not embarrassed about admitting to his condition to his men friends; he was open on the subject of regular sexual activity being essential for men's health. At the time he was complaining of the medication to Beard, he told Wills, 'I don't think I am any better'.[33] Forster too had been made aware: 'I have been getting on in health very slowly and irksome botheration enough. But I think I am round the corner.'[34] Still not improved by mid-August, Dickens wrote to Wilkie Collins that he would visit him in Broadstairs if he believed that 'taking a tumble in the sea [would be of benefit] but I suppose there is no nitrate of silver in the Ocean?'[35]

When Dickens first consulted Frank Beard he asked him to visit him at the office of *All the Year Round* rather than at home, which would have helped to keep his illness confidential. As it proved resistant to treatment, Dickens was still taking medication when he returned to Gad's Hill, informing Frank Beard that he was continuing to take both of the remedies but neither of them were making a difference. How open was he with Georgina about the reason his doctor was prescribing him medicine? Dickens always kept Georgina updated on his state of health, but an STD may have been too personal. It was not that Dickens was reserved about mentioning sexual matters to his sister-in-law and wife. He told Georgina that Wilkie Collins had apparently lost his virginity in Rome to a woman three times his age, and in 1853 had written to Catherine saying that on arrival in Capri he had been greeted with the gossip that two of Mrs Norton's sons had been having sex with local girls. Dickens had no qualms about the boys having sexual relations outside marriage but strongly disapproved when one of them married his 'bare-footed [beach] girl'.[36]

Dickens suffered from the STD on and off for eighteen months, but all that can be gleaned from his letters to Georgina is that she knew he was being treated for some undisclosed illness. On returning to London in January 1860 he reported to her, 'I don't feel quite so well today, but I think it is the Medicine'.[37] When a further recurrence appeared later in the year, she was told, 'I have to see Frank Beard again on Monday morning', but he reassured her that he was not in pain and, 'If you have the least doubt about me, I am open to inspection … But be sure that if I wanted any nursing, I should say so, and should resort to you sooner than to anybody on earth.'[38]

If Dickens aspired to put his relationship with Nelly on a more intimate level, then having gonorrhoea would have put any plans on hold, but only for a while. In getting closer to Nelly he set in motion the potentially cataclysmic events of 1862–3. If it had not been for these events, then the one-sided nature of Dickens and Georgina's relationship, where both of them were focused on his needs, would most likely have continued. Instead, Dickens's revelations resulted in Georgina having a dramatic mental and physical breakdown. His anxiety at the prospect of losing this devoted friend brought about a rebalancing of their alliance.

Georgina's breakdown was a result of her misguided trust in her brother-in-law's honesty about his involvement with Nelly Ternan. Dickens gave the appearance of being, as he protested, simply a mentor and guardian to the Ternans. He helped them find suitable housing accommodation, used his influence to secure acting roles for Maria and Nelly, and assisted Fanny Ternan by paying for her to receive coaching in Florence to help her fulfil an ambition to become a professional singer. As Nelly was Dickens's particular 'pet', there would have been no surprise at his buying the lease on 2 Houghton Place for the Ternans, only for it to revert solely to Nelly when she came of age.[39] Singling out one person for special attention was not remarkable in the Dickens household. For instance, when Charley had children, Georgina, Dickens and Mamie thought it appropriate to discuss which child they liked best.

Dickens was not the only person to have deceived Georgina. By 1862, Georgina had established what was to be a lifelong friendship with Nelly. Despite Georgina being twelve years older than Nelly, the two women had much in common. Nelly, like Georgina, was a good mimic, loved books and had an interest in theatre and politics. Georgina may even have stepped in to act as chaperone to Nelly and her sister Maria while their mother was in Florence with her eldest daughter Fanny. Mrs Ternan would have needed assurance that leaving her daughters under Dickens's guardianship would not damage their reputations; after all, the neighbours would have been rightly scandalised to have witnessed a middle-aged man frequently climbing the steps to the door of two young, unchaperoned girls. In later years, Nelly showed a picture of Gad's Hill to a young friend, telling her that she had been there many times; some of these visits may have been to stay with Georgina and Mamie when Dickens was on his reading tours. In many ways, Nelly was similar to Mamie. Both had a love of music, were devoted to dogs and were skilled horse riders. Unlike Georgina, who thrived on winning Dickens's approval through her domestic management, neither Nelly or Mamie had much interest or talent in cookery or running a house.

Did Georgina ever suspect Dickens was sexually interested in Nelly? His lavish praise of Nelly would not have been anything to go by, and both women were aware of Dickens's habit of extolling their qualities. Georgina confessed she was 'astonished' by the admiration Dickens publicly expressed for her, saying his words were 'far more than [she] deserved', while Nelly reported that Dickens similarly overrated her.[40] She confessed to accepting Dickens's flattery because her weakness was 'vanity combined with a desire for a competence'.[41] Georgina also saw that Nelly possessed characteristics Dickens would not have liked; she could be imperious at times, something of a tease, moody and had a volatile temper when she did not get her own way.[42] Nor was there any reason for Georgina to suppose Nelly had any romantic feelings for Dickens. There is no evidence that Nelly ever appeared to be in love with Dickens and no reason for Georgina to suspect that the young girl's relationship with him was any different to that of her sisters, Maria and Fanny.

If there was one thing that may have given Georgina cause to question Dickens's motives, it would have been the amount of money he was expending on the Ternans. His generosity had already prompted an enquiry from Richard Spofford, a Boston lawyer, who was suspicious about why Dickens was prepared to spend so much money on his cousin Fanny Ternan, in paying for her to receive professional voice coaching in Italy. Dickens wrote Spofford a long reply, equating his concern for the Ternan girls to that of a father by referring to Mamie and Katey, and condemning the gossip as a 'kind of evil' which occupied 'a dark place in the social life of many countries, and especially of America'.[43] Yet anyone who knew Dickens well would have understood Spofford's unease. Georgina had heard Dickens complain regularly about the number of relatives who kept coming to him for money, and now here he was splurging extravagantly on non-family members. On top of the expenses incurred in sending Fanny and her mother to Florence, he also paid for Nelly to travel there for a short visit. Georgina might not have known that Dickens had given the theatre manager John Buckstone a cheque for £50 for engaging Nelly to act in a one-act farce. Nor do we know if Georgina was aware Dickens intended handing over the remaining thirty-seven years of the lease on Tavistock House for a nominal rent to Mrs Ternan when she arrived back from Italy. Forster and W. H. Wills urged him to consider how such an action would create unwanted speculation, which is why he instead bought the lease of 2 Houghton Place, Ampthill Square.

The lead-up to Georgina's breakdown began in the early months of 1862 when there was a detectable change in Dickens's mood. It was a sentimental Dickens who presented W. H. Wills with a solid silver claret jug, 'expressive of our friendship. I have had your name and mine set upon it, in token of our many years of mutual reliance and trustfulness.'[44] He enthused about Maria Ternan's assets, going above and beyond her acting abilities, claiming she was 'one of the best and bravest of little spirits and most virtuous of girls'.[45] A sense of endings and beginnings could explain this more emotional Dickens. The unexpected deaths of the Rev. James White in March and of an American friend, Cornelius Felton, in April contrasted with a second, new life for the elderly William Macready with the birth of his son, following his marriage to the much younger Cecile Spencer. Georgina and Dickens were asked to be the boy's godparents. If there is any truth in the speculations of many scholars on Dickens and Nelly's relationship, this is the period when he succeeded in seducing her.[46] Any pleasure this gave him was short-lived when he discovered that, not only was he going to be a grandfather for the first time, he was also an expectant father.

Although, on its own, nothing can be read into a note Dickens sent to the actor Charles Fechter, arranging to see him at 5.30 on Friday 23 May at the office of *All the Year Round*, it marks the beginning of a series of unexplained disappearances. Dickens warned Fechter, '[i]t is possible – but not very probable – that some private business may take me out of town in the course of the next week'.[47] He was out of the office on that day and there is no surviving correspondence for the seven days from Thursday 22 May until the following Wednesday, 28 May. Silences like these usually indicated he was somewhere with Nelly. The first sign that something was really worrying Dickens appears on 31 May, in a letter to his recently widowed sister, Letitia: 'I have been hoping to come to you every day since I saw you; but I have been sorely worried and distressed of late'.[48] Dickens hoped to be at her house the following day, but never arrived. This was the same day, 1 June, when the family left what Dickens called the 'odious' 16 Hyde Park Gate, the house he had leased to allow Mamie to enjoy the London season, to return to Gad's Hill.

As far as we know, Georgina was in good health. Just over a week after their return to Gad's Hill, guests arrived for a Monday–Thursday stay between 9 and 12 June. Georgina appeared to be well and happy. One of the visitors, Frank Finlay, editor of the Belfast *Northern Whig*, described Georgina as 'a really delightful person … totally unaffected and of singularly pleasant and easy manner'.[49] He talked about Georgina accompanying the party on walks, playing whist and sitting up late into the evening, chatting and exchanging stories. His account helps to pinpoint the moment when Georgina's health suddenly broke down. Finlay reports that all the guests left on the morning of Thursday 12 June, when Georgina appeared her usual self. He certainly made no comment about any change in her manner, health or appearance. It was Dickens's habit to take a long afternoon walk with Georgina and there is no reason to suppose they did anything differently that Thursday afternoon. Something happened between the time the guests left on Thursday morning and the following day. Dickens may have taken the opportunity on their walk, out of earshot of the servants and the rest of the family, to impart news concerning

Nelly to Georgina. The very next morning Dickens reported that Georgina was 'far from well'.[50] Letitia heard from her brother a week later, 'I have been so anxious and distressed about Georgina (who has some affection of the heart), that I have been altogether dazed'.[51] Her symptoms included breathlessness and chest pains and, in keeping with medical advice, Dickens decided that the following Friday, 20 June, he would 'take Miss Hogarth ... away for a week, in the hope of doing her service through a little change'.[52] Initially, they headed for Dover, which provided the recommended bracing sea air, but they were there for just one night before going over to Paris. Given that Baron Haussmann's renovations had turned the centre of Paris into a building site, there is a question as to why Dickens subjected his ill sister-in-law to such an unsanitary environment, unless he needed her help with a problem.

The writer Robert Garnett has analysed Dickens's trips to Paris and his findings suggest that this was the time when Nelly was pregnant and gave birth.[53] A pregnant Nelly had to leave London as it would not be long before people discovered the 'virtuous and spotless' girl had been compromised.[54] She needed to be removed to a place she was not known and where Dickens would stand less chance of being recognised when he visited. France was the most obvious choice but, even there, someone might report the presence of the famous author seeking to rent a secluded house for a mother and daughter. Far less noticeable would be if Georgina searched out a possible property and did the negotiations. After all, she spoke fluent French and knew northern France well. The house had to be private, but with access to local doctors, midwives and nurses. For Georgina to make discreet enquiries about arrangements for the lying-in of a woman friend would not provoke suspicion. If Dickens had to enlist Georgina's help, there was no way he could gloss over the fact he was having a sexual relationship with Nelly.

How upset and shocked Georgina was by Nelly's pregnancy is obvious from her visceral reactions. She either did not, or had chosen not to, regard Nelly as a threat to her life with Dickens.

One reason was the age difference between Nelly and Dickens. Their twenty-six-year age-gap was larger than that between R. H. Horne and his wife Kate Horne, whom Georgina once scathingly referred to as 'young enough to be his daughter'.[55] Georgina was to say later, 'I confess I cannot reconcile myself to these violently unnatural *disparities* in marriage'.[56] Yet Georgina's breakdown on hearing of Dickens's impending fatherhood is an extreme reaction that implies more than a disapproval of age differences.

Whether Georgina acknowledged it to herself or not, Dickens had duped her. Over the years she had lived with Dickens, he had represented many significant male figures to her, as a companion, protector and friend, and she had developed strong emotional feelings for him. His revelations did more than shatter her trust in him as she was forced to deal with the emotional trauma of possibly losing him and everything she loved. There were real, practical worries about how her life was about to be overturned again and so soon after the upheaval of the Dickenses' marital separation. What would her family, friends and the newspapers say about her when it was discovered that Dickens had a mistress after all? As Dickens had protested Georgina's, as well as Nelly's, innocence and purity, it was perfectly feasible for others to believe that he had lied about his relations with Georgina too. Would Georgina end up in court accused of engaging in an incestuous affair? What if Dickens loved Nelly enough to weather the damage to his career and instigate a divorce from Catherine? If Dickens and Nelly married, where would that leave her? Perhaps Dickens might find her a house on her own where she would have to live alone, humiliated and ostracised by society. The only way Georgina could help herself was to bury her worries and assist Dickens and Nelly in trying to hide the pregnancy from the eyes of everyone. Six years later she reflected back on her devotion to Dickens, admitting, 'God knows how faithful my love was for him'.[57]

From 20 to 26 June, Dickens and Georgina were in Paris, or more accurately as he reported to Letitia, 'a week's wandering in the strangest towns in France'.[58] He did not tell Letitia what they were doing, just that 'Georgina is better, but we have cause for great anxiety about her', then adding, 'I go back again for another adventure next week – this day week probably'.[59] He was increasingly vague, telling a part-truth alongside a misleading assertion. In a letter sent between his first and second visits, he told an acquaintance, 'I am away to France forthwith for a holiday, and am not likely to be in London for many weeks to come. It is some years since I was last across the channel.'[60] He had in fact been in France less than two weeks earlier. Georgina did not accompany him on his second visit. When they had arrived back to Gad's Hill following the 'week's wandering' expedition, Dickens insisted that Georgina see their old family doctors, Frank Beard and John Elliotson.[61]

At the age of thirty-five, Georgina was diagnosed with 'degeneration of the heart' and declared 'quite unfit' to cope with guests, so prospective visitors found their invitations to Gad's Hill cancelled.[62] For all that Dickens had been emotionally absorbed by Nelly, Georgina's rapid deterioration raised the possibility that he might lose her. He wrote anxiously to William Macready on 2 July, 'I (who know her best, I think) see much in her that fills me with uneasiness'.[63] Dickens may have been unwittingly thinking back to his own euphoric mood in May that year when he reflected back on Georgina's mood at the time: 'The change that two months have made is extraordinarily great. All that alacrity and "cheer of spirit" that used to distinguish her are gone … And she is very low about herself, almost as soon as one has ceased to speak to her, after brightening her up.'[64]

Georgina went to be looked after in Letitia's home while Dickens took off for France again on 10 July for five days. During Dickens's absence, or shortly after his return, concern for Georgina increased and she was taken to a heart and lung specialist, Dr Archibald Billing. This time the diagnosis, aneurism of the aorta, was life-threatening. The symptoms are those Georgina was experiencing, including hoarseness and difficulty breathing, numbness, chest pain and nausea. Of course, what no one knew at the time was that Georgina would live to the age of ninety and never suffer any heart problems after 1862. An alternative diagnosis which explains her reactions only became known to medical science in the 1980s. The signs of a panic attack are noticeably similar to those of heart problems, including palpitations, chest pains, feeling faint, numbness, sweating, trembling, a choking sensation and nausea. The threat of what would happen to her should news of Nelly's pregnancy be discovered, and of losing Dickens, could understandably have triggered panic attacks.

Around the time Georgina was seeing Dr Billing, Dickens heard that his old friend William de Cerjat was coming over to England with his daughters. Despite Georgina's illness, she welcomed the prospect of seeing them, but he needed to warn Cerjat they would have to delay a visit to Gad's Hill as he was 'obliged to go away on a distant engagement until Saturday afternoon'.[65] He then squeezed in a third journey to France, just before Cerjat and his family arrived on the afternoon of Saturday 26 July. This was the trip that would have delivered Nelly and Mrs Ternan to their new house in the French countryside. Back at Gad's Hill, in time for a welcome dinner for Cerjat and his family, Dickens witnessed Georgina having another attack. In panic, Dickens shot off a note to Wilkie Collins: 'Georgina, very, very poorly. Excruciating pain in the left breast is the last symptom. It seized her at dinner.'[66] This appears to be one of the last occasions when she had an attack. Throughout August and September she slowly improved although, as Dickens wrote to Collins, she remained 'very weak'.[67] At the beginning of August, Georgina's mother died, never having reconciled with her younger daughter, followed a month later by Dickens's mother, Elizabeth.

It was not only Georgina's health that was on Dickens's mind. He confessed to Wilkie Collins: 'I have some rather miserable anxieties which I must impart one of these days when I come to you or you come to me. I shall fight out of them, I dare say: being not easily beaten – but they have gathered and gathered.'[68]

Between August and October, Dickens crossed over to France for days at a time. Letitia asked to accompany him in early September but he put her off, pretending he would not be returning to France until October, when the family would be relocating to Paris. Again he was obfuscating as he was in France the following week. Dickens announced he would be taking Georgina on a short break to Dover between 24 September and 1 October. Dover being his usual departure port for France, it is feasible he took Georgina to visit Nelly. Dickens next planned a longer stay in France, intending that Georgina, Mamie and himself take up residence in Paris from the middle of October until shortly before Christmas.

It is doubtful that Mamie had any idea Nelly and Mrs Ternan were living in the vicinity, and Georgina would not have told her. Besides, Mamie was busy with her own life. She was often with her friends Maria and William Humphrey in Hampshire, or her other good friend, Nina Lehmann. Given that she regarded Georgina as an aunt 'par excellence', Mamie acted somewhat selfishly during Georgina's illness by her frequent absences.[69] Often Dickens complained he did not know Mamie's whereabouts. Arriving back at Gad's Hill in October, Dickens was displeased to find that Georgina had been left alone and unwell for days.

In France, they heard that Dickens had become a grandfather and Georgina a great-aunt when Charley's wife gave birth to Mary Angela (known as Mekitty). They – Dickens, Georgina and Mamie – were back at Gad's Hill for Christmas 1862. The plans for the new year were kept private. Dickens told one person they would be home for a week and then go over to Paris until February, and another that he was going alone. In reality there was no chance that Georgina could leave Gad's Hill as the boys were all at home. Dickens wrote that '[t]he house is pervaded by boys', and he took off for Paris on 8 January, accompanied by his valet, John

Thompson.[70] It was not easy to get away to see Nelly as he gave three readings at the British Embassy, alerting people to his presence in Paris. As a result, he was 'beset by mysterious adorers', requiring him to 'smuggle myself in and out of the house in the meanest and basest manner'.[71] If Robert Garnett's analysis is correct, then Nelly's due date was around the end of January 1863. It was at this time that Dickens left Paris. He did not return to England for either Georgina's birthday on 22 January, which was most unusual, or for his own birthday celebrations on 7 February. There are no records proving that Nelly gave birth, suggesting that if there had been a baby, it was still-born or lived for only a short time. As he did in arranging for Catherine to recuperate at the seaside after baby Dora's death, Dickens proposed a change of scene for Nelly. Without saying who was accompanying him, Dickens wrote to Mamie, 'my project is to send John home on Thursday and then to go on a little perfectly quiet tour for about ten days, touching the sea at Boulogne'.[72]

If there is any accuracy in this reading between the lines of Dickens's letters and Georgina's illness, it raises the question of how Georgina overcame her extreme anxiety so that she no longer suffered panic attacks.[73] She would have needed reassurance that her life was not to be upended. A short story written by Dickens between mid-September and 8 October 1862, when Nelly was supposedly pregnant, gives a clue as to how a child might be explained in a way that would not provoke scandal. Dickens penned 'His Boots' for the Christmas number of *All the Year Round*.[74] Set in a small northern French town, a middle-aged Englishman espies a French soldier playing with a little girl. On investigation, the Englishman, Mr Langley, discovers that the infant is illegitimate and although the barber's wife is paid a small fee to look after her, she neglects the child. The French soldier, Corporal Theophile, informally adopts the girl, known as Bebelle, making sure she is clean and fed. When the town suffers a major fire, Theophile dies helping to fight the blaze. When Langley discovers Bebelle weeping at the grave of Corporal Theophile, he rescues her, decides to become her guardian and takes her back to England. Was Dickens playing with the idea of emulating Langley and 'adopting' Nelly's child, claiming the baby had been orphaned in France? Alternatively, there were many examples where a single woman passed off her own child as a foundling, orphan or a distant relative that she had adopted.

If this crisis left Georgina feeling insecure and vulnerable about her place in Dickens's life, then she need not have worried. He had long made a point of lavishing affection on her, implying that she occupied a central place in his heart, calling her, as he did Nelly, 'my dearest girl' and signing off his letters by sending his love 'to all the boys – and most of all to you', and 'I send my love …. To dear Mamie and Katey, and to yourself of course, in the first degree'.[75] After her breakdown, Dickens drew Georgina closer into his confidence. He confessed to her how upset he was at a performance of *Faust* which he saw in Paris at the time Nelly was due to give birth. *Faust* is the story of a man who seduces a beautiful and innocent girl and, in so doing, destroys her life. Dickens admitted, 'I could hardly bear the thing; it affected me so, and sounded in my ears so like a mournful echo of things that lie in my own heart'.[76]

From 1863 onwards, Dickens became more solicitous towards Georgina, paying her little attentions such as arranging for photographs to be taken of her at Gad's Hill. He insisted she consult health practitioners, with the tacit understanding that he would pay the medical bills:

> I am very sorry to hear such bad tidings of that unfortunate mouth of yours. It is, in the main, some remainder (I think) of that severe influenza, or catarrh, or what not, that has so longed troubled you. I would by all means go to Cartwright [Dickens's dentist] as soon as the swelling subsides. Also I would see Frank Beard and try quinine, or a new tonic that they give now to people who cannot take quinine.[77]

Dickens flirted with Georgina, writing a teasing note referring to her mimicry skills after being away from her for just a couple of days: 'Last evening I missed you so much, that I was obliged to go to the Olympic. Charles Mathews ... played most admirably.'[78] On a reading tour, he remarked that his manager, George Dolby, had purchased some Everton toffees as a gift, knowing she liked them, reiterating how '[t]he excellent Dolby has become quite "spooney" on my informing him of the immediate occasion of my writing to you'.[79] Reminding her how important she was to him, Dickens sent her fulsome greetings on a rare occasion when he could not be home for her birthday: 'This is to wish you many happy returns of tomorrow, and to send you my deepest love and attachment.'[80]

There is evidence that Dickens took steps to protect her feelings by adopting an element of secrecy. When he wanted to prevent her knowing how much time he was spending with Nelly, he would come up with an excuse.[81] A note sent on a Wednesday from the office of *All the Year Round* saying that work would prevent him from getting to Gad's Hill until the following Monday, hid his intention to take Nelly to the theatre and work at her home in Slough.[82] One Friday evening he wrote claiming that a painful foot made movement so difficult he had decided to remain at his comfortable rooms at the office 'with the view of keeping myself and my foot quiet, I think I will not come to Gad's until Monday ... I couldn't walk a quarter of a mile tonight for £500'.[83] He did not stay in the Wellington Street office but was with Nelly in Slough.

There have been rumours that Dickens and Nelly had a second child. One rumour stems from entries in Dickens's pocket diary for 1867. He wrote the word 'arrival' against Saturday 13 April and 'loss' a week later on 20 April. Some scholars have interpreted these cryptic entries as the delivery of a child, followed a week later by the baby's death.[84] Yet efforts to find something to confirm this conjecture have come to nothing. In his analysis of Dickens's movements in 1867, David Pipes convincingly argues that 'arrival' refers to the return home of his son Sydney from the Royal Navy, and 'loss' to the day on which he inadvertently left his knapsack containing a book and manuscripts in a hansom cab between the train station and the office.[85] A second rumour, this time of a baby born in February 1868, was sparked by the discovery at the Charles Dickens Museum of two letters from C. E. S. Chambers, the great-nephew of Janet and W. H. Wills. Chambers had inherited the complete archive of Dickens's letters to Wills. One concerned Dickens's instructions sent when on his American reading tour 'regarding the welfare of a certain lady' who was due to give birth imminently.[86] The circumstances preclude Nelly from being the woman having a baby as she was visiting her sister in Italy and the pregnancy of a single woman would have been the subject of gossip. Nevertheless, this fact has not prevented the belief that when Dickens wrote to Wills about an impending birth, he was referring to Nelly.

Dickens's letters to Georgina in February 1868 make it clear who the mystery woman was. He had been on a second reading tour of America for several months, accompanied by his reading manager, George Dolby. Dolby's wife was due to be confined with the couple's second child early in February. On 7 February 1868 Dickens wrote to Georgina, 'You will know, no doubt, of Mrs. Dolby's having a boy.'[87] He evidently wanted to ensure Mrs Dolby and the baby were looked after in George Dolby's absence. Dickens asked W. H. Wills to mark the birth of Dolby's new son by purchasing the handsomest pony he could find, and sending him with his trappings complete as a present with 'the Chief's love'.[88] Dickens also wanted to have a photograph taken of Dolby's nephew holding the pony and for Wills to forward the photograph on to Dolby in America.

During and following the Dickenses' marital separation Georgina proved to Dickens she was steadfast and devoted. She put his happiness and needs above everything and everyone. The same can be said of Dickens in those early years after he parted from

Catherine; that is, he put his own interests above all else. There had always been the chance during the separation that Georgina could lose the love and protection of the man on whom she was completely dependent. When the fear almost became a reality because of his intimacy with Nelly, she had a mental and physical breakdown. Between 1858 and 1862 the relationship between Georgina and Dickens was the most unequal it had ever been, or ever would be in the future. Georgina's illness brought about a change in that Dickens became more thoughtful towards her. However much he loved Nelly, it could not match his need for the adoration of his readers, the admiration of his audiences and the approbation of his fellow writers. Despite his folly, he was not going to sacrifice all the success he had achieved through toil and effort over the years, nor risk destroying the, albeit unconventional, family home he had established at Gad's Hill.

Chapter 8

'His own decision will be the best' (1864–70)

It took several years for Georgina to recover from her breakdown. Photographs Dickens arranged to have taken of her in September 1863 show the thirty-six-year-old appearing older than she was. Physically, her health was restored by 1866 and the images taken that year portray a far more youthful Georgina.[1] Yet she never appeared to regain her energy fully. Dickens's observation about Georgina losing her enthusiasm and cheerfulness was as accurate in the late 1860s as it was when she first became ill. She was no longer the 'lively damsel' who enjoyed parties, now saying that she preferred 'living in the country [having] got quite out of the habit of living in town'.[2] Georgina later told a friend, 'I ... look back and think how often I used to be *un*happy and fretted and anxious about things'.[3] Her subdued demeanour was evident to the guests visiting Gad's Hill. Introduced to Georgina for the first time, an American woman commented that she was 'quiet, but most hospitable'.[4] Dickens was always concerned for her health, advising her on various medicines and urging her to consult doctors when he thought she needed to, but he was often away from Gad's Hill. When it was evident she was struggling, he would intervene: 'My sister in law has been very unwell ... and is recommended a brisk change ... I mean to bring her to Ireland with me.'[5] Georgina might have revived her spirits had life returned to normal after the events of 1862–3. However, everything had changed and a

159

combination of circumstances coalesced to impede Georgina's convalescence. Why did Georgina fail to recover her emotional equilibrium after her breakdown? What were the signs that her devotion to Dickens was turning into a fixation?

When Georgina first became ill in June 1862 and was unable to fulfil her housekeeping responsibilities, invitations to Gad's Hill ceased. When guests returned, it seemed Georgina was once again Dickens's efficient housekeeper. George Dolby, Dickens's reading manager, described the attention given to his comfort during a stay at Gad's Hill.[6] On entering his room, there was a sofa, cosy bed and writing table, generously supplied with various sizes of paper, envelopes and quill pens which were changed every day. Two cane-bottomed chairs, of the kind Dickens himself favoured, were placed near the desk. Dickens had persuaded the postal services to install a post box outside his house so that guests did not have to make the three-mile trek into Rochester with their letters. For relaxation, visitors were provided with a miniature library in their bedrooms, stocked with a selection of books chosen by Dickens specifically for them. In winter, a fire was lit and a copper kettle placed in the hearth. Cups, saucers, a tea caddy, teapot, sugar and milk were laid out on a side table so that a warm drink could be made without calling for a servant.

Given Dolby's description of his stay at Gad's Hill, one wonders why Dickens's grandson insisted Georgina was not a good house-keeper. In the years before her illness, Dickens had lavished praise on Georgina for organising and managing his household, and he emphasised her impeccable home-making skills when he was searching for reasons why his marriage was not successful. At that time, Dickens condemned Catherine as an unfit wife and mother by contrasting her with the allegedly domestically dedicated Georgina. After her breakdown, Georgina became a more anxious, unsure person and appeared to make no domestic decisions herself, relying entirely on Dickens's instructions. The comfortable stay George Dolby described was a result of Dickens's edicts about what their guests should find in their rooms, while it was Georgina's job to put it all in place. There is a chance that Georgina's loss of confidence coincided with the period when Dickens was not as distracted by worries over Nelly as he had been; consequently he reasserted himself in the domestic running of the household. Where it used to be Catherine he micromanaged, it was now Georgina.

When Georgina reported that the French fabrics ordered to cover an armchair in his room had arrived, he corrected her: 'There is no chair whatever to be covered *in my room*. Curtains are to be made to the large windows … and the new sofa is to be covered. That is all!' And to be sure she had read his instructions, he repeated, '[t]here is no chair to be covered'.[7] Nor did he leave her to launder his clothes, giving her a step-by-step guide as to what to do: 'In the middle drawer of my wardrobe are a dress coat and a pair of dress trousers … will you with the end of a clean towel and Eau de Cologne from my scent case – cleanse them, *by daylight*, where they are splashed.'[8] The Gad's Hill account books reveal that Georgina did not keep them, as most housekeepers would do; rather, Dickens oversaw them with Georgina only making entries in the last two months of his life. His constant vigilance and correction were a stark contrast to her always having been lauded by Dickens for her housekeeping talents.

One housekeeping area where Georgina genuinely required help was in managing the servants. Originally, Dickens gave Mamie responsibility for overseeing the servants but, like almost everything to do with the domestic running of Gad's Hill, the job fell to Georgina. Over the years Dickens expanded the number of staff he employed at Gad's Hill to nine, plus his manservant, John Thompson. Some of the servants would take advantage of Dickens's frequent absences. On one occasion when the family were in London, a neighbour informed Dickens that the cook and the groom, James Marsh, had been sighted wearing Dickens's and Mamie's riding habits and racing around the local countryside on the master's horses.[9] At another time, Georgina was at home when Dickens heard from a different neighbour that boozy parties, fuelled by the contents of the Gad's Hill wine cellar, were being held at a local cottage. Dickens had thought the stocks of champagne were going down rather quickly and suspected Marsh. He instructed Georgina to purchase an additional padlock for the wine cellar door and get Marsh to affix it so that he would know they were onto him. Dickens admonished Georgina by saying that if the servants could simply help themselves, then 'I particularly wish you to consider whether you are in the habit of leaving the cellar-key in any places, from which it could be taken by any one'.[10]

Marsh was willing to take advantage of Georgina even when she was unwell. It was shortly after her breakdown, when Mamie and Dickens were away and she was alone, that she heard Marsh crying out from the kitchen, 'I am dead!'[11] Georgina dashed to the servants' quarters to find him languishing in an armchair while the women-servants shouted at him that he was not dying. A more gullible Georgina believed Marsh's claim that he was having a heart attack and sent for the doctor, who duly arrived and diagnosed dyspepsia. Despite Marsh constantly abusing his position, Dickens seemed as reluctant to sack him as he had been to dismiss his valet, John Thompson, for stealing.[12] This was either Dickens being an extremely tolerant employer or an anxious one who was wary of upsetting any servant who might repeat what they knew about his relationship with Nelly.[13]

Aside from Dickens's surveillance of her housekeeping, Georgina found her opinions under tighter scrutiny. It was as if Dickens had substituted his wife with his sister-in-law as the person he needed to keep in check. Ever since she was a teenager, Georgina's sharp observations had sometimes got her into trouble with Dickens. For the most part she had learned how to avoid annoying him, but Dickens's notoriously mercurial temperament made it difficult to judge when he might find a comment amusing. With Dickens often staying over at the office or with Nelly, letters between them were gossipier than just dealing with household matters. Dickens would make backhanded compliments about friends, as when he declared the second Mrs Macready to be 'quite perfect' if only 'not half so pretty or so buxom' as the first Mrs Macready.[14] He could be unkind too, as he showed when talking of Georgina's friend Eliza Forster. Dickens was at dinner with the Forsters when Eliza regaled him with her visit to the Lord Mayor's show. Eliza had a speech impediment whereby she pronounced 'n' as 'l' and he reported how: 'Mrs. Forster gave me a tremendous narrative, in her feebly and unaccountably triumphant manner of "brigil up the Lord Chief Barrel's youlgest childrel to see the Lorl Mayor's Show;" of which I comprehended exactly that much and no more.'[15] After Dickens's death, when reviewers of Georgina and Mamie's edited collection of Dickens's letters commented on his scathing observations, Georgina defended him, saying these were 'little jokes which he may have made without the smallest unkindness or idea of disloyalty to his friends'.[16] Yet while she dismissed 'little jokes' on Dickens's part, similar observations on her part drew his criticism.

Georgina's wit was similar to Dickens's in that she would often follow a compliment with a cutting remark. When a friend sent a wedding gift for Katey Dickens of a painting by a renowned American artist, Georgina wrote, 'I told you how much I liked the picture *myself*, when I acknowledged its arrival here ... It is a very nice one – of course the *idea* is not quite original – but it is very sweet.'[17] In a similar vein, Georgina recounted a conversation with Dickens and Mamie which shows how cruel comments passed between them as humour. Their discussion concerned young Charley Dickens's daughters. Describing one-year-old Ethel as 'not at all nice. She is the coarsest little creature I ever saw in my life – and not at all pretty', Georgina went on to say:[18]

At first we [Dickens, Georgina and Mamie] all kept up a fiction it was necessary we *must* love both little girls equally, but lately we have relieved our minds with one consent, by throwing off the manner and owning to each other what we all feel – that the eldest is a dear child, and the second is not.[19]

Despite sharing her brother-in-law's sarcastic sense of humour, Georgina could find herself being severely reprimanded by Dickens. When she decried the lack of finesse in a letter they had received from William Macready's second wife, Cecile, Dickens snapped back:

> You were a little hasty about Mrs. Macready's first letter. It was disagreeable, but I have always observed that she writes as one conscious of a letter-writing reputation … and that she founds her sentences on the Elegant Extracts and Speaker. This last letter being written wholly under emotion has no such drawback.[20]

Dickens criticised Georgina for repeating opinions he had himself expressed. He could be extremely disparaging about his sons, telling W. H. Wills of the distaste he felt towards 'my boys with a curse of limpness on them … You don't know what it is to look round the table and see reflected from every seat at it (where they sit) some horribly well remembered expression of inadaptability to anything.'[21] Georgina shared Dickens's disappointment with friends, remarking acerbically to Annie Fields on the news that Harry had secured a place at Cambridge University, 'It [is] quite a new sensation for Charles to have one of his sons distinguish himself.'[22] But when a homesick Plorn wrote a despondent letter from Australia and Georgina criticised the boy in some way, Dickens leaped to his son's defence: 'In judging of Plorn's letter, we must remember the entirely new circumstances surrounding him, and the flutter of spirits consequent on writing at all.'[23] Trying to keep in Dickens's good books was like walking a tightrope wearing a blindfold.

Georgina spent considerable amounts of time alone with just the servants for company. There were weekend guests when Dickens was at Gad's Hill, but he was often elsewhere.[24] Dickens's sister, Letitia Austin, and sister-in-law, Harriet Lovell, visited when he was away, and Marguerite Power, niece of the Countess of Blessington, stayed for prolonged periods.[25] Gad's Hill had become an 'empty nest' as, with the exception of Plorn, the children were in their teens and twenties. Most of the boys were either finishing school or starting their careers, and Katey was married. Even Plorn, the most home-loving of all the children, had eventually found a boarding school that he could accept. As Mamie was the officially designated mistress of her father's house, she was expected to be at Gad's Hill to act as hostess. Nonetheless, whenever she could, Mamie would disappear somewhere, to be either with Katey in London or with friends. Dickens acknowledged that his family were all going their separate ways and it was 'Georgina holding them all together, and perpetually corresponding with the distant ones'.[26]

Georgina may have found it easier to be on her own at Gad's Hill than having to confront the increasingly wayward behaviour of her niece. Her role as Mamie's chaperone had been taken over by Mamie's friends, Maria Humphrey and Nina Lehmann. As married women, they were regarded as more respectable chaperones than a single woman (especially one living with her brother-in-law). This meant there were fewer occasions when Georgina was able to observe her niece over-imbibing at social functions. However, there was at least one occasion when Mamie was at Gad's Hill when she had a riding accident that was possibly connected to her drinking. When Georgina and a groom set out to rescue her after receiving a message from Mamie that her horse had gone down on a stone, Dickens informed Wilkie Collins that they had 'found [Mamie] in a public house … wonderfully taken care of and looked after'.[27] Not that Mamie was a drunk and she moved in circles where alcohol was always available and plentiful at social events. Her riding habit was torn to pieces, she had a deep cut above her knee and had to use crutches for several weeks.

As she reached the age of twenty-seven, Mamie's drinking was being noticed by friends, and she was starting to become a social embarrassment. Fred Lehmann told his wife, Nina, of his concern for both Dickens girls. He suggested they were losing their reputations, having heard from several third parties that 'society is beginning to fight very shy of them'.[28] At one social gathering,

Lehmann was disturbed to see Mamie behaving rudely by 'shaping her mouth all the time for the word "beast" whenever [Henry] Chorley, looked away from her'.[29] He added that 'Mamie, who looked round and matronlike ... may blaze up in a firework any day'.[30] Katey Dickens was aware that Mamie was acting impetuously and made a mysterious comment about her sister: 'She takes her happiness when she can, and a few visits to town lately have given her all she cares for.'[31] Katey's biographer, Lucinda Hawksley, believes that Katey was referring to an affair. Certainly, something or someone was exciting Mamie, who wrote a letter to Nina Lehmann describing herself as being 'in paradise'.[32] At a Lord Mayor's ball in Covent Garden, where Mamie was so drunk she passed out in the toilets and had to be carried out by several attendants, she blamed the leather smell of the new boots and pouches of the military volunteers for causing her to faint.[33] It is highly likely that Georgina was aware of her niece's use of alcohol, but it was only in the years after Dickens's death that she began to speak openly about it.

Of all the many changes to occur as Georgina recovered from her breakdown, the most significant were brought about by Dickens's alliance with Nelly. Despite Dickens's evident concern and care for Georgina, his preoccupation with Nelly altered the pattern of his and, therefore, Georgina's daily life.

In January 1865, Dickens wrote a cryptic note to Georgina saying, '[t]he mysterious "arrangement" is, I hope, by no means a bad one'.[34] He planned to bring Nelly and her mother back from France to live in England. On their return journey to London, Dickens, Nelly and Mrs Ternan were involved in a train accident at Staplehurst in which ten people were killed and Nelly herself injured, with long-term consequences. By the end of June, mother and daughter were installed in a house Dickens had leased in Slough.[35] Having Nelly living within a reasonable travelling distance of London made it easier for Dickens to see her on a weekly basis rather than making a dash across the Channel whenever he could find a few days. With Nelly's return and the popularity of the reading tours,

Dickens divided his time between Nelly's house, the office at 26 Wellington Street, the reading tours and Gad's Hill.[36] Georgina was no longer Dickens's main emotional support as she had been before and during the marital breakdown. He had Nelly to talk to and George Dolby to take care of him on his reading tours. Dickens's peripatetic arrangements meant Georgina rarely had the opportunity to travel; there were no more family holidays in Boulogne or Broadstairs, no more weekend excursions to Paris and only occasional trips outside London to hear Dickens read.

After the Staplehurst rail accident, Dickens was wary of train travel, but this did not stop him wanting to get away from family life. He confessed: 'If I had no boys holding on to the skirts of my coat, I think I should keep a yacht and go sailing about' and 'if Mary were to marry (which she won't), I should sell [Gad's Hill], and go genteelly vagabondising over the face of the earth'.[37] Annie Fields, a great friend, worried about the effects that listening to Dickens's restlessness had on his children: 'Nobody can say how much too much of this the children have to bear.'[38] Annie could have said the same thing about Georgina. How much of hearing Dickens talk about wanting to leave Gad's Hill did Georgina find unnerving? Regardless of Dickens's reassurance of his affection, Georgina must surely have worried he might one day sell Gad's Hill and leave her in order to be with Nelly.

Was Georgina jealous of Nelly? Georgina's biographer, Arthur Adrian, claims that 'the attachment she displayed for women of whom Dickens had been fond – romantically or otherwise – suggests that her own devotion, though fervent to the point of obsession, partook of no jealous female possessiveness'.[39] Dickens's biographer Michael Slater agrees, saying she displayed 'freedom from any touch of jealousy' by making friends with the women Dickens enthused over, which included Annie Fields, Mary Boyle and Nelly.[40] Yet Georgina did get jealous. In later life she explained her feelings to a friend, admitting: 'I get every year more and more jealous of the tender *personal* remembrance of him'.[41] In other words, she was protective of the special relationship they shared. Over the course of twenty-eight years they had been there for one another, first as almost father and daughter, then friends, social companions, master of the house with his housekeeper/nurse, and confidants. Georgina had helped take care of his children, taken responsibility for communicating with his wider family, acted as his personal assistant and given him the support he needed in order to lead a secret life with Nelly. In return, Dickens made Georgina feel uniquely important, as he showed when declaring she had 'a higher claim' on him 'than anyone else in this world'.[42] For Georgina, the only reason for becoming jealous of the women Dickens was close to was if they usurped her particular roles. When Dickens was alive, Georgina made every effort to get on with them and forge genuine friendships. After his death, she minimised or disregarded the significance of any woman who might have been considered to supersede her in Dickens's affections. She suggested Catherine was incapable, called Maria Beadnell Winter 'silly' and never publicly acknowledged the existence of Christiana Weller, Augusta de la Rue or Nelly, let alone Dickens's feelings towards them.

How did the changed circumstances affect Georgina? What were the signs that Georgina was becoming fixated on Dickens? She displayed several symptoms, from veering between a need to protect Dickens while also acting as overly dependent on him, displaying low self-esteem and having difficulty in maintaining contact with others because of her obsession. Georgina's reactions before and during Dickens's second reading tour of America in 1867–8 was a period when all these signals could be seen.

Hearing from others that Dickens was planning a reading tour of America lasting six months, Georgina was stricken with anxiety. She immediately wrote to check the truth of the rumour. Dickens reassured her he had no intention of going, saying, '*You have no fear about America*', but a year later he changed his mind.[43] Financially, Dickens needed to boost his income as he was maintaining three households, as well as supporting his children and several relatives.

The money he could earn in America proved too tempting even though it would put additional pressure on his health.

Throughout the 1860s, Dickens's health was on a slow decline. Constantly battling a string of ailments, Dickens provided Georgina with regular updates on his various illnesses. When he was fifty-two he suffered from endless bouts of coughs, sore throats and colds. At fifty-three, the first signs of gout appeared, although Dickens refused to accept them as gout. He blamed his symptoms on having acquired a frostbitten foot while walking in the snow. Finding he was unable to wear a shoe after late afternoon, he had a special protective boot made. Dickens took small doses of laudanum for the pain. Georgina supervised his medication and was ever watchful of his progress. When forced to turn down an invitation to the Adelphi Theatre because of gout pain, he wrote to the manager: 'My Nurse thinks that on the first day of going out, my foot is not well enough to come up and down your stairs.'[44]

Georgina's fears about the America tour were not solely about whether Dickens's health could withstand the strain. She was worried how she would fare without him. Her anxiety showed when she appeared too intimidated to ask Dickens a slight favour. As the date of his departure for America drew near, Georgina and her nieces attended the farewell banquet in London, along with nearly 500 others. A more private farewell dinner was to be held in Liverpool the night before he set sail for Boston. Georgina told a family friend, Percy Fitzgerald, she had hoped to go to the private Liverpool dinner but evidently did not feel able to ask Dickens if she might attend: 'I don't think he means to take us – at least he has said nothing about it yet. So I imagine not. His own decision will be the best on the subject.'[45] In another letter, Georgina was yearning for Dickens's return and mourning his absence even before he had left:

> Yes Charles's going is indeed settled – and is a very miserable prospect for the coming winter! … on the whole I shall be very thankful now, *once* he is *gone*. I think the time before that in preparation is

always so miserable and when he is once off the time will be going on to his return – please God! at the end of May or beginning of June.[46]

Although Dickens was in America for Christmas 1867, the usual group of people assembled at Gad's Hill for the festivities. Georgina had always loved Christmas but on this occasion, 'it will be very sad, that party without the *Head* – and I shall be very glad when it is over – and we shall have begun another year'.[47] She refused to be distracted from her feelings of loneliness. Taking pity on her, Percy Fitzgerald's mother invited Georgina for a short holiday in Dublin, but she declined, saying she did not like 'to go far from home' during Dickens's absence.[48] In January 1868, she accepted an invitation to spend a few days with their good friends the Forsters. While they had been 'the *kindest of the kind*', Georgina admitted she was 'ashamed to say that I was glad to get home again – but I don't know why', adding that she found it 'a trial … to stay in that home'.[49] Was the trial being in the Forster's home without the company of Dickens?

Dickens returned from his second reading tour of America on 1 May 1868. He disembarked in Liverpool and went off immediately to be with Nelly. The tour had been a success but taken a huge toll on him. The physical efforts needed had been great and, if the tour itself was not demanding enough, he had the added psychological strain of acquiring a stalker.[50] Dickens was, though, keen to deny any suggestion that he had been overtaxed by the tour and claimed that when his doctor first saw him, he was shocked – '"Good Lord!" he said, recoiling, "Seven years younger".'[51] The pressures Dickens put himself under showed on his face and for some years he had looked much older than he actually was. His attempts to appear more youthful had the reverse effect. When the author of *Little Women*, Louisa May Alcott, went to hear Dickens reading, she was horrified to see her hero: 'youth and comeliness were gone, but the foppishness remained, and the red-faced man, with false teeth … had his scanty grey hair curled … there was nothing genuine about him'.[52]

Once Dickens returned to Gad's Hill, Georgina was able to focus all her efforts on helping him to recover his energies and making him comfortable. Every day she would make a trip across the lawn in front of the house and through the tunnel to take a small bunch of fresh flowers for his desk in the writing chalet.[53]

Guests from America began to arrive at Gad's Hill, and it was the visit of the poet Henry Wadsworth Longfellow and his daughters that illustrates Georgina's absorption in her brother-in-law. She showed that she was echoing Dickens's opinions, looking at the world through his eyes, never deviating or offering an alternative view. Dickens said of Longfellow that he was a man who had little to say for himself. Writing to Georgina from America, Dickens told her of his meeting with Longfellow's daughters, commenting that the eldest girl possessed an odd appearance: 'If you saw her eyes looking through a chink, you would say she was lovely. You see her whole squeezed face and don't know … whether to decide that she is pretty or plain.'[54] Georgina met Henry Longfellow in July 1868 and in her own letter to a family friend wrote: 'Mr. Longfellow is not particularly *interesting*, somehow', adding, '[t]he daughters are very odd … the eldest only 17 – not pretty but with good faces'.[55] In other letters Georgina rarely expressed herself as herself. Rather than giving her own views by using 'I', she wrote as if she and Dickens were one and the same person: 'we have been following you in (our) imaginations'; 'We doubt you remember that situation'; 'we can only understand'.[56] Similarly, Georgina spoke of a man who had been a close friend of Dickens's when she was still a teenager, saying, '[h]e used to be, years ago, one of our *most* intimate friends'.[57]

Exactly one year after arriving back from his America tour, in May 1869, Dickens's Boston hosts, James and Annie Fields, came to England. There was a rumour going around London society that Annie had fallen in love with Dickens.[58] She was certainly smitten, but Annie was devoted to her husband. It seems Annie worshipped Dickens almost as much as Georgina did. Annie and Georgina's mutual adoration of Dickens drew the women together and they became lifelong friends. During the Fieldses' visit, the women would sit together sewing while the men went out for walks or rides in London and the Kent countryside. Annie knew about Dickens's love for Nelly but, although there has been speculation that she and Georgina talked about Dickens's 'dear girl', the evidence suggests otherwise. In later years, when Georgina wrote to Annie of her holidays in Margate, she never said she was staying with Nelly. Georgina mentioned Nelly, although never by name, telling Annie only that 'a friend' had helped her copy out letters for the edited collection, and that she was having to visit 'a friend' who was ill.

Annie Fields was in a unique position in that she knew and was very fond of Georgina and adored Dickens. As a writer and diarist at the heart of Boston's cultural and literary circles, she offers an intimate analysis of the relationship between Dickens and Georgina and how it was viewed by others. Ten years after the Dickenses' separation, Annie recorded how Dickens's closest friends continued to feel uncomfortable about his living arrangements with Georgina. Annie hosted a luncheon attended by several of Dickens's men friends, including Wilkie Collins and Charles Fechter, during which the conversation turned to Dickens. The men deliberated on Dickens's home life. Henry Longfellow spoke of Dickens's 'restlessness, of his terrible sadness', to which Charles Fechter added '[y]es, yes, all his fame goes for nothing since he has not the one thing. He is very unhappy in his children'.[59] Annie was struck how none of them mentioned Georgina, despite knowing her well. She despaired for Georgina, realising: '[T]o how little purpose poor Miss Hogarth spends her life hoping to comfort and care for him. I never felt more keenly her anomalous position in the household. Not one mentioned her name; they could not have, I suppose lest they might do her wrong.'[60]

The gossip about Georgina's unconventional position was something Annie was well aware of. The American feminist writer Mary Abigail Dodge, once a good friend of Annie's, chose to malign Georgina in order to attack Dickens. In a piece for *Harper's Weekly*, Dodge referred to Georgina's continued presence in the family home after the Dickenses' separation: 'To make the affair still more notorious, a young lady, Mrs. Dickens' sister, had undertaken to "keep house" for Dickens and his daughters. The whole affair is very repugnant to our idea of matrimonial constancy.'[61] Later, Dodge wrote scathingly that the great author had no shame at having:

> another woman [–] also in his house, holding in regard to both himself and his children a position which belonged to the legal wife and mother. England is beating her obstinate head against marriage with a deceased wife's sister; but here it is a living wife's sister superseding the living wife.[62]

Annie found it galling to see the single Georgina, who did not have either the will or the platform to defend her reputation, being abused by a woman suffragist. Annie extolled the dignified way in which Georgina responded to the attacks on her character, writing to her mother and sister how she proved herself to be 'equal to her position which is saying *everything*'.[63] It was an indication, though, that Georgina's reputation was continuing to be sullied abroad as well as in Britain.

The Fieldses said their sad farewells to Dickens and Georgina, setting off for Boston in October 1869. They would never see Dickens again. Dickens's health was increasingly causing Georgina concern. He was unable to take part in the Christmas festivities of 1869 to the same extent as usual, as Georgina reported:

> [H]is foot was bad and for the first Christmas Day that even I remember, he had to keep [to] the house. I sat with him all day in the library – and kept his foot poulticed – he was able to appear at dinner but with his poor foot bandaged and obliged to keep it up on a chair – but otherwise he was so bright and cheerful![64]

Dickens was, however, fit enough to continue the readings, maintain his editing of *All the Year Round* and meet the deadlines for a new novel, *Edwin Drood*. The readings put a strain on his voice, resulting in frequent hoarseness, gout gave him continuous foot pains and he had backaches, a pain in his eye, and piles. Earlier, in 1866, Frank Beard had diagnosed 'degeneration of some functions of the heart', for which Dickens was prescribed iron, quinine, digitalis and alcohol.[65]

Dickens was known for being an abstemious drinker, but this has to be put in the context of the time when frequent and heavy drinking was acceptable. This was a period when doctors recommended the use of alcohol and opiates for medicinal purposes and the health dangers of drinking even relatively moderate amounts on a daily basis were unrecognised. Georgina's 'Recipe Book for Drinks' even contains the instruction to include a quart of brandy in the children's ginger beer.[66] Dickens might not have been a heavy drinker, but he always made sure he had alcohol with him when he was away from home, not least because he liked to make punch for guests invited to his hotel room following a performance. He frequently sent notes to Georgina asking her to 'bring up to town with you 2 more bottles of the very old brandy' or 'half a dozen bottles of Madeira, and half a dozen bottles of the old brandy'.[67] She had to make sure when packing his bags for a reading tour that she included 'a bottle or two of Whiskey and Eau d'Or as liqueurs'; there were occasions when he confessed to solitary drinking: 'I took to drinking after dark. Made a jug of whiskey punch.'[68] George Dolby recalled how, when touring, Dickens would take 'a dozen oysters and a little champagne' during the interval and a draught of brandy after an hour's travelling by train.[69] If Georgina was concerned about Dickens's drinking, it was most likely because the doctors thought Dickens so unwell they needed to prescribe rum at breakfast, sherry at lunchtime, a pint of champagne at dinner, sherry with an egg beaten into it at 8 p.m. and 'soup, and anything to drink that I can fancy' last thing at night'.[70] Biographer Claire Tomalin recounts one weekend visit when, knowing the abstemious habits of the host, Dickens took the precaution of bringing his own supply. As she observes, 'packing a private bottle and planning a secret drink does suggest that his need for alcohol had become a serious dependence'.[71]

Dickens suffered a stroke in April 1869 when on a reading tour in the north of England. In the lead-up to this he had a number of issues, starting with a fall where he hurt his shin and had to have it bound up, followed by a bout of painful haemorrhoids and the problems with his foot. A few days later he told Georgina he was experiencing numbness down his left side, feeling extremely giddy and 'if I don't look at anything I try to touch with my left hand, I don't know where it is'.[72] Frank Beard insisted that Dickens immediately cease the reading tour and return home to rest. Either Georgina did not know it was a slight stroke or played it down, reporting that he was not 'suffering from any direct ailment', and had 'simply *over* done [the] travelling and Reading combined'.[73]

Over the next few months, Dickens made some adjustments to his lifestyle, asking Georgina to cut tea and coffee from his diet and instead 'get in some of that Homeopathic Cocoa, and let me have a jug or pot of it containing 2 large cups – always boiled with milk, and no water – on the table at breakfast always'.[74] Yet these were minor concessions as he continued to work and travel constantly between Gad's Hill, the office and Peckham (where Nelly was now based). Georgina wanted to remain at Gad's Hill rather than taking a house for the season, but as Dickens was giving twelve readings around the capital, it made sense to rent 5 Hyde Park Place. She expected to attend all the final readings but an official mourning period following the sudden death of her father, caused by falling down the stairs at the offices of the *Illustrated London News* in February 1870, meant she had to miss three of them. Nelly attended at least one of the readings. Dickens's health was not improving. On stage, he stumbled over his words, using Pecknicks, Pickwicks or Pickswick instead of Pickwick; in his letters he referred to Georgina as his sister, and made errors in the names and addresses of people he wrote to.[75] He found laudanum was the only medication that offered some relief from his hoarseness, sore throat and the perpetual pain in his foot. Unable to cope with any more socialising, Dickens, accompanied by Georgina, left for home on 25 May 1870, leaving Mamie to stay with Katey in London.

Georgina remained at Gad's Hill when Dickens went up to London on 2 June to meet George Dolby at the office of *All the Year Round*. Dolby noticed he was in low spirits and quite tearful. That evening, Dickens went to see Mamie and Katey acting in some private theatricals at the home of Sir Charles and Lady Freake in Cromwell Road. Afterwards, Charley Collins found him wandering around, sleepy and confused, believing himself to be home at Gad's Hill. They insisted he did not return to Kent that night and so he slept at the office. Overnight he regained his strength and Georgina, oblivious to what had occurred the previous evening, saw no cause for alarm when he returned home. The following day, Saturday 4 June, Katey arrived for the weekend. After Georgina and Mamie had gone to bed, Katey sat talking with her father until 3 a.m. She had wanted to discuss a contract she had been offered to join a theatre company. Dickens warned her against it, telling her she was too sensitive to deal with some of the people she would encounter and that she was clever enough to do something else. Realising it was probably because she needed to earn money, Dickens offered to help her. Perhaps it was talking about the life of an actress that led him to confess he and Nelly had had a son together, but that the boy had died. Deeply reflective, Dickens admitted to his daughter how much he wished he had been 'a better father – a better man'; most tellingly, he said of the book he was writing, *Edwin Drood*, that he hoped it would be a success 'if, please God, I live to finish it … I say if because you know, my dear child, I have not been strong lately'.[76]

On the morning of Monday 6 June, Katey and Mamie were due to set off back to London. Usually they would not disturb

Dickens when he was working. On this occasion, possibly in the light of their frank conversation overnight, Katey decided to run through the tunnel to the writing chalet to say goodbye. Instead of proffering his cheek for a kiss as he would normally do, Dickens embraced her. After writing the latest number of *Edwin Drood* on Tuesday 7 June, Dickens took the carriage to Cobham Woods with Georgina. He left her to take the carriage home, wanting to make the four mile walk back on his own. That night they lingered in the dining room after dinner to admire the Chinese lanterns hung in the adjoining conservatory. Wednesday 8 June began with Dickens writing letters, one to Emma Christian (*née* Picken) saying that he was unable to help her friend secure a pension, others refusing invitations for his bust to be made or photograph taken, sorting out an overpayment of a band for his foot, correcting a correspondent's misreading of a scriptural reference in *Edwin Drood* and postponing a meeting with an old family friend, Charles Kent. He dropped into the Falstaff Inn over the road from Gad's Hill to cash a cheque for £22 and returned to the house for lunch at 1 p.m. Unlike his usual work patterns, Dickens went back to the writing chalet to continue work on *Drood*. Georgina was waiting when Dickens returned at 6 p.m.

As they sat down for dinner, Georgina saw he looked unwell and that he had tears in his eyes. Within minutes he had a fatal stroke. She gave slightly varying accounts of his reactions as the stroke was occurring, but her main account of what transpired was that she asked him if he felt ill and he responded, '[y]es, very ill for the last hour'. She suggested calling the doctor but he wanted to continue with dinner, then started rambling about a neighbour's house, pain in his jaw, needing to go to London. Standing up, he staggered and Georgina said, '[c]ome and lie down'. 'Yes, on the ground', he replied as he fell to the floor.[77] Georgina told Annie Fields, 'It was impossible to move him after he fell – we got a sofa into the Dining Room and lifted him upon it – and there he lay – unconscious.'[78]

Georgina called for the local doctor; Dr Stephen Steele was at Gad's Hill by 6.30. She also sent for the family doctor, Frank Beard, plus Charley, Mamie and Katey, and almost certainly Nelly. Katey was in her bedroom in London, Mamie in the connecting dressing room, both having a nap before going to a friend's party, when the telegram arrived. They dashed down to Gad's Hill immediately with Frank Beard, and Nelly too arrived that evening. Georgina wrote that they were still hopeful: 'We had had a Bed brought in … in the hope that he would become sensible – and better and could be moved on to that.'[79] But Dickens was showing signs of approaching death. Apart from the coma, his feet were cold and the women applied hot bricks to try and warm them. Nelly left before Charley arrived the next morning, 9 June. At Dr Steele's request, Charley sent a telegram to the office of *All the Year Round* asking for a cardiac specialist, Dr Russell Reynolds, to be asked to attend immediately. By the time Reynolds arrived, Nelly was back at Gad's Hill, and Mary Boyle had come to see her old friend. Reynolds took one look at Dickens and gave them the news they were dreading, that he could not live. Dickens died at 6.10 p.m., when Georgina told a friend, 'He *was* moved on to the bed … I still feel, as I write that word, as if it *could* not be true!'[80] It was almost exactly twenty-four hours after the stroke, and coincidentally five years to the day since the Staplehurst train crash, that Dickens died. Georgina's purpose in life died that day too.

Chapter 9
'A hard, hard trial' (1870–1917)

Georgina was forty-three when Dickens died. The suddenness of his death catapulted her into the same depths of despair that the forty-two-year-old Queen Victoria suffered after the demise of Prince Albert. Unlike Queen Victoria, Georgina felt unable to express the depth of her loss, confessing to Annie Fields that she found it a 'hard, hard trial' having 'to try to take an interest in life for the sake of the people about one' and, worse, 'it must all be borne and *kept to myself*'.[1] Why, when Georgina was living in a period in which public displays of bereavement were commonplace, did she feel she had to keep her grief to herself? Was she trying to protect the children by appearing strong and dependable? Was she worried that if she showed how distraught she was, it might revive gossip about her and Dickens?

A private funeral took place at 9.30 a.m. on 14 June 1870 at Westminster Abbey, which Catherine was either discouraged or forbidden from attending.[2] Dickens's death had created two widows: his official wife, Catherine, and his lifelong companion, Georgina. In many ways Georgina had been his unofficial platonic wife; while Georgina was not subject to the legal and cultural constraints imposed on Catherine, she had fulfilled many of the expectations of a dutiful, adoring spouse. The mutual loss of the man they loved did nothing to unite the sisters. When they finally met up, it was not a comfortable experience and both denied being the one to initiate the reunion. Charles William Shirley Brooks, editor of *Punch* and a great friend of Catherine's, stated that Georgina made the first move. Shirley Brooks evidently shared Catherine's enmity towards Georgina, reporting that 'Miss H. has also visited her – I will not write about this, but the affair is to the honour of Mrs. D.s heart'.[3] However, Georgina claimed that Catherine instigated the contact:

> We went to see her – by her own desire ... a few days after dearest Charles' death – and we have been seeing her occasionally ever since. She comes to dinner with us – and we go to her – from time to time. I cannot say we get much pleasure out of it.[4]

There was scope for resentment on both sides. Dickens's final words in his will could only have exacerbated ill feelings. His lauding of Georgina's devotion to the children and calling her the 'best and truest friend man ever had' contrasted starkly with his insinuation that Catherine was self-centred and a burden. Dickens repeated the misleading claim that they had 'separat[ed] by consent', following which Catherine received what he regarded as a generous annual income 'while all the great charges of a numerous and expensive family have devolved wholly upon myself'.[5] A further insult to Catherine was the naming of Georgina as guardian to those of his children who were not yet legally classed as adult. However, it was Catherine who was accorded public recognition as his official widow, receiving condolences from Queen Victoria and being consulted by one of Dickens's first biographers just months after his death.

The practical tasks of widowhood fell to Georgina to deal with. She was the one who had to sort through his clothes, giving his old elastic stockings to the poor around Gad's Hill and wondering what to do with new clothing that arrived the day after his death. While Catherine might have felt bitter that her sister was performing these final, personal gestures for her husband, at least she did not have the trauma of losing her home. Under the terms of Dickens's will, his estate was to be converted into money, which meant selling Gad's Hill and its contents. Georgina had to itemise all the furnishings, artwork and the contents of the wine cellar in her much-loved home. She rented Monument House at Weybridge for herself, Mamie, Harry and three of the servants, but because Dickens had determined everything had to be sold, they had nothing to furnish it with: 'Mamie and I bought all our furniture, plates and linens at a valuation from the dear old house – before the Sales'.[6]

At the time of Dickens's death, Georgina and Catherine were already in full mourning for their father who had died just four months earlier. Victorian widows were expected to enter a two-year mourning period during which they wore only black clothes, used mourning stationery for their letters and avoided being seen in public for twelve months. For a brother-in-law, Georgina should have been following these rituals for six months, the end of which would have coincided with the time when she would have come out of the deep period of mourning for her father. Yet she clung onto the official trappings of bereavement for much longer, continuing to use the black-bordered letter paper two years on, eschewing social gatherings and agreeing to dine only 'once a year' with Mamie at the Lehmanns' house in Highgate.[7] One explanation for what turned out to be a long and intense mourning period is that Georgina was experiencing 'complicated grief'.[8] The triggers for this include a family history of extreme reactions to bereavement (which Mrs Hogarth had displayed), excessive dependency on the lost loved one, insecure childhood attachments, and multiple bereavements. Georgina had experienced a series of losses within a few months. In February, her eighty-six-year-old father had died at Catherine's house a few weeks after falling down the stairs at work; in April it was the turn of Daniel Maclise, the handsome and famous artist from her youth; the following month, Mark Lemon, an old friend associated with some of her happiest memories of Devonshire Terrace, died suddenly. The final catalyst was the unexpected death of Dickens. Her complete dependence on him left her bereft and ill equipped to take on the responsibilities she was left with.

Two days before Dickens's funeral, Georgina had been shocked to discover that she, along with John Forster, was an executor of his will: 'I wish he had not given me so great a trust and responsibility. If I had ever had the least idea of such an intention on his part, I would have begged him to reconsider it.'[9] Included in his bequests to Georgina were £8,000 (just over £1 million) and responsibility for his personal belongings and 'all my private papers whatsoever and wheresoever'.[10] Not only was Dickens's generosity towards his sister-in-law destined to attract attention, but giving Georgina such a prominent position in his will brought her 'unnatural position' in his home under scrutiny once again.[11] Several of Dickens's friends were annoyed with him on her behalf. Charles Fechter complained the will was written in a way to 'give colour to the senseless and cruel accusations against Miss Hogarth'.[12] Others were more suspicious. In America, John Bigelow recorded in his diary a conversation he had with Wilkie: 'Collins intimates … that Dickens's sister-in-law, to whom he leaves all his private papers and whom he pronounces the best friend man ever had, was very fond of him. The impression seems to be that they were too intimate.'[13]

Not wanting anyone around her to know the extent of her grief, Georgina confided her emotions to Annie Fields, who, thousands of miles away in Boston, could be relied upon to keep her confidences. Over and again Georgina displayed her distress, lamenting the emptiness she still felt in 1871: 'life is so blank! And it is so hard to care *enough* for anything that is left in the world.'[14] A year later she continued to struggle to accept Dickens's absence, 'to realise fully the blank that was made in life'.[15] Occasionally Georgina exerted ownership as his 'widow', referring to him lovingly as '*my* dearest Charles'.[16]

Four years on, Georgina's chronic grief was just as raw: 'it is the continuance of living without *the* thing that made life interesting and *worth* living!'[17] As the fifth anniversary of Dickens's death came into sight, Georgina recognised how the bereavement was affecting her: '[T]he *bitterness* I suppose of sorrow is over but the sorrow with one will be life long. Nothing will ever fill up that empty place – nor will life ever again have any *real* interest for me.'[18] Finally, she acknowledged that she had been suffering from depression: 'I suppose in fact I am just recovering from the *shock* which though it had no apparent physical effect at the time, I have no doubt did strike a bodily blow as well as a mental one.'[19]

During the 1870s, Georgina's grief left her with only enough energy to deal with the most immediate family matters. Prior to his death, Dickens made his wishes clear as to what was to happen after he had gone. Within days, Charley started to complicate matters in ways that his father would not have approved of. Dickens wanted to be buried in the vicinity of his home; however, Forster and Charley joined forces with the dean of Westminster and arranged for the abbey to be his final resting place.[20] Then, instead of allowing Gad's Hill to be sold to an outside buyer, thereby raising much-needed funds for the estate, Charley intervened and bought the property for himself.[21] The fact that he could not afford it caused more problems, since, if he failed to find the money, the property reverted to the family at a depreciated price. Relations between Charley and the woman he always addressed simply as 'Gina', really soured when he made plans to sell Dickens's writing chalet to a man who intended touring it round the country. It was only when the exhibitor asked for it to be furnished with artefacts owned by Dickens that Charley thought this was too much and agreed to sell it back to Georgina. Assuming the children would want to help repurchase the writing chalet, Georgina asked each for a contribution. To her anger and disappointment, Frank and Sydney both refused. Telling Annie Fields that they 'have no more *feeling* in the matter than Charley has', she was sadly disappointed 'to find so *many* unworthy sons of their great Father'.[22] It was Sydney's turn to cross his aunt when she tried to raise money for Dickens's penurious sister, Letitia Austin, to whom Dickens had left nothing in his will.[23] At Georgina's behest, Frederic Ouvry wrote to each of the children, suggesting that £125 be withheld from each of their shares. Sydney replied he was 'not disposed at present to place this sum in the hands of Mrs. Austin' and asked for a cheque for the deducted £125 to be forwarded.[24] Georgina was furious: 'It *is* too disgusting, I have no words to express what I think.'[25]

Apart from reporting on Catherine's health after she was diagnosed with cervical cancer, Georgina rarely spoke of the Hogarth family. In over forty years' correspondence with Annie Fields, Georgina only mentions the death of her 'good old father' and that her niece, May Roney, stayed with her for the Christmas festivities of 1874.[26] It is impossible to say how much contact Georgina had with her relatives when Dickens was alive. His antipathy towards her younger sister Helen would have deterred Georgina from seeing her regularly, if at all, but she would have been aware that she had married, had a little girl and was widowed when the child was only three years old. Helen worked as a singing teacher to support herself and daughter May, but began to have financial worries after George Hogarth died. As Dickens's death meant a reduction in Catherine's income, Helen no longer had either her father or sister to help ease her money worries. Georgina's bank account reveals that she stepped in to assist Helen, but this went against what she knew Dickens would have wanted. He had despised Helen, the woman he called 'the little serpent'.[27]

By the time that Helen needed financial support, Georgina had elevated Dickens to a god-like figure, most likely a symptom of her extreme grief. Everything about Dickens was spoken of as 'sacred', deserving of 'reverence' and 'veneration'. Every object from his desk and study was 'a sacred possession'; the writing chalet where he was working on *Edwin Drood* on his final day became a 'dear little sacred place', and each birthday and 9 June kept as a 'sacred anniversary'.[28] She warmed only to those who showed an 'intense veneration' for Dickens's memory, so it seems strange that, despite treating everything about him with divine respect, she used his money to give the detested Helen a quarterly allowance of £4 (£500). On top of the allowance, Georgina made two payments to Helen totalling £50 (£6,600) after Catherine's death. Maybe her generosity was the consequence of guilt at having sided with Dickens against her family, or, perhaps Georgina's practical common sense came to the fore, placing her sister's needs over a point of principle.

Helen was not the only Hogarth to benefit from Dickens's bequest to Georgina. Her brother William had returned penniless from Australia and approached her for assistance. When her nephew Plorn, who managed to get through his own inheritance within a short space of time, wrote to ask for a loan, Georgina had to tell him that she was unable to grant his request:

> We require every penny we have to live … your Uncle William is getting old, and his health is failing and … then I should have to do what I could for him, and my sister Helen and little May are far from well off and … I have had to help them.[29]

After Helen died in 1890, Georgina continued financially supporting her daughter, a now married May Leon. In 1897, Georgina gave May £150 (£20,800), possibly as a share transfer, at a time when she could ill afford it. As the years passed, Georgina experienced severe financial difficulties, yet she never ceased to support her Hogarth relatives.

Until Georgina began to emerge from her depression and deep mourning, she relied on John Forster and Frederic Ouvry to exercise executor powers on her behalf. When she discovered Dickens's play *The Strange Gentleman* (1836) was going to be performed without permission, she asked Frederic Ouvry to intervene. Telling Ouvry that Dickens had disliked the play and said he would not have seen it repeated if offered a thousand pounds, Georgina suggested 'a little *mild and judicious* … legal intimidation' be used to threaten the producer.[30] On a number of occasions, Georgina suggested to Annie

Fields that she or her publisher husband challenge articles in American publications that she disapproved of. For instance, when James Fields's *Atlantic Monthly* reported on a walking competition organised by Dickens to amuse the men during their leisure time while on the reading tour of 1867–8, Georgina somewhat archly wrote, '[t]here are *some* things Mamie and I would rather not have had published, as you imagine – the Walking Match for one thing – it was so entirely a *joke* – that it seems to me as if the Public had no business with it'.[31]

The one task delegated to her that she could not hand over, and which was more onerous than Dickens might have anticipated, was having to deal with his personal belongings. Fanny Ternan Trollope told her stepdaughter that 'all the trifling objects that he had personally used were to be distributed at Georgina's discretion to those friends who value them'.[32] It was a delicate task to decide who should or should not receive a personal artefact, as well as what should be sent. The jewellery was shared amongst the family, with Georgina choosing a diamond ring for herself. She and Mamie had cut several locks of hair from Dickens's head to be given to special friends, and they obtained numerous copies of photographs of Dickens, the writing chalet and his study desk. Each item Georgina gave out was accompanied by a personal note, explaining what she was sending and why. Dickens's most dearly loved items were well-used, 'utterly *valueless* and shabby', which, she explained, would make them more important to his dearest friends.[33] A cigar case and medicine chest went to his old friend and doctor, Frank Beard; a cloak, table ornament and lock of hair was handed to Charles Fechter; his dear friend Thomas Carlyle received a walking stick; and Charles Reade a pen tray. James and Annie Fields were sent a paper knife, given to Dickens many years earlier in Scotland, together with some photographs. Not everyone prized the mementos they received in the way she hoped. Georgina was dismayed to discover the 'magnetic' Charles Fechter left his keepsakes behind when he went to America. He made matters worse by opening a parcel and letter handed to him by Georgina intended for Mrs Fechter and their son. According to a servant, Fechter took out what he wanted and set the rest to one side, having no intention of delivering the packet.

A particular quandary was what to give the Ternans. Visiting Nelly and Fanny at the lodgings they had taken in Kensington in the weeks after Dickens's death, Georgina brought with her the mementos she had chosen. The pen Dickens was using on his final day went to Nelly. What or whether to give something to Fanny was a problem. She had married the author Thomas Trollope and, soon after, had fallen out with Dickens. Whatever the cause, he told a friend the year after her marriage, 'I don't in the least care for Mrs. T. T. … She is infinitely sharper than the Serpent's Tooth.'[34] Given that he despised Fanny, Dickens would have deemed her unworthy of receiving a remembrance. However, Fanny wrote to tell her stepdaughter that Georgina handed her 'a little medal for Papa and a paper weight for me'.[35] Georgina may have heard Dickens express the attitude that, 'for the magic [i.e. Nelly's] sake, I scrupulously try to do her [Fanny] justice, and not to see her – out of my path – with a jaundiced vision'.[36] By making sure she included Fanny in the distribution of Dickens's personal belongings, Georgina avoided fuelling any existing ill feeling between the families.

Grief shaped Georgina's life in the early 1870s. She took a week to commemorate Dickens's death, visiting the gravestone in the abbey most days, remaining there for hours, looking at the flowers that had been left, eagerly reading any cards, and comforted by the fact that he had not been forgotten. She repeated the exercise on his birthday.

After the family's temporary stay at Monument House, Georgina leased 81 Gloucester Terrace for her, Mamie and Harry, together with the servants.[37] It was the kind of large, grand abode Dickens would have rented for the London season. Georgina soon realised that the house was costing far more than they could afford but was unable to rally the energy to do something about it: 'I hope the house will work out all right – and I wish with all my heart I could get myself to feel any interest as to whether it does or not!'[38] Like most Victorian women, Georgina lacked a financial education and so had no experience of paying insurances, medical payments or planning for all the unforeseen bills of a large household. She had never held a bank account and had no idea of stocks and shares. With Ouvry's guidance, her £8,000 legacy was invested, mainly in the railways. The interest was at 5 per cent, giving Georgina the £400 a year she believed she could live on. However, although she knew she had to manage on a significantly smaller budget than the one she had been used to, she made little attempt to alter the family's lifestyle. Georgina attributed her reckless spending to wanting to keep a grieving Mamie happy, describing how 'she has expensive tastes, especially as to house and furniture, which I have not had the heart to refuse to join her in indulging'.[39] The fact was that, even with Mamie and Harry's contributions, she was spending more than twice the amount she had anticipated on their domestic arrangements and within the first couple of years she was digging into the capital.

While Georgina continued to be consumed by her loss, others began to move on. Katey was widowed and married a second time, to fellow artist Carlo Perugini in 1873; Nelly married in 1876, and a few months later, Harry wed Marie Roche. The announcement of Harry's impending wedding in September 1876 came as a shock to Georgina. Only weeks earlier, she had written to Annie Fields that in August 'Harry will go into Switzerland again … with a friend for his long vacation'.[40] Unlike her delight at hearing of Katey's second marriage, Georgina was not at all pleased. She made excuses that she was worried that 'dear Harry' had overlooked his father's religious beliefs when proposing, since his fiancée's Catholicism 'would have been a terrible blow to Harry's Father'.[41] As Dickens had encouraged Mamie to consider marrying Percy Fitzgerald, a Catholic, Georgina's reaction might have had more to do with jealousy at losing another beloved man. Sounding somewhat insincere, she wrote to Plorn in Australia claiming she was 'always wishing I could like [Marie] more, at all events find her more interesting and sympathetic'.[42] Georgina added that there was: 'something dry and unyouthful (to coin a word) about Marie which prevents one feeling that spontaneous affection for her which we should like to feel for our dear Harry's wife'.[43]

Catherine had a very different opinion, regarding her new daughter-in-law, Marie, as 'a very charming girl'.[44] Engagements tended to be short in the nineteenth century, but the fact that Harry met and married Marie within a few short months suggests the wedding was planned hurriedly. The birth of their first child, Enid, came just eight months after the wedding.

Harry's unexpected marriage meant Georgina was forced to look for new accommodation. The grand townhouse at Gloucester Terrace was too large and expensive for just her and Mamie. They took temporary rooms in Harley Street and then Sloane Street. Given Georgina's depressed mental state, she had little interest in where they lived. In 1877, on the advice of Frederic Ouvry, Georgina made the decision to use some of her capital to buy, rather than lease, a house. She chose 11 Strathmore Gardens, in a small, quiet cul-de-sac. It was a large double-fronted house of five storeys, newly built between 1868 and 1870, and close to the home of John and Eliza Forster. This was not, though, the lifetime home for her and Mamie that Georgina intended it to be. Mamie stayed with friends for long periods of time. Although in the first few years after Dickens's death, she accompanied Georgina to take wreaths and bouquets to Westminster Abbey on her father's anniversaries, once Mamie began to emerge from her grief, she became less fixated on maintaining these vigils.

In complete contrast to her niece, during the 1870s, Georgina became progressively more obsessed with Dickens, making increasingly determined efforts to protect his legacy and prevent his achievements from being overshadowed. On hearing that Wilkie Collins planned a reading tour of America, Georgina repeatedly denigrated him: 'I *cannot* imagine that he will be successful as a lecturer or Reader!', 'I never heard him read – but I cannot imagine him reading *well* – he seems to me to have no physical qualification for it' and 'I cannot imagine that any reading of his could ever give me the slightest pleasure'.[45]

Georgina tried to dissuade Annie Fields from attending a lecture by Edmund Yates, fearing he might make some non-reverential observation about Dickens. She dismissed Yates's planned American lecture trip, disdainfully observing that she was 'not by any means confident that his Lectures will be in good *taste* – and I am *sure* I would rather not hear them'.[46]

Nelly was the one person whom Georgina was happy to see distance herself from Dickens. Nelly met her clergyman husband, George Wharton Robinson, the year after Dickens's death. However, she seemed to be enjoying her independence, spending considerable time at Fanny's house in Italy, and it was not until 1874 that they became engaged. Nelly had been suffering from ill health since the Staplehurst rail accident and, around the time of her engagement, underwent a painful operation, probably related to the injuries she sustained to her arm. After the operation, Georgina would visit her 'invalid friend' twice a week. At least initially, George Robinson knew nothing of Nelly's relationship with Dickens, other than that she was on good terms with the Dickens family. Georgina stayed with the couple at their home in Margate and, when they started a school, she was the guest of honour, handing out prizes to pupils on sports day. As a way of legitimating her friendship with Dickens, Nelly claimed she was like a goddaughter to him and pretended to be fourteen years younger than she actually was.[47] With several years taken off her age, no one could suspect Nelly and Dickens of having an affair; after all, a fifty-eight-year-old Dickens was hardly likely to have been intimate with a girl who claimed she was only five when he separated from Catherine. Lying about her age also meant that George Robinson was unaware his wife was older than he was.

On the 1876 marriage certificate of Nelly Ternan and George Wharton Robinson no age is recorded. However, in the 1881 census, Nelly's age is given as twenty-eight (real age, forty-two) and George is thirty. According to Claire Tomalin in *The Invisible Woman*, Nelly frequently gave different birth years in the census, eventually settling around ten years younger than George. For once, Georgina was unlikely to have disapproved of a marriage between an older woman and a much younger man. She had said of marriages where the woman was older than the man, 'I think even a *few* years disparity on the *wrong* side is dangerous because a woman is always *older* than a man – even if they are the same age – and I think when a woman marries a man who might be her *Son* – it becomes *very* risky'.[48]

Covering over the unaccounted years required the complicity of all those who knew about Nelly's life with Dickens. Georgina knew Nelly could rely on her sisters' discretion, but the servants knew about the relationship and their loyalty could not be taken for granted. Jane Wheeler was sixteen years old when she began working for Mrs Ternan and Nelly and had remained with Nelly after Dickens's death. When Nelly returned to London after living with her sister Maria Ternan Taylor in Oxford, Jane had stayed on. In 1876, after Maria left her husband and Nelly was about to marry George Wharton Robinson, Jane found herself unemployed. Nelly may have worried about the potential slip-ups that might arise from taking into her new marital home a servant employed during the period she was with Dickens.[49] With Georgina's assistance, a plan was made to ensure that Jane was kept close.

Georgina was following Dickens's example; Dickens had taken the precaution of securing the loyalty of his manservant John Thompson after Thompson left his service. Biographer Claire Tomalin attributes Dickens's tolerance of the arrogant servant to the fact he knew all about Dickens's secret relationship, as he was often sent to deliver messages or do errands for Nelly. Thompson had no respect for Dickens and was caught stealing money from the cashbox at the office of *All the Year Round*. Instead of dismissing him without a reference, Dickens instructed W. H. Wills to find him another job. When Wills told the thief that he was to be employed as a waiter at the Reform Club, Thompson had the temerity to refuse on the grounds that he did not feel he could, or wanted to, do such work. Dickens then took the extraordinary step of setting him up as self-employed with his own small business. It is difficult to see this as anything other than hush money.[50] Jane was genuinely loyal to Nelly, but there was a risk of something being inadvertently revealed if she worked for a new employer. Georgina found a solution by employing Jane as a cook, who remained in her employment for the next twenty years. When Jane married the widower William Brown, he moved into Georgina's house – an unusual step since William did not start working for Georgina, but continued in his job as a cabinet French polisher. The couple remained with Georgina, moving from house to house, eventually finding their own home when Jane resigned in 1898. At the time, Georgina told friends that Jane was retiring because of ill health but, still aged only forty-nine, Jane went back into service a few years later and returned to Nelly's employment in 1913.

A comfortable accord between the Dickens/Hogarth and Robinson families had developed as the next generation began to appear. With the exception of Katey, the women of both families socialised and kept in touch with one another. On what would have been Dickens's seventieth birthday, Mamie compiled *The Charles Dickens Birthday Book*. Mamie provided short passages for the birthdays of friends and family (with the notable exception of Catherine). Georgina's birthday includes the line 'best and truest friend' and a quotation from *Oliver Twist*: 'devoted to us … that perfect sacrifice of self', while Nelly's carries a phrase from *The Old Curiosity Shop* on how charmingly pretty Nelly looked.[51] These birthday books were laid out as diaries or calendars to provide space for the owner's entries. Nelly signed her name on Letitia Austin's copy and the birthdays of both Letitia and Harriet Lovell Dickens appear in Nelly's book.

Harry Dickens's family enjoyed a convivial friendship with the Robinsons. There were holidays together when Harry and Marie's children played on the sands at Boulogne with the Robinson youngsters. Georgina went too, enjoying her time at this favourite haunt of Dickens with 'Harry and his wife and sweet children'.[52] Although she thought Marie 'has had too many babies – *too fast*', the pleasure she took from them helped to bring her out of her long bereavement.[53] Ongoing intimacy between the Dickens/Hogarth and Robinson families continued long after these seaside holidays. Nelly's 1912 address book include details for Harry and Marie and three of their married children (Henry Charles Dickens, listed as 'Hal'; Olive Shuckburgh and Enid Hawksley). Alongside an entry for Georgina, there was one for 'Georgy's doctor', showing the openness between the two women in discussing their medical conditions.

John Forster's death in 1876 was followed by Frederic Ouvry's in 1881, leaving Georgina as the only person left to whom Dickens had entrusted his legacy. Being the sole executor coincided with the period when Georgina finally emerged from her deep grief. After visiting Westminster Abbey in 1882 on the anniversary of what would have been Dickens's seventieth birthday, Georgina was able to say, 'I came away with a feeling of deep depression which is, thank God! not common to me now'.[54]

Georgina's idea for producing a book of Dickens's letters was the first sign that she was embarking on a more active role as executor and guardian of his memory. Her motivations for the collection were prompted partly by a desire to keep Dickens in the public eye, partly by financial need and partly, it appears, by a wish to denigrate Catherine. Percy Fitzgerald first suggested to Georgina in 1877 that she put together a volume of Dickens's letters. The fact she considered it is surprising, given that she knew Dickens was against biographers using the confidential letters of famous men. She was at Gad's Hill in September 1860 when Dickens had a bonfire in the garden, destroying twenty years of letters and papers, determined there would be no such abuse of the correspondence he received from notable figures. Believing that the public had no right to see private communication, Dickens undoubtedly wished others would do the same and burn his letters after they had been read. Practical reasons, together with an increasingly imperious approach to protecting Dickens's name, were what convinced Georgina to go ahead with the publication. She was spending more than her income and told Percy Fitzgerald, 'if any money is to be made by them, it might as well be made by me as by any one else'.[55] She may have had to reassure herself that Dickens would not have objected if he knew his loving sister-in-law and dutiful daughter Mamie were responsible for the project. After making up her mind to proceed, Georgina justified her decision by saying that Forster's biography felt 'incomplete as a *Portrait* … Charles was a man who expressed his individuality so strongly in his letters that … a collection of these to various people on various subjects will supply a want'.[56] On an emotional level, editing Dickens's letters offered a means of breathing life into the memories of 'dearest Charles' and an opportunity to put forth her version of the man she wanted the public to remember.

While Georgina claimed that she and Mamie 'ought to produce a wonderful Book – like a new one from the dear dead Hand!', they went at the task with scissors and paste, wreaking editorial havoc in order to create a suitably 'reverent' image of the 'Inimitable'.[57] They combined letters of different dates, changed the wording and failed to indicate when they were cutting out sections. Any references to Nelly, Dickens's eating and drinking indulgences, or talk about his earnings from the American and British reading tours, were censured. Any possibility that Dickens's fondness for Georgina might be misread was expunged. When Dickens wrote to W. H. Wills from Paris describing the filthiness of the house he had rented, he continued: 'But Sir [–] when Georgina, the servants and I were here for the first night (Catherine and the rest being at Boulogne), I heard my little right hand restless [saying] "Oh it's dreadfully dirty. I can't sleep for the smell of the room".'[58] The phrase 'little right hand' was replaced with 'Georgy'.

Misleadingly, Georgina edited the letters to support Dickens's narrative of his marriage. On reading the chapter covering the separation in Forster's biography, Georgina was annoyed that Dickens's side of the marital breakdown could not be told: 'what I feel to be *hard*', she wrote, 'is that proper justice cannot be done to Charles'.[59] Her statement is ironic given that the only account of the separation the public had heard was Dickens's self-justificatory version in which he completely maligned Catherine. Georgina went on to say that, as Catherine was still alive, Forster was unable to 'comment on the peculiarities of her character' but if these 'could be fairly set against *his* would I think require no comment – and would be an explanation for a great deal'.[60]

According to Katey Dickens, she took Georgina to see Catherine in 1878 with a view to ending the ill feeling between the sisters. Each thought the other was to blame. Georgina considered Catherine an emotionally flawed character, telling Annie Fields:

> As to my sister – it is a subject I don't want ever to say much upon – but I hate all false pretences … she is a very curious person – unlike any one else in the world – and I feel from the way you write that you have an entirely mistaken idea of the state she is in. – Naturally, as you don't know her.[61]

Katey implied that Catherine regarded Georgina as a troublemaker, as when they were reunited, 'Mrs. Dickens forgave her sister for those things which happened in the past'.[62] In reality, Katey's attempts at reconciliation were far from successful and Georgina and Catherine continued to harbour a mutual antagonism. Editing the letters provided Georgina with an opportunity to secure 'proper justice' for Dickens, and she and Mamie utilised Dickens's letters to Catherine cautiously. As well as using the edited collection to produce a version of Dickens she approved of, Georgina took advantage of the opportunities she had in interviews with Dickens's biographers to shape the narrative of his relationship with Catherine. No wonder that authors and critics found Georgina a willing interviewee; it was a chance for her 'truth' to prevail. This can be seen in A. W. Ward's *Dickens* (1882), which acknowledges Georgina as a main source. Incorrectly, Ward asserts that 'Mrs. Dickens left her husband', going on to say, 'If he had ever loved his wife ... there is no indication of it in any of his numerous letters addressed to her.'[63] It was to be another fifty-three years before Dickens's letters to Catherine were published in full, suggesting that, as K. J. Fielding has argued, Ward 'was strongly influenced by Miss Hogarth' and it was 'improbable that he formed his judgement' based on the twenty edited letters in Georgina and Mamie's collection.[64]

It was only when Catherine developed terminal cervical cancer that Georgina's attitude towards her softened, calling her 'my poor sister' and saying how she '[bore] her great pain wonderfully'.[65] At the same time, their brother Edward and his wife, who lived a few streets away from Catherine, were dying of consumption. As Georgina dashed between their homes, nursing her ailing siblings and trying to prepare the Dickens letters for publication, it was almost certainly Nelly who was the 'kind friend' who stepped in to transcribe the remaining correspondence.[66] When Catherine died in November 1879, her bequests gave a clue as to how reconciled and forgiving she felt towards Georgina. It was the youngest sister, Helen, who received all Catherine's most treasured reminders of Mary and Mrs Hogarth and those of her deceased sons Walter and Sydney. Catherine left Georgina two items: a photograph of Walter in his uniform and an enamel snake ring. Why Catherine left a photograph of Walter (yet nothing of Sydney's) to Georgina is surprising and intriguing. There is no record of Georgina having a particularly soft spot for this nephew. It might simply be that Georgina had admired the photograph during the time she was nursing Catherine or it may have been Catherine's way of reminding her sister that she was the children's mother. Walter was the only one of the Dickens children who had left home prior to his parents' separation so was never under Georgina's sole care.

Catherine's bequeathing of the blue enamel snake ring to Georgina may have been symbolic. It had been a gift from Count D'Orsay, whom Georgina barely knew, in the mid-1840s. Prince Albert had given an enamel diamond snake engagement ring to Queen Victoria in 1839, popularising the design. The snake was a symbol of eternal love but also conveyed an alternative meaning. As Rosemary Ashton has pointed out, the adulterous wife in Augustus Egg's *Past and Present* (1858) lies weeping on the floor, wearing bracelets of snake motifs.[67] If Catherine left her sister a pointed reminder that she thought her duplicitous, Georgina remained equally aggravated. Her warmer attitude towards Catherine during her illness did not last. She rarely mentioned her after Catherine's death, but the testimony of Lisa Puckle describing Georgina's fireside chats with Lisa's grandmother, Cecile Macready, when Catherine was lambasted for being an attention seeking 'whiney woman', implies ongoing resentment. Georgina never forgave Catherine for not being the kind of wife she thought Dickens deserved.

Catherine died in November 1879, the same week the first two volumes of Dickens's letters were published. This time marks the emergence of a more vocal Georgina, the one who was to become recognised as the 'guardian of the beloved memory'.[68] Following a six-month mourning period for Catherine, a different Georgina to the rather subdued woman of the Gad's Hill years appeared. She no longer had to fear she might do or say something that might incur a rebuke or cost her Dickens's affection. Emboldened in her official role as executor, Georgina began to make her voice heard. In the absence of John Forster and Frederic Ouvry, she enlisted Harry's assistance in making formal challenges regarding Dickens's estate. When the carelessness of Frederic Ouvry's executors in 1883 allowed a bundle of personal letters to be sold to an

American dealer, she denounced attempts to publish them. Many of those from Dickens's father were seen as embarrassing since they recorded his frequent requests for loans from his son's publishers. On another occasion, she requested Harry issue a condemnatory response to the editors of *Harper's* over a piece written by someone the Dickens family and Georgina had regarded as a good friend. Percy Fitzgerald should have known better than to assert Mary Hogarth had secretly loved Dickens for years but stood aside for Catherine. Georgina declared him an '*Idiot*' and swore she would 'never have any further acquaintance with him'.[69]

Georgina did not seek Harry's assistance when firing off complaints that had no grounds other than that she objected to certain (accurate) revelations about Dickens's lifestyle. She was angry with the writer F. G. Kitton when he pointed out in his book how a photograph in Forster's *Life of Charles Dickens* had been doctored to give Dickens a more wholesome image. The original photograph showed Dickens standing on the porch at Gad's Hill holding a glass of wine, but the American edition of Forster's *Life* altered the image to one Georgina approved, which replaced the glass of wine with a book. Annoyed with Kitton and the publisher for making it known that the original photograph had Dickens with a wineglass, she despatched an angry letter, full of exclamation marks, indicating her frustration at how she and the author had 'totally different points of view!'; how some of the comments 'give an entirely false impression of him!' and included too many voices 'whether they really knew anything … or … did *not*!'.[70]

Sometimes she was unable to make any official challenge and had to content herself with complaining to friends. When one-time friend and ex-employee R. H. Horne retold an incident in a *Temple Bar* journal article, in which he had witnessed Dickens struggling to contain his laughter on seeing Forster 'in a new pair of glazed leather shoes, the toes of which were at least two inches beyond his own' and clumsily demonstrating some newly learned dance steps, Georgina was apoplectic. Horne had gone on to say that, when he asked 'Miss G___' who had taught Forster this rather odd dance, Georgina responded, 'I really can't tell you ... but his absurdities are a constant source of amusement to us'.[71] The fact is that there were occasions when Forster's pomposity was a source of amusement to those who knew him. However, because Horne had offered the general public sight of a Dickens who could make fun of his friends, Georgina denounced Horne as 'one of the most contemptible and despicable of mankind' but admitted that it was, 'not so much ... what he says of Forster as by the use he makes of Charles's name – and even of mine'.[72]

This more purposeful and assertive Georgina did not appear to be worried about endearing herself to friends. While she had often admonished Percy Fitzgerald before cutting him off altogether, and there was no love lost with R. H. Horne after he abandoned his wife Kate, her possessive defence of Dickens's memory undoubtedly risked alienating some people. Georgina remained friends with Maria Beadnell Winter until her death in 1886, but she did not allow this long association to deflect her from her determination to preserve her image of Dickens. When Maria Beadnell's letters to Dickens were published in America, newspaper headlines made Dickens appear weak and vulnerable. The *New York Times* declared: 'Love Letters of Dickens to "Dora"; Revelation of a Pathetic Romance in the Novelist's Youth That Influenced His Life's Work'.[73] The introduction to the book describes a sharp-witted Maria and her friend cruelly toying with the hapless Dickens and, when it was all over, 'the girls probably got together and had a good laugh at Dickens' expense'.[74] Georgina and Harry prevented the book being distributed for sale in Britain, but she obtained a copy for herself from America. After reading it, she wrote a response in the form of a memorandum. Extracts from this were used when the letters were eventually made public in Britain, nineteen years after Georgina's death. Georgina disparaged her old friend Maria, describing her as a 'kind, goodnatured woman, but fearfully silly' and observed how 'very fat' and 'quite commonplace' she had become.[75] Georgina told a story of how, after they had visited Maria and her husband, Dickens had laughed about this girlfriend from his youth in the carriage going home. Georgina talks of an ageing Maria as a romantic who 'liked to talk a good deal about her early love'.[76] In truth, Georgina would have known of Dickens's youthful heartbreak and observed his excitement in 1855 at the prospect of meeting his first love again. Fearing that Dickens's lovelorn letters would make him look foolish and not show sufficient reverence for his hallowed memory, she got her digs in first.

This was far from the only occasion when Georgina felt she needed to pre-empt what she regarded as undesirable revelations of Dickens's life, but events were often beyond her control. In the mid-1890s, Georgina learned of a one-act play that had been performed in Melbourne called 'Dickens: A Comedy' which was set in Manchester and involved the cast of *The Frozen Deep*.[77] It appears there was nothing salacious in the play, but one of the characters was a 'Miss Ternan' and in his book *Dickens and Drama*, S. J. Adair-Fitzgerald commented that 'round this actress and Dickens is woven a slight love affair'.[78] There is no record of Georgina's response, but she would surely have acted to quash Adair-Fitzgerald's assertions. When news reached her in 1893 that Thomas Wright had uncovered a story of Nelly confessing to her local parish priest of an intimate relationship with Dickens, she immediately tackled him. Wright later remarked that Georgina had written '"furiously", to him ... demanding that he abandon his project'.[79] It was to be another forty-three years, long after Georgina's death, before Wright went ahead with the publication of his astonishing revelations about Nelly being the mistress of Charles Dickens.

Relations between Georgina and Nelly were not always harmonious. Nelly was known to be wilful and Georgina judgemental, so there were moments of frostiness. When in 1886 Nelly loaned Mamie £800 (£110,800), there was no reason why either of them should have consulted Georgina. Yet it created bad feeling when she became aware of it. Writing of their dispute, Gail David-Tellis comments that the ever-watchful Georgina 'must have feared that should word of the loan spread, there would be a flare-up of the old scandal'.[80] After all, she argues, what else, other than a substantial legacy from Dickens, could explain Nelly's affluent financial position and her largesse to Mamie?[81] There are other indications suggesting that between the mid-1880s and early 1890s there were tensions between Georgina and Nelly. Jane Brown (*née* Wheeler) had remained very fond of Nelly and her decision to leave Georgina's employment might have been influenced by the fact she was in an awkward position – torn between two women who were not getting on. It would not be surprising if an assertive Nelly and censorious Georgina found each other exasperating at times and avoided disputes by acting coolly towards each other. Helen Wickham, a friend of Nelly's daughter Gladys, 'particularly noticed that on her return ... from several visits to Miss Hogarth in 1900, Ellen made no comment whatsoever'.[82] These tensions in Georgina and Nelly's friendship must have resolved themselves because convivial relations were eventually restored. The two women could bond over their shared health problems, with Nelly diagnosed with breast cancer in 1907 and Georgina in 1912.

More upsetting for Georgina than any tension with Nelly was Mamie's growing coolness. Her niece went from relying on Georgina after her father's death ('She clings to me just now ... She thinks of nothing but staying quietly with me. So I must consider myself bound to her') to avoiding her.[83] Mamie had started to become more unpredictable in the 1860s after her parents separated. The child who Dickens nicknamed 'Mild Glo'ster' because she was so quiet, became bolder and increasingly capricious. In her twenties, she experimented with her appearance by adopting the fashion of dyeing her hair blonde with a streak of auburn, which both shocked and amused Wilkie Collins and Fred Lehmann, and she started to drink more. Household accounts show that in the years 1873–4 when Georgina, Mamie and Harry were living at Gloucester Terrace, the wine merchant's bill was over £74 (£8,900).

As Mamie saw her contemporaries embark upon marriage, her future prospects as companion to a grieving aunt looked grim. Mamie was not ready to settle for this and, almost as soon as Georgina had purchased Strathmore Gardens, she began spending long periods away from London. The attraction was the Reverend Thomas Hargraves and his wife Marie at Penton Mewsey in Hampshire, whom she had met while staying with her friends the Humphreys.[84] At first Georgina saw a positive change in the health and emotional state of her niece, telling Annie Fields that 'Mamie is very well – and very "gay" just now'.[85] The Hargraveses were over ten years younger than Mamie and she thrived on their devotion to their religious work and enthusiasm for outdoor sporting pursuits. However, on meeting the couple, Georgina took an immediate dislike to them, calling Thomas Hargraves 'detestable' and 'unworthy' and describing Marie as a 'poor woman' with a 'sad life'.[86] A particular worry to her was that they all drank to excess. Mamie's weight fluctuated dramatically and she increasingly appeared drawn and unhealthy. Since Mamie rarely came home to Strathmore Terrace, Georgina tried her best to get her to recognise the extraordinary financial strain placed on both of them by living apart while incurring the expenses of a joint household. When, for the second year in succession, Mamie failed to return to London to lay flowers on Dickens's gravestone, Georgina wrote a bitter, despairing letter to Annie Fields:

> [M]y life is so bound up with this other – *his* Daughter – whose welfare I must also (if it is possible that such things can be known and can affect those who are gone from us!) be his desire! that I have this peculiar feeling which binds me more to Mamie than my feeling for *herself* does. Because I must own that though I *love* her as much as ever, I feel that she has shown – and *does* show, so little consideration for me, that, as far as *she* is personally concerned, I sometimes get so angry that I think I *will* make up my mind to think only of *my*self! And insist on breaking off – and going on my own way. Then this other thought and love comes in – and until *she* wishes it too! I cannot make the separation.[87]

It was to be another three years before Mamie agreed that Georgina could sell Strathmore Terrace. Sad though it was to acknowledge that Mamie had chosen to desert her, having separate households helped to ease the financial strain.

At the age of sixty-one, Georgina reported that she was 'in a healthier state both of mind and body than I have been for years'.[88] In 1886, Georgina had moved from Strathmore Gardens into a large flat at 70 Wynnstay Gardens with her live-in maid, Emma Durnford. Jane Brown and her husband found alternative accommodation and her services as a cook were not required during this period. Unable to settle into Wynnstay Gardens, Georgina decided to sub-let and made a temporary move to Harry and Marie's house in 1887, which lasted just a few months. Although they made her feel welcome, with their constantly expanding family and Georgina's wish for 'a little place *of my own*', she took a house at 55 Oakley Street, on the same road in which her old friend Mary Boyle lived.[89] Emma Durnford moved with Georgina and they were immediately joined by Jane and William Brown.

When she was not scouring newspapers for anything relating to Dickens and his legacy, or advising Dickens's biographers, Georgina had an active social life. Apart from daily visiting and hosting callers to her home on Wednesdays, she spent hours with her great-nieces and great-nephews and was a regular theatre-goer. There were twice-weekly shopping trips to the Army & Navy department store and Harvey Nichols; a photograph of the eighty-six-year-old shows she was still keen to appear fashionable. Georgina is pictured wearing the latest in day wear: a white cotton pin-tuck blouse with a straight skirt and decorative belt.

Georgina made new friends as more of those associated with the old days passed away. She wrote to recent friends Jane Pym and her husband Horace, a solicitor and avid collector of Dickens memorabilia, that she felt some relief on hearing of the death of Wilkie Collins, who had been suffering dementia, as 'no one who loved him could have wished his life to be prolonged for the *mind*

30 Georgina Hogarth in 1912

was dead! and who could desire the body to outlive it'.[90] She kept in regular contact with long-standing friends like Mary Boyle, Eliza Forster and Janet Wills (the latter two both widows). She and Janet had set up a fund in 1884 to assist Kate Horne, whom Dickens and Wills had tried to help after she was deserted by her husband in 1854. The women regularly visited each other and helped support one another through bouts of ill health. Georgina missed out on spending a luxurious Christmas at Foxwold with the Pyms, opting instead to spend part of the day with Mary Boyle after 'promising faithfully to stay in London' after her friend had had a cataract removed, 'and be as much with her as I can while she is laid up after the operation'.[91] Annie Fields invited Georgina many times to visit her in America but she always made an excuse, first saying that Mamie was scared to cross the ocean, then claiming she had to look after the house and servants, and finally admitting she did not want to make the journey. Annie was more adventurous and made three trips to London, calling on a delighted Georgina. Even though Annie was a Dickens devotee whom he had regarded as 'one of the dearest little women in the world' and trusted enough to speak about Nelly, Georgina remained tight-lipped about her brother-in-law's young mistress.[92] In their forty-four years of correspondence, Georgina never referred to Nelly by name, only ever making vague references to 'a friend'. Perhaps it was because Annie and Georgina's lifelong friendship, based on what Annie's biographer described as a 'quasi-religious awe' of Dickens, precluded them talking about his relationship with Nelly since this would have required them to acknowledge Dickens's flaws.[93]

As Georgina embarked upon her seventies, Dickens had been dead for nearly thirty years and while she continued to dedicate herself to his memory, she no longer echoed his every opinion; Dickens's views on royalty being one example. Dickens had not held the monarchy in any great esteem so neither had Georgina. When Dickens was alive, she described Edward, Prince of Wales, as 'a disgrace', noting that he was rightly 'hooted in the street and hissed at the Theatre' when named in the Mordaunt divorce case as Lady Mordaunt's lover.[94] Shortly after this, Dickens had an audience with the fifty-one-year-old Queen Victoria. Reporting on this meeting, Georgina told a friend that Dickens had thought her 'strangely *shy* and like a girl in manners', adding the comment, 'I think, you know, that the *honour* conferred by the visit was all on "the Queen's side"!'[95] Yet when it was the Queen's Diamond Jubilee in 1897, Georgina wrote excitedly of the preparations and expressed great pleasure at being able to watch the procession, Harry having obtained tickets for 'seats in St. Martin's churchyard where I hope we shall see well'.[96] In the year Victoria died and Edward came to the throne, Georgina showed that she had clearly altered her views on the monarch and her son. She attended the funeral procession of Queen Victoria with Jane Pym, writing of the event to Annie Fields:

> The mourning for her is universal – and it is *genuine*. I saw the Funeral Procession … It was a most solemn and deeply touching sight … I have a great belief in the new King. I think he has some very fine *Royal* qualities – and he certainly inherits much of his Mother's tact and *sympathy*. But I don't think there will be quite the same intense feeling of love and loyalty for any other Monarch in our country or in any others as had grown up and developed for Queen Victoria. She was such a real *Woman!*[97]

What Dickens would have said to his sister-in-law on her newly acquired monarchist sympathies can only be imagined.

Throughout her eighth decade, Georgina was preoccupied by health and financial worries. In 1900, aged seventy-three, her eczema worsened, she was diagnosed with hardening of the arteries and began to develop debilitating headaches and blackouts. She moved house again, this time taking rooms at 31 Egerton Terrace, just steps away from Harry and Marie's home. Built in the 1840s, the white stucco, double-fronted terraced house was a smaller, but grander, edifice than her previous homes. Egerton Terrace would become one of the most expensive streets in London and even at the turn of the century Georgina could only afford to rent rooms. Worsening health incurred large medical bills, putting more strain on her limited income, and she was increasingly reliant on loans and advances on her investments. Yet, despite having a small budget, Georgina continued to help others. Aside from providing money to her brother, sister and niece, she continued to make donations to a range of charities, including the Working Ladies' Guild, which assisted unmarried or widowed women, and the Babies' Home and Day Nursery. More significant was the long-term support to her, Catherine and Dickens's old friend and servant Anne Cornelius and her daughter, first setting up a fund and, when that ran out, giving them £15 (£2,100) of her own money.

Dickens may have been anticipating a time when an older, single Georgina would need help, when he wrote his will, urging his children 'always to remember how much they owe to the said Georgina Hogarth, and never to be wanting in a grateful and affectionate attachment to her'.[98] Dickens frequently spoke of his children's 'devotion' and 'tenderest affection' for 'Aunty', yet the fact he felt it necessary to remind them of their duty implies that he either believed his children had little sense of responsibility, or thought that they would choose their mother's side. In the years when Georgina's health and financial position were seriously deteriorating, many of the Dickens children were not able to help, should they have wanted to. Georgina kept in contact with them all, sharing family news but having different relationships with each one.[99]

As the eldest and nearest in age to her, Charley's connection with 'Gina' was cordial but not particularly warm. He was always protective of his mother and fully aware of the tensions between the sisters.[100] Their relationship, which had started to deteriorate over his mishandling of the sale of Gad's Hill, was made worse by the sale of the writing chalet. With some misgivings, but wanting to help the persistently cash-strapped Charley, Georgina and Mamie gave him the contract to print the three volumes of their collected letters. It had been agreed that the women would cover the cost of the printing themselves. Just when Georgina was struggling to manage her finances, Charley made life more difficult by proving to be a demanding creditor, insisting she paid what she owed. When he died at the age of fifty-nine, Georgina expressed sorrow, especially as he left behind a wife and seven daughters, but there was never any indication that she grieved for a beloved nephew.

For the eighteen years between leaving London and her death, Mamie lived with the Hargraveses, moving from one ministry to another and avoiding Georgina and the rest of her family. However, in the final two weeks of her life when she was dying of liver cirrhosis caused by her alcoholism, Katey and Georgina arrived to take care of her. As she lay in bed at the home she shared with the Hargraveses in Farnham Royal Village, Slough, Mamie would have been in considerable pain and barely aware of what was happening around her. Mamie died in 1896 at fifty-eight, the same age as her father, and on the day of her brother Charley's funeral. In the family correspondence, no one mentioned the cause of her death. Harry avoided providing any details, writing to his brother Alfred that 'Mamie faded gradually away'.[101] Georgina told Plorn's wife, Connie, 'My love for Mamie … was most true and tender … But the loss … is not so great as it would have been years ago – For it is long since she ceased to be my companion.'[102]

Georgina's relationship with Katey was less close than with Mamie, but their attachment had been strong enough for her younger niece to entrust with a secret. When Charley Collins died in 1873, Katey should have been in mourning until 1875. However, Lucinda Hawksley's research into her three-times great-aunt Katey revealed that she had married fellow artist Carlo Perugini just five months later, in September 1873.[103] The likelihood is that this was because she was pregnant. Georgina dealt with questions as to why she and Mamie had remained in London during the summer, describing how 'Katy had a good deal of business to settle … and our plans were always postponed on her account'.[104] Katey had acquired something of a reputation amongst London circles for having affairs prior to Collins's death, so Georgina welcomed her marriage to the 'sensible, good, honourable and upright' Perugini.[105] If Katey was pregnant, she lost the baby, and the couple had a second, public marriage in June 1874, attended by Georgina, Mamie, Harry, Frank and the artist John Millais. Katey suffered another miscarriage at the end of 1874 but was pregnant again by spring the following year. Despite being on good terms with her mother, Katey asked Georgina to attend the birth of her son and always turned to her when she was ill. Despite Georgina being unable to manage her own finances, Katey relied on her aunt to hold money on her behalf. A married woman was not allowed to have a bank account in her own name and as Carlo Perugini did not want to have the money Katey received from Dickens's estate signed over to him, Georgina was able to help. As a single woman, Georgina, together with Henry Dickens and John Millais, opened a joint bank account and were able to withdraw funds on Katey's behalf.[106]

Katey grew into a very different woman to her mother and aunt. She wrote notes for a lecture in 1920 called 'On Women Old and New' in which she criticised the narrow, mundane existences that Victorian middle-class women were forced to live, and she took to task women who meekly complied. Apparently including her mother and aunt as part of her analysis, she condemned the ploys they adopted to get around men's edicts, rather than challenging them directly. Katey developed a close friendship with Jane Carlyle and shared her views on the unfairness of women's position in society. Yet although Katey was forward thinking and sympathetic to the challenges faced by women, she does not appear to have considered how these constraints affected the unmarried Georgina. She was always more circumspect about Aunty Georgy than her sister and brothers were. When she discovered that Georgina had criticised her for being intolerant towards Harry's wife, when in truth it was Georgina who was being far more judgemental, Katey justifiably observed that 'Aunty was not quite straight, and I often stood up to her; *that* is why she called me "intolerant"'.[107] An elderly Georgina dined with the Peruginis once a week, arriving in a cab, dressed in her finery with rings on every finger. A set of little stool steps were placed at the carriage door to help the very plump seventy-five-year-old descend to the pavement.

Little is known about how attached Frank and Sydney were to Aunty Georgy. Sydney, the seafaring fifth son, got himself into so much debt that Dickens banned him from returning to Gad's Hill when he came ashore. Dickens told another son, Alfred, 'I fear Sydney is much too far gone for recovery and I begin to wish that he were honestly dead'.[108] Sydney gave his official home address as 70 Gloucester Crescent, his mother's home. When he arrived back in England six months after his father's death, seeing how wretched and repentant he was, Georgina felt sorry for him. Sydney died at sea in 1872, prompting Georgina to recall tender memories of him as 'the sweetest little child'. However, her grief was channelled through the lens of Dickens's anger with his son for running up debts, and she told Annie Fields, 'I fear we *must* feel that his being taken away early is the most merciful thing that could have happened to him – but it was very, very sad to have to feel this'.[109]

Frank had been serving in the Bengal Constabulary for seven years when he came back to London for a six-month leave in 1871. Like Sydney, he apparently chose to base himself with his mother as Georgina noted rather disconsolately, '[w]e don't *see* very much of him – he seems affectionate and pleased to see us when we do – but I don't think he cares much about any one'.[110] Frank was one of her nephews who had angered Georgina by saying that he did not wish to give any money to repurchase the writing chalet from Charley. Having received his inheritance, Frank started acting recklessly; he overstayed his leave of absence, gave up his position in the police and, when his sisters tried to help him find more work, he failed to attend appointments. His behaviour prompted Georgina to remark to Frederic Ouvry, 'I think he is mad – I really do'.[111] Frank disappeared from sight and was found by the family in 1874, poor and apologetic. He was around long enough to give Katey away at her second wedding. With Mamie's connections, he obtained an appointment in the Northwest Mounted Police, and Georgina, together with his brothers and sisters (with the exception of Charley), advanced him money to get him started on his new life in Canada. The last mention Georgina made of Frank was in 1875, describing how well and happy he was in his job. There are no surviving letters from Georgina around the time Frank died in 1886, making it impossible to gauge the state of their bond.

Forty-five years after he left England, Georgina saw Alfred again. He was on a lecture tour of Australia, Europe and America, giving readings on his father's life and works. Due to her ill health, Georgina was unable to travel to hear him speak. Alfred had endeared himself to Aunty Georgy by asking Ouvry shortly after Dickens's death whether he needed to provide financial support for Georgina and Mamie from his share of the estate. Both Alfred and Plorn, the 'Australian boys', as she called them, willingly contributed to repurchasing the writing chalet and helped provide a fund for their Aunt Letitia.

Plorn was still a minor at the time of Dickens's death, but he decided not to return to England, eventually getting over his crippling homesickness and marrying in Australia. Georgina wrote warm letters to him, including one saying she wanted to send him a wedding present that 'will last for ever, and be always in your house, as a remembrance of the "Aunty" and friend who loves you with all her heart'.[112] Another letter was uncharacteristically open about the Hogarth family finances, possibly because her struggling brothers, William and James, were also in Australia and were no doubt in contact with their equally cash-strapped nephews.

Georgina and Harry were always close. She adored him and, despite her initial reservations, it was the once much-criticised Marie Dickens who was kinder to Georgina than any of her nieces. Georgina had seemed resentful of Marie's relationship with Harry and looked for reasons to fault her: as well as blaming Marie for the seven children she and Harry had in quick succession, Georgina accused her of being over-sensitive about her children's health and fussing too much over them. In time, though, she began to rely on the kind and caring Marie. Despite coping with a large and busy family, Marie arranged for Georgina to live with them when she was ill, included her in family holidays and would collect her in her carriage to take her round London for afternoon calls on friends. Harry, together with Marie and their children, turned out to be the most loving of the Dickens siblings towards Aunty Georgy, not only watching over her but also loaning her money.

In a letter to Harrison Ainsworth's youngest daughter, Georgina expressed surprise to find 'I shall be 81! Next week! *That* sounds a formidable age! And it seems to me incredible that I should be so old! I don't feel it – in my *mind* at all!'[113] Georgina was safe in the knowledge that Dickens's legacy was well established. She had witnessed the establishment of the Boz Club in 1900, followed two years later by the Dickens Fellowship, of which Georgina was made an honorary fellow. The Charles Dickens' Birthplace Museum was established in 1903 and *The Dickensian* journal in 1905. On a personal level, she was far less fortunate and making ends meet was a constant problem. Georgina did her best to remain solvent by selling many of her treasured Dickens mementos. Walter Spencer, a bookshop owner, described how in 1906: '[S]he began to send her maid to my shop once or twice a week with Dickens relics, a practice she followed for eight or nine years. Sometimes I purchased from her to the extent of £40 in a week.'[114]

Despite selling items and receiving loans from her nephew Harry and her friend Jane Pym, Georgina's finances continued to deteriorate. In 1910, she left her elegant home in Egerton Terrace and moved to a small flat above a shop at 64A Kenway Road, Earls Court, with a maid, Ellen Andrew (Emma Durnford having long retired). In her eighty-fourth year, Georgina had cataracts in both eyes that hampered her reading and prevented her writing her once-monthly letters to Annie. The following year, she was diagnosed with breast cancer and had a mastectomy. She accrued huge medical bills and was forced to part with the manuscript of *The Cricket on the Hearth*, left to her by John Forster, which she had hoped to pass on to Harry. The script sold for £1,000, but her medical bills by then were £800 and rising. She retreated again into Harry and Marie's care, but only for a short period. While clearly vulnerable and experiencing increasing periods lost to dementia, Georgina insisted on having her own establishment. In 1916, she rented a small, neat, two-storey house at 72 Church Street, Kensington.

Georgina's senility had been causing concern to the family from around 1913 because, predictably, some people were willing to capitalise on her frailty. After Ellen Andrew, Georgina had a maid who took advantage of her helplessness. Harry once arrived at his aunt's to find unprincipled dealers in the house, about to take away valuable possessions.[115] No one could be certain how much more the maid had managed to sell off before she was caught. Katey described how Georgina would stand by the window, bowing to an imagined Lord Kitchener or convinced that fighting was going on outside her house. Dickens, too, occupied many of her delirious outbursts. Gladys Storey described how,

> in her times of unconsciousness she would rave about C.D. and K[ate] P[erugini] prays that she may not go so out of her mind for fear of *lifting* lifting the veil of truth ... Coming out of a stupor Georgina said "Tell me, my child, is it a boy or a girl?"[116]

It is unclear whether Storey's duplication and emphasis of the word 'lifting' indicates that she wondered whether there was any truth in rumours of an illicit relationship between Georgina and Dickens. Any suspicion Storey had of Georgina's place in Dickens's affections was an echo of the doubts that continued to be associated with her name. On joining the Dickens Fellowship, Walter Dexter describes being 'rather surprised, and very interested, to see' Georgina Hogarth sitting alongside the Dickens family at a birthday dinner in 1905 as he, 'in common with many people of the time', had long assumed that 'it was she who was the cause of the estrangement between Dickens and his wife!'[117]

It was Marie Dickens who was with Georgina when she died, aged ninety, in the evening of 19 April 1917, having suffered a stroke eight days earlier. Her death certificate listed cause of death as arterio-sclerosis (hardening of the arteries) and 'senectus' or old age. The sofa from Gad's Hill on which Dickens had died was one possession Georgina could never bring herself to sell, and she left it in her will to the Dickens' Birthplace Museum. Katey inherited Georgina's jewellery and share in the copyright of *The Charles Dickens Letters*, and the manuscript of *The Life of Our Lord* was bequeathed to Harry. She left a cryptic message to Harry: 'I hope that it may be possible for him to carry out the wishes expressed in any memorandum prepared by me or on my behalf that may be found among my papers at my death'.[118] Presumably there was also something in the memorandum mentioning her niece, May. Her estate was valued at £317 (£23,400).

Georgina was buried in Mortlake Cemetery near to the plot in which Charley Dickens lay. The epitaph on her gravestone, chosen by Katey and Harry, reads 'In loving memory of Georgina Hogarth. "Aunty"'. At the very bottom, under the dates of her birth and death, is 'Sister-in-law of Charles Dickens'. If Georgina had been allowed a say, the designations would have been the reverse as she always proudly defined herself, first and foremost, by her relation to Dickens. In the days following the passing of her 'dearest Charles', Georgina offered up a rare insight into her thoughts on her position in the Dickens household. She admitted it was not easy and that she had to put up with much that made her life difficult. Even so, she would have had it no other way.

> *My* comfort is now in the feeling that I would not give up *a day of the past* ... My life has been a curious one – and not the ideal of a happy woman's existence – and I have often felt it hard – and wondered whether it was *all* a mistake – and a waste! *Now* I feel that with all its difficulties and drawbacks, I would not change it – I would not have it altered for the brightest and most prosperous existence any woman could have had'.[119]

Chapter 10

Aftermath

Georgina is acknowledged today as Dickens's companion, confidante and housekeeper.[1] Yet, despite their close and varied friendship, outside the world of Dickens scholars her name rarely comes up other than in relation to the collapse of the Dickenses' marriage. There was a period in the twentieth century when she was pigeon-holed as either an impressionable devotee or a shrewd and self-centred woman; to the present day, guides at the Charles Dickens Museum continue to be asked, 'Did Dickens have an affair with his sister-in-law?' Her unsisterly behaviour towards Catherine suggests someone who was capable of betrayal. Even the descendants of Dickens have wondered whether there was something in the gossip. In 2011, Lucinda Hawksley, Dickens's great-great-great granddaughter, remembers as a young girl being told by an aunt that Dickens had had an affair with Georgina: 'It was one of those stories handed down in the family. She said Georgina was his mistress and I remember asking my father what that meant.'[2] Given that no one amongst Dickens's set of friends suggested they believed he was physically attracted to, let alone had a sexual relationship with, Georgina, it is surprising how long the rumours have lasted. The assumption that Dickens and Georgina were sexually intimate is often accepted as fact by those who should know better. In 2005, an expert on the BBC *Antiques Roadshow* programme confirmed that the buttons from Dickens's smoking jacket were genuine because

215

they were accompanied by 'a letter of provenance signed by Georgina Hogarth, his wife's sister, his mistress'.[3]

The longevity of the gossip about an affair is partly due to Charley Peters (aka 'Hector Charles Bulwer Lytton Dickens'), a man who alleged he was the son of Dickens and Georgina. In 1908 Harry Dickens had been contacted by the Society for the Protection of Children based in Calcutta (Kolkata), asking if he could verify the identity of 'Hector Charles Bulwer Lytton Dickens'. The man, 'Hector Dickens', had approached the society asking for money to help support his son, supposedly the grandson of Charles Dickens and Georgina Hogarth.

According to Hector, he was born in 1854 and Georgina brought him to Gad's Hill in 1857, the year before the Dickenses separated. His story was accompanied by claims that Catherine had erupted at the discovery of her husband and sister's illegitimate child and left home. Dickens had, apparently, wanted to marry Georgina but the laws of incest forbade it. Hector went on to say that when Dickens died, the rest of the family turned Georgina and her son out of Gad's Hill. He claimed that when he was sixteen, he travelled to Australia, where he met up with his 'half-brothers', Alfred and Plorn. Maintaining they had known each other since their days at Gad's Hill, Hector argued that the Dickens boys naturally accepted him as a stepbrother as they knew about his 'father's' relationship with his 'mother'. After reacquainting himself with his Dickens brothers, Hector married, had a child and moved his new family from Australia to India. Explaining that he was finding it difficult to look after his family, Hector had to resort to charity. The application he presented was accompanied by letters from various Australian notables who all believed 'Hector' was the badly treated, biological son of Dickens.

Harry instigated an investigation into this brother he had never heard of and hastily despatched a denial, along with supporting evidence, to the society in Calcutta (Kolkata). Harry wrote to B. W. Matz, editor of *The Dickensian*, 'It makes one's blood boil to think my dear revered old aunt should be made the subject of such a scandalous story.'[4] 'Hector Charles Bulwer Lytton Dickens', or rather Charley Peters, apparently succeeded in misleading the members of his own family since they reappeared at various times over future years to assert their place as long-lost relatives.

Charles Thomas Peters (born 1854) was a bootmaker living in Melbourne, Australia at the same time as Dickens's son Alfred. Little is known about Alfred Dickens in the late 1880s other than that he married for a second time in 1888 and was having significant financial difficulties. Alfred's auctioneering business collapsed as a consequence of the failure of the banks and he lost all his financial investments. Looking for ways of raising money, he decided to give readings of his father's work and may also have sold off some of his personal possessions (the boys were given family keepsakes when they left home). Alfred had already auctioned his household goods before leaving the town of Hamilton and moving two hundred miles to Melbourne.

Charley Peters claimed to have a ring given by the poet Tennyson to Dickens, which he had bought in 1890 from his alleged half-brother, Alfred.[5] Peters seems to have been sufficiently acquainted with knowledge about Alfred's home life in England to have concocted the story he was to tell eighteen years later – that he, Charley, was the illegitimate son of Georgina and Dickens. Peters moved to Townsville, North Queensland, in 1896 and took the relocation as an opportunity to change his name to 'Hector Charles Bulwer Lytton Dickens'.

Three years later, in 1899, twenty-four-year-old Edith Vernon arrived in Townsville on an assisted passage from Gloucester, England. She began the journey giving her occupation as servant but, by the time she arrived in Townsville, had changed it to nurse. We do not know if Edith's willingness to reinvent herself meant she knew that the man she married in 1900 as 'Hector Dickens' was once Charley Peters or whether he deceived her. Whichever it was, the descendants of the couple seemed genuinely convinced they were a branch of the Dickens family. Edith was pregnant when she and 'Hector' married and, after giving birth to a son, whom they called Charles Tennyson Dickens, they remained in Townsville until 1905.

The Peters family emigrated to Calcutta (Kolkata), India, and it was here in 1908 that 'Hector' applied to the Society for Protection of Children for financial assistance. During the early 1920s he was managing the Goodwood Hotel in Simla, but by 1924 was making his way back to England. An inventory of his family possessions in 1924 included a gold watch, purportedly a gift from Plorn, and a tie pin he alleged had belonged to Walter. There is no evidence of what happened to these items or anything to support their authenticity. However, in 1862, Walter had sold off anything of value in Calcutta (Kolkata) to pay his debts just before his death, so his possessions were on the open market. Charley Peters' ownership of these family keepsakes suggest that he had set about amassing as many items as he could afford to support the claim he was related to Dickens. Peters eventually returned to England, residing with his wife's niece and dying in Bournemouth in 1932, aged seventy-eight, using the name of 'Charles B. L. Dickens'. His son, Charles Tennyson Dickens, married in India in 1920 and, together with his wife Elsie Evans, relocated to Durban, South Africa, where they remained for the rest of their lives.

It was the relatives of this family that attracted media attention in 2009 when they put the Tennyson–Dickens ring up for auction. Georgina's reputation was again impugned with headlines declaring '"Proof" that Dickens fathered illegitimate child to be auctioned'.[6] In 2011, to resolve the ongoing claim of 'Hector Dickens's' family that they were related through Georgina and Dickens, Mark Dickens and his cousin took DNA tests which decisively proved there were no links.[7] Yet, there may be more still to discover about 'Hector Dickens's' endeavours to link his family to Charles Dickens.

In 2017 a portrait of Dickens by Margaret Gillies was discovered in a box of bric-a-brac from a house contents sale in Pietermaritzburg (less than fifty miles from Durban where 'Hector's' son and his wife had lived). Painted in 1843, the portrait had disappeared without trace. Initially, it had remained in the ownership of the artist, but Margaret Gillies was unable to say what had happened to it after 1846. How it ended up in South Africa is a mystery. Investigations by art historians have offered one possible explanation.[8] Lawrence Hendra, one of the art historians looking into the painting, suggests Gillies may have given it to her adopted daughter. Hendra goes on to propose that, in the mid-1860s, Gillies's daughter sent the portrait to her brothers-in-law, Thornton and Herbert Lewes, who were then seeking their fortunes in South Africa. Having fallen on hard times, the Lewes brothers may have either sold or given the picture of the famous novelist away. In the absence of any more information, Lawrence Hendra had to leave the matter there. However, in researching this book and having tracked Charley Peters and his son from Townsville, Australia, to Durban, South Africa, another possibility arises. Having read 'Hector's' handwritten inventory of Dickens keepsakes, it is clear he was taking every opportunity to buy up Dickens family memorabilia. On that basis I want to offer two alternative and equally speculative explanations as to how the missing portrait ended up in South Africa.

After Margaret Gillies lost sight of the painting in 1846, it may have come into Dickens's possession and he could have given it to either Sydney, Alfred or Plorn as a family memento when the boys left home in the 1860s. All three sold off their belongings to raise money to pay their debts wherever they were in the world. Alfred and Plorn sold their belongings in Australia while Sydney's naval career took him all over the world, including to West Africa and India (although he was probably too ill to disembark here). It could well have been another item that Charley Peters purchased in a sale in his bid to authenticate his Dickens heritage.

A second explanation involves Richard H. Horne, the journalist for *Household Words* who angered Dickens and W. H. Wills in 1852 when he abandoned his wife to make his fortune in Australia.

Horne took money from Dickens and Wills to cover the costs of the trip and asked for his earnings for articles sent back from Australia for *Household Words* to be paid to his wife, Kate. Assuring Kate he would send for her once he settled, he wrote only one article, thereby leaving her financially unsupported. His willingness to abuse the kindness of Dickens, Wills and his wife makes him a rather questionable character. Before his marriage, Horne spent the year 1846 living with Margaret Gillies and her sister Mary in their Highgate house. He regarded Mary Gillies as his 'oldest and truest friend'.[9] Indeed, Kate moved in with the Gillies sisters for a time after Horne left and, despite his treatment of his wife, Mary Gillies remained fond of him. Perhaps Horne was given, or had appropriated, the portrait of Dickens when he moved out of the Gillies sisters' home to marry Kate in 1847. He might have taken the painting with him when he emigrated to Australia, settling in Melbourne and selling it when money became tight before he returned to London in 1869. It is not unrealistic to suggest that, at some point, 'Hector' bought the small portrait in a sale in Melbourne, which he passed on to his son and daughter-in-law when they moved to South Africa. This is undoubtedly a questionable speculation but no more so than the version of the painting being acquired by two men who were not acquainted with the then still living author.

The DNA test taken by Mark Dickens and his cousin established that Georgina and Dickens were not parents to 'Hector', but this fact is unlikely to prevent ongoing media conjecture about whether they had an affair. Nor can confirmation of Georgina's innocence rectify the impression given in many twentieth-century biographies that, at best, she occupied a minor place in Dickens's life or, at worst, she tried to manipulate her sister and brother-in-law.

After the death in 1933 of Dickens's last surviving child, Harry, there was no one left of the original Dickens family able to comment on the character of their 'dear Aunt Georgina' and her role in the household.[10] Polarised opinions of her appeared over the years.

Aftermath

Following Georgina's demise in 1917, a warm tribute was paid in *The Dickensian* recalling her as 'kind-hearted, gentle, amiable and attractive to all with whom she came in contact … Cheerful and bright always, she was loved by all, young and old, who knew her.'[11] It is no surprise that kind words were expressed on her passing, but the impression of Georgina as a pleasant, good-hearted woman was evident before then. In the 1870s, a female American journalist who got to know Georgina well said she was 'one of the best of women' and, in 1882, a newspaper reporter referred to her as the 'charming Miss Hogarth'.[12] Even at the time of the marital separation in 1858, friends of Catherine who were vehemently opposed to Dickens spoke cordially of Georgina, referring to her as 'good and faithful', and an 'excellent aunt'.[13] Her great-nephew remembered the elderly Georgina as 'a dear, sweet, Victorian, kind-hearted, charming lady. She was quite incapable of spite and I am absolutely certain that she was incapable of doing anybody any unkindness.'[14]

There was, though, acknowledgement of another side to Georgina. An editor of *The Dickensian* recalled visiting Georgina in 1913 at her home at 72 Church Street when he was a boy. He describes meeting 'a little old lady in a quaint lace cap, with twinkling eyes', but his question about whether Dickens based the character of Agnes Wickfield in *David Copperfield* on her 'arouse[d] a little asperity'.[15] A sharp-tongued Georgina was observed at a train station after she had spent the weekend at Horace and Jane Pym's Foxwold home. A fellow guest, the author Thomas Anstey Guthrie, was with Georgina awaiting the return train to London when a local businessman approached her asking about the Druce case. This was a ridiculous lawsuit being taken through the courts where the deceased Lord Portland was accused of leading a double life as Thomas Druce, the co-owner of a London upholstery firm. The claimants alleged that Dickens was a witness to this subterfuge. According to Anstey Guthrie, the man at the station 'bustled up to her importantly' and in a hectoring tone demanded, 'Well, Miss

Hogarth, what about this Druce case eh? Think your friend Charles Dickens knew anything of it?' Noting that 'Miss Hogarth was not at all given to bristling, but she bristled on that occasion', Georgina snapped back, 'He was my brother-in-law', adding, 'these people's stories are all lies'.[16] On the whole, people who had met or knew Georgina gave the impression that she was generally a decent person but not the meek, self-sacrificing saint of Dickens's letters and public statements.

In the late 1920s, depictions of Georgina as a weak and featureless devotee began to appear in biographical accounts of Dickens's life. None of the authors suggested they had spoken to people who knew Georgina; consequently it is difficult to understand where this view of her came from. Perhaps Dickens's eulogising of Georgina gave writers the idea that such a paragon of virtue must be bland, even vacuous. Carl Bechhofer Roberts's novelised account of Dickens's life, *This Side Idolatry* (1928), depicts Georgina as 'all admiration and compliance, "tittering" dutifully at her adored brother-in-law's facetiousness'.[17] Six years later, Hugh Kingsmill in *The Sentimental Journey: A Life of Charles Dickens* (1934), describes Georgina as a weak person 'magnetised by Dickens's self-pity' and taken advantage of by Dickens, who used 'his sense of power to exploit an unmarried woman's instinct of self-sacrifice'.[18]

A completely opposite view of Georgina, but one which proved equally as dominant, emerged in Gladys Storey's *Dickens and Daughter* (1939). Based on Storey's conversations with her friend Katey Dickens, Georgina is shown as far from vacuous. The relationship between Dickens and Georgina was discussed directly: 'at one period it was an outside opinion that he was in love with her; that opinion was purely supposition; though there is no doubt she possessed a great love for him'.[19] Katey spoke of Aunty Georgy as a reliable, integral member of the family but evidently harboured doubts about her trustworthiness and was especially indignant about her disloyalty to Catherine. Stressing that Georgina was helpful to Catherine, 'but that was all', Katey was particularly upset by the memory of how Georgina, together with Forster and her father, shut her mother out from any discussions to do with the house or the children.[20] Any misgivings were confirmed when, after Georgina's death, Katey bought a letter at auction sent by Aunty Georgy to Plorn. The letter had been written just before Harry's marriage to Marie Roche. Prior to sending this letter, Georgina had written to Annie Fields expressing her worries about Marie's Catholicism. In the missive to Plorn, Georgina repeated her reservations about Marie but, rather than acknowledging these were her views, she named Katey as the one to have had doubts and implied these were not shared by all family members. The reservations Katey harboured about Aunty's perfidy may explain why she blamed Georgina for events which were not of her doing. Storey records that, after the separation when the Dickens boys were despatched to various parts of the world, '[m]embers of the family attributed this exodus of his sons to the influence of their aunt, Georgina Hogarth'.[21] Storey decided that Katey was criticising her aunt unfairly, arguing that, although Georgina was 'clever and wise', the accusation 'she was the actual cause for his sending his sons away came not from his [Dickens's] lips'.[22] Storey had a point: Dickens was hardly likely to be dictated to by Georgina or anyone else. Besides, as Dickens explained to Fred Lehmann, he was 'afraid to keep my boys about London' because 'I am afraid of their spoiling one another', so if he 'could get [them] abroad therefore, I should prefer it much'.[23]

Unsurprisingly, the next generation of biographers seized on the comments from Katey which hinted at a less saintly Georgina. As mentioned earlier, in the mid-1890s Thomas Wright had incurred Georgina's wrath when she heard that he proposed to disclose Dickens's relationship with Nelly. Wright delayed publication of *The Life of Charles Dickens* (1936) until three years after Harry's death. Adopting a similar stance to Gladys Storey, Wright saw Georgina's intentions during the run-up to the Dickenses' marital separation 'as certainly good' and she was 'perfectly correct as to her moral conduct' but that she deliberately 'shuts her eyes to the mistake she is making in permitting herself to take the place in the home which was rightly Mrs. Dickens and which Mrs. Dickens most certainly desired to retain'.[24] After Wright's biography, there was a series of scathing assessments of Georgina's character and motivations.

Gender stereotyping in the 1950s predicted that single women would become sour and unfulfilled, and without a husband and children they would turn into self-centred, cold, ruthless characters. Georgina was cast in all these roles. According to Una Pope-Hennessy in *Charles Dickens* (1945), Georgina was 'planting ideas in Dickens's head about blocking doors in the bedroom', had 'Mamey and Katey under her thumb' and 'levered the mother of her nephews and nieces out of the house of which she remained the permanent and apparently satisfied inmate'.[25] Four years later, Hesketh Pearson's book painted a picture of a sexually jealous woman, embittered towards Catherine and Nelly, and even resenting Dickens for casting her in a 'virtuous part' when she had the responsibilities of a household without the 'pleasures of marriage'.[26] In *Charles Dickens and His Family* (1956), W. H. Bowen decided after studying the Maclise sketch of Dickens, Catherine and the sixteen-year-old Georgina, that she looked 'impersonal' and 'acquiescent' and lacked the 'understanding and … sympathy that are the bedrock of a mother's strength and power'.[27] A cool-headed Georgina who made the decision not to marry, preferring 'her life as the effective mistress of Dickens's household' and, for that reason 'can hardly be classed as a victim', appears in Felix Aylmer's *Dickens Incognito* (1959).[28] Alongside the biographies were Hebe Elsna's fictionalised narratives, *Consider These Women* (1952) and *Unwanted Wife: A Defence of Mrs. Charles Dickens* (1963). As a reviewer of *Unwanted Wife* pointed out, since the publication of Thomas Wright's book, the characterising of a 'scheming Georgina Hogarth' had been 'taken up and embroidered by numerous biographers' and she was personified as 'cold-blooded, ambitious and dominating both her sister and brother-in-law'.[29] Writing against the tide of opinion of Georgina as a manipulator was Edgar Johnson, who pointed out, 'there is no evidence for depicting her as a scheming intriguer and Kate [Catherine Dickens] as her helpless victim'.[30]

In complete contrast to the vilification of Georgina was Arthur Adrian's *Georgina Hogarth and the Dickens Circle* (1957). In Adrian's telling of Georgina's life, an amiable young girl becomes a sweet-natured, devoted young woman, then a warm-hearted, caring aunt and friend, and finally a 'guardian of the beloved memory'. Yet, in presenting Georgina as the absolute opposite of the image created in Dickens biographies of this period, Adrian denied any sense of her as a human being with desires, fears and opinions. It was not until the publication of Michael Slater's *Dickens and Women* (1983) that Dickens's relationship with Georgina received a more considered contextual analysis. Slater recognised that Georgina's 'choice' to remain with Dickens was not determined by vindictiveness, jealousy or because she was too feeble to make a stand, but that financial need, personal emotions and enjoyment of a privileged lifestyle all played a part. Subsequent Dickens biographers have followed Slater's interpretation, and twenty-first-century authors present a Georgina who is neither saint nor sinner but one who could be charming but also sharp; an efficient housekeeper, but within limits.[31] While acknowledging that Georgina had a certain element of freedom as a single woman in comparison to the married Catherine, it was still restricted. Unless the constraints of an unmarried, financially dependent, middle-class, middle-aged Victorian woman are acknowledged, discussing Georgina's actions at the time of the Dickenses' separation as a 'decision' or 'choice' attributes her with an autonomy she did not possess.

Despite feminist scholarship which points to the restrictions on women's lives imposed by Victorian gender roles, contemporary historians and literary biographers have often found it difficult to sympathise with Georgina's position. That said, the person who presented Georgina in a particularly negative light is Georgina herself. Her letters to Annie Fields, made available to the public in 1944, together with those Georgina wrote to Percy Fitzgerald and her correspondence to the Pyms, include several snippy comments about friends and family.[32] Georgina was, though, not the only family member who occasionally made harsh observations. The only defence that can be made of Georgina's inclination to adopt a judgemental tone is that she appears to have generally confined it to her correspondence. Hans Christian Andersen, himself a difficult character, is the one person on record who experienced and complained of a brusque Georgina.

In the 1990s Georgina was again implicated in a controversy. The paperback edition of Claire Tomalin's *The Invisible Woman* included a postscript featuring information that had come to light regarding Dickens's death. Tomalin was approached by J. C. Leeson, who told her that, in 1872, his great-grandfather, Reverend J. Chetwode Postans, had been minister of Linden Grove Congregational Church, located opposite Ellen Ternan's home, Windsor Lodge, in Peckham. The church caretaker had, for some reason, decided to disclose to the Rev. Postans the information that Dickens had been taken ill, not at Gad's Hill, but at another house nearby, 'in compromising circumstances'.[33] The allegation – that Dickens had a stroke while having sexual relations with Nelly – was made in 1959 when J. C. Leeson sent a letter to the *Sunday Times*. The newspaper chose to ignore it, probably because it sounded unconvincing. When Claire Tomalin learned of the report she decided 'it was a wild and improbable story, but not an entirely impossible one'.[34] Tomalin speculated about what might have happened if there was any truth in the tale, which involved Nelly sending Georgina a telegram to prepare her for the arrival of a carriage carrying a mortally sick Dickens. To do this, the assistance of several people would have been needed to load, then transport, a practically lifeless body twenty-seven miles, then unload and deposit Dickens on a sofa in the dining room. Georgina and Nelly would have had not only to deny a seriously ill Dickens immediate medical help in order to move him, but also to persuade the servants to maintain the elaborate ruse. Although Dickens scholars have given no credence to such an unlikely event, Michael Slater observed in *The Great Charles Dickens Scandal* that 'this more thrilling version of Dickens's death has caught the public's imagination and will continue … to run and run'.[35]

Slater's prediction has proved accurate. In *The Mystery of Charles Dickens* (2020), A. N. Wilson favours the more salacious description of the hours leading up to Dickens's demise. For Wilson, evidence of its authenticity is provided by the fact that Georgina reported to Frederic Ouvry that she had found only just over £6 when she went through the pockets of the clothes Dickens was wearing the day he collapsed. The mystery Wilson refers to here is that on the morning of Dickens's stroke, 8 June 1870, he had drawn a cheque for £22 at the Falstaff Inn, the public house on the opposite side of the road from Gad's Hill. Where had the rest of the money gone? Wilson argues that, after cashing the cheque, Dickens did not return to the writing chalet to continue with *Edwin Drood*, but took the train to Peckham and 'paid [Nelly] her housekeeping money – which would account for the substantial sum of more than £15 missing from his pockets'.[36]

There are several problems with this alternative version of Dickens's last day. Given the number of people who would have had to have known about the shocking treatment of one of England's greatest authors, it is impossible to believe it was kept quiet for nearly ninety years. Also, if Georgina had agreed with Nelly to produce a fabricated account of Dickens's stroke happening at Gad's Hill, then she would presumably have stuck exactly to their story. Instead, Georgina gave three slightly varying descriptions. She reported Dickens at dinner that evening starting to ramble and become incoherent. In one account Georgina refers to him wondering whether Macready's son was with him at Cheltenham, while in another she talks of him standing up suddenly from the dinner table and saying he had to go to London straightaway. In a third version, Georgina reports that Dickens was complaining of toothache.[37] Dickens probably made confusing mention of all of these and it was simply that Georgina did not recall everything when she retold the event to different people. As for the unaccounted £15, Georgina never suggested that she believed money to be missing, but merely reported to the solicitor what cash she had found on Dickens and how much was in the family purse. It may be that Georgina knew where the money had gone. Georgina told a friend that Dickens 'was doing accounts up to within half an hour of his fatal attack' and could have used some of it to help pay towards the wedding of the parlour maid (due to get married on 10 June) or given her a few pounds as a gift or left money in his desk for household bills.[38] None of these eventualities would Georgina have thought necessary to mention to Ouvry.

There remain aspects of Georgina's life with Dickens still to be discovered. In 1999, Sotheby's auction house sold 120 letters from Georgina to Charles Kent. A journalist and minor poet, Charles Kent met Dickens after his glowing review of *Dombey and Son* was printed in the *Sun* newspaper in 1846. The two men developed a firm friendship and Kent was a regular visitor to Gad's Hill. Charles Kent received one of the last letters Dickens wrote and, after 1870, he maintained a correspondence with Georgina spanning the next thirty years. The letters from Georgina to him were full of reminiscences about Dickens and reports of the lives of the Dickens children and, according to a person who read the correspondence, provided 'an untapped resource of biographical information'.[39] These letters were sold on 15 July 1999 at Sotheby's to Roy Davids Limited. The company was later wound up due to the ill health of the owner. When the Roy Davids Collection came up for sale at Bonhams in 2013 there was no trace of Georgina's letters. The trail has gone cold and it can only be hoped that one day these letters will re-emerge. While the loss of so many letters is regrettable, if anything can be learned from Georgina's cautiousness in her correspondence with her close female friend, Annie Fields, these letters were unlikely to contain any significant revelations.

Aftermath

Georgina's bank accounts contain two mysteries. The first mystery is the entries which simply say HIM. As the withdrawals are for the same amount of £5 (£650) and occur in February and June, the anniversaries of Dickens's birthday and death, they are most likely related to purchases or donations in his memory. The second mystery relates to large, regular payments made to two unknown women. In 1884, despite experiencing financial difficulties, Georgina began making two, sometimes three, payments a year to a Miss Goddard for amounts totalling anything from £14 (£1,900) to £45 (£6,000). These continued for seventeen years, until 1901. As the payments to Miss Goddard ceased, regular contributions to a Miss Elliott began but for smaller totals of between £12 (£1,500) to £26 (£3,400). It was possible to eliminate servants' wages, medical attendance or extravagant dressmaker bills. The only clue is the word 'exoro' against Miss Goddard's name for a 1901 entry. The translation from Latin means to beg successfully or obtain by entreaty, so it could be an invoice or equally a request for a charitable donation. The fact that the payments often include odd shillings and pence rather than rounded up to a whole amount seems significant in that this suggests bills rather than bequests. Walter Spencer in *Forty Years in My Bookshop* declared Georgina spent a great deal of money on flowers, but the amounts seem excessive if they were payments to a florist. Despite exhaustive research, this remains an intriguing puzzle.

Still to be resolved is the matter of Georgina's authentication cards and the sale of Dickens memorabilia. In 1870, when Georgina set about distributing Dickens's belongings to family, friends and others, she included a letter giving its history and place in Dickens's life. Over the years, as the initial recipients died and passed these mementos on, these letters have been used as provenance when the keepsakes were put up for sale. When Georgina found herself short of money she was forced to sell her own precious Dickens memorabilia. For each item she would provide an authentication card, written in her own hand, giving a short history of the item.

Walter Spencer maintained that Georgina began selling objects to him in 1906 and continued to do so until 1914–15. This latter date is questionable as Georgina was severely limited by her dementia at this point. His starting date is also uncertain as she was having significant money worries by 1900. Georgina was also offering items to Maggs Bros, antiquarian booksellers. It is strange that the accompanying authentication cards are all written on the same cardboard. Over such a long period, Georgina would be expected to have used different types of card.

It is not only the authentication cards that are a mystery. Some of the mementos accompanied by Georgina's official verification appear to be of a later date than the date she gave. For example, an object engraved with an 1840s date has silvermarks from the 1890s. One conclusion is that Georgina could not bear to part with the keepsakes from Dickens so she had copies made. It is not completely out of the question, as other members of the family were known to do something similar. In 1888, Horace Pym wrote to Georgina to see if she knew what had happened to the sundial that had stood in the grounds of Gad's Hill. Georgina replied:

> I suppose Charley sold it as he did most things! before he left the place! If he had taken care to sell things to people who would have a reverence for them I should not so much mind. But I fear he never troubled himself very much about that. I was obliged to tell Captain Budden [owner of Gad's Hill] that even the grave stone over 'little Dick' is *not* the original one![40]

The fact that Georgina was so annoyed with Charley Dickens suggests that she would never bring dishonour to Dickens's name by replacing originals with imitations. Also, when Georgina died in 1917 there was no evidence that she owned anything that had once belonged to Dickens, apart from his couch. On the other hand, she was desperate for money and this may have encouraged her to behave in ways she would once have thought unthinkable. The amount of Dickens memorabilia that she appeared to have had is astonishing, especially as she suggested to Annie Fields that most items were distributed immediately after Dickens's death. How then did she still own the large number of objects required that allowed her to offer something for sale to Walter Spencer once or twice a week for many years?[41] One possibility may be that she had been given some additional items by well-wishers such as Jane Pym. Horace Pym died in 1896 having amassed a considerable amount of Dickens memorabilia. Jane lent Georgina money and may have supplemented these loans with items from Horace's vast collection for her to use as she chose.

Another explanation is that Georgina's authentication cards were not always related to keepsakes she personally owned. Georgina was not the only woman amongst her friends to have money problems. Nelly Ternan's husband had a breakdown in 1886. They gave up the school they ran and struggled to manage on a small income. After George Wharton Robinson's death in 1910, Nelly's finances became even tighter. She must have owned jewellery, trinkets and other objects given to her by, or belonging to, Dickens, but for her to have provided authentication cards would have drawn attention and sparked gossip. However, her good friend Georgina could, and no doubt willingly would, provide the necessary verification – and who was to know if Nelly had a copy of the item made, to allow it to be sold twice over?

With few exceptions, Georgina has rarely generated any sympathy. Dickens's grandson described Georgina as a single 'ordinary mid-Victorian lady', which is not precisely accurate as she enjoyed many more privileges than others of her status because of her sister's marriage.[42] Her failure to defend Catherine is, understandably, one reason why so few biographers have recognised and commiserated with her predicament. Yet, it is also the case that the relationship with Dickens came with some significant costs. The fact that Dickens was a privileged man and Georgina a dependent woman in itself meant they were never going to experience a friendship of equals. Her intense personal investment in Dickens far outweighed his affection for her and Georgina was the one to make the necessary compromises to accommodate the way he wanted to be seen by the outside world.

Although I have emphasised the significance of the social and cultural context in assessing Georgina and Dickens's relationship, their characters of course played a part. From the moment Georgina joined the Dickens household, she was awestruck by 'men of genius' and especially Dickens. Like any teenage fan, she was absorbed in the life of her hero, but living with Dickens added another level of intensity. It was an intensity that she never grew out of. Georgina thrived and delighted in Dickens's tendency to overemphasise her wit, domestic skills and talents. While Dickens had a mercurial temperament, he was generally a kind person. If he realised the depth of Georgina's feelings for him (and how could he not?) then he would have tried to treat her with compassion, but his own needs would always take priority. The intelligent Georgina must have recognised that, in Dickens's life, Dickens would always put himself first, and that fact made her vulnerable. After Dickens's death, when Georgina no longer had to worry about the stability of his affections and her home, she emerged a more determined and outspoken character. Georgina's significance in Dickens's personal history is undeniable, as captured by a newspaper reporter in 1882 who, on seeing her at the Royal Academy, described her as, 'Miss Georgina Hogarth who years hence will be a personage in literary history, merely from the fact that she is the "Georgie" who was so beloved'.[43] Readers should make up their own minds as to how beloved she was as a sister and aunt, but to Dickens she was indeed the 'best and truest friend man ever had'.

Who's who

Abbreviations: C.D. = Charles Dickens; G.H. = Georgina Hogarth

Charles Dickens's family

Alfred Allen Dickens (1814–14): brother, died as a baby.

Alfred Lamert Dickens (1822–60): brother. Railway engineer. Married Helen Dobson in 1846, five children.

Alfred D'Orsay Tennyson Dickens (1845–1912): son. Station agent in Australia and later a lecturer. Married Jessie Devlin in 1873, two daughters. Married second wife, Emily Riley, in 1888.

Anna Delancey Dickens (*née* Weller) (1830–91): sister-in-law. Pianist and singer. Sister of Christiana Weller. Wife of Fred Dickens, from whom she obtained a judicial separation in 1858.

Augustus Newnham Dickens (1827–66): brother. Short-term jobs as newspaper editor, store owner, land manager. Married Harriet Lovell in 1848, deserted her by absconding to America with partner, Bertha Phillips.

Beatrice Dickens (1869–1937): granddaughter. Sixth child of Charles Culliford Dickens. Goddaughter of G.H.

Bertha Phillips Dickens (1829–68): common-law wife of Augustus Dickens, four children, two dying in infancy. Died of a morphine overdose on Christmas Eve 1868.

Bessie Dickens (*née* Evans) (1838–1907): daughter-in-law, wife of Charles Culliford Dickens. Seven daughters (Mary Angela (Mekitty), Ethel, Sydney Margaret, Dorothy, Beatrice, Cecil Mary) and one son, Charles. Her father was Fred Evans, who with his partner William Bradbury was Dickens's publisher from 1844 to 1858.

Catherine Dickens (*née* Hogarth) (1815–79): wife. Mother of ten children. Sister of G.H.

Charles (Charley) Culliford Dickens (1837–96): eldest son. Married Bessie Evans in 1861, to his father's displeasure as C.D. had fallen out with his daughter-in-law's father at the time of his separation from Catherine. Charley had seven daughters and one son.

Dora Dickens (1850–51): ninth child and youngest daughter.

Edward Bulwer Lytton (Plorn) Dickens (1852–1902): son. Station manager in Australia, later entered politics. Married Constance Desailly in 1880. No children.

Elizabeth Dickens (*née* Barrow) (1789–1863): mother.

Enid Dickens (later Hawksley) (1877–1950): granddaughter, eldest daughter of Marie and Henry Fielding Dickens. Married Ernest Hawksley.

Frances (Fanny) Dickens (later Burnett) (1810–48): sister. Pianist and singer. Married Henry Burnett in 1837, one son, Henry, who died a year after his mother.

Francis Jeffrey Dickens (1844–86): son. Served in mounted police in India and Canada.

Frederick Dickens (1820–68): brother. Clerk. Married Anna Delancey Weller in 1848 and separated from her in 1858.

Harriet Dickens (*née* Lovell) (1828–late 1880s): sister-in-law. Financially independent, wife of Augustus Dickens. Lost her sight after her marriage. Deserted by Augustus.

Helen Dickens (*née* Dobson) (1823–1915): sister-in-law. Wife of Alfred Lamert Dickens, five children.

Henry Charles Dickens (1878–1966): grandson, son of Henry Fielding Dickens. Barrister.

Henry (Harry) Fielding Dickens (1849–1933): son. Barrister, received a knighthood in 1922. Married Marie Roche in 1876, eight children.

John Dickens (1785–1851): father. Clerk in Royal Navy pay office. Married Elizabeth Barrow in 1809.

Katey Dickens (later Collins, later Perugini) (1839–1929): daughter. Artist. Married Charles Collins in 1860; after his death she married Charles (Carlo) Perugini in 1874 and they had a son who died at the age of seven months.

Letitia Dickens (later Austin) (1816–93): sister. Married Henry Austin in 1837.

Mamie Dickens (1838–96): eldest daughter.

Marie Dickens (*née* Roche) (1852–1940): daughter-in-law. Wife of Henry (Harry) Fielding Dickens, eight children.

Mary Angela (Mekitty) Dickens (1862–1948): granddaughter, eldest daughter of Charles (Charley) Culliford Dickens. Novelist and journalist.

Sydney Smith Haldimand Dickens (1847–72): son. Royal Navy officer.

Walter Landor Dickens (1841–63): son. Junior officer in the British Army.

Georgina Hogarth's family

Catherine Hogarth (later Dickens) (1815–79): eldest sister. Wife of C.D.

Edward Norris Hogarth (1833–79): youngest brother and twin of Helen Hogarth. Journalist. Married Matilda Howell in 1867.

George Hogarth (1783–1870): father. Lawyer, music critic and editor. Married Georgina Thomson in 1814, ten children.

George Hogarth (1821–41): older brother.

Georgina Thomson Hogarth (1793–1863): mother.

Helen Hogarth (later Roney) (1833–90): youngest sister and twin of Edward Hogarth. Music teacher and performer. Married Richard Cusack Roney in 1864, one daughter, May Roney.

James Ballantyne Hogarth (1825–76): older brother. Emigrated to Australia.

Mary Scott Hogarth (1817–18): older sister, died before G.H. was born.

Mary Scott Hogarth (1819–37): older sister. Close sisterly relationship with Catherine, adored by C.D.

Robert Hogarth (1816–43): older brother. Emigrated to Mexico, then worked in government service in Jamaica.

William Hogarth (1823–95): older brother. Emigrated to Australia and returned to London in 1870s.

May Roney (1865–1925): niece, daughter of Helen Hogarth. Chorister with D'Oyly Carte touring companies. Married William Leon.

Richard Cusack Roney (1840–68): brother-in-law, married to Helen Hogarth. Journalist.

Helen Thomson (1795–?): aunt. Older sister of Mrs Hogarth (Georgina Thomson Hogarth).

Friends, colleagues and others

Ainsworth, William Harrison (1805–82): popular novelist and great friend of C.D. in late 1830s and early 1840s. They had little to do with each other from the 1850s but his youngest daughter, Blanche Swanson, exchanged letters with G.H. in 1908.

Andersen, Hans Christian (1805–75): novelist. Great admirer of C.D. Stayed with G.H. and rest of Dickens family at Gad's Hill in summer 1857.

Austin, Henry (1812–61): brother-in-law of C.D., married Letitia Dickens in 1837. Civil engineer, who oversaw the building renovations at Tavistock House. He was later secretary of the first

Board of Health. Early suitor of Maria Beadnell and long-standing friend of C.D.

Austin, Letitia – *see* Letitia Dickens (in C.D. family section above)

Barrett Browning, Elizabeth (1806–61): poet. Married to Robert Browning. They were acquainted with C.D. Lived in Italy, knew Thomas Trollope. Robert exchanged several gossipy letters with novelist Isa Blagden about the Trollope/Ternan/C.D. relationships.

Beadnell, Maria (later Winter) (1810–86): daughter of a senior bank clerk. Spurned C.D.'s affections in 1832 and married Henry Winter in 1845. Inspired the characters of Dora Spenlow (*David Copperfield*) and Flora Finching (*Little Dorrit*).

Beard, Frank (1814–93): brother of Thomas Beard. Physician. Became C.D.'s doctor around 1858.

Beard, Thomas (1807–91): brother of Frank Beard. Journalist. Best man at wedding and lifelong friend of C.D.

Bentley, Richard (1794–1871): publisher of *Oliver Twist* in *Bentley's Miscellany*. C.D. was its first editor. The two men had a fractious relationship culminating in C.D. buying himself out of his contract and purchasing the copyright of *Oliver Twist*.

Bigelow, John (1817–1911): American lawyer and historian. Met C.D. in 1867. C.D. liked and sympathised with Bigelow, but disliked John's wife, Jane Bigelow, who stalked him in New York.

Blessington, Marguerite, Countess of (1789–1849): novelist and literary hostess. Controversially lived with her son-in-law, Count D'Orsay. Her niece was Marguerite Power, who often stayed for weeks at a time with G.H. at Gad's Hill and was one of the few friends C.D. introduced to Ellen Ternan.

Boyle, Mary Louisa (1810–90): writer, amateur actor, cousin of Lavinia Watson. Devoted to C.D. and great friends with G.H.

Brooks, Charles William Shirley (1816–74): succeeded Mark Lemon on his death in 1870 as editor of the satirical journal *Punch*.

Brown, Anne – *see* Cornelius, Anne.

Brown, Colin Rae (1821–97): journalist and publisher. He founded or edited several periodicals, including the *North British Daily Mail*, the *Daily Bulletin*, the *Scottish Banner* and the *Workman*. He was also a published poet.

Brown, Jane (*née* Wheeler) (1849–1920s?): trusted servant of Nelly Ternan and her mother from age of sixteen, then cook to G.H. Later returned to Nelly's service. Married William Brown in 1886.

Buckstone, John (1802–79): long-time friend of C.D. Actor, playwright, comedian, theatre manager.

Bulwer-Lytton, Edward (1803–73): successful novelist and playwright. Met C.D. in 1837 but developed a friendship in 1850. Attractive to women, G.H. was fascinated by him.

Burdett-Coutts, Angela (1814–1906): heiress and philanthropist. Good friend of C.D. Worked together on several projects, notably Urania Cottage. Friendship cooled when C.D. separated from Catherine.

Burnett, Henry (1811–93): brother-in-law of C.D., married Frances (Fanny) Dickens in 1837. Singer and musician.

Carlyle, Jane Welsh (1801–66): known for her letters and diaries. Married to C.D.'s good friend, Thomas.

Carlyle, Thomas (1795–1881): renowned historian. Married Jane Welsh in 1826.

Cerjat, William W. F. de (?–1869): friend of C.D. living in Switzerland.

Chorley, Henry (1808–72): literary, art and music critic. Friend of the Dickens family, particularly fond of Mamie, to whom he left a generous legacy in his will.

Christian, Eleanor Emma – *see* Picken, Emma.

Colden, Frances Wilkes (1796–1877): with husband David Cadwallader Colden hosted C.D. on first American tour.

Collins, Charles Allston (1828–73): son-in-law of C.D., married Katey Dickens in 1860. Younger brother of Wilkie Collins. Artist linked to Pre-Raphaelite Brotherhood.

Collins, Kate – *see* Katey Dickens (in C.D. family section above).

Collins, Wilkie (1824–89): novelist. Intimate friend of C.D. during the 1850s. Although relations cooled after his brother married Katey D, he remained friends with C.D. and G.H. until his death.

Cornelius, Anne (*née* Brown) (b. circa 1821): trusted maid to Dickens household from 1840. She established a friendship with Catherine Dickens and G.H. Later married Edward Cornelius and had a daughter she named Catherine Georgina Ann.

Cowden-Clarke, Mary (*née* Novello) (1809–98): writer, acted in Dickens's amateur productions, devotee.

Dallas, Eneas Sweetland (1828–79): Scottish journalist and author. He contributed to the *Daily News*, the London *Saturday Review*, the *Pall Mall Gazette* and the *World*.

de la Rue, Augusta (*née* Granet) (1810–97): married Emile in 1832. One son. Mesmerised by C.D. to cure various illnesses. C.D. was intrigued by her illnesses; she was fascinated by him.

de la Rue, Emile (1802–70): Swiss banker. Met the Dickenses in Genoa in 1844. Married to Augusta. One son.

Dobson, Helen – *see* Helen Dickens (in C.D. family section above).

Dolby, George (1831–1900): manager of Dickens's reading tours from 1866. Good friend and confidant of C.D. Wrote a memoir of their travels. A drinker and a spender, he died in a paupers' hospital.

D'Orsay, Count Alfred (1801–52): lived with his step-mother-in-law, the Countess of Blessington. His dandified appearance was emulated by Ainsworth, Dickens, Disraeli and Bulwer-Lytton. Moved to Paris in 1849 after being made bankrupt. He gave Catherine Dickens the serpent ring she later bequeathed to G.H.

Durnford, Emma (1833–1907): maid and companion to G.H. Joined Dickens household at Gad's Hill in 1866, left service sometime after 1901.

Egg, Augustus (1816–63): noted painter of literary and historical subjects. While at the Royal Academy formed 'The Clique' with fellow artists, William Powell Frith and Richard Dadds. From 1847 to 1857 he appeared in many of Dickens's amateur theatricals. Proposed to G.H. Married a solicitor's daughter in 1860.

Elliotson, John (1791–1868): physician to C.D. from early days of the Dickenses' marriage. Friend and godfather to Walter Dickens. Introduced C.D. to mesmerism. His love of novelty stretched the boundaries of acceptable medical research and resulted in him losing his post as head of University College Hospital.

Evans, Fred (1803–70): printer. Bradbury and Evans were C.D.'s printers from 1836 and publishers 1845–58. C.D. cut off all contact in 1858 when the publisher refused to print his statement on the end of his marriage. C.D.'s son Charley married Evans's daughter, Bessie, and C.D. refused to attend the wedding.

Faucit, Helen (later Helena Saville Faucit, Lady Martin) (1817–98): actress. William Macready's main leading lady 1836–45. Acquaintance of the Dickenses, often invited as a guest to the entertainments at their home. Married Ralph Martin in 1851.

Fechter, Charles Albert (1822–79): Anglo-French actor. Became friend of C.D. Gave the writing chalet as a gift to C.D. G.H. found him 'magnetic' but shallow and untrustworthy.

Fechter, Charlotte Eléonore Rabut (1819–94): minor actor. Married Charles Fechter in 1847, two children. Fechter was an unfaithful husband.

Felton, Cornelius (1807–62): president of Harvard University. C.D. and G.H. both regarded him as a friend. G.H. maintained contact with his daughter Mary Felton until the late 1870s.

Fields, Annie Adams (1834–1915): American writer. At the centre of Boston literary society with husband, James. Happily married but adored C.D. Hosted C.D. during second reading tour of America. Became good friends with G.H. and they corresponded for over forty years.

Fields, James (1817–81): C.D.'s friend and American publisher. Husband of Annie. Editor of the *Atlantic Monthly*.

Finlay, Frances Dalzell, Jr: editor of the Belfast newspaper *Northern Whig*, which he inherited from his father. Invited to stay at Gad's Hill, where he described a charming and convivial G.H. just hours before she had a physical breakdown.

Fitzgerald, Percy Hetherington (1834–1925): Irish lawyer, later writer. Friend of the Dickens family and G.H. A suitor for Mamie Dickens. G.H. fell out with him after he published an article making untrue claims about her sisters and C.D.

Forster, Eliza (previously Colburn) (*née* Crosbie) (1815–94): wife of John Forster. Previously married to the publisher Henry Colburn. Friend of G.H.

Forster, John (1812–76): C.D.'s adviser, literary executor, biographer and closest lifelong male friend. Married Eliza Colburn in 1856. G.H. too regarded Forster as a good friend and relied on him in the years following C.D.'s death.

Franklin, Eliza (later Trix) (1813–89): became friends with Catherine Dickens when the Hogarths moved to Exeter. Eliza was eighteen and Catherine sixteen. Eliza married John Trix, a chemist, in 1843.

Frith, Isabella (*née* Baker) (1823–80): wife of artist William Powell Frith. Good friend of Catherine. Ten children, including the writer Jane Panton.

Frith, William Powell (1819–1909): artist. Met C.D. when commissioned to paint Kate Nickleby and Dolly Varden.

Gaskell, Elizabeth (1810–65): novelist and regular contributor to *Household Words*. Initially had a warm friendship with C.D. but this soured due to a difficult working relationship.

Gillies, Margaret (1803–87): painter. Lived with sister, Mary, in north London. Painted portrait of C.D. in 1843.

Hargraves, Thomas (1850–1905): clergyman. Mamie Dickens left her home with G.H. in 1878 to live with him and his wife Marie Benyon Hargraves (1850–1927).

Holman Hunt, William (1827–1910): artist and a founder of the Pre-Raphaelite Brotherhood. Best man to Charles Collins on his marriage to Katey Dickens.

Horne, Catherine (Kate) Clare St George (*née* Foggo) (1826–93): wife of Richard Horne, married 1847. C.D. admired and helped support her after she was deserted by her husband. G.H. and Janet Wills oversaw the Horne Fund, set up to ensure she had an income.

Horne, Richard Hengist (1802–84): poet, journalist, author. Member of staff at *Household Words*. Took part in C.D.'s amateur theatricals. Deserted his wife and joined the Australian gold rush. Much disliked by G.H.

Humphrey, Maria (*née* Cubitt) (1828–97): niece of the builder Thomas Cubitt who worked on the renovations of Tavistock House for C.D. Married to William Humphrey. Great friend of Mamie Dickens.

Humphrey, Sir William Henry (1827–1909): Conservative politician, MP for Andover and High Sheriff of Hampshire 1872–3. Married to Maria Cubitt and lived at Penton Lodge, Hampshire.

Jerrold, Douglas (1803–57): dramatist, writer and journalist. Friend of C.D. since 1836. C.D. was instigator of the Douglas Jerrold Fund to raise money for the family after his death, although Jerrold's son insisted they did not need it.

Kent, Charles (1823–1902): writer and journalist. Friend and admirer of C.D. He exchanged many letters with G.H. in which she gave news of the family; the letters were sold at Sotheby's in 1999 but have since disappeared from public view.

Knight, Charles (1791–1873): author and publisher. Took part in at least one of C.D.'s amateur theatricals. Contributor to *Household Words*. On friendly terms with the Dickens family.

Leech, John (1817–64): illustrator. Contributor to *Punch*. Long-term friends with C.D. His family holidayed with the Dickenses.

Lehmann, Frederick (1826–91): businessman and liberal politician. Friend of Dickens family. Married to Nina Chambers.

Lehmann, Nina (*née* Chambers) (1830–1902): musician. Niece of Janet Wills. Married to Frederick. Great friends with Mamie Dickens.

Lemon, Mark (1809–70): playwright, first editor of *Punch*. Close family friend of the Dickenses. Acted on Catherine's behalf in separation, which ended friendship with C.D.

Lemon, Nelly (*née* Romer) (1817–90): married Mark in 1839. Talented amateur singer. Got to know the Dickenses in 1841. Two years later the families became intimate, living near each other and holidaying together. Like her good friend Catherine, she had ten children.

Linton, Eliza Lynn (1828–98): novelist, journalist, contributor to *Household Words* and *All Year Round*. On the death of her father, she inherited Gad's Hill, which she sold to C.D.

Longfellow, Henry Wadsworth (1807–82): American poet. Met C.D. on first visit to America in 1842. Visited C.D. in London and at Gad's Hill. G.H. always enquired after him and his family in her correspondence with Annie Fields, speaking of them as kind friends.

Maclise, Daniel (1806–70): artist. Lived with his family in Russell Place, Fitzroy Square, where his sister Isabella kept house for him. From 1837 to late 1840s he formed a trio with Forster as C.D.'s closest male friends.

Macready, Catherine Francis (*née* Atkins) (1806–52): professional actress before her marriage to William Macready. A good friend and confidante of Catherine Dickens. Had ten children.

Macready, Cecile Louise Frederica (*née* Spencer) (1827–1908): second wife of William Macready. C.D. and G.H. were godparents to their son Neville. Good friends with G.H.

Macready, William (1793–1873): actor. Long-time friend of C.D. and Georgina. Married first to Catherine Atkins and after her death, Cecile Spencer.

Martineau, Harriet (1802–76): social theorist, feminist, writer. Contributed series of articles to *Household Words* but only slight personal acquaintance with the Dickenses. She and C.D. had a public dispute in 1855–6 on industrial safety which arose from their differing understandings of liberalism.

Millais, Effie (previously Ruskin, *née* Gray) (1828–97): Married John Millais in 1855 following annulment of her first marriage to John Ruskin on the grounds of non-consummation. After death of C.D. and Millais, Effie and her family maintained a friendship with G.H.

Millais, John Everett (1829–76): artist. Became friends with C.D. in 1855. Mentored Katey Dickens's artistic ambitions. Sketched Dickens the day after he died.

Norton, Caroline (*née* Sheridan) (1808–77): novelist, wrote on rights of married women. Granddaughter of the playwright Richard Brinsley Sheridan. Separated from husband and had affair with Lord Melbourne. Enjoyed warm relations with C.D. and Catherine.

Olliffe, Laura (1823–98): daughter of William Cubitt, MP, niece of the builder Thomas Cubitt, sister of Maria Humphrey. Wife of Sir Joseph Olliffe (1808–69), physician to the British embassy in Paris.

Ouvry, Frederic (1814–81): C.D.'s solicitor from 1856, acted for G.H. from 1870.

Panton, Jane (*née* Frith) (1847–1923): writer. Daughter of Isabella and William Powell Frith. Sympathetic to Catherine Dickens's situation but also made kind comments about G.H.

Perugini, Charles Edward (1839–1918): Italian-born painter. Known by G.H. as Carlo, second husband of Katey Dickens.

Perugini, Kate – *see* Katey Dickens (in C.D. family section above).

Peters, Charley (1854–1932): changed his name around 1896 to Hector Charles Bulwer Lytton Dickens, later known as Charles Dickens the Younger. Attempted to extract money from charities by claiming he was the illegitimate son of C.D. and G.H.

Picken, Emma (1820–98): met C.D. and Catherine in 1840. Married Edward Christian in 1842. Wrote two articles on her recollections of the Dickenses in the late 1880s.

Powell, John Hill: sub-editor of the *Morning Chronicle* and editor of the *Evening Chronicle* in 1830s. Employed by C.D. as a sub-editor on the *Daily News* in 1846.

Power, Marguerite (1815–67): writer, poet and traveller. Niece of Marguerite, Countess of Blessington. Moved with her aunt and sister to Paris in 1849, later returning to England. One of the few people C.D. introduced to Ellen Ternan. Good friends with G.H. and a regular visitor to Gad's Hill.

Pym, Horace (1844–96): solicitor, book collector. Revered C.D. Became good friends with G.H.

Pym, Jane (*née* Fox) (1852–1912): second wife of Horace Pym. Close friend of G.H. and lent her money.

Robinson, Ellen (Nelly) – *see* Ternan, Ellen.

Robinson, George Wharton (1851–1910): clergyman and schoolmaster. Married Ellen Ternan in 1876 apparently unaware of the extent of her intimacy with C.D. His family holidayed with the Henry Dickens family and G.H. stayed at his house in Margate on several occasions.

Smith, Arthur (1825–61): C.D.'s reading tour manager in 1858 and 1861.

Smithson, Elizabeth (*née* Thompson) (1810–60): sister of T. J. Thompson. Married to Charles, business partner of C.D.'s friend and solicitor, Thomas Mitton. Friend of Catherine.

Stanfield, Clarkson (1793–1867): marine artist. Provided scenery for C.D.'s theatricals. Devoted friend to C.D.

Stanfield, Rebecca (*née* Adcock) (1808–75): actress prior to marriage. Second wife of Clarkson. Good friend of Catherine. Because of affection between Clarkson and C.D., she was one of the few supporters of Catherine who continued to be invited to Gad's Hill.

Swanson, Anne Blanche (*née* Ainsworth) (1830–1908): youngest daughter of William Harrison Ainsworth. Ainsworth's biographer, S. M. Ellis, put G.H. in contact with Blanche, whom she had not seen since the 1850s.

Tagart, Rev. Edward (1804–58): Unitarian minister at Great Portland Street when C.D. and G.H. worshipped in 1842.

Tagart, Helen (previously Martineau, *née* Bourn) (1797–1879): married second husband, Edward, in 1828 following death of her first husband, James Martineau, brother of Harriet. Introduced Elizabeth Gaskell to the Dickenses. Remained friends with Catherine after the separation.

Talfourd, Judge Thomas (1795–1854): radical politician and author. As an MP, he first introduced a copyright bill in 1837 (although a law was not passed until 1842) and served as Dickens's counsel in the suit that the author brought in 1844 against publishers who plagiarised his books.

Tennyson, Lord Alfred (1809–92): poet. Mutual admiration between Tennyson and C.D. However, G.H. was scathing of his acceptance of a peerage in 1883.

Ternan, Ellen (*née* Ternan) (1839–1914): actress. Met C.D. in 1857 and was financially supported by him from around this time. Married George Wharton Robinson in 1876. They had two children, Geoffrey and Gladys.

Ternan, Fanny – *see* Trollope, Frances.

Ternan, Mrs Frances (*née* Jarman) (1802–73): actress. Mother of Fanny, Maria and Ellen.

Ternan, Maria (later Taylor) (1837–1904): actress and journalist. Second daughter of Mrs Frances Ternan. Married son of a brewer, William Rowland Taylor in 1863, leaving him in 1873. Lived in Rome and travelled in North Africa.

Thackeray, Anne (later Ritchie) (1837–1919): writer. Eldest daughter of William Thackeray. Lifelong friends with Katey Dickens.

Thackeray, William Makepeace (1811–63): novelist. Ongoing spats with C.D. despite warmth between the families. Fond of Catherine and G.H. and eager not to be seen to be taking sides.

Thompson, Amelia (Millie) (1809–65): sister of Elizabeth Smithson and T. J. Thompson. Looked after her nieces following the death of their parents.

Thompson, Christiana – *see* Weller, Christiana.

Thompson, Thomas James (1812–81): inherited a considerable fortune. T. J. was a widower when he met and became friends with the Dickenses in 1837. Married Christiana Weller. Lived in Italy.

Touchet, Eliza Buckley (1792–1869): wife of James Touchet, William Harrison Ainsworth's second cousin. Following the death of her husband and Ainsworth's separation from his wife, she and her sister Anne went to live with him at Kensal Lodge.

Trollope, Frances (Fanny) (*née* Ternan) (1835–1913): novelist. Eldest daughter of Frances Ternan. Despite a twenty-five-year age-gap, she became second wife of Thomas Trollope in 1866. She and C.D. grew to dislike each other.

Trollope, Thomas (1810–92): writer, brother of writer Anthony Trollope. First wife died and he married his daughter's music teacher, Fanny Ternan. Introduced to each other by C.D.

Watson, Lavinia (*née* Quin) (1816–88): wife of Richard Watson (1800–52), MP for Peterborough. Cousin of Mary Boyle. Lived at Rockingham Castle. Met C.D. and G.H. in Switzerland in 1846. Trusted female friend of C.D.

Weller, Anna Delancey – *see* Anna Delancey Dickens (in C.D. family section above).

Weller, Christiana (1825–1910): pianist. C.D. was smitten on first meeting her but his ardour cooled when she married his friend, T. J. Thompson in 1845. Had two famous daughters, the artist Elizabeth Butler and the poet Alice Meynell.

Wheeler, Jane – *see* Brown, Jane.

White, Rosa (*née* Hill) (1805–82): inherited two farms in Bonchurch on the Isle of Wight. Married to Rev. James White (1803–62). Two daughters who both died of consumption. Good friend of G.H. G.H. frequently visited her for holidays when Rosa moved to Devon.

Wigan, Alfred (1814–78): actor-manager. Was managing the Olympic Theatre when Dickens approached him for recommendations for actresses for *The Frozen Deep*.

Wills, Janet (*née* Chambers) (1812–92): daughter of Edinburgh publisher Robert Chambers. Married William in 1846. They had no children. Was impatient with Catherine Dickens.

Wills, William Henry (1810–80): trusted assistant editor of *Household Words* and *All the Year Round* and good friend of C.D. Married Janet Chambers.

Winter, Maria – *see* Beadnell, Maria.

Yates, Edmund (1831–94): journalist and novelist. Contributor to *Household Words* and *All the Year Round*. Friend of C.D. Katey Dickens developed a teenage crush, despite the fact he was married. G.H. complained that his articles about C.D. were too gossipy.

Notes

References to *The Pilgrim Edition of the Letters of Charles Dickens* are abbreviated to *P*, followed by the volume number.

Introduction

1 The purchasing power equivalent today can be found at www.officialdata.org/UK-inflation (accessed 15 October 2022). Recent equivalent figures are rounded to the nearest £100.

2 Census returns for the Dickens household, 1861.

3 John Butt, 'Reviews: Georgina Hogarth and the Dickens Circle', *Review of English Studies*, 10:38 (1959), p. 207.

4 Pauline Simonsen, 'Elizabeth Barrett Browning's Redundant Women', *Victorian Poetry*, 35:4 (1997), p. 509.

5 Elizabeth Langland, 'Nobody's Angels: Middle Class Women and Domestic Ideology in Victorian Culture', *PMLA*, 107:2 (1992), p. 291.

6 Kay Boardman, 'The Ideology of Domesticity: The Regulation of the Household Economy in Victorian Women's Magazines', *Victorian Periodicals Review*, 33:2 (2000), p. 154.

7 Lillian Nayder, *The Other Dickens: A Life of Catherine Hogarth* (Ithaca, NY: Cornell University Press, 2011), p. 199 and p. 200.

8 Kathryn Hughes, 'Gender Roles in the 19th Century', *Discovering Literature: Romantics and Victorians*, British Library website (2014), www.bl.uk/romantics-and-victorians/articles/gender-roles-in-the-19th-century.

9 John Forster, *The Life of Charles Dickens*, 3 vols (London: Chapman and Hall, 1874), Vol. 3, p. 473.

10 Henry Charles Dickens, 'Presidential Address to the Dickens Fellowship Conference in 1946', *The Dickensian*, 42:280 (1946), p. 190.

11 Forster, *The Life of Charles Dickens*, Vol. 3, p. 486.

12 Dickens to Angela Burdett-Coutts, 25 October 1853, in Charles Dickens, *The Pilgrim Edition of the Letters of Charles Dickens* ed. Madeleine House et al., 12 vols (Oxford: Clarendon Press, 1965–2002) (hereafter *P*), VII, p. 172.

13 Dickens to Mrs Ternan, 16 September 1857, *P*, XII, p. 679; Francis Finlay and Others, 'Guests at Gad's Hill', in Philip Collins (ed.), *Dickens: Interviews and Recollections*, Vol. 2 (London: Macmillan Press, 1981), p. 287.

14 Nancy Weston, *Daniel Maclise: Irish Artist in Victorian London* (Dublin: Four Courts Press, 2000), p. 114.

15 J. W. T. Ley, 'Father and Daughter', *The Dickensian*, 35:252 (1939), p. 252; W. H. Bowen, *Charles Dickens and his Family* (Cambridge: W. Heffer and Sons, 1956), p. 93; Hesketh Pearson, *Dickens: His Character, Comedy and Career* (London: Methuen and Co., 1949), p. 248.

16 Claire Tomalin, *Charles Dickens: A Life* (London: Penguin, 2011), p. 396; A. N. Wilson, *The Mystery of Charles Dickens* (London: Atlantic, 2020), p. 13.

17 Arthur Adrian, *Georgina Hogarth and The Dickens Circle* (London: Oxford University Press, 1957), p. 205.

18 Gladys Storey, *Dickens and Daughter* (London: Frederick Muller Ltd, 1939), p. 24.

19 Ada Nisbet, *Dickens and Ellen Ternan* (Berkeley, CA: University of California Press, 1952), p. 31.

20 I have relied upon Arthur Adrian's deciphering of Georgina's writing in her letters to Percy Fitzgerald. See Arthur Adrian, 'Georgina Hogarth to Percy Fitzgerald: Some Unpublished Letters', *The Dickensian*, 88:1 (1992), pp. 5–18.

21 Lucinda Hawksley describes Georgina's letters to Connie Dickens – Plorn's wife whom she never met – as revealing: 'very intimate family secrets … Her letters seem to have been her way of dealing with grief or disappointment; perhaps the knowledge that she was unlikely ever to meet Connie made it easier to confide in her'. Lucinda Hawksley, *Katey: The Life and Loves of Dickens's Artist Daughter* (London: Doubleday, 2006), p. 305.

22 Storey, *Dickens and Daughter*, p. 100; Patricia Ingham, *Dickens, Women and Language* (Toronto: University of Toronto Press, 1992), p. 72; A. N. Wilson, 'Charles Dickens the Misogynist', *Mail on Sunday* (23 May 2020), www.dailymail.co.uk/news/article-8351467/Charles-Dickens-cruel-wife-hated-mother-affair-writes-N-WILSON.html.

23 Margaret MacMillan, *History's People* (London: Profile Books, 2015), p. 5.

Chapter 1: The Hogarths and Dickens become in-laws

1 There were two Mary Hogarths. Mr and Mrs Hogarth named their second daughter Mary, but she lived less than a year. It was common in

the Victorian period to pass the name of a child who died in infancy on to a future child. See Hogarth family tree.

2 A detailed account of Catherine and Georgina Hogarth's ancestry is provided by Nayder, *The Other Dickens.*

3 Charles Dickens, 'Speech: Edinburgh, June 25, 1841', in Charles Dickens, *Speeches: Literary and Social*, pp. 3–4, www.public-library.uk/ebooks/90/39.pdf.

4 E. E. Christian, 'Recollections of Charles Dickens: His Family and Friends', *Temple Bar*, 82 (April 1888), p. 495.

5 William F. Long, 'Passages in the Life of Mr George Hogarth – 2: Mr Hogarth Goes to Prison', *The Dickensian*, 112:499 (2016), p. 122.

6 Charles Dickens Jr, 'Brompton', in *Dickens's Dictionary of London* (London, 1879), www.victorianlondon.org/dickens/dickens-bic.htm.

7 Mamie Dickens, *Charles Dickens by his Eldest Daughter* (London: Cassell and Co., 1885), p. 35.

8 William F. Long, 'Passages in the Life of Mr George Hogarth – 1: Mr Hogarth Applies for a Chair', *The Dickensian*, 498:112 (2016), p. 28.

9 Ibid.

10 Michael Slater, *Dickens and Women* (London: J. M. Dent and Sons, 1983), p. 367 and p. 369.

11 Ibid., p. 81.

12 British Library, London (hereafter BL), RP 9217, Pym, Horace N., Dickens, Charles, 7 autograph letters signed from Mamie Dickens and 24 autograph letters signed from Georgina Hogarth to Pym and his wife, including numerous references to Charles Dickens, his life and books. With autograph envelopes, Georgina Hogarth to Jane Pym, 5 April 1902.

13 Philip Collins (ed.), *Dickens: Interviews and Recollections*, 2 vols (London: Macmillan Press, 1981), Vol. 1, pp. 16–17.

14 Slater, *Dickens and Women*, p. 81.

15 Dickens to an unknown correspondent, 8 June 1837, *P*, I, p. 268.

16 Barry Newport, 'The Death of Mary Hogarth: A New Explanation', *The Dickensian*, 111:496 (2015), pp. 142–5.

17 Dickens reluctantly relinquished this plan when Mary's brother died in 1841, to allow George to be buried alongside his sister.

18 Slater, *Dickens and Women*, p. 82.

19 Ibid., p. 81.

20 'In memory of my dear Sister M.S.H. May 7th 1837 C. D.', ibid., p. 85.

21 Nayder, *The Other Dickens*, p. 129.

22 R. Giddings, 'Dickens and the Great Unmentionable' (paper presented at 'Dickens and Sex' Conference, University of London Institute of English Studies, 20 March 2004); Paul Schlicke (ed.), *The Oxford Companion to Charles Dickens* (Oxford: Oxford University Press, 2011), pp. 533–6; Robert Garnett, *Charles Dickens in Love* (New York: Pegasus Books, 2012), p. 154.

23 Dickens to Mrs Hogarth, ? June 1837, *P*, I, p. 275.

24 Long, 'Passages in the Life of Mr George Hogarth – 2: Mr Hogarth goes to Prison', pp. 118–29.

25 Judith Flanders, *The Victorian House* (London: Harper Perennial, 2003), p. 94.

26 Thea Holme, *The Carlyles at Home* (Oxford: Oxford University Press, 1965).

27 William F. Long and Mairi E. Chong, 'Letter to the Editor: Sudden Death in the Hogarth Family', *The Dickensian*, 111:497 (2015), pp. 267–8.

28 Ibid.

29 'Peeps at Dickens: Pen Pictures from Contemporary Sources. XXVII – Hans Andersen to his Sister', *The Dickensian*, 30:229 (1933), p. 58; B. W. Matz, 'Miss Georgina Hogarth', *The Dickensian*, 13:5 (1917), p. 122; H. C. Dickens, 'Presidential Address 1946', p. 190.

30 Nayder, *The Other Dickens*, p. 29.

31 Slater, *Dickens and Women*, p. 104.

32 Henry E. Huntington Library, Art Collections, and Botanical Gardens, San Marino, California, Annie Adams Fields Papers (hereafter Huntington Library), MS FI 2708, Georgina to Annie Fields, 18 August 1871.

33 A note from Catherine which was included in a letter Dickens sent from Baltimore to his brother Fred back in London on 22 March 1842, *P*, III, pp. 149–50; Catherine's note written on p. 1 of a folded sheet from Dickens to Fred, 4 April 1842, *P*, III, p. 189.

Chapter 2: Friends and flirting

1 Dickens to David Colden, 31 July 1842, *P*, III, p. 291.

2 George Pierce Baker, *Charles Dickens and Maria Beadnell: Private Correspondence* (Boston, MA: Bibliophile Society, 1908), p. 141.

3 K. J. Fielding, 'Dickens and his Wife: Fact or Forgery?', *Etudes Anglaises*, 8 (1955), p. 216.

4 Dickens to Catherine, late May 1835, *P*, I, p. 62.

5 Simonsen, 'Elizabeth Barrett Browning's Redundant Women', p. 509.

6 Daniel Maclise to John Forster, 'I am out of favour with Grim'. See Dickens to Daniel Maclise, 30 or 31 January 1842, note 1, *P*, III, p. 41.

7 Henry Dickens, *The Recollections of Sir Henry Dickens, K.C.* (London: William Heinemann, 1934), p. 51.

8 See Chapter 5. Dickens reminded Catherine that his name gave her 'station better than rank', 5 December 1853, *P*, VII, p. 198.

9 Kathy Chamberlain, *Jane Welsh Carlyle and her Victorian World* (London: Duckworth, 2017), p. 29.

10 Rosemary Ashton, *Thomas and Jane Carlyle* (London: Random House, 2002), p. 172.

11 Ibid., p. 200.

Notes

12 Nayder, *The Other Dickens*, p. 34; Ashton, *Thomas and Jane Carlyle*, pp. 15–16.
13 Isabella Beeton, *Beeton's Book of Household Management* (London: Jonathan Cape, 1861). Although Mrs Beeton's advice first appeared in 1857, she was reiterating much of the guidance given in earlier etiquette books such as Arthur Freeling, *The Ladies Pocket Book of Etiquette* (Waltham Saint Lawrence: Golden Cockerel Press, 1928; first published 1838); An American Lady, *A Handbook of Etiquette for Ladies* (New York: Leavitt and Allen, 1847); Sarah Stickney Ellis, *The Women of England: Their Social Duties and Domestic Habits* (London: Fisher and Son, 1839).
14 Chamberlain, *Jane Welsh Carlyle and her Victorian World*, p. 47.
15 Jane Carlyle to John Forster, 16 October 1840, Carlyle Letters Online, https://carlyleletters.dukeupress.edu/home.
16 Holme, *The Carlyles at Home*, p. 110.
17 Catherine Peters, *The King of Inventors: A Life of Wilkie Collins* (London: Secker and Warburg, 1991), pp. 350–1.
18 Ibid.
19 Ashton, *Thomas and Jane Carlyle*, p. 238.
20 Ibid., pp. 237–8.
21 Charles and Mary Cowden-Clarke, *Recollections of Writers* (London: S. Low, Marston, Searle and Rivington, 1878), p. 295.
22 F. G. Kitton, *Charles Dickens: His Life, Writings and Personality* (London: T. C. and E. C. Jack, 1902), p. 439.
23 David Simkin, *Portraits of Charles Dickens (1812–1870)*, www.photohistory-sussex.co.uk/DickensCharlesPortraits.htm.
24 Henry Burnett, 'The Young Novelist at Work and Play', in Philip Collins (ed.), *Dickens: Interviews and Recollections*, Vol. 1 (London: Macmillan, 1981), p. 22.
25 Dickens to William Harrison Ainsworth, 30 October 1837, *P*, I, p. 326.
26 Dickens to William Harrison Ainsworth, 30 October 1837, note 2, Anne Buckley to her niece, Mary Anne Harrison, 8 November 1837, *P*, I, p. 324.
27 Christian, 'Recollections of Charles Dickens', p. 481.
28 E. E. C., 'Reminiscences of Charles Dickens from a Young Lady's Diary', *Englishwoman's Domestic Magazine*, 10 (1871), p. 336.
29 Slater, *Dickens and Women*, pp. 358–9.
30 Christian, 'Recollections of Charles Dickens', p. 484.
31 E. E. C., 'Reminiscences of Charles Dickens from a Young Lady's Diary', pp. 338–9.
32 Ibid., p. 339.
33 Ibid.
34 Christian, 'Recollections of Charles Dickens', p. 492.
35 Ibid.
36 Ibid., p. 493.

37 Ibid.
38 E.E.C., 'Reminiscences of Charles Dickens from a Young Lady's Diary', p. 342.
39 Ibid.
40 Ibid.
41 D. Parker, A. Wilson and R. Wilson, 'Letters of a Guest at Devonshire Terrace', *The Dickensian*, 95:447 (1999), p. 57.
42 Ibid., p. 56.
43 E. E. C., 'Reminiscences of Charles Dickens from a Young Lady's Diary', p. 343.
44 Christian, 'Recollections of Charles Dickens', p. 497.
45 Edgar Johnson, *Charles Dickens: His Tragedy and Triumph*, 2 vols (New York: Simon and Schuster, 1952), Vol. 1, p. 383.
46 Dickens to John Forster, 24 April 1842, *P*, III, pp. 204–5.
47 Collins, *Dickens: Interviews and Recollections*, Vol. 1, p. 53. The young lady reporting the occasion was Elizabeth Wormeley, who was staying with the publisher George Ticknor and attended the dinner for 'the leading literary characters of Boston'. She described the incident in E. Wormeley Latimer, 'A Girl's Recollections of Dickens', *Lippincott's Magazine* (September 1893), pp. 338–9.
48 Collins, *Dickens: Interviews and Recollections*, Vol. 1, pp. 52–3.
49 Johnson, *Charles Dickens*, Vol. 1, p. 422.
50 Dickens to Frances Wilkes Colden, 15 July 1842, *P*, III, p. 271.
51 Dickens to Emma Mordecai, 19 March 1842, *P*, III, p. 140.
52 Minnie (Thackeray) Stephens reported that according to Katey Dickens, 'her mother did not drink but is heavy and unregardful of her children and jealous of her husband', George Curry, 'Charles Dickens and Annie Fields', *Huntington Library Quarterly*, 51:1 (1988), p. 32; Mrs Thomas Whiffen, *Keeping Off the Shelf* (New York: E. P. Dutton and Co., 1928), p. 53.
53 R. E. Francillon, *Mid-Victorian Memories* (London: Hodder and Stoughton, 1914), p. 252.
54 Slater, *Dickens and Women*, p. 141.

Chapter 3: Dickens and his 'little Pet'

1 The time Georgina moved in permanently can be deduced from Dickens's letter to Henry Wadsworth Longfellow, 29 December 1842, *P*, III, p. 409: 'I wish you had seen her sister, who is usually with us, as she is now; but was with her mother when you were here'.
2 Huntington Library, MS FI 2697, Georgina to Annie Fields, 31 December 1872.

Notes

3 *Charles Dickens* by Daniel Maclise, 1839, National Portrait Gallery. Referred to as the 'Nickleby' portrait. It was commissioned by the publishers, Chapman and Hall, and presented to Dickens at the dinner on 5 October 1839 to mark the publication of the novel *Nicholas Nickleby*.

4 Dickens preferred to take a cold shower first thing but he had to wait until the family moved to Tavistock House to have that luxury installed.

5 Mamie Dickens, *My Father as I Recall Him* (London: Roxburghe Press, 1897), pp. 10–11.

6 Mamie Dickens, 'Charles Dickens at Home', *Cornhill Magazine*, 4 (January 1885), p. 33.

7 W. J. Carlton, '"Old Nick" at Devonshire Terrace', *The Dickensian*, 59:341 (1963), pp. 142–3. The two known Maclise portraits of Catherine Dickens have been dated around 1846/7. However, according to Carlton, the reference to Catherine's portrait comes from an article, 'Souvenirs de Londres' by Paul Emile Daurand Forgues in the journal *L'Illustration* dated 1844, suggesting an earlier date.

8 Henry F. Dickens, *Memories of my Father* (London: Victor Gollancz, 1928), p. 12.

9 Dickens to Angela Burdett-Coutts, 12 November 1842, *P*, III, p. 367.

10 Kate Perugini, 'On Women Old and New', *The Dickensian*, 29:227 (1933), p. 185.

11 Dickens to John Forster, 12 February 1843, *P*, III, p. 440.

12 See Hogarth family tree.

13 Slater, *Dickens and Women*, p. 164.

14 Dickens to Mrs Hogarth, 8 May 1843, *P*, III, p. 483.

15 Edgar F. Harden (ed.), *The Letters and Private Papers of William Makepeace Thackeray*, Vol. 1 (New York and London: Garland, 1994), p. 184.

16 Dickens to Catherine, 9 January 1849, *P*, V, pp. 471–2.

17 Dickens to Emile de la Rue, 28 July 1845, *P*, IV, p. 339; 24 March 1847, *P*, V, p. 41.

18 Adrian, *Georgina Hogarth and the Dickens Circle*, p. 41.

19 Sarah Stickney Ellis, *The Daughters of England: Their Position in Society, Character and Responsibilities* (London: Fisher, Son and Co., 1842), p. 308.

20 E. E. C., 'Reminiscences of Charles Dickens from a Young Lady's Diary', p. 338. Although the thought of a naked man nearby might be both disturbing and provoking to the sensibilities of young Victorian ladies, when Dickens was growing up it was considered unmanly for men to wear any kind of swimwear. See Louise Allen, *The Georgian Seaside* (CreateSpace, 2016), p. 60.

21 J. A. V. Chapple and A. Pollard (eds), *The Letters of Mrs. Gaskell* (Manchester: Manchester University Press, 1966), letter 195, pp. 286–91.

22 Jane Carlyle to Jeannie Welsh, 28 December 1843. Carlyle Letters Online.

Notes

23 William Toynbee, *The Diaries of William Charles Macready, 1833–1851* (New York: G. P. Putnam's Sons, 1912), pp. 179–80.

24 Dickens to Douglas Jerrold, 24 October 1846, *P*, IV, p. 645.

25 Winifred Gerin, *Anne Thackeray Ritchie: Journals and Letters* (Oxford: Oxford University Press, 1981), p. 46.

26 Forster, *The Life of Charles Dickens*, Vol. 2, p. 436.

27 Elaine Showalter and English Showalter, 'Victorian Women and Menstruation', in Martha Vicinus (ed.), *Suffer and Be Still* (Bloomington, IN: Indiana University Press, 1973), p. 84.

28 Ibid.

29 Deborah Gorham, 'The Victorian Girl and the Feminine Ideal', in Martha Vicinus (ed.), *Suffer and Be Still* (Bloomington, IN: Indiana University Press, 1982), p. 87.

30 Sanitary protection was not commercially available until the 1880s so women had to fashion themselves a kind of adult nappy made out of rags which were then rinsed, either in the water closet or the privy, and put to soak in copper washtubs. In houses employing servants, the job of washing the napkins of the female family members was undertaken by the maids.

31 Dickens to Georgina, 4 February 1845, *P*, IV, p. 261.

32 Dickens to Catherine Macready, 26 April 1847, *P*, V, pp. 60–1.

33 Flanders, *The Victorian House*, pp. 258–9.

34 Augustus Egg produced this intimate sketch of a domestic Georgina around the time he proposed to her. It is unlikely he intended it to be read as an indicator that Georgina was more like a servant than a family member.

35 Ya-Lei Yen, 'Clothing Middle-Class Women: Dress, Gender and Identity in Mid-Victorian England c. 1851–1875' (PhD dissertation, Royal Holloway, University of London, 2014).

36 Senate House Library, University of London, London, MS1003, Katharine Longley, *A Pardoner's Tale*, p. 416.

37 Caroline Norton's reputation was demolished after an alleged affair with Prime Minister Lord Melbourne and leaving her abusive husband. Dickens was always kind, inviting her to parties at Devonshire Terrace, and she told friends she could always depend on Dickens and his 'dear little wife' to visit her. The actress Helen Faucit had been the subject of newspaper speculation when she was alleged to have been pregnant with the child of the married William Macready (see Chapter 2).

38 S. M. Ellis, *William Harrison Ainsworth and his Friends*, Vol. 2 (London: John Lane, Bodley Head, 1911), pp. 37–8.

39 Case Western Reserve University, Cleveland, Ohio, Arthur Adrian Papers, Box 3HA6, Georgina to Blanche Swanson, 17 January 1908.

40 Dickens to Charles Sumner, 31 July 1842, *P*, III, note 9, Caroline Norton to Catherine Dickens, *P*, III, p. 297.

41 Huntington Library, MS FI 2784, Georgina to Annie Fields, 2 April 1873.

42 Dickens to Edward Bulwer-Lytton, 6 February 1851, *P*, VI, p. 281.

43 Huntington Library, MS FI 2703, Georgina to Annie Fields, 21 November 1870.

44 Gordon N. Ray (ed.), *The Letters and Private Papers of William Makepeace Thackeray*, 4 vols (Oxford: Oxford University Press, 1945), Vol. 1, p. 287.

45 Forster, *The Life of Charles Dickens*, Vol. 1, p. 158.

46 Ibid.

47 Royal Archives, Windsor, Queen Victoria's Journals, Lord Esher's typescripts, RA VIC/MAIN/QVJ (W), 2 February 1839, www.queenvictoriasjournals. org/home.do.

48 Dickens to Thomas Hood, 30 November 1842, *P*, III, p. 386.

49 Often known as 'Girl at the Waterfall'. Georgina always referred to the picture as 'Nymph of the Waterfall'. Interviewing Georgina in 1911, Richard Renton incorrectly recorded her reference to Maclise's work as 'Nymph *at* the Waterfall'. Richard Renton, *John Forster and his Friendships* (London: Chapman and Hall, 1912), p. 63. For an alternative analysis of the history of this painting, see Gail David-Tellis, 'Dead Girl Rising: Georgina Hogarth as "the Girl at the Waterfall"', *The Dickensian*, 117:514 (2021), pp. 122–31.

50 Maclise made the sketch *Charles Dickens, his Wife and her Sister*, 1843 in a pub in Richmond on the day Dickens wrote to Forster that he was unable to write and had dashed off with his 'pair of petticoats'. Dickens to John Forster, 12 February 1843, *P*, III, p. 440.

51 Jan Marsh, *Jane and May Morris* (Horsham: Printed Word, 2000), p. 14.

52 Peters, *The King of Inventors*, p. 63.

53 E. Thornwell, *The Ladies Guide to Perfect Gentility* (New York: Derby and Jackson, 1857), p. 80.

54 Dickens to Daniel Maclise, 12 July 1841, note 3, DM to CD, 16 July 1841, *P*, II, p. 331.

55 Dickens to Daniel Maclise, 16 August 1841, *P*, VII, p. 831.

56 Weston, *Daniel Maclise: Irish Artist in Victorian London*, p. 137.

57 Kate Perugini, 'Dickens as a Lover of Art and Artists', *Magazine of Art*, 28 (1903), p. 127.

58 Letter from Charles Dickens to the sender mistakenly attributed to be John Forster, on 3 August 1844, *P*, IV, p. 165. A note from the editors say they think this letter was actually to Maclise on the basis of 'the joking reference to "Miss H"'.

59 Renton, *John Forster and his Friendships*, p. 66. See also Perugini, 'Dickens as a Lover of Art and Artists'. In the article on her father and his artist friends Katey provides an affectionate portrayal of Maclise as a young man. As Katey was only an infant in the years she writes about, the only

person still alive who would remember him and able to give the kind of information that appears in the piece was Georgina.

60 Dickens to Augusta de la Rue, 27 September 1845, *P*, IV, p. 390.

61 Dickens to Georgina, 9 March 1847, *P*, V, p. 33; Dickens to Catherine, 24 June 1850, *P*, VI, p. 117.

62 F. G. Kitton, *Dickens and his Illustrators* (London: George Redway, 1899), p. 170.

63 Dickens to Cornelius Felton, 1 September 1843, *P*, III, p. 551.

64 Middle-class mothers had the assistance of their own attendant, known as a 'monthly nurse', for the weeks following delivery.

65 Walter Dexter (ed.), *Dickens to his Oldest Friend* (New York: Haskell House, 1973), p. 272.

66 Dickens to Jane Carlyle, 27 January 1844, *P*, IV, p. 33.

67 Dickens to Fanny Burnett, 1 March 1844, *P*, IV, p. 57.

68 Dickens to Maclise, 2 March 1844, *P*, IV, p. 59; Dickens to T. J. Thompson, 28 February 1844, *P*, IV, p. 55.

69 Slater, *Dickens and Women*, p. 88.

70 Pearson, *Dickens*, p. 128; David H. Paroissien, 'Charles Dickens and the Weller Family', *Dickens Studies Annual*, 2 (1972), p. 7.

71 Nayder, *The Other Dickens*, p. 126; Fred Kaplan, *Dickens: A Biography* (London: Hodder and Stoughton, 1988), p. 606; Johnson, *Charles Dickens*, Vol. 2, p. cxciv.

72 Dickens to Christiana Weller, 8 April 1844, *P*, IV, p. 99.

73 Johnson, *Charles Dickens*, Vol. 1, p. xli.

74 Paroissien, 'Charles Dickens and the Weller Family', p. 10.

75 Ibid.

76 Dickens to Macready, 17 October 1845, *P*, IV, p. 406.

77 Dickens decided to take the family to live in Italy for a year partly because living on the continent was cheaper, and partly to collect material for a travelogue (*Pictures from Italy*). His fortunes had taken a hit when the initially low sales figures of *Martin Chuzzlewit* resulted in the publishers deducting £50 a month from his income. The phenomenal success of *A Christmas Carol* in 1843 had yielded little profit because Dickens insisted on a high-quality production of the small volume.

78 Paroissien, 'Charles Dickens and the Weller Family', p. 6.

79 Ibid., p. 14.

80 Georgina to Christiana Weller, 16 October 1845, *P*, IV, note 3; Dickens to Macready, 17 October 1845, *P*, IV, p. 407.

81 Dickens to Emile de la Rue, 17 August 1846, *P*, IV, p. 604.

82 Dickens to Thomas Mitton, 30 August 1846, *P*, IV, p. 615.

83 Nayder, *The Other Dickens*, p. 131.

84 Dickens to Catherine, 8 November 1844, *P*, IV, p. 215.

Notes

85 Huntington Library, MS FI 2770, Georgina to Annie Fields, 28 December 1900.

86 Dickens to Emile de la Rue, 14 February 1845, *P*, IV, p. 267.

87 Dickens to Douglas Jerrold, 14 February 1847, *P*, V, p. 29; Forster, *The Life of Charles Dickens*, Vol. 1, p. 39.

88 Dexter, *Charles Dickens to his Oldest Friend*, p. 274.

Chapter 4: 'A lively young damsel'

1 Dickens to Angela Burdett-Coutts, 25 October 1853, *P*, VII, p. 172.

2 Edmund Yates, *Edmund Yates: His Recollections and Experiences* (London: R. Bentley and Son, 1884), p. 305.

3 Huntington Library, MS FI 2773, Georgina to Annie Fields, 15 June, 1875, and MS FI 2716, 17 October 1873.

4 Phebe A. Hanaford, *The Life and Writing of Charles Dickens: A Woman's Memorial Volume* (Augusta, ME: E. C. Allen and Co., 1875), p. 359; H. S. Solly, *The Life of Henry Morley, LL.D.* (London: Edwin Arnold, 1898), p. 200; Yates, *Edmund Yates: His Recollections and Experiences*, p. 256.

5 Frank's birth in January 1844 was followed by: Alfred in October 1845, Sydney in April 1847, a miscarriage in autumn 1847, Henry (known as Harry) in January 1849 and Dora in 1850.

6 For Dickens's involvement with Urania Cottage, see Jenny Hartley, *Charles Dickens and the House of Fallen Women* (London: Methuen, 2008).

7 Dickens to W. H. Wills, 29 August 1850, *P*, VI, p. 158.

8 Slater, *Dickens and Women*, p. 177.

9 Leslie C. Staples, 'Some Early Memories of the Dickens Fellowship', *The Dickensian*, 73:383 (1977), p. 134.

10 Nayder, *The Other Dickens*, p. 152.

11 Dickens to William Bradbury, 29 October 1849, *P*, V, p. 633.

12 Kaplan, *Dickens*, p. 246.

13 The job of the bathing women was to look after the valuables of the ladies and lower the bathing machine to the edge of the water. Some were also 'dippers' – well-built, strong women who would help lift the lady into the water.

14 Dickens often called himself 'the Inimitable' in letters to friends in remembrance of a joke dating from the time of *Pickwick* when some newspapers spoke of him as 'the Inimitable Boz'. Georgina Hogarth and Mamie Dickens, *The Letters of Charles Dickens* (London: Macmillan and Co., 1903), p. 211.

15 Dickens to John Leech, 9 October 1849, *P*, V, p. 624.

16 Dickens to W. W. F. de Cerjat, 29 December 1849, *P*, V, p. 683.

Notes

17   J. W. T Ley, *The Dickens Circle: A Narrative of the Novelist's Friendships* (New York: E. P. Dutton, 1919), p. 283.

18   Peters, *The King of Inventors*, p. 131.

19   William Powell Frith, *My Autobiography and Reminiscences*, Vol. 3 (London: Richard Bentley and Son, 1888), p. 217.

20   Ibid.

21   Johnson, *Charles Dickens*, Vol. 2, p. 719.

22   Dickens to Maclise, 16 September 1850, *P*, VI, p. 170.

23   Dickens to Mrs Lemon, 3 November 1850, note 5, *P*, VI, p. 203.

24   Dickens to Mrs Richard Watson, 23 November 1850, *P*, VI, p. 216.

25   Hertfordshire Archives and Local Studies, Hertford, DE/K/C4/134, Georgina Hogarth to Edward Bulwer-Lytton, 23 November 1850.

26   Dickens to Bulwer-Lytton, 6 February 1851, *P*, VI, p. 281.

27   Ibid.

28   Huntington Library, MS FI 2711, Georgina to Annie Fields, 21 February 1873.

29   Dickens to Emile de la Rue, 28 July 1845, *P*, IV, p. 339; 24 March 1847, *P*, V, p. 41.

30   Dickens to Angela Burdett-Coutts, 25 October 1853, *P*, VII, p. 172.

31   Ibid.

32   Huntington Library, MS FI 2700, Georgina to Annie Fields, 5 June 1871; Case Western Reserve University, Arthur Adrian Papers, Box 3HA6, Georgina to Blanche Swanson, 8 January 1908.

33   Dickens to Catherine, 16/17 October 1853, *P*, VII, p. 167.

34   Cowden-Clarke and Cowden-Clarke, *Recollections of Writers*, p. 323.

35   Donald J. Gray, 'The Uses of Victorian Laughter', *Victorian Studies*, 10:2 (1966), p. 146.

36   Dickens to Angela Burdett-Coutts, 25 October 1853, *P*, VII, p. 172; Dickens to Georgina, 25 October 1853, *P*, VII, p. 176.

37   Dickens to Georgina, 25 November 1853, *P*, VII, p. 211.

38   Charles Dickens, 'Violated' letter, 25 May, 1858, *P*, VIII, Appendix F, pp. 740–1.

39   Dickens to Catherine, 11 September 1851, *P*, VI, p. 482. A garniture is a decoration, ornament or embellishment; the *Scarlet Letter* is a book by Nathaniel Hawthorne.

40   Alfred Tennyson Dickens, 'My Father and his Friends', *Nash's Magazine*, 4 (September 1911), p. 640.

41   Huntington Library, MS FI 2738, Georgina to Annie Fields, 26 June 1878.

42   Courtney Boyle (ed.), *Mary Boyle: Her Book* (London: John Murray, 1902), p. 247.

43   Tomalin, *Charles Dickens*, p. 228.

44   Nayder, *The Other Dickens*, p. 203.

45   Dickens to Catherine, 21 August 1850, *P*, VI, p. 153.

Chapter 5: Dickens's mid-life crisis

1   Dickens to Angela Burdett-Coutts, 16 March 1852, *P*, VI, p. 627.
2   Dickens to John Leech, 23 May 1853, *P*, VII, p. 92.
3   Dickens to Mark Lemon, 3 July 1853, *P*, VII, p. 109.
4   Robert Douglas-Fairhurst, *The Turning Point* (London: Penguin, 2021), p. 125.
5   Dickens first grew a moustache in 1844 but shaved it off soon after. Lillian Nayder, '"*He Has a Moustache*"; or "Earth Will Not Hold Us Both"; Charles Dickens and the Problem of Fred', *Dickens Quarterly*, 30:2 (2013), pp. 141–53.
6   Dickens to R. H. Horne, 2 March 1853, note 4, *P*, VII, p. 34; Nayder, *The Other Dickens*, pp. 219–20.
7   Dickens to Thomas Beard, 22 July 1852, note 1, *P*, VI, p. 720. Catherine (Kate) Horne (*née* Foggo, 1826–93) married the journalist and writer for *Household Words*, Richard Hengist Horne. (1802–84). He was more than twice her age. They married in 1847, only for Horne to abandon her, travelling to Australia in 1852 on the pretext of collecting material for articles for *Household Words*. Dickens, as his editor, and W. H. Wills, felt responsible for looking after Kate.
8   Dickens to Wilkie Collins, 19 January 1856, *P*, VIII, p. 30.
9   Dickens to George Putnam, 24 July 1851, Vol. 6, *P*, p. 442.
10   Dickens to Georgina, 22 July 1854, *P*, VII, p. 377.
11   Dickens to Wilkie Collins, 22 April 1856, *P*, VIII, p. 95.
12   Dickens to William Howard Russell, 30 May 1857, *P*, VIII, p. 337.
13   Kathryn Hughes, 'The Middle Classes: Etiquette and Upward Mobility', *Discovering Literature: Romantics and Victorians*, British Library website (2014), www.bl.uk/romantics-and-victorians/articles/the-middle-classes-etiquette-and-upward-mobility.
14   Dickens to Forster, 24 February 1856, *P*, VIII, p. 63; Dickens to Georgina, 10 January 1862, *P*, X, p. 12.
15   Eliza Lynn Linton, *My Literary Life* (London: Hodder and Stoughton, 1899), p. 63.
16   Susan Chitty, *The Beast and the Monk: A Life of Charles Kingsley* (London: Hodder and Stoughton, 1974), p. 174.
17   Dickens to Catherine, 3 September 1850, *P*, VI, p. 161.
18   Dickens to Dr William Brown, 1 August 1853, *P*, VII, p. 123.
19   Charles Dickens Museum, London, Gladys Storey Papers, Envelope PP, Hester Fuller to Gladys Storey, 16 July 1939.
20   Michael Slater, *The Great Charles Dickens Scandal* (London: Yale University Press, 2012), p. 159.
21   Dickens to Catherine, 27 November 1853, *P*, VII, p. 216.
22   Dickens to Catherine, 5 December 1853, *P*, VII, p. 224.
23   Dickens to Emile de la Rue, 14 November 1853, *P*, VII, p. 194.

Notes

24 Dickens to W. H. Wills, 12 Aug 1852, *P*, VI, p. 739.

25 Dickens to Georgina, 25 November 1853, *P*, VII, p. 211.

26 Dickens to Angela Burdett-Coutts, 25 October 1853, *P*, VII, p. 172.

27 Slater, *Dickens and Women*, p. 166.

28 Charles Dickens, *Bleak House*, ch. 35.

29 Slater, *Dickens and Women*, p. 167.

30 Ibid.

31 Dickens to John Forster, 3 and 4 February 1855, *P*, VII, p. 523.

32 Dickens to Maria Winter, 22 February 1855, *P*, VII, p. 545.

33 Ibid., p. 544.

34 Baker, *Charles Dickens and Maria Beadnell: Private Correspondence*, pp. 120–3; Hogarth and Dickens (eds), *The Letters of Charles Dickens*, p. 350.

35 Dickens to W. H. Wills, 27 April 1856, *P*, VIII, p. 99.

36 Dickens to Wilkie Collins, 24 March 1855, *P*, VII, p. 575.

37 Dickens to W. H. Wills, 20 April 1854, *P*, VII, p. 320.

38 Dickens to Georgina, 22 July 1854, *P*, VII, p. 376.

39 Ibid.

40 Dickens to Catherine, 7 February 1856, *P*, VIII, p. 47.

41 The nervous tic was a temporary condition that cleared up after a few months.

42 Elizabeth Sanders Arbuckle (ed.), *Harriet Martineau's Letters to Fanny Wedgwood* (Stanford, CA: Stanford University Press, 1983), p. 196.

43 Nayder, *The Other Dickens*, p. 219.

44 Ibid.

45 Storey, *Dickens and Daughter*, p. 23.

46 Christian, 'Recollections of Charles Dickens: His Family and Friends', p. 481; Curry, 'Charles Dickens and Annie Fields', p. 32.

47 Arbuckle, *Harriet Martineau's Letters to Fanny Wedgwood*, p. 196.

48 Dickens, 'Violated' letter.

49 Nayder, *The Other Dickens*, p. 202.

50 Ibid.

51 Arthur Adrian, *Mark Lemon: First Editor of Punch* (London: Oxford University Press, 1966), p. 21.

52 Jane Panton, *Leaves from a Life* (London: Eveleigh Nash, 1908), pp. 229–30.

53 Hester Thackeray Fuller and Violet Hammersley, *Thackeray's Daughter*, 2nd edn (London: W. J. Pollock and Co., 1952), pp. 61–2.

54 Philip Collins, 'W. C. Macready and Dickens: Some Family Recollections', *Dickens Studies*, 11:2 (1966), p. 54; See also, Case Western Reserve University, Arthur Adrian Papers, Box 3HA6, Arthur Adrian interview notes of his conversation with Lisa Puckle, William Macready's granddaughter by his second wife, Cecile Macready. Lisa Puckle told Adrian that she had heard the comment about Catherine from her grandmother, Cecile. However, Cecile and Georgina were close friends and Lisa remembers

spending many afternoons listening to the two old ladies chatting by the fireside. Cecile Macready never lived in London where Catherine resided and she married William Macready three years after the Dickenses' separation so it is highly unlikely Cecile ever met Catherine. William was always fond of Catherine and it would be surprising if he had passed this scathing opinion of Catherine on to Cecile. The most likely source for the observation that Catherine was a 'whiney woman' who wanted attention is Georgina. For one thing, both Kitty Macready and Catherine Dickens are accused of expecting and wanting more attention than their 'men of genius' husbands, and Georgina also openly criticised Catherine to friends, such as Cecile. Cecile may, in turn, have repeated this negative view of Catherine to her granddaughter.

55 'Mr Wilkie Collins's "Frozen Deep"', *Leader*, 8: 335 (10 January 1857), p. 44.

56 Adrian, *Georgina Hogarth and the Dickens Circle*, p. 38.

57 Dickens had come across Gad's Hill as a nine-year-old boy out walking with his father. John Dickens said if he worked hard enough he might live there one day and when Dickens found out it was up for sale he had to buy it, paying the owner, fellow writer Eliza Lynn Linton, £1,790 (£198,000).

58 Elias Bredsdorff, *Hans Christian Andersen* (London: Phaidon Press, 1975), p. 212.

59 H. F. Dickens, *The Recollections of Sir Henry Dickens*, p. 35.

60 Elias Bredsdorff, *Hans Andersen and Charles Dickens: A Friendship and its Dissolution* (Cambridge: W. Heffer and Sons, 1956), p. 73, p. 74, p. 78.

61 Hawksley, *Katey: The Life and Loves of Dickens's Artist Daughter*, p. 114.

62 Dickens to Angela Burdett-Coutts, 10 July 1857, *P*, VIII, p. 372.

Chapter 6: Loyalty and disloyalty

1 The performances were held on Friday 21 and Saturday 22 August, with a third on Monday 24 August 1857.

2 Hawksley, *Katey: The Life and Loves of Dickens's Artist Daughter*, p. 130.

3 Dickens to Frank Stone, 17 August 1857, *P*, VIII, p. 412.

4 Una Pope-Hennessy, *Charles Dickens* (London: Chatto and Windus, 1945), p. 391. It should be noted that Pope-Hennessy does not cite the source of this information.

5 Dickens to Angela Burdett-Coutts, 5 September 1857, *P*, VIII, pp. 432–3.

6 Dickens to Wilkie Collins, 29 August 1857, *P*, VIII, p. 423.

7 Ibid.

8 Dickens to Henry Austin, 2 September 1857, *P*, VIII, p. 427.

9 Dickens to Georgina, 9 September 1857, *P*, VIII, p. 438.

Notes

10 Dickens to Georgina, 15 September 1857, *P*, VIII, p. 448.

11 Dickens's letter to W. H. Wills sent from Doncaster suggests his motives towards an unnamed person were not innocent: 'I wish I was as good a boy in all things as I hope I have been, and mean to be in this. But Lord bless you, the strongest parts of your present correspondent's heart are made up of weaknesses. And he just come to be here at all (if you knew it) along of his Richard Wardour! Guess *that* riddle, Mr Wills!' (Dickens to W. H. Wills, 17 September 1857, *P*, VIII, p. 449). Three days later he told Wills he had plans 'to take the little – riddle – into the country this morning' and then, hinting at more devious intentions, 'So let the riddle and riddler go their own wild way, and no harm come of it!' (Dickens to W. H. Wills, 20 September 1857, *P*, VIII, pp. 450–1). Dickens added that he had decided to remain in Doncaster longer than planned. However, his plans did not work out and he unhappily returned to London on the Monday, as arranged.

12 Michael Slater, *Charles Dickens* (London: Yale University Press), p. 435.

13 Storey, *Dickens and Daughter*, p. 96.

14 Dickens to Richard Spofford, 15 July 1858, *P*, VIII, p. 605.

15 Claire Tomalin, *The Invisible Woman* (London: Viking, 1990), p. 111.

16 Storey, *Dickens and Daughter*, p. 96.

17 Nayder, *The Other Dickens*, p. 248.

18 Charles Dickens and Wilkie Collins, *The Lazy Tour of Two Idle Apprentices* (Richmond: Alma Books, 2018), p. 90.

19 Ibid., p. 71.

20 Ibid., p. 68, p. 70, p. 71.

21 Dickens to Emile de la Rue, 23 October 1857, *P*, VIII, p. 472.

22 For discussion of Dickens's attempt to have Catherine certified, see John Bowen, 'Madness and the Dickens Marriage: A New Source', *The Dickensian*, 115:507 (2019), pp. 5–20.

23 Leslie Mitchell, *Bulwer Lytton: The Rise and Fall of a Victorian Man of Letters* (London: Hambledon and London, 2003), p. 63.

24 Fielding, 'Dickens and His Wife', p. 216.

25 Storey, *Dickens and Daughter*, pp. 23–4.

26 David Parker and Michael Slater, 'The Gladys Storey Papers', *The Dickensian*, 76:390 (1980), p. 7.

27 Dickens, 'Violated' letter; Deborah Anne Logan (ed.), *The Collected Letters of Harriet Martineau*, Vol. 4 (London: Routledge, 2007), pp. 97–8.

28 Logan, *The Collected Letters of Harriet Martineau*, pp. 97–8.

29 Slater, *Dickens and Women*, p. 137.

30 Dickens to Angela Burdett-Coutts, 9 May 1858, *P*, VIII, pp. 558–60.

31 Fielding, 'Dickens and His Wife', p. 215.

32 Dickens to Emile de la Rue, 23 October 1857, *P*, VIII, p. 472.

Notes

33 John Bigelow, *Retrospections of An Active Life, 1822–1879*, 4 vols (New York: Baker and Taylor, 1909–13), Vol. 1, p. 264.

34 Ray, *The Letters and Private Papers of William Makepeace Thackeray*. Vol. 4, p. 86.

35 Dickens to Arthur Smith, 25 May 1858, *P*, VIII, p. 568; Dickens, 'Violated' letter. Forster said that the letter was intended 'as an authority for correction of false rumours and scandals' and Arthur Smith gave a copy of it, with like intention, to the [New York] *Tribune* correspondent in London. It actually appeared in the paper, and was then copied by other American and English papers, on 16 August 1858 (without Dickens's permission, hence he called it the 'Violated' letter).

36 Ibid.

37 Ibid.

38 Ibid.

39 Baker, *Charles Dickens and Maria Beadnell: Private Correspondence*, pp. 140–2.

40 Fielding, 'Dickens and his Wife', p. 216.

41 Ibid.

42 Dickens to Edmund Yates, 11 August 1858, *P*, VIII, p. 623.

43 Nayder, *The Other Dickens*, p. 261.

44 Ibid., pp. 261–2.

45 Dickens, 'Personal' statement, *P*, VIII, Appendix F, p. 744.

46 Dickens, 'Violated' letter.

47 Dickens to William Holman Hunt, 20 April 1858, *P*, VIII, p. 548.

48 K. J. Fielding, 'Dickens and the Hogarth Scandal', *Nineteenth-Century Fiction*, 10:1 (1955), pp. 71–2.

49 Ibid.

50 Baker, *Charles Dickens and Maria Beadnell: Private Correspondence*, p. 142.

51 Dickens had turned to Unitarianism after being impressed by the Unitarians he met in Boston during his first trip to America. On his return he began attending the chapel in Little Portland Street, where he met and became lifelong friends with its minister, the Reverend Edward Tagart.

52 Sophia Hankinson, 'A Brother Lost and Found: The Tale of Edward Tagart, Helen Bourn Martineau, Charles Dickens, Beatrice Potter and Transylvania', *Martineau Society Newsletter* (31 June 2012), p. 8.

53 Dickens to W. W. F. de Cerjat, 7 July 1858, note 1, *P*, VIII, p. 597.

54 Panton, *Leaves from a Life*, p. 143.

55 Clara Paterson, *Angela Burdett-Coutts and the Victorians* (London: John Murray, 1953), p. 154.

56 Ashton, *Thomas and Jane Carlyle*, p. 397.

57 Thomas Carlyle was writing love letters to Lady Harriet Baring. When Jane became distressed about his relationship with Lady Baring, Thomas 'played the Dickens' quite literally by accusing her of being deluded. How

dare she think there was anything romantic going on, 'what a *daft* creature art thou in thy sick imaginations!' See Thomas Carlyle to Jane Carlyle, 20 August 1846, quoted in Ashton, *Thomas and Jane Carlyle*, p. 271.

58 Panton, *Leaves from a Life*, p. 145.

59 Ray, *The Letters and Private Papers of William Makepeace Thackeray*, Vol. 4, p. 131.

60 Slater, *The Great Charles Dickens Scandal*, p. 28.

61 John Lehmann, *Ancestors and Friends* (London: Eyre and Spottiswoode, 1962), p. 231.

62 Bowen, *Charles Dickens and his Family*, p. 178; Pearson, *Dickens*, p. 255; Pope-Hennessy, *Charles Dickens*, pp. 405–6.

63 Sharon Marcus, *Between Women* (Woodstock: Princeton University Press, 2007), p. 1.

64 Case Western Reserve University, Arthur Adrian Papers, Box 3HA6, Lisa Puckle to Arthur Adrian, 1 April 1954.

65 Huntington Library, MS FI 2738, Georgina to Annie Fields, 26 June 1878.

66 Fielding, 'Dickens and his Wife', p. 216.

67 Huntington Library, MS FI 2715, Georgina to Annie Fields, 30 August 1873.

68 Fielding, 'Dickens and his Wife', p. 215.

69 Dickens, 'Violated' letter.

70 Fielding, 'Dickens and his Wife', p. 216.

71 Storey, *Dickens and Daughter*, p. 24.

72 Simonsen, 'Elizabeth Barrett Browning's Redundant Women', p. 510.

73 Perugini, 'On Women Old and New', p. 185.

74 See note 11, this chapter.

75 Nayder, *The Other Dickens*, p. 205.

Chapter 7: 'Poor Miss Hogarth'

1 Storey, *Dickens and Daughter*, p. 94.

2 Curry, 'Charles Dickens and Annie Fields', p. 24, p. 52.

3 Dickens to Georgina, 5 August 1858, *P*, VIII, p. 617.

4 Baker, *Charles Dickens and Maria Beadnell: Private Correspondence*, pp. 140–2.

5 Dickens to Frank Beard, 14 February 1859, *P*, IX, p. 27; Dickens to W. F. de Cerjat, 1 February 1859, *P*, IX, p. 21.

6 Dickens to Mamie, 23 September 1860, *P*, IX, p. 314.

7 Dickens to Georgina, 27 December 1860, *P*, IX, p. 356.

8 Dickens to Georgina, 28 January 1862, *P*, X, p. 25.

9 Dickens to Georgina, 8 November 1858, *P*, VIII, p. 698.

10 Hertfordshire Archives and Local Studies, DE/K/025/196, Georgina to Edward Bulwer-Lytton, 26 November 1858.

Notes

11 Curry, 'Charles Dickens and Annie Fields', p. 5.

12 Dickens to Georgina, 9 January 1861, *P*, IX, p. 365. Laura Olliffe, daughter of the politician William Cubitt and niece of the builder Thomas Cubitt, who renovated Tavistock House.

13 Nayder, *The Other Dickens*, pp. 275–6.

14 Ibid., p. 276; H. F. Dickens, *The Recollections of Sir Henry Dickens*, p. 19.

15 Dickens fell out with Mark Lemon (who acted for Catherine in negotiating the official separation) for refusing to publish his 'Personal' statement in *Punch*. Both Lemon and the publishers, Bradbury and Evans, thought it unsuitable for the pages of a comic magazine.

16 Dickens to W. W. F. de Cerjat, 3 May 1860, *P*, IX, p. 247.

17 Chapple and Pollard, *The Letters of Mrs. Gaskell*, p. 535.

18 Kate Dickens Perugini, 'I Loved him for his Faults', in Philip Collins (ed.), *Dickens: Interviews and Recollections*, Vol. 1 (London: Macmillan Press, 1981), pp. 154–5.

19 Adrian, *Mark Lemon, First Editor of Punch*, p. 135.

20 Harden, *The Letters and Private Papers of William Makepeace Thackeray*, pp. 846–7.

21 Storey, *Dickens and Daughter*, p. 105.

22 Slater, *Dickens and Women*, p. 174.

23 Dickens to J. C. Parkinson, 9 August 1860, *P*, IX, p. 285.

24 Dickens to Georgina, 15 February 1867, *P*, XI, p. 314.

25 Dickens to Georgina, 24 January 1862, *P*, X, p. 22.

26 Ibid.

27 Dickens to Georgina, 1 August 1866, *P*, XI, p. 228.

28 H. B. Macphail to Charles Dickens, 14 October 1858, *P*, VIII, p. 754.

29 Harry Dickens told Gladys Storey that a certificate confirming Georgina's virginity was in the family papers although no trace of it can now be found. See Slater, *Dickens and Women*, p. 415.

30 Dickens was somewhat inconsistent on the matter of prostitution, regarding sexual activity as important to 'good health' and referring to prostitutes as 'conveniences', yet troubled enough to join Angela Burdett-Coutts in setting up Urania Cottage which included 'fallen women' amongst its residents.

31 Dickens to Frank Beard, 25 June 1859, *P*, IX, p. 84.

32 Dickens to Frank Beard, 1 July 1859, *P*, IX, p. 88.

33 Dickens to W. H. Wills, 30 June 1859, *P*, IX, p. 87.

34 Dickens to John Forster, 9 July 1859, *P*, IX, p. 92.

35 Dickens to Wilkie Collins, 16 August 1859, *P*, IX, p. 106.

36 Dickens to Georgina, 25 November 1853, *P*, VII, p. 210; Dickens to Catherine, 14 November 1853, *P*, VII, p. 195.

37 Dickens to Georgina, 1 January 1860, *P*, IX, p. 188.

38 Dickens to Georgina, 28 December 1860, *P*, IX, pp. 355–6.

Notes

39 Nelly appears to have stopped living at 2 Houghton Place, Ampthill Square, in 1862 when she disappears from all records. Fanny was living there in 1865. Nelly retained ownership, but rented the house out until selling it in 1901.

40 Adrian, 'Georgina Hogarth to Percy Fitzgerald: Some Unpublished Letters', p. 15.

41 Thomas Wright, *The Life of Charles Dickens* (London: H. Jenkins Ltd, 1935), pp. 82–3.

42 Tomalin, *The Invisible Woman*, p. 242.

43 Dickens to Richard Spofford, 15 July 1858, *P*, VIII, pp. 604–5.

44 Dickens to W. H. Wills, 5 April 1862, *P*, X, p. 67.

45 Dickens to Yates, 3 April 1862, *P*, X, p. 64.

46 Tomalin, *The Invisible Woman*, p. 133, p. 136; Garnett, *Charles Dickens in Love*, p. 224.

47 Dickens to Charles Fechter, 16 May 1862, *P*, X, p. 83.

48 Dickens to Letitia Austin, 31 May 1862, *P*, X, p. 88.

49 Finlay and Others, 'Guests at Gad's Hill', p. 282.

50 Dickens to John Poole, 13 June 1862, *P*, X, p. 93.

51 Dickens to Letitia Austin, 20 June 1862, *P*, X, p. 95.

52 Dickens to John Poole, 13 June 1862, *P*, X, p. 93.

53 Robert Garnett, 'The Crisis of 1863', *Dickens Quarterly*, 23:3 (2006), pp. 181–91.

54 Dickens, 'Violated' letter, p. 741.

55 Huntington Library, MS FI 2745, Georgina to Annie Fields, 15 May 1876.

56 Huntington Library, MS FI 2729, Georgina to Annie Fields, 22 May 1880.

57 Adrian, 'Georgina Hogarth to Percy Fitzgerald: Some Unpublished Letters', p. 15.

58 Dickens to Letitia Austin, 3 July 1862, *P*, X, p. 102.

59 Ibid.

60 Dickens to James Sheridan Knowles, 7 July 1862, *P*, X, p. 103.

61 Dickens to Letitia Austin, 3 July 1862, *P*, X, p. 102.

62 Dickens to William Macready, 2 July 1862, *P*, X, p. 99.

63 Ibid.

64 Ibid., pp. 99–100.

65 Dickens to W. W. F. de Cerjat, 20 July 1862, *P*, X, p. 108.

66 Dickens to Wilkie Collins, 27 July 1862, *P*, X, p. 113.

67 Dickens to Wilkie Collins, 20 September 1862, *P*, X, p. 129.

68 Ibid.

69 M. Dickens, *My Father as I Recall Him*, p. 90.

70 Dickens to Mary Boyle, 27 December 1862, *P*, X, p. 183.

71 Dickens to Mamie, 16 January 1863, *P*, X, p. 194.

72 Dickens to Mamie, 1 February 1863, *P*, X, p. 204.

73 See also Garnett, *Charles Dickens in Love*, ch. 7.

74   'His Boots' was one of a group of stories called *Somebody's Luggage* published in the Christmas edition of *All the Year Round* in 1862. For discussion see John Bowen, 'Bebelle and "His Boots": Dickens, Ellen Ternan and the Christmas Stories', *The Dickensian*, 96:452 (2000), pp. 197–208.

75   Dickens to Georgina, 20 August, 25 August, 29 August 1858, *P*, VIII, p. 629, p. 639, p. 642. It is interesting to note that these endearments escaped Georgina's scissors when she was editing Dickens's letters. Although Georgina told Frederic Ouvry that she either destroyed or edited many letters she regarded as particularly personal, she could not resist allowing some expressions of intimacy to remain, thereby preserving her place in Dickens's affections for posterity.

76   Dickens to Georgina, 1 February 1863, *P*, X, p. 206.

77   Dickens to Georgina, 14 December 1868, *P*, XII, p. 244.

78   Dickens to Georgina, 10 August 1867, *P*, XI, p. 411. Charles Mathews was an actor famous for his 'monopolylogues': farces in which he played all the characters.

79   Dickens to Georgina, 21 January 1869, *P*, XII, p. 279.

80   Ibid., p. 278.

81   It is not easy to be precise about where Dickens was at any particular time as he used Gad's Hill letterhead when he evidently was not at home and was presumably with Nelly. The ruse is apparent by examining his collected letters which show the occasions when he writes to Georgina enquiring about a matter when he was ostensibly at home. For example, he asks her about an unexpected caller arriving at the house on a day that he was supposedly working in his study, and would have seen the man coming up the driveway. On another occasion Georgina sends him news of the sudden illness of a servant – an event which occurred when his letters suggest he was writing from home.

82   Dickens to Georgina, 8 May 1867, *P*, XI, p. 364.

83   Dickens to Georgina, 2 August 1867, *P*, XI, p. 406.

84   Felix Aylmer, *Dickens Incognito* (London: Rupert Hart-Davis, 1959), pp. 49–61.

85   David J. V. Pipes, *Charles Dickens in 1867* (CreateSpace, 2018), p. 53.

86   Slater, *The Great Charles Dickens Scandal*, p. 158.

87   Dickens to Georgina, 7 February 1868, *P*, XII, p. 40.

88   Dickens to W. H. Wills, early February 1868, *P*, XII, p. 43.

Chapter 8: 'His own decision will be the best'

1   See Figure 18 of Georgina in the early 1860s, when she is in mourning dress, and Figure 23, taken in 1866. Figure 23 is likely to have been taken at the same sitting as that of three photographs of Charles Dickens

at Robert Mason's Bond Street studio, either on 14 November 1866 or later. The background and studio props are identical to the one in this photograph of Georgina. For information on the place and timing of the Dickens photographs, see Leon Litvack, 'Dickens in the Eye of the Beholder: The Photographs of Robert Hindry Mason', *Dickens Studies Annual*, 47 (2017), pp. 180–1.

2   Yates, *Edmund Yates: His Recollections and Experiences*, p. 256; Huntington Library, MS FI 2694, Georgina to Annie Fields, 28 December 1869.

3   Huntington Library, MS FI 2702, Georgina to Annie Fields, 10 October 1871.

4   Finlay and Others, 'Guests at Gad's Hill', p. 284.

5   Dickens to F. D. Finlay, 1 January 1869, *P*, XII, p. 264.

6   Finlay and Others, 'Guests at Gad's Hill', p. 282.

7   Dickens to Georgina, 7 November 1866, *P*, XI, pp. 266–7.

8   Dickens to Georgina, 9 January 1867, *P*, XI, p. 296.

9   Dickens to W. W. F. de Cerjat, 1 February 1861, *P*, IX, p. 381.

10   Dickens to Georgina, 19 February 1862, *P*, X, p. 37.

11   Dickens to Letitia Austin, 7 October 1862, *P*, X, p. 135.

12   Biographer Claire Tomalin attributes Dickens's tolerance of the arrogant Thompson to the fact he knew all about Dickens's secret relationship as he was often sent to deliver messages or do errands for Nelly.

13   In her later years, Nelly admitted she had visited Gad's Hill many times and would have been a familiar sight to the servants.

14   Dickens to Georgina, 3 January 1862, *P*, X, p. 3.

15   Dickens to Georgina, 14 November 1860, *P*, IX, p. 339.

16   Huntington Library, MS FI 2745, Georgina to Annie Fields, 15 May 1876.

17   Huntington Library, MS FI 2782, Georgina to Annie Fields, 18 July 1874.

18   Adrian, 'Georgina Hogarth to Percy Fitzgerald: Some Unpublished Letters', p. 7.

19   Ibid.

20   Dickens to Georgina, 4 April 1869, *P*, XII, pp. 323–4.

21   Dickens to W. H. Wills, 6 June 1867, *P*, XI, p. 377.

22   Huntington Library, MS FI 2785, Georgina to Annie Fields, 15 June 1869.

23   Dickens to Georgina, 25 February 1869, *P*, XII, p. 297.

24   Dickens continued to write at Gad's Hill, completing the first numbers of *Our Mutual Friend* in January 1864.

25   Marguerite's reputation had once suffered simply because, as a young girl, she had moved in with her aunt, the Countess of Blessington, and Count D'Orsay. Dickens liked Marguerite enough to introduce her to Nelly, and to use a pet name in their correspondence: 'Would you like to come here next Monday and dine with us at 1, and go over to Madame

Celeste's opening? The charmer is coming, and Georgy will be here all day.' Dickens to Marguerite Power, 25 September 1860, *P*, IX, p. 318.

26 Dickens to W. W. F. de Cerjat, 25 October 1864, *P*, X, p. 444.

27 Dickens to Wilkie Collins, 24 October 1860, *P*, IX, p. 329.

28 Lehmann, *Ancestors and Friends*, p. 211.

29 Ibid., p. 210.

30 Ibid., p. 211.

31 Ibid.

32 R. C. Lehmann, *Familiar Letters: N. L. to F. L., 1864–1867* (London: Ballantyne, Hanson and Co., 1892), p. 19.

33 Dickens to W. W. F. de Cerjat, 3 May 1860, *P*, IX, p. 248.

34 Dickens to Georgina, 31 January 1865, *P*, XI, p. 13.

35 The train that brought Dickens, Nelly and her mother back from France on Friday 9 June 1865 was crossing a viaduct at Staplehurst, Kent when it left the rails and plunged into the stream below. Ten people were killed and fourteen others severely wounded. Dickens was unhurt and clambered out of the carriage window, taking his flask of brandy, to give aid to those needing help. Mrs Ternan was shaken and Nelly injured her arm, very probably breaking it and leaving her with permanent damage. Dickens never recovered from the post-traumatic stress he developed, caused by the shock of the Staplehurst crash.

36 Dickens sold Tavistock House in 1860.

37 Dickens to Thomas Mitton, 28 April 1865, *P*, XI, p. 37; Dickens to W. W. F. de Cerjat, 4 January 1869, *P*, XII, p. 268.

38 Curry, 'Charles Dickens and Annie Fields', p. 52.

39 Adrian, *Georgina Hogarth and the Dickens Circle*, p. 205. See also Wilson, *The Mystery of Charles Dickens*, p. 134.

40 Slater, *Dickens and Women*, p. 176.

41 Huntington Library, MS FI 2733, Georgina to Annie Fields, 23 June 1877.

42 Dickens, 'Violated' letter.

43 Dickens to Georgina, 24 May 1866, Vol. 11, p. 204.

44 Dickens to Benjamin Webster, 25 February 1865, *P*, XI, p. 20.

45 Adrian, 'Georgina Hogarth to Percy Fitzgerald: Some Unpublished Letters', p. 9.

46 Ibid., p. 8.

47 Ibid., pp. 9–10.

48 Ibid., p. 9.

49 Ibid., p. 11.

50 Dickens immediately liked John Bigelow when he met him in Boston, but did not warm to his wife Jane. When the Bigelows returned home to New York at the same time as Dickens arrived there, Jane decided she had the right to monopolise him and believed he should see her whenever she chose. She kept up a surveillance of his hotel room and saw a Mrs Hertz,

a widowed friend of the hotel manager, arrive to have lunch with Dickens. As Mrs Hertz left, Jane Bigelow pounced, screaming and hitting her with her fists. Dickens's reading manager, George Dolby, posted guards at the hotel doors and on several occasions they prevented Jane Bigelow from gaining access to Dickens.

51 Johnson, *Charles Dickens*, p. 1097.

52 Louisa May Alcott, 'A Dickens Day', *Independent*, 19: 995 (26 December 1867). Another American commented on Dickens's preoccupation with his hair. Discovering Dickens was a fellow diner, the American was dismayed to see him looking 'very little like a gentleman, and to our amazement, took out a pocket-comb and combed his hair and whiskers, or rather his goatee, at the table. And yet this is the celebrated man that ridiculed the manners of the Americans!', Collins, *Dickens: Interviews and Recollections*, Vol. 2, p. 339.

53 The writing chalet was a miniature Swiss chalet, a gift from the actor Charles Fechter, which Dickens had erected on a plot of land over the road from Gad's Hill.

54 Dickens to Georgina, 6 December 1867, *P*, XI, p. 505.

55 Adrian, 'Georgina Hogarth to Percy Fitzgerald: Some Unpublished Letters', p. 11.

56 Huntington Library, MS FI 2785, Georgina to Annie Fields, 15 June 1869; MS FI 2694, 28 Dec 1869; MS FI 2695, 4 May 1870.

57 Huntington Library, MS FI 2695, Georgina to Annie Fields, 4 May 1870.

58 Chitty, *The Beast and the Monk: A Life of Charles Kingsley*, p. 287.

59 Curry, 'Charles Dickens and Annie Fields', p. 52.

60 Ibid.

61 'Dickens's Household Trouble', *Harper's Weekly* (24 July 1858), p. 471, https://archive.org/details/harpersweekloobonn/page/470.

62 Dodge wrote this piece under her pseudonym of Gail Hamilton. Sydney P. Moss and Carolyn J. Moss, *American Episodes Involving Charles Dickens* (Troy, NY: Whitston, 1999), pp. 152–60.

63 Curry, 'Charles Dickens and Annie Fields', p. 43.

64 Huntington Library, MS FI 2703, Georgina to Annie Fields, 21 November 1870.

65 Dickens to Georgina, 9 February 1866, *P*, XI, p. 155.

66 Charles Dickens Museum, XB88, Georgina Hogarth's 'Recipe Book for Drinks'.

67 Dickens to Georgina, 26 February 1869, *P*, XII, p. 299; 23 October 1867, *P*, XI, p. 459.

68 Dickens to Georgina, 31 January 1861, *P*, IX, p. 380; 25 November 1861, *P*, IX, p. 522.

69 Tomalin, *Charles Dickens*, p. 353.

70 Dickens to Mamie, 7 April 1868, *P*, XII, p. 92.

71 Tomalin, *Charles Dickens*, p. 381.

72 Dickens to Georgina, 21 April 1869, *P*, XII, p. 339.

73 Adrian, 'Georgina Hogarth to Percy Fitzgerald: Some Unpublished Letters', p. 13.

74 Dickens to Georgina, 12 November 1869, *P*, XII, p. 439.

75 Tomalin, *Charles Dickens*, p. 387; Dickens to Thomas Hyde, 10 February 1870, *P*, XII, p. 476; Dickens to S. L. Fildes, 13 March 1870, *P*, XII, p. 489.

76 Storey, *Dickens and Daughter*, p. 134; Adrian, *Georgina Hogarth and the Dickens Circle*, p. 135.

77 Tomalin, *Charles Dickens*, p. 395.

78 Huntington Library, MS FI 2779, Georgina to Annie Fields, 4 July 1870.

79 Ibid.

80 Ibid.

Chapter 9: 'A hard, hard trial'

1 Huntington Library, MS FI 2778, Georgina to Annie Fields, 29 September 1870; MS FI 2703, 21 November 1870.

2 The mourners were Georgina, Nelly, Charley and his wife Bessie, Katey and Charles Collins, Mamie, Harry, his sister Letitia, cousin Edmund Dickens and friends Frederic Ouvry, Frank Beard, Wilkie Collins and John Forster.

3 George Somes Layard, *Shirley Brooks of Punch: His Life, Letters and Diaries* (New York: Henry Holt and Co., 1907), p. 416.

4 Huntington Library, MS FI 2701, Georgina to Annie Fields, 5 August 1872.

5 Forster, *The Life of Charles Dickens*, Vol. 3, p. 517.

6 Huntington Library, MS FI 2774, Georgina to Annie Fields, 15 August 1870. Two auctions were held at Christie's. The sale of the pictures and art objects raised £9,460 (over £1.1 million today). At the second auction, the property sold for £8,647 (over £1 million). The furnishings and wines made £2,270 (just under £300,000 today). See Adrian, *Georgina Hogarth and the Dickens Circle*, p. 155, p. 159.

7 Huntington Library, MS FI 2705, Georgina to Annie Fields, 16 February 1872.

8 E. A. Lobb et al., 'Predictors of Complicated Grief: A Systematic Review of Empirical Studies', *Death Studies*, 34:8 (2010), pp. 673–98.

9 Adrian, *Georgina Hogarth and the Dickens Circle*, p. 147.

10 Forster, *The Life of Charles Dickens*, Vol. 3, p. 515. Catherine was also left £8,000, but her legacy was placed in a trust which Charley and Harry

managed. It worked out at £240 per annum, far less than the £600 a year Dickens had paid her.

11 Curry, 'Charles Dickens and Annie Fields', p. 52; Moss and Moss, *American Episodes Involving Charles Dickens*, p. 157.

12 Curry, 'Charles Dickens and Annie Fields', p. 58.

13 Bigelow, *Retrospections of an Active Life, 1867–1871*, Vol. 4, p. 383.

14 Huntington Library, MS FI 2699, Georgina to Annie Fields, 20 April 1871.

15 Huntington Library, MS FI 2707, Georgina to Annie Fields, 18 June 1872.

16 Huntington Library, MS FI 2711, Georgina to Annie Fields, 21 February 1873, my italics; see also Adrian, *Georgina Hogarth and the Dickens Circle*, p. 171.

17 Huntington Library, MS FI 2711, Georgina to Annie Fields, 21 February 1873.

18 Huntington Library, MS FI 2782, Georgina to Annie Fields, 18 July 1874.

19 Huntington Library, MS FI 2776, Georgina to Annie Fields, 17 March 1875.

20 Leon Litvack, 'Dickens's Burial in Westminster Abbey: The Untold Story', in L. Litvack and N. Vanfasse (eds), *Reading Dickens Differently* (Chichester: Wiley Blackwell, 2020). Georgina, the girls and Harry wanted Dickens to be buried at Rochester Cathedral.

21 For details of Charley Dickens's purchase of Gad's Hill, see Adrian, *Georgina Hogarth and the Dickens Circle*, p. 159.

22 Huntington Library, MS FI 2699, Georgina to Annie Fields, 20 April 1871.

23 Lillian Nayder discusses whether Dickens deliberately omitted this once-loved sister from his will as a punishment for the fact Letitia continued on good terms with Catherine after the separation. Lillian Nayder, '"The Omission of his Only Sister's Name": Letitia Austin and the Legacies of Charles Dickens', *Dickens Quarterly*, 28:4 (2011), pp. 251–60.

24 Charles Dickens Museum, Ouvry Papers, Farrer Ouvry Envelope 15, 15.37.

25 Adrian, *Georgina Hogarth and the Dickens Circle*, p. 171.

26 Huntington Library, MS FI 2780, Georgina to Annie Fields, 25 February 1870.

27 Dickens to Edmund Yates, 11 August 1858, *P*, VIII, p. 623.

28 Huntington Library, MS FI 2774, Georgina to Annie Fields, 15 August 1870; MS FI 2698, 1 March 1871; MS FI 2746, 26 June 1880.

29 Plorn's financial difficulties were caused by a combination of 'business failures, gambling losses and unpaid debts' (see Adrian, *Georgina Hogarth and the Dickens Circle*, p. 254); Charles Dickens Museum, Gladys Storey Papers, Envelope Q, Georgina to Edward (Plorn) Dickens, 29 May 1884.

Notes

30 Adrian, *Georgina Hogarth and the Dickens Circle*, p. 231.
31 Huntington Library, MS FI 2702, Georgina to Annie Fields, 10 October 1871.
32 Senate House Library, MS1003, Longley, *A Pardoner's Tale*, p. 416.
33 Huntington Library, MS FI 2774, Georgina to Annie Fields, 15 August 1870.
34 Dickens to Frances Elliott, 4 July 1867, *P*, XI, p. 389.
35 Senate House Library, MS1003, Longley, *A Pardoner's Tale*, p. 416.
36 Dickens to Frances Elliott, 4 July 1867, *P*, XI, p. 389.
37 The servants were: the cook Catherine Earle, housemaid Emma Durnford and page (houseboy) Isaac Armitage.
38 Charles Dickens Museum, Ouvry Papers, Farrer Ouvry Envelope 4, 14.25, Georgina to F. Ouvry.
39 Adrian, *Georgina Hogarth and the Dickens Circle*, p. 164.
40 Huntington Library, MS FI 2783, Georgina to Annie Fields, 24 June 1876.
41 Huntington Library, MS FI 2731, Georgina to Annie Fields, 16 January 1877.
42 Charles Dickens Museum, Gladys Storey Papers, Envelope Q, Georgina to Edward (Plorn) Dickens, 22 July, 1877.
43 Ibid.
44 Nayder, *The Other Dickens*, p. 329.
45 Huntington Library, MS FI 2713, Georgina to Annie Fields, 12 May 1873; MS FI 2715, 30 August 1873; MS FI 2717, 24 November 1873.
46 Huntington Library, MS FI 2709, Georgina to Annie Fields, 13 November 1872.
47 Nelly was twelve years older than George Wharton Robinson.
48 Huntington Library, MS FI 2741, Georgina to Annie Fields, 30 October 1877.
49 Towards the end of her life, Jane left a message for Nelly's daughter, Gladys, that her 'dear mother never lived with Charles Dickens'. J. W. T. Ley, an ardent Dickensian, was thoroughly convinced no sexual relationship existed between Dickens and Nelly and amended this statement given to him by Gladys Wharton Robinson. His version read, 'that her dead mother never was the mistress of Charles Dickens'. See Slater, *The Great Charles Dickens Scandal*, p. 182.
50 For discussion of John Thompson, see Tomalin, *Charles Dickens*, p. 357.
51 Senate House Library, MS1003, Longley, *A Pardoner's Tale*, note 26, p. 461.
52 Huntington Library, MS FI 2764, Georgina to Annie Fields, 14 December 1883.
53 Huntington Library, MS FI 2759, Georgina to Annie Fields, 27 February 1883.

54 Huntington Library, MS FI 2749, Georgina to Annie Fields, 10 February 1882.

55 Adrian, 'Georgina Hogarth to Percy Fitzgerald: Some Unpublished Letters', p. 15.

56 Huntington Library, MS FI 2737, Georgina to Annie Fields, 22 March 1878.

57 Huntington Library, MS FI 2739, Georgina to Annie Fields, 11 August 1878.

58 Dickens to W. H. Wills, 21 October 1855, *P*, VII, p. 724.

59 Huntington Library, MS FI 2715, Georgina to Annie Fields, 30 August, 1873.

60 Ibid.

61 Huntington Library, MS FI 2701, Georgina to Annie Fields, 5 August 1872.

62 Storey, *Dickens and Daughter*, pp. 163–4.

63 A. W. Ward, *Dickens* (Franklin Square: Harper and Brothers, 1882), p. 144.

64 K. J. Fielding, *Charles Dickens: Writers and their Works, No. 37* (London: British Council and National Book League, Longmans, Green and Co., 1953), p. 15.

65 Huntington Library, MS FI 2740, Georgina to Annie Fields, 19 September 1878; MS FI 2742, 11 November 1878.

66 Huntington Library, MS FI 2736, Georgina to Annie Fields, 27 February 1879.

67 Rosemary Ashton, *One Hot Summer: Dickens, Darwin, Disraeli, and the Great Stink of 1858* (London: Yale University Press, 2017), pp. 38–9.

68 Adrian, *Georgina Hogarth and the Dickens Circle*, ch. 14.

69 BL, RP 9217, Georgina to Mrs J. Pym, 5 April 1902.

70 Adrian, *Georgina Hogarth and the Dickens Circle*, p. 238.

71 R. H. Horne, 'John Forster; His Early Life and Friendships', *Temple Bar* (April 1876), p. 499.

72 Huntington Library, MS FI 2745, Georgina to Annie Fields, 15 May 1876.

73 'Love Letters of Dickens to "Dora": Revelation of a Pathetic Romance in the Novelist's Youth that Influenced his Life's Work', *New York Times*, 27 September 1908, www.nytimes.com/1908/09/27/archives/love-letters-of-dickens-to-dora-revelation-of-a-pathetic-romance-in.html.

74 Harry B. Smith (ed.), *The Dickens-Kolle Letters* (New York: Bibliophile Society, 1910), p. xi.

75 Walter Dexter, *The Love Romance of Charles Dickens* (London: Argonaut Press, 1936), p. 79, p. 93.

76 Ibid., pp. 115–16.

Notes

77 Georgina heard about this play from Mary Cowden-Clarke, a long-term friend and admirer of Dickens. Mary had been asked to write the introduction to John Garraway's play, *Dickens: A Comedy*. See Senate House Library, MS1003, Longley, *A Pardoner's Tale*, p. 416.

78 Slater, *The Great Charles Dickens Scandal*, p. 47.

79 Ibid., pp. 51–2.

80 Mamie used the £1,500 legacy bequeathed to her from the estate of John Forster to be paid on the death of his wife Eliza, as security. It was the same year Mamie relinquished any interest in the house in Strathmore Gardens which Georgina had purchased for them and when she and her 'new family', the Hargraveses, moved to Manchester. See Gail David-Tellis, 'Breach of Code: The Rift between Mamie Dickens and Georgina Hogarth', *The Dickensian*, 115:509 (2019), pp. 230–1.

81 Ibid.

82 Senate House Library, MS1003, Longley, *A Pardoner's Tale*, p. 513.

83 Huntington Library, MS FI 2779, Georgina to Annie Fields, 4 July 1870.

84 Catherine Marie Hargraves preferred to be known by her second name. For discussion of Mamie's relationship with Thomas and Marie Hargraves see Christine Skelton, 'Mamie Dickens: The Later Years', *The Dickensian*, 113:506 (2017), pp. 252–60.

85 Huntington Library, MS FI 2750, Georgina to Annie Fields, 23 May 1877.

86 Mary Lazarus, *A Tale of Two Brothers* (Sydney: Angus and Robertson, 1973), p. 194.

87 Huntington Library, MS FI 2759, Georgina to Annie Fields, 27 February 1883.

88 Huntington Library, MS FI 2771, Georgina to Annie Fields, 19 January 1888.

89 Huntington Library, MS FI 2760, Georgina to Annie Fields, 13 June 1887.

90 BL, RP 9217, Georgina to Horace and Jane Pym, 26 September 1889.

91 Ibid.

92 Dickens to Georgina, 22 December 1867, *P*, XI, p. 518.

93 Rita Gollin, *Annie Adams Fields* (Amherst and Boston, MA: University of Massachusetts Press, 2002), p. 69.

94 Huntington Library, MS FI 2780, Georgina to Annie Fields, 25 February 1870.

95 Huntington Library, MS FI 2695, Georgina to Annie Fields, 4 May 1870.

96 Huntington Library, MS FI 2763, Georgina to Annie Fields, 17 June 1897.

Notes

97 Huntington Library, MS FI 2767, Georgina to Annie Fields, 23 February 1901.

98 Forster, *The Life of Charles Dickens*, Vol. 3, p. 517.

99 For discussion of the Dickens children after their father's death, see Robert Gottlieb, *Great Expectations: The Sons and Daughters of Charles Dickens* (New York: Farrar, Straus and Giroux, 2012).

100 In addition, Georgina had taken Dickens's part in initially snubbing Charley's bride, Bessie, because she was the daughter of his once publisher, Fred Evans (who had offended Dickens by refusing to support the publication of his 'Personal' statement). Charley and Bessie could not fail to notice, too, how Georgina treated their girls differently. In one of the many versions of her own will, Georgina instructed that the money she had intended leaving to her goddaughter Beatrice, Charley's fifth daughter, was instead to be shared with Mekitty on the basis that she 'is the one I like best – and the most interesting of his children'. Charles Dickens Museum, Ouvry Papers, Farrer Ouvry Envelope 30, 37.15, Georgina to F. Ouvry.

101 Lazarus, *A Tale of Two Brothers*, p. 147.

102 Ibid., p. 194.

103 Hawksley, *Katey: The Life and Loves of Dickens's Artist Daughter*, pp. 254–5.

104 Huntington Library, MS FI 2716, Georgina to Annie Fields, 17 October 1873.

105 Huntington Library, MS FI 2722, Georgina to Annie Fields, 13 May 1874.

106 Huntington Library, MS FI 2723, Georgina to Annie Fields, 9 June 1874. A bank account in the names of Miss Georgina Hogarth, John Everett Millais Esq. and Henry Fielding Dickens Esq. was opened in 1874. In 1888, there was £5,515 (just over £644,000). In January 1912, the balance of £9.15.6d (around £1,000) was withdrawn and the account closed. Royal Bank of Scotland Archives, Edinburgh (1878–1914), Coutts Bank, London, Accounts Ledgers of Miss Georgina Hogarth (1870–8).

107 Storey, *Dickens and Daughter*, p. 212.

108 Dickens to Alfred Dickens, 20 May 1870, *P*, XII, p. 530.

109 Huntington Library, MS FI 2707, Georgina to Annie Fields, 18 June 1872.

110 Huntington Library, MS FI 2699, Georgina to Annie Fields, 20 April 1871.

111 Adrian, *Georgina Hogarth and the Dickens Circle*, p. 180.

112 Charles Dickens Museum, Gladys Storey Papers, Envelope Q, Georgina to Edward (Plorn) Dickens, July 1880.

113 Case Western Reserve University, Arthur Adrian Papers, Box 3HA6, Georgina to Blanche Swanson, 17 January 1908.

114 Walter T. Spencer, *Forty Years in my Bookshop* (London: Constable and Co., 1923), pp. 98–9.

115 Adrian, *Georgina Hogarth and the Dickens Circle*, p. 265.
116 Charles Dickens Museum, Gladys Storey Papers, Envelope C.
117 Walter Dexter, 'Twice Twenty-One: The Fellowship in Retrospect', *The Dickensian*, 40:269 (1943), p. 26.
118 Author copy of Georgina Hogarth's Last Will and Testament.
119 Huntington Library, MS FI 2778, Georgina to Annie Fields, 29 September 1870.

Chapter 10: Aftermath

1 'Georgina Hogarth', *Oxford Dictionary of National Biography*, www.oxforddnb.com/.
2 Richard Brooks, 'Dickens's Racy Tale of Two Sisters', *Sunday Times* (2 October 2011) p. 18, www.thetimes.co.uk/article/dickenss-racy-tale-of-two-sisters-2lf78020glw.
3 BBC *Antiques Roadshow*, Series 28, No. 11, Chelsea Pensioners Royal Hospital, Chelsea, London, 13 November 2005.
4 Adrian, *Georgina Hogarth and the Dickens Circle*, p. 256.
5 Leonee Ormond, 'Charles Dickens and Alfred Tennyson', *Tennyson Research Bulletin*, 10:1 (2012), pp. 71–9. Ormond argues that it was uncharacteristic of Tennyson to give such a gift. However, Tennyson had great affection for Dickens and may have been influenced to present him with a ring by a member of his wider family, Mary Boyle.
6 Alison Flood, '"Proof" that Dickens Fathered Illegitimate Child to be Auctioned', *Guardian* (15 January 2009), www.theguardian.com/books/2009/jan/15/dickens-sister-child-auction; for Hector Dickens's inventory of Dickens's possessions see Dan Newling, 'Is this Ring For Sale Proof Charles Dickens Had an Illegitimate Son with Sister-in-Law?' *MailOnline* (15 January 2009), www.dailymail.co.uk/news/article-1117405/Is-ring-sale-proof-Charles-Dickens-illegitimate-son-sister-law.html.
7 Simon Worrall, 'Charles Dickens's Great-Great-Grandson: Author Was "World's First Superstar"', *National Geographic* (24 December 2014), www.nationalgeographic.com/adventure/article/141225-charles-dickens-christmas-carol-ellen-ternan-pickwick-papers.
8 Lawrence Hendra, 'The Lost Portrait: A Note on Provenance', in Emma Rutherford, Lawrence Hendra, Lucinda Dickens Hawksley and Louisa Price, *Charles Dickens: The Lost Portrait Catalogue* (London: Philip Mould and Co., 2018), pp. 20–9.
9 Dickens to W. H. Wills, 29 December 1852, note 8, *P*, VI, p. 841.
10 H. Dickens, 'The Recollections of Sir Henry Dickens, K.C.', p. 20.
11 Matz, 'Miss Georgina Hogarth', p. 122.
12 British Newspaper Archive, 'London Gossip', *Hampshire Telegraph*, 10 May 1882; Moss and Moss, *American Episodes Involving Charles Dickens*, p. 155.

Notes

13 Panton, *Leaves from a Life*, p. 144; S. M. Ellis, *A Mid Victorian Pepys: The Letters and Memoirs of Sir William Hardman 1863–1865* (London: Cecil Palmer, 1923), p. 8.

14 H. C. Dickens, 'Presidential Address to the Dickens Fellowship Conference in 1946', p. 190.

15 Staples, 'Some Early Memories of the Dickens Fellowship', p. 134.

16 F. Anstey, *A Long Retrospect* (London: Oxford University Press, 1936), p. 291.

17 Carl Bechhofer Roberts, *This Side Idolatry* (Indianapolis, IN: Bobbs-Merrill Co., 1928).

18 Hugh Kingsmill, *The Sentimental Journey: A Life of Charles Dickens* (London: Wishart and Co., 1934), p. 135.

19 Storey, *Dickens and Daughter*, p. 124.

20 Ibid., p. 24.

21 Ibid., p. 124.

22 Ibid.

23 Dickens to Frederick Lehmann, 8 January 1863, *P*, X, p. 191.

24 Wright, *The Life of Charles Dickens*, p. 163, p. 263.

25 Pope-Hennessy, *Charles Dickens*, p. 399, p. 401, p. 405–6.

26 Pearson, *Dickens*, p. 255.

27 Bowen, *Charles Dickens and his Family*, p. 93, p. 178.

28 Aylmer, *Dickens Incognito*, p. 81.

29 Pansy Pakenham, 'Hebe Elsna's Defence of Mrs Dickens', *The Dickensian*, 59:340 (1963), pp. 125–6.

30 Johnson, *Charles Dickens*, Vol. 2, p. 907.

31 Azure Engelbrecht, 'Neo-Victorian Dickens(es): The Hogarth/Dickens Circle and Recent Biofiction' (PhD dissertation, University of Auckland, 2016); Wilson, *The Mystery of Charles Dickens*; Cenarth Fox, *Aunt Georgy* (Fox Plays, 2009), www.yumpu.com/en/document/read/13324893/aunt-georgy.

32 Annie Adams Fields Papers, gifted by Boylston A. Beal and Zabdiel B. Adams, in 1944, to Massachusetts Historical Society, now housed at the Henry E. Huntington Library; Adrian, 'Georgina Hogarth to Percy Fitzgerald: Some Unpublished Letters', pp. 5–18; BL, RP 9217, 22 November 1888; 5 May 1890.

33 Slater, *The Great Charles Dickens Scandal*, p. 177.

34 Tomalin, *Charles Dickens*, p. 396.

35 Slater, *The Great Charles Dickens Scandal*, p. 179.

36 Wilson, *The Mystery of Charles Dickens*, p. 13.

37 Emily Bell, 'Writing the Death of Dickens', *Victoriographies*, 10:3 (2020), p. 275.

38 Huntington Library, MS FI 2779, Georgina to Annie Fields, 4 July 1870.

39 Robert Patten, 'The Dickens Archive and the Sotheby's Sale', *The Dickensian*, 95:449 (1999), p. 257.

Notes

40 BL, RP 9217, Georgina to Horace Pym, 22 November 1888.

41 I am grateful to Andrew Maywood for sharing his research findings into Georgina's authentication cards.

42 Dickens's grandson described Georgina as an 'ordinary mid-Victorian lady and rather helpless and inefficient. Indeed, she was no great figure in history at all'. See H. C. Dickens, 'Presidential Address to the Dickens Fellowship Conference in 1946', p. 190.

43 British Newspaper Archive, 'London Gossip', *Hampshire Telegraph*, 10 May 1882.

Bibliography

Archive sources

British Library, London, RP 9217, Pym, Horace N., Dickens, Charles, 7 autograph letters signed from Mamie Dickens and 24 autograph letters signed from Georgina Hogarth to Pym and his wife, including numerous references to Charles Dickens, his life and books. With autograph envelopes.

British Newspaper Archive, www.britishnewspaperarchive.co.uk.

Case Western Reserve University, Cleveland, Ohio, Arthur Adrian Papers, Box 3HA6.

Charles Dickens Museum, London, Ouvry Papers, Farrer–Ouvry, envelopes 1–41, Autograph and typescript letters.

Charles Dickens Museum, London, Storey Papers, Envelopes C, PP, Q, Autograph and typescript letters.

Henry E. Huntington Library, Art Collections, and Botanical Gardens, San Marino, California, Annie Adams Fields Papers, MSS FI.

Hertfordshire Archives and Local Studies, Hertford, Bulwer-Lytton, Edward, Letters Received, DE/K/C4/134, 23 November 1850; DE/K/025/196, 26 November 1858.

Royal Archives, Windsor, Queen Victoria's Journals, Lord Esher's typescripts, RA VIC/MAIN/QVJ (W), www.queenvictoriasjournals.org/home.do (accessed 15 October 2022).

Royal Bank of Scotland Archives, Edinburgh (1878–1914), Coutts Bank, London, Accounts ledgers of Miss Georgina Hogarth (1870–78).

Senate House Library, University of London, London. Longley Collection, MS1003, Longley, Katharine, *A Pardoner's Tale*.

Primary and secondary sources

Adrian, Arthur, *Georgina Hogarth and the Dickens Circle* (London: Oxford University Press, 1957).

Bibliography

Adrian, Arthur, *Mark Lemon: First Editor of Punch* (London: Oxford University Press, 1966).

Adrian, Arthur, 'Georgina Hogarth to Percy Fitzgerald: Some Unpublished Letters', *The Dickensian*, 88:1 (1992), pp. 5–18.

Alcott, Louisa May, 'A Dickens Day', *Independent*, 19: 995 (26 December 1867).

Allen, Louise, *The Georgian Seaside* (CreateSpace, 2016).

An American Lady, *A Handbook of Etiquette for Ladies* (New York: Leavitt and Allen, 1847).

Anstey, F., *A Long Retrospect* (London: Oxford University Press, 1936).

Arbuckle, Elizabeth Sanders (ed.), *Harriet Martineau's Letters to Fanny Wedgwood* (Stanford, CA: Stanford University Press, 1983).

Ashton, Rosemary, *Thomas and Jane Carlyle: Portrait of a Marriage* (London: Random House, 2002).

Ashton, Rosemary, *One Hot Summer: Dickens, Darwin, Disraeli, and the Great Stink of 1858* (London: Yale University Press, 2017).

Aylmer, Felix, *Dickens Incognito* (London: Rupert Hart-Davis, 1959).

Baker, George Pierce, *Charles Dickens and Maria Beadnell: Private Correspondence* (Boston, MA: Bibliophile Society, 1908).

Beeton, Isabella, *Beeton's Book of Household Management* (London: Jonathan Cape, 1861).

Bell, Emily, 'Writing the Death of Dickens', *Victoriographies*, 10:3 (2020), pp. 270–91.

Bigelow, John, *Retrospections of an Active Life, 1822–1879*, 4 vols (New York: Baker and Taylor, 1909–13).

Boardman, Kay, 'The Ideology of Domesticity: The Regulation of the Household Economy in Victorian Women's Magazines', *Victorian Periodicals Review*, 33:2 (2000), pp. 150–64.

Bowen, John, 'Bebelle and "His Boots": Dickens, Ellen Ternan and the *Christmas Stories*', *The Dickensian*, 96:452 (2000), pp. 197–208.

Bowen, John, 'Madness and the Dickens Marriage: A New Source', *The Dickensian*, 115:507 (2019), pp. 5–20.

Bowen, W. H., *Charles Dickens and his Family* (Cambridge: W. Heffer and Sons, 1956).

Boyle, Courtney (ed.), *Mary Boyle: Her Book* (London: John Murray, 1902).

Bredsdorff, Elias, *Hans Andersen and Charles Dickens: A Friendship and its Dissolution* (Cambridge: W. Heffer and Sons, 1956).

Bredsdorff, Elias, *Hans Christian Andersen* (London: Phaidon Press, 1975).

Brooks, Richard, 'Dickens's Racy Tale of Two Sisters', *Sunday Times* (2 October 2011) p. 18, www.thetimes.co.uk/article/dickenss-racy-tale-of-two-sisters-2lf78020glw (accessed 15 October 2022).

Burnett, Henry, 'The Young Novelist at Work and Play', in Philip Collins (ed.), *Dickens: Interviews and Recollections*, Vol. 1 (London: Macmillan, 1981).

Butt, John, 'Reviews: Georgina Hogarth and the Dickens Circle', *Review of English Studies*, 10:38 (1959), pp. 207–9.

Carlton, W. J., '"Old Nick" at Devonshire Terrace', *The Dickensian*, 59:341 (1963), pp. 138–44.

Carlyle Letters Online, https://carlyleletters.dukeupress.edu/home (accessed 15 October 2022).

Chamberlain, Kathy, *Jane Welsh Carlyle and her Victorian World* (London: Duckworth, 2017).

Chapple, J. A. V. and Pollard, A. (eds), *The Letters of Mrs. Gaskell* (Manchester: Manchester University Press, 1966).

'Charles Dickens – His Methods and Habits', *Brooklyn Daily Eagle* (16 August 1882), http://afflictor.com/2011/12/07/old-print-article-charles-dickens-his-methods-and-habits-brooklyn-daily-eagle-1882/ (accessed 15 October 2022).

Chitty, Susan, *The Beast and the Monk: A Life of Charles Kingsley* (London: Hodder and Stoughton, 1974).

Christian, E. E., 'Recollections of Charles Dickens: His Family and Friends', *Temple Bar*, 82 (April 1888), pp. 481–506.

Collins, Philip, 'W. C. Macready and Dickens: Some Family Recollections', *Dickens Studies*, 11:2 (1966), pp. 51–6.

Collins, Philip (ed.), *Dickens: Interviews and Recollections*, 2 vols (London: Macmillan Press, 1981).

Cowden-Clarke, Charles and Cowden-Clarke, Mary, *Recollections of Writers* (London: S. Low, Marston, Searle, and Rivington, 1878).

Curry, George, 'Charles Dickens and Annie Fields', *Huntington Library Quarterly*, 51:1 (1988), pp. 1–71.

David-Tellis, Gail, 'Breach of Code: The Rift between Mamie Dickens and Georgina Hogarth', *The Dickensian*, 115:509 (2019), pp. 223–36.

David-Tellis, Gail, 'Dead Girl Rising: Georgina Hogarth as "the Girl at the Waterfall"', *The Dickensian*, 117:514 (2021), pp. 122–31.

Dexter, Walter, *The Love Romance of Charles Dickens* (London: Argonaut Press, 1936).

Dexter, Walter, 'Twice Twenty-One: The Fellowship in Retrospect', *The Dickensian*, 40:269 (1943), pp. 25–35.

Dexter, Walter (ed.), *Dickens to his Oldest Friend* (New York: Haskell House, 1973).

Dickens, Alfred Tennyson, 'My Father and his Friends', *Nash's Magazine* 4 (September 1911), p. 640.

Dickens, Charles, *The Pilgrim Edition of the Letters of Charles Dickens*, ed. Madeleine House et al., 12 vols (Oxford: Clarendon Press, 1965–2002).

Dickens, Charles, 'Speech: Edinburgh, June 25, 1841', in Charles Dickens, *Speeches: Literary and Social*, pp. 3–4, www.public-library.uk/ebooks/90/39.pdf (accessed 15 October 2022).

Bibliography

Dickens, Charles and Collins, Wilkie, *The Lazy Tour of Two Idle Apprentices* (Richmond: Alma Books, 2018).

Dickens Jr, Charles, 'Brompton', in *Dickens's Dictionary of London* (London, 1879), www.victorianlondon.org/dickens/dickens-bic.htm (accessed 15 October 2022).

Dickens, Henry, *The Recollections of Sir Henry Dickens, K.C.* (London: William Heinemann, 1934).

Dickens, Henry Charles, 'Presidential Address to the Dickens Fellowship Conference in 1946', *The Dickensian*, 42:280 (1946), pp. 188–91.

Dickens, Henry F., *Memories of my Father* (London: Victor Gollancz, 1928).

Dickens, Mamie, 'Charles Dickens at Home', *Cornhill Magazine*, 4 (January 1885), pp. 31–55.

Dickens, Mamie, *Charles Dickens by his Eldest Daughter* (London: Cassell and Co., 1885).

Dickens, Mamie, *My Father as I Recall Him* (London: Roxburghe Press, 1897).

'Dickens's Household Trouble', *Harper's Weekly* (24 July 1858), p. 471, https://archive.org/details/harpersweekloobonn/page/470 (accessed 15 October 2022).

Douglas-Fairhurst, Robert, *The Turning Point* (London: Penguin, 2021).

Downer, Alan S., *The Eminent Tragedian* (London: Oxford University Press, 1966).

E. E. C., 'Reminiscences of Charles Dickens from a Young Lady's Diary', *Englishwoman's Domestic Magazine*, 10 (1871), pp. 336–44.

Ellis, S. M., *William Harrison Ainsworth and his Friends*, Vol. 2 (London: John Lane, Bodley Head, 1911).

Ellis, S. M., *A Mid Victorian Pepys: The Letters and Memoirs of Sir William Hardman 1863–1865* (London: Cecil Palmer, 1923).

Ellis, Sarah Stickney, *The Women of England: Their Social Duties and Domestic Habits* (London: Fisher and Son, 1839).

Ellis, Sarah Stickney, *The Daughters of England: Their Position in Society, Character and Responsibilities* (London: Fisher, Son and Co., 1842).

Engelbrecht, Azure, 'Neo-Victorian Dickens(es): The Hogarth/Dickens Circle and Recent Biofiction' (PhD dissertation, University of Auckland, 2016).

Fielding, K. J., *Charles Dickens: Writers and their Works, No. 37* (London: British Council and National Book League, Longmans, Green and Co., 1953).

Fielding, K. J., 'Dickens and his Wife: Fact or Forgery?', *Etudes Anglaises*, 8 (1955), pp. 212–22.

Fielding, K. J., 'Dickens and the Hogarth Scandal', *Nineteenth-Century Fiction*, 10: 1 (1955), pp. 64–74.

Finlay, Francis, and Others, 'Guests at Gad's Hill', in P. Collins (ed.), *Dickens: Interviews and Recollections*, Vol. 2 (London: Macmillan Press, 1981).

Flanders, Judith, *The Victorian House* (London: Harper Perennial, 2003).

Bibliography

Flood, Alison, '"Proof" that Dickens Fathered Illegitimate Child to be Auctioned', *Guardian* (15 January 2009), www.theguardian.com/books/2009/jan/15/dickens-sister-child-auction (accessed 15 October 2022).

Forster, John, *The Life of Charles Dickens*, 3 vols (London: Chapman and Hall, 1872–4).

Fox, Cenarth, *Aunt Georgy* (Carnforth: Fox Plays, 2009), www.yumpu.com/en/document/read/13324893/aunt-georgy (accessed 15 October 2022).

Francillon, R. E., *Mid-Victorian Memories* (London: Hodder and Stoughton, 1914).

Freeling, Arthur, *The Ladies' Pocket Book of Etiquette* (Waltham Saint Lawrence: Golden Cockerel Press, 1928; first published 1838).

Frith, William Powell, *My Autobiography and Reminiscences*, Vol. 3 (London: Richard Bentley and Son, 1888).

Fuller, Hester Thackeray and Hammersley, Violet, *Thackeray's Daughter*, 2nd edn (London: W. J. Pollock and Co., 1952).

Garnett, Robert, 'The Crisis of 1863', *Dickens Quarterly*, 23:3 (2006), pp. 181–91.

Garnett, Robert, *Charles Dickens in Love* (New York: Pegasus Books, 2012).

Gerin, Winifred, *Anne Thackeray Ritchie: Journals and Letters* (Oxford: Oxford University Press, 1981).

Giddings, R., 'Dickens and the Great Unmentionable' (paper presented at 'Dickens and Sex' Conference, University of London Institute of English Studies, 20 March 2004).

Gollin, Rita, *Annie Adams Fields* (Amherst and Boston, MA: University of Massachusetts Press, 2002).

Gorham, Deborah, *The Victorian Girl and the Feminine Ideal*, in Martha Vicinus (ed.), *Suffer and Be Still* (Bloomington, IN: Indiana University Press, 1982).

Gottlieb, Robert, *Great Expectations: The Sons and Daughters of Charles Dickens* (New York: Farrar, Straus and Giroux, 2012).

Gray, Donald J., 'The Uses of Victorian Laughter', *Victorian Studies*, 10:2 (1966), pp. 145–76.

Hanaford, Phebe A., *The Life and Writing of Charles Dickens: A Woman's Memorial Volume* (Augusta, ME: E. C. Allen and Co., 1875).

Hankinson, Sophia, 'A Brother Lost and Found: The Tale of Edward Tagart, Helen Bourn Martineau, Charles Dickens, Beatrice Potter and Transylvania', *Martineau Society Newsletter* (31 June 2012).

Harden, Edgar F. (ed.), *The Letters and Private Papers of William Makepeace Thackeray*, Vol. 1 (New York and London: Garland, 1994).

Hartley, Jenny, *Charles Dickens and the House of Fallen Women* (London: Methuen, 2008).

Hawksley, Lucinda, *Katey: The Life and Loves of Dickens's Artist Daughter* (London: Doubleday, 2006).

Hendra, Lawrence, 'The Lost Portrait: A Note on Provenance', in Emma Rutherford, Lawrence Hendra, Lucinda Dickens Hawksley and Louisa

Bibliography

Price, *Charles Dickens: The Lost Portrait Catalogue* (London: Philip Mould and Co., 2018).

Hogarth, Georgina and Dickens, Mamie (eds), *The Letters of Charles Dickens* (London: Macmillan and Co., 1903).

Holme, Thea, *The Carlyles at Home* (Oxford: Oxford University Press, 1965).

Horne, R. H., 'John Forster: His Early Life and Friendships', *Temple Bar* (April 1876), pp. 491–505.

Hughes, Kathryn, 'Gender Roles in the 19th Century', *Discovering Literature: Romantics and Victorians*, British Library website (2014), www.bl.uk/romantics-and-victorians/articles/gender-roles-in-the-19th-century (accessed 15 October 2022).

Hughes, Kathryn, 'The Middle Classes: Etiquette and Upward Mobility', *Discovering Literature: Romantics and Victorians*, British Library website (2014), www.bl.uk/romantics-and-victorians/articles/the-middle-classes-etiquette-and-upward-mobility (accessed 15 October 2022).

Ingham, Patricia, *Dickens, Women and Language* (Toronto: University of Toronto Press, 1992).

Johnson, Edgar, *Charles Dickens: His Tragedy and Triumph*, 2 vols (New York: Simon and Schuster, 1952).

Kaplan, Fred, *Dickens: A Biography* (London: Hodder and Stoughton, 1988).

Kenyon, L. B. (ed.), *Letters of Elizabeth Barrett Browning*, Vol. 2 (London: Smith Elder, 1897).

Kingsmill, Hugh, *The Sentimental Journey: A Life of Charles Dickens* (London: Wishart and Co., 1934).

Kitton, F. G., *Dickens and his Illustrators* (London: George Redway, 1899).

Kitton, F. G., *Charles Dickens: His Life, Writings and Personality* (London: T. C. and E. C. Jack, 1902).

Langland, Elizabeth, 'Nobody's Angels: Middle-Class Women and Domestic Ideology in Victorian Culture', *PMLA*, 107:2 (1992), pp. 290–304.

Layard, George Somes, *Shirley Brooks of Punch: His Life, Letters and Diaries* (New York: Henry Holt and Co., 1907).

Lazarus, Mary, *A Tale of Two Brothers* (Sydney: Angus and Robertson, 1973).

Lehmann, John, *Ancestors and Friends* (London: Eyre and Spottiswoode, 1962).

Lehmann, R. C., *Familiar Letters: N. L. to F. L., 1864–1867* (London: Ballantyne, Hanson and Co., 1892).

Ley, J. W. T., *The Dickens Circle: A Narrative of the Novelist's Friendships* (New York: E. P. Dutton, 1919).

Ley, J. W. T., 'Father and Daughter', *The Dickensian*, 35:252 (1939), pp. 250–3.

Linton, Eliza Lynn, *My Literary Life* (London: Hodder and Stoughton, 1899).

Litvack, Leon, 'Dickens in the Eye of the Beholder: The Photographs of Robert Hindry Mason', *Dickens Studies Annual*, 47 (2017), pp. 165–99.

Bibliography

Litvack, Leon, 'Dickens's Burial in Westminster Abbey: The Untold Story', in L. Litvack and N. Vanfasse (eds), *Reading Dickens Differently* (Chichester: Wiley Blackwell, 2020).

Lobb, E. A., Kristjanson, L. J., Aoun, S. M., Monterosso, L., Halkett, G. K. and Davies, A., 'Predictors of Complicated Grief: A Systematic Review of Empirical Studies', *Death Studies*, 34:8 (2010), pp. 673–98.

Logan, Deborah Anne (ed.), *The Collected Letters of Harriet Martineau*, Vol. 4 (London: Routledge, 2007).

'London Gossip', *Hampshire Telegraph* (10 May 1882).

Long, William F., 'Passages in the Life of Mr George Hogarth – 1: Mr Hogarth Applies for a Chair', *The Dickensian*, 498:112 (2016), pp. 22–30.

Long, William F., 'Passages in the Life of Mr George Hogarth – 2: Mr Hogarth Goes to Prison', *The Dickensian*, 112:499 (2016), pp. 118–29.

Long, William F. and Chong, Mairi E., 'Letter to the Editor: Sudden Death in the Hogarth Family', *The Dickensian*, 111:497 (2015), pp. 267–8.

'Love Letters of Dickens to "Dora": Revelation of a Pathetic Romance in the Novelist's Youth that Influenced his Life's Work', *New York Times* (27 September 1908), www.nytimes.com/1908/09/27/archives/love-letters-of-dickens-to-dora-revelation-of-a-pathetic-romance-in.html (accessed 15 October 2022).

MacMillan, Margaret, *History's People* (London: Profile Books, 2015).

Marcus, Sharon, *Between Women* (Woodstock: Princeton University Press, 2007).

Marsh, Jan, *Jane and May Morris* (Horsham: Printed Word, 2000).

Matz, B. W., 'Miss Georgina Hogarth', *The Dickensian*, 13:5 (1917), pp. 122–3.

Mayhew, Henry, *London Labour and the London Poor* (London: Charles Griffin and Co., 1851).

Mitchell, Leslie, *Bulwer Lytton: The Rise and Fall of a Victorian Man of Letters* (London: Hambledon and London, 2003).

Moss, Sydney, P. and Moss, Carolyn J., *American Episodes Involving Charles Dickens* (Troy, NY: Whitston, 1999).

'Mr Wilkie Collins's "Frozen Deep"', *Leader*, 8: 335 (10 January 1857), p. 44, https://ncse.ac.uk/periodicals/l/issues/vm2-ncseproduct2175/page/20/ (accessed 15 October 2022).

Nayder, Lillian, *The Other Dickens: A Life of Catherine Hogarth* (Ithaca, NY: Cornell University Press, 2011).

Nayder, Lillian, '"The Omission of his Only Sister's Name": Letitia Austin and the Legacies of Charles Dickens', *Dickens Quarterly*, 28:4 (2011), pp. 251–60.

Nayder, Lillian, '"*He Has a Moustache*"; or "Earth Will Not Hold Us Both"; Charles Dickens and the Problem of Fred', *Dickens Quarterly*, 30:2 (2013), pp. 141–53.

Newling, Dan, 'Is this Ring For Sale Proof Charles Dickens Had an Illegitimate Son with Sister-in-Law?' *MailOnline* (15 January 2009), www.dailymail.co.uk/

news/article-1117405/Is-ring-sale-proof-Charles-Dickens-illegitimate-son-sister-law.html (accessed 15 October 2022).

Newport, Barry, 'The Death of Mary Hogarth: A New Explanation', *The Dickensian*, 111:496 (2015), pp. 142–5.

Nisbet, Ada, *Dickens and Ellen Ternan* (Berkeley, CA: University of California Press, 1952).

Ormond, Leonee, 'Charles Dickens and Alfred Tennyson', *Tennyson Research Bulletin*, 10:1 (2012), pp. 71–9.

Oxford Dictionary of National Biography, www.oxforddnb.com/ (accessed 15 October 2022).

Pakenham, Pansy, 'Hebe Elsna's Defence of Mrs Dickens', *The Dickensian*, 59:340 (1963), pp. 125–6.

Panton, Jane, *Leaves from a Life* (London: Eveleigh Nash, 1908).

Parker, David and Slater, Michael, 'The Gladys Storey Papers', *The Dickensian*, 76:390 (1980), pp. 3–16.

Parker, D., Wilson, A. and Wilson, R., 'Letters of a Guest at Devonshire Terrace', *The Dickensian*, 95:447 (1999), pp. 51–60.

Paroissien, David H., 'Charles Dickens and the Weller Family', *Dickens Studies Annual*, 2 (1972), pp. 1–38.

Paterson, Clara, *Angela Burdett-Coutts and the Victorians* (London: John Murray, 1953).

Patten, Robert, 'The Dickens Archive and the Sotheby's Sale', *The Dickensian*, 95:449 (1999), pp. 257–8.

Pearson, Hesketh, *Dickens: His Character, Comedy and Career* (London: Methuen and Co., 1949).

'Peeps at Dickens: Pen Pictures from Contemporary Sources. XXVII – Hans Andersen to his Sister', *The Dickensian*, 30:229 (1933), pp. 58–9.

Perugini, Kate, 'Dickens as a Lover of Art and Artists', *Magazine of Art*, 28 (1903), pp. 125–30.

Perugini, Kate, 'On Women Old and New', *The Dickensian*, 29:227 (1933), pp. 185–7.

Perugini, Kate Dickens, 'I Loved him for his Faults', in Philip Collins (ed.), *Dickens: Interviews and Recollections*, Vol. 1 (London: Macmillan Press, 1981).

Peters, Catherine, *The King of Inventors* (London: Secker and Warburg, 1991).

Pipes, D. J. V., *Charles Dickens in 1867* (CreateSpace, 2018).

Pope-Hennessy, Una, *Charles Dickens* (London: Chatto and Windus, 1945).

Ray, Gordon N. (ed.), *The Letters and Private Papers of William Makepeace Thackeray*, 4 vols (Oxford: Oxford University Press, 1945).

Renton, Richard, *John Forster and his Friendships* (London: Chapman and Hall, 1912).

Roberts, Carl Bechhofer, *This Side Idolatry* (Indianapolis, IN: Bobbs-Merrill Co., 1928).

Sala, George Augustus, 'My Master in Letters', in Philip Collins (ed.), *Dickens: Interviews and Recollections*, Vol. 2 (London: Macmillan, 1981).

Bibliography

Schlicke, Paul (ed.), *The Oxford Companion to Charles Dickens* (Oxford: Oxford University Press, 2011).

Showalter, Elaine and Showalter, English, 'Victorian Women and Menstruation', in Martha Vicinus (ed.), *Suffer and Be Still* (Bloomington, IN: Indiana University Press, 1973).

Simkin, David, *Portraits of Charles Dickens (1812–1870)*, www.photohistory-sussex.co.uk/DickensCharlesPortraits.htm (accessed 15 October 2022).

Simonsen, Pauline, 'Elizabeth Barrett Browning's Redundant Women', *Victorian Poetry*, 35:4 (1997), pp. 509–32.

Skelton, Christine, 'Mamie Dickens: The Later Years', *The Dickensian*, 113:506 (2017), pp. 252–60.

Slater, Michael, *Dickens and Women* (London: J. M. Dent and Sons, 1983).

Slater, Michael, *Charles Dickens* (London: Yale University Press, 2009).

Slater, Michael, *The Great Charles Dickens Scandal* (London: Yale University Press, 2012).

Smith, Harry B. (ed.), *The Dickens-Kolle Letters* (New York: Bibliophile Society, 1910).

Solly, H. S., *The Life of Henry Morley, LL.D.* (London: Edwin Arnold, 1898).

Spencer, Walter T., *Forty Years in my Bookshop* (London: Constable and Co., 1923).

Staples, Leslie C., 'Some Early Memories of the Dickens Fellowship', *The Dickensian*, 73:383 (1977), pp. 132–7.

Storey, Gladys, *Dickens and Daughter* (London: Frederick Muller Ltd, 1939).

Thornwell, E., *The Ladies Guide to Perfect Gentility* (New York: Derby and Jackson, 1857).

Tomalin, Claire, *The Invisible Woman* (London: Viking, 1990).

Tomalin, Claire, *Charles Dickens: A Life* (London: Penguin, 2011).

Tosh, John, 'Domesticity and Manliness in the Victorian Middle Class', in M. Roper and J. Tosh (eds), *Manful Assertions: Masculinities in Britain since 1800* (London: Routledge, 1991).

Toynbee, William, *The Diaries of William Charles Macready, 1833–1851* (New York: G. P. Putnam's Sons, 1912).

Ward, A. W., *Dickens* (Franklin Square: Harper and Brothers, 1882).

Weston, Nancy, *Daniel Maclise: Irish Artist in Victorian London* (Dublin: Four Courts Press, 2000).

Whiffen, Mrs Thomas, *Keeping Off the Shelf* (New York: E. P. Dutton and Co., 1928).

Wilson, A. N., *The Mystery of Charles Dickens* (London: Atlantic, 2020).

Wilson, A. N., 'Charles Dickens the Misogynist', *Mail on Sunday* (23 May 2020), www.dailymail.co.uk/news/article-8351467/Charles-Dickens-cruel-wife-hated-mother-affair-writes-N-WILSON.html (accessed 15 October 2022).

Wormeley Latimer, E., 'A Girl's Recollections of Dickens', *Lippincott's Magazine* (September 1893). pp. 338–9.

Bibliography

Worrall, Simon, 'Charles Dickens's Great-Great-Grandson: Author Was "World's First Superstar"', *National Geographic* (24 December 2014), www.nationalgeographic.com/adventure/article/141225-charles-dickens-christmas-carol-ellen-ternan-pickwick-papers (accessed 15 October 2022).

Wright, Thomas, *The Life of Charles Dickens* (London: H. Jenkins Ltd, 1935).

Ya-Lei Yen, 'Clothing Middle-Class Women: Dress, Gender and Identity in Mid-Victorian England c. 1851–1875' (PhD dissertation, Royal Holloway, University of London, 2014).

Yates, Edmund, *Edmund Yates: His Recollections and Experiences* (London: R. Bentley and Son, 1884).

Index

Note: 'n' after a page reference indicates the number of a note on that page
Abbreviations: C.D. = Charles Dickens; G.H. = Georgina Hogarth

Index

Index

Index

Elliotson, Dr John 53, 54, 55, 151, 240
Ellis, Sarah Stickney 31, 52, 253n.13
Elsna, Hebe 224
English Woman's Journal 142
etiquette 4, 7, 8, 31, 55, 58, 63, 139, 253n.13
Evans, Bessie *see* Dickens, Bessie
Evans, Fred 105, 136, 234, 240, 252n.33,
    278n.100
Evening Chronicle 14, 16, 245
Every Man in His Humour 64, 81

Fairhurst, Robert Douglas 93
Faithfull, Emily 142–3
Falstaff Inn 177, 227
Faucit, Helen 31, 33, 58, 240, 256n.37
Faust 155
Fechter, Charles 60, 147–8, 172, 182, 186–7,
    240, 272n.53
Felton, Cornelius 147, 240
Fields, Annie Adams 133, 164, 167, 173, 177,
    185–6, 188, 190, 206, 225–6, 228,
    230–1, 240
    adoration of C.D. 171–2
    friendship with G.H. 10, 167, 184, 204–5
    G.H. confides in 179, 182, 183, 195, 202,
        210, 223
    observations of C.D. 132, 135
    worries about G.H. 132, 172
Fields, James 171, 186, 240
Finlay, Frances D. 148, 240
Fitzgerald, Percy 10, 169, 170, 188, 193–4, 198,
    199, 226, 241, 250n.20
Forster, Eliza Crosbie (previously Colbourn)
    163, 170, 189, 204, 241
Forster, John 7, 42, 43, 62, 65, 77, 96, 183, 193,
    198–9, 241, 243
    advises C.D. 118, 125, 147
    biography of C.D. 6, 47–8, 194–5, 198
    and Catherine Dickens 94, 98, 119–20,
        222–3
    C.D. confides in 102, 143
    and G.H. 60–1, 72–3, 80, 170, 182, 185,
        197, 212
Foxwold 204, 221
Franklin, Eliza 36–7, 38–9, 41, 61, 136, 137, 241
Freake, Sir Charles 176
Frith, Isabella 107, 127, 241, 244
Frith, William Powell 52, 81, 107, 239, 241, 244
The Frozen Deep 108, 110, 111, 112, 200, 248
Furnival's Inn 17, 58

Gad's Hill
    auction of contents 181, 273n.6
    Ellen Ternan visits 145
    hospitality at 160

housekeepers 133, 161, 165
    as main home of C.D. 142
    purchase of 263n.57
    renovation of 134
    sale of 183, 207
    as summer home 58, 108, 131
Garnett, Robert 149, 154
Garrick Club 121
Gaskell, Elizabeth 53, 138, 241, 246
Genoa 71, 72, 73, 76, 97, 99, 103, 118, 239
Gillies, Margaret 218–19, 220, 241
Gillies, Mary 220
Girl at the Waterfall see Waterfall at St. Nighton's
    Kieve, near Tintagel
Gloucester Crescent, No. 70 111, 127, 133, 137,
    209
gonorrhoea *see* sexually transmitted disease
Guthrie, Thomas Anstey 221

Halifax Guardian 14
Hargraves, (Catherine) Marie and Rev.
    Thomas 202, 207, 208, 241,
    277n.84
Harrison, Mary Anne 35, 253n.26
Haussmann, Baron George-Eugene 149
Hawksley, Enid *see* Dickens, Enid
Hawksley, Lucinda 112, 166, 208, 215, 250n.21
Hayes, Catherine 54
Hendra, Laurence 219
Hogarth, Catherine *see* Dickens, Catherine
Hogarth, Edward 16, 21, 135, 196, 235
Hogarth, George (G.H. father) 13, 30, 48, 70, 235
    and C.D. marriage breakdown 121, 124,
        129–30
    character 15, 23
    death 181
    financial difficulties 20, 47, 74, 103
    as newspaper editor 14, 16, 20–1
Hogarth, George (G.H. brother) 20, 21, 22, 235
Hogarth, Mrs Georgina (*née* Thomson) 69,
    196, 235
    and C.D. 20, 23, 103, 104, 123–5
    character 23
    death 152
    and G.H. 63, 121, 122–3, 129–30
Hogarth, Georgina
    allowance and finances 90, 185, 188, 206,
        212, 229–31
    amateur theatricals 81–2, 107–8
    appearance and dress 269–70n.1
    and Catherine Dickens 180, 195–6
        friendship groups 89, 106–7, 128–9
        sisterly bond 3, 53–4, 74, 88–9, 92, 98,
        109, 111–12
    character 23, 59, 74, 220–1

Index

Index

Melbourne, Lord William Lamb 59, 244, 256n.37
'men of genius' 12, 28, 29, 31, 33, 45, 75, 81, 83, 106, 107, 122, 129, 232, 262–3n.54
    definition 6–7
menstruation 54–5, 256n.30
mesmerism *see* Dickens, Charles
middle-class women *see* women
Millais, Effie 142, 244
Millais, John Everett 208, 209, 244, 278n.106
Mitton, Thomas 70, 245
Mordecai, Emma 44
Morning Chronicle 13, 14, 16, 48, 245

Nayder, Lillian 5, 71, 78, 91, 100, 105, 106, 274n.23
nicknames *see* Hogarth, Georgina, nicknames
'Nickleby' portrait 48, 62, 255n.3
'Nymph of the Waterfall' *see Waterfall at St. Nighton's Kieve, near Tintagel*
Norton, Caroline 8, 44, 58, 59–60, 144, 244, 256n.37

Olliffe, Lady Laura (*née* Cubitt) 136, 244, 267n.12
Osnaburgh Street, No. 25 24
Ouvry, Frederic 9, 10, 24, 184, 185, 188, 189, 193, 197, 210, 211, 227, 228, 249, 269n.75, 273n.2

Panton, Jane (*née* Frith) 127, 244
Paris 65, 74, 90, 149, 150, 153–4, 155, 167, 194
Paroissien, David 68, 69
Pearson, Hesketh 224
Peckham 175, 226, 227
'Personal' statement 125, 126, 128, 267n.15, 278n.100
Perugini, Carlo 188, 208–9, 244
Perugini, Kate *see* Dickens, Katey
Peters, Charley 216–19, 244
Picken, (Eleanor) Emma (later Christian) 36–42, 48, 53, 61, 66, 67, 70, 118, 177, 244
Pipes, David 156–7
Pope-Hennessy, Una 224, 263n.4
Postans, Rev. J. Chetwode 226
Powell, John 14, 16, 245
Power, Marguerite 164, 237, 245
prostitutes 63, 267n.30
Puckle, Lisa 197, 262n.54
Punch magazine 107, 180, 237, 242, 243, 267n.15
Pym, Horace 11, 203, 204, 221, 226, 230, 231, 245
Pym, Jane 11, 203, 204, 206, 212, 221, 226, 231, 245

Reade, Charles 186
Reynolds, John Russell 178
Reynolds's Weekly Newspaper 126
Ritchie, Anne *see* Thackeray, Anne
Roberts, C. E. Bechhofer 222
Robinson, Ellen *see* Ternan, Ellen
Robinson, George Wharton 190–1, 231, 245, 275n.47
Robinson, Gladys 201, 275n.49
Roche, Marie *see* Dickens, Marie
Rochester, Kent 118, 160, 274n.20
Rockingham Castle 89, 247
Roney, Helen *see* Hogarth, Helen
Roney, May (later Leon) 184, 185, 214, 236
Royal Academy of Arts 39, 64, 80, 107, 232, 239
Ruskin, John 142, 244

Saint Georges, Marguerite 95
Scott, Walter 14, 15
Scribe, Augustin Eugène 95
séance *see* table-turning
servants 5, 21, 49, 55
    C.D. household 17, 47, 48, 87, 105, 119, 133, 134, 160, 161, 226–7, 256n.30
    G.H. household 181, 187, 191, 205, 212–13, 229, 275n.37
    see also Brown, Jane; Cornelius, Anne; Marsh, James; Thompson, John
sewing 21, 57, 81, 172
sexually transmitted disease 143–4
Seymour, Robert 28
Shuckburgh, Olive (*née* Dickens) 193
single women *see* women
Slater, Michael 16, 67, 77–8, 101, 167, 225, 227
Slough 156, 166, 208
Smith, Arthur 122, 123, 245, 265n.35
Smith, Sydney 60, 88
Smithson, Elizabeth (*née* Thompson) 36, 37, 38, 245
Sotheby's 228, 242
Spencer, Walter 212, 229–30, 231
Spofford, Richard 146
Stanfield, Clarkson 62, 245
Stanfield, Rebecca 126, 245
Staplehurst rail accident 166,167, 178, 190, 271n.35
Steele, Dr Stephen 178
Stephens, Minnie *see* Thackeray, Minnie
Storey, Gladys 213, 223, 267n.29
Stowe, Harriet Beecher 94
The Strange Gentleman 185
Summerson, Esther 78, 100–2
Sutherland, Harriet, Duchess of 44
Swanson, (Anne) Blanche (*née* Ainsworth) 59, 211–12
Sykes, Lady Henrietta 61

Index

table-turning 93
Tagart, Rev. Edward 126, 246, 265n.51
Tagart, Helen 126, 246
Talfourd, Judge Thomas 32, 246
Tavistock House 103, 108, 118, 119, 147, 236,
  242, 255n.4, 267n.12, 271n.36
  description of 87–8
Tennyson, Alfred 67, 217, 218, 246, 279n.5
Ternan, Ellen (later Robinson) 1, 111, 115, 246,
  268n.39, 270n.13, 270n.25, 271n.35
  acting career 112, 147
  and alleged child with C.D. 148–9, 154,
    156–7, 176
  and C.D. death 178, 226–7, 273n.2
  and Dickens family 192–3
  financial difficulties 231
  and friendship with G.H. 145, 172, 197,
    200–1
  health 166, 190, 201
  and Mamie Dickens 145–6, 200–1
  marriage 188, 190–1, 275n.47
  meeting C.D. 112–13, 114–16
  in Peckham 175, 226, 227
  in Slough 156, 166
  temperament 146, 200–1
Ternan, Fanny (later Trollope) 145, 146–7, 186,
  187, 247
Ternan, Mrs Frances 111, 113, 145, 147, 152,
  166, 191, 246, 271n.35
Ternan, Maria 111, 112–13, 115, 145, 147, 191,
  246
Thackeray, Anne (later Ritchie) 53–4, 98, 107,
  246
Thackeray, Minnie (later Stephens) 53–4, 247,
  254n.52
Thackeray, William 51, 61, 121, 127–8, 139,
  246
Thompson, Christiana *see* Weller, Christiana
Thompson, John 153–4, 161, 162, 191–2,
  270n.12, 275n.50
Thompson, Millie 36, 37, 41
Thompson, Thomas James 36, 42, 66, 67, 68,
  70, 133, 247
Thomson, George 22
Thomson, Helen 121, 130, 236
Thomson, Katherine 22
Tomalin, Claire 90, 175, 191, 226, 270n.12
Touchet, Elizabeth 58–9, 247
Trollope, Frances *see* Ternan, Fanny
Trollope, Thomas 187, 237, 245
Turning the Tables 82

unmarried women *see* women
Urania Cottage 77, 92, 238, 259n.6, 267n.30

Vernon, Edith 217
Victoria, Queen 61, 108, 179, 180, 197, 205,
  206
Victorian gender and social codes of conduct
  45, 55, 57, 79, 225
'Violated' letter 122, 127, 128, 265n.35
virgin *see* Hogarth, Georgina, virginity
visiting cards *see* calling cards

Waterfall at St. Nighton's Kieve, near Tintagel 62–4,
  257n.49
Watson, Lavinia 89, 135, 237, 247
Watson, Richard 89
Weller, Anna 69
  see also Dickens, Anna
Weller, Christiana (later Thompson) 66–71, 75,
  133
Wellington Street, No. 16 90
Wellington Street, No. 26 156, 167
Western Luminary 14
Westminster Abbey 179, 183, 189, 193, 274n.20
Wheeler, Jane *see* Brown, Jane
White, Rev. James 89, 98, 147
White, Rosa 89, 98, 128, 247
Wickfield, Agnes 77, 221
Wickham, Helen 201
Wigan, Alfred 111, 248
Wills, Janet (*née* Chambers) 128, 204, 242, 243,
  248
Wills, William Henry 90, 99–100, 128, 131,
  147, 157, 164, 192, 194–5, 219–20,
  248, 261n.7, 264n.11
Wilson, A. N. 227
Winter, Maria *see* Beadnell, Maria
women
  married 4–5, 31, 45, 208–9
  middle-class 4, 8, 21–2, 50, 55, 57, 258n.64
  as mistress of the house 49, 58
  and respectability 8, 33
  single/unmarried 4–5, 28, 55, 78, 79, 91,
    129, 130
  see also law of coverture
Wormeley, Elizabeth 44, 254n.47
Wright, Thomas 200, 223–4
writing chalet 171, 177, 183, 184, 186, 207, 210,
  211, 227, 240, 272n.53

Yates, Edmund 76, 120, 123, 190, 248

Cambridge El

Elements in Metaphysics
edited by
Tuomas E. Tahko
University of Bristol

TRUTHMAKING

Jamin Asay
Purdue University, Indiana

Shaftesbury Road, Cambridge CB2 8EA, United Kingdom

One Liberty Plaza, 20th Floor, New York, NY 10006, USA

477 Williamstown Road, Port Melbourne, VIC 3207, Australia

314–321, 3rd Floor, Plot 3, Splendor Forum, Jasola District Centre,
New Delhi – 110025, India

103 Penang Road, #05–06/07, Visioncrest Commercial, Singapore 238467

Cambridge University Press is part of Cambridge University Press & Assessment,
a department of the University of Cambridge.

We share the University's mission to contribute to society through the pursuit of
education, learning and research at the highest international levels of excellence.

www.cambridge.org
Information on this title: www.cambridge.org/9781009112031

DOI: 10.1017/9781009109987

First published 2023

A catalogue record for this publication is available from the British Library.

ISBN 978-1-009-11203-1 Paperback
ISSN 2633-9862 (online)
ISSN 2633-9854 (print)

Truthmaking

Elements in Metaphysics

DOI: 10.1017/9781009109987
First published online: January 2023

Jamin Asay
Purdue University, Indiana

Author for correspondence: Jamin Asay, jfasay@purdue.edu

Abstract: Truthmaking is the metaphysical exploration of the idea that what is true depends upon what exists. Truthmaker theorists argue about what the truthmaking relation involves, which truths require truthmakers, and what those truthmakers are. This Element covers the dominant views on these core issues in truthmaking. It also explores some key metaphysical topics and debates that are usefully approached by employing the tools of truthmaker theory: the debate between presentists and eternalists over the existence of entities from the past, and the debate between actualists and possibilists over merely possible states of affairs. In the final section, the Element explores how to think about truthmakers for truths involving social constructions.

Keywords: truth, truthmaking, presentism, eternalism, modality, possibility, social construction, metaphysics, ontology

ISBNs: 9781009112031 (PB), 9781009109987 (OC)
ISSNs: 2633-9862 (online), 2633-9854 (print)

Contents

1 Introduction

Metaphysics is the philosophical study of reality, and truthmaking is the bridge connecting two aspects of it. On one side is the *stuff* of reality: the things that populate the universe, the objects we bump into, think about, and engage on a daily basis. *Ontology* is the branch of metaphysics that argues about what is included in the inventory of the universe. Do numbers exist? Objective moral values? God? On the other side are the *truths* about reality, those claims that accurately describe it. Echidnas can swim. Two is a prime number. If the Chicxulub asteroid hadn't collided with Earth, it wouldn't have caused a mass extinction. Truthmaking is the study of how these two dimensions of reality – what exists, and what is true – are related.

A common way of describing the relationship between what exists and what is true is in terms of dependence: what is true depends upon what exists, but not vice versa. Aristotle (1984: 22) captured the basic idea with an example along the following lines. Consider the island of Tasmania. The island belongs to the ontological inventory of the world: it's a real place, not a mere fiction. Furthermore, the sentence "Tasmania exists" is true. If the island didn't exist, the sentence wouldn't be true. And if the sentence weren't true, the island wouldn't exist. So this tiny bit of existence and truth go hand in hand; you can't have one without the other. Yet there is also an asymmetry between them. The island doesn't exist because the sentence about it is true. The sentence's being true isn't what accounts for or explains the existence of the island. (Consult a geologist for a better answer.) Instead, the sentence is true because the island exists. The sentence says that Tasmania exists, and so Tasmania itself is directly responsible for the truth of the sentence. The island, in other words, makes the sentence true: it is its truthmaker. In this way, existing objects are prior to, or more fundamental than, the truth of the claims involving those objects. *Truth depends on being* is thus a useful slogan for truthmaker theory.

Slogans are fine (and I imagine few would disagree with this one), but the real promise of truthmaker theory lies in its ability to deepen our understanding of truth, ontology, and the relationship between them. I contend that truthmaking can be wielded in a way that advances ontological debates and captures the metaphysical underpinnings of the various domains of our thought. This Element develops those goals, and thereby defends the utility of truthmaking. It first covers some foundational issues for truthmaking. Section 2 introduces the dominant perspectives on what truthmaking is, and Section 3 tackles the contentious issue of whether all truths have truthmakers. Truthmaking is then put to work. Section 4 explores the debate between presentism and eternalism over the reality of the past and future, showing how truthmaking is central to that dispute. Section 5 covers some truthmaking issues raised by nonactual possibilities. Finally, Section 6 connects truthmaking to social constructions, exploring how truthmaking relates to questions of race and gender.

2 Truthmakers and Truthmaking

Imagine you are the creator of a universe and have hired an accountancy firm to organize the inevitable loads of paperwork involved. Before you activate the universe, bringing it into being by snapping your omnipotent fingers, you meticulously plan it out in advance. As you draw up and revise your plans, your new accountants keep a comprehensive record of your universe. The firm's ontology department is charged with keeping track of all the things you've created within the universe. If something exists in the universe, it belongs on the ontology department's master inventory. Meanwhile, the clerks over in the truth department are busy compiling all the truths for the universe. As you add to the universe and rearrange your creation, the truth department is constantly updating its work. Their goal is to write the master book of your universe, which collects everything true about it.

Notice that these two departments need to work together. Suppose you decide to create an orca and name her "Oriana." The ontology department adds Oriana to their database, and the truth department adds "Oriana exists," "Oriana is an orca," and others to their manuscript. If you change your mind about including Sharko and remove him from your blueprints, the ontology department will strike him from their records and the truth department will erase "Sharko is one of the sharks" from its book. In general, any time the ontology needs adjusting, so too will the truths. (Whether the converse is true is more contentious.)

Truthmaking is, at least at a minimum, the project of developing the correct equilibrium between the ontology and truth departments. Sometimes that task is straightforward; if you create two sharks for your world, you've added "There are two sharks" as a truth about it. Similarly, if you want it to be true that there are at least seven red pandas, you'll need to create at least seven red pandas. But suppose you want your world to be one where copper conducts electricity, the square of three is nine, and the moral arc of the universe bends toward justice. You instruct the truth department to add these to the list. What, if anything, does the ontology department need to do in response? The answer isn't obvious; it requires philosophical argument. Engaging in such argument is engaging in truthmaking.

As with most philosophy, there is little that truthmaker theorists agree on, even with respect to the foundational issues for truthmaking. Differences over the nuts and bolts of truthmaking can have dramatic consequences when it comes to the ontological implications we should draw from a certain body of truths. In the remainder of this section I'll cover some of the basic questions that any truthmaker theorist must consider.

2.1 What Are Truthmakers?

Suppose the ontology department has finished its accounting. It has produced an exhaustive list of all the "furniture" of your universe. All the truthmakers for your universe are found on that list. Something can't *be* a truthmaker if it has no *being*. But is everything on the list a truthmaker?

Some say "no." On this view, truthmakers are a special or specific kind of entity. For example, it has been claimed that truthmakers must be *fundamental* entities: something is a truthmaker only if it is fundamental (Cameron 2008c, Schaffer 2010, Rettler 2016). What counts as fundamental is highly disputed. Perhaps the smallest pieces of the universe (elementary particles, say) constitute the fundamental, or perhaps the largest object of all – the entire cosmos – is singlehandedly the fundament (Schaffer 2010). Other views find the fundamental somewhere in the "middle" (see Inman 2017 and Bernstein 2021). In any event, the tape dispenser on my desk isn't a fundamental element of reality on anyone's view, and therefore doesn't make anything true, not even "The tape dispenser on my desk exists." What makes it true instead are whatever pieces of fundamental reality are responsible for the tape dispenser.

Some say "yes," and I believe that is the better answer.[1] Ontology is the study of what exists, and there's more to existence than just the fundamental. Metaphysicians are *also* concerned with fundamental ontology, but that doesn't mean they are not concerned with the derivative, nonfundamental features of reality (cf. Barnes 2014). Likewise, particle physics may be the fundamental science, but chemistry, biology, and psychology remain indispensable to the scientific enterprise.[2] Most of the truths that we believe do not concern the fundamental dimensions of reality, and the ontologically curious wonder how those truths line up with nonfundamental reality. Section 6, for instance, investigates the ontology behind social constructions, which – being *constructions* – are not fundamental.

Hence, I argue that literally everything in the universe is a truthmaker. For any object φ, it is a truthmaker for at least one sentence, namely, "φ exists." Truthmakers, then, are not a distinctive subset of what there is. One advantage of this perspective is that it demonstrates that the notion of a truthmaker is ontologically neutral. Regardless of what kinds of objects you have in your

---

[1] See Asay 2020a: 22–24 and Schipper 2021.
[2] See Tahko 2021 on the relationships between the sciences vis-à-vis fundamentality.

ontology, you have an ontology filled with truthmakers. Truthmaking can thus be utilized regardless of one's antecedent ontological views. All are invited to the truthmaking table: realists and anti-realists, nominalists and Platonists, rationalists and empiricists. Signing up for truthmaking is not signing up for distinctive, theoretically optional entities called "truthmakers."

Everything may be a truthmaker, but that doesn't begin to settle the question of what falls under "everything." Do we need natural laws, numbers, and deities within our ontologies? Truthmaker theorists argue over what we do and don't need to include within our ontological inventories in order to arrive at an equilibrium between our beliefs about what is true and our beliefs about what exists. Crucial to those arguments is a perspective on the relationship between a truth and its truthmaker. Suppose Opal is, unlike Oriana, an actual orca. She is a truthmaker because there are some truths she makes true, such as "Opal exists" and "There are orcas." But that she makes *some* claims true doesn't mean she makes *every* true claim true. She is a truthmaker, but not for "Bucharest is the capital of Romania." What, then, accounts for which truths an object makes true?

2.2 What Is Truthmaking?

Opal is a truthmaker for "There are orcas" but not "There are sharks." Why? The explanation turns on the nature of the truthmaking relationship: if some object φ is a truthmaker for some sentence S, then they stand in the truthmaking relation.[3] If we knew what that relation was, we could make a start at determining which objects are related to which truths via truthmaking.

2.2.1 Necessitation

As we've seen, the basic idea behind truthmaking is that sentences are true because of the objects that exist in the world. Truthmakers are the entities that are in some sense "responsible" for the truth of sentences. One way to unpack this metaphor is to imagine what the world would have been like had certain things not existed, or certain sentences not been true. In the actual world, Opal

---

[3] I have chosen to restrict my discussion of truthmaking to sentences. This is solely for simplicity. True sentences are only one kind of truth: There are also true beliefs, true statements, true propositions, etc. (assuming, of course, that there are such things as beliefs, statements, and propositions). Truthmaker theorists sometimes argue about which *truth-bearers* are required for or fundamental to truthmaking; see Asay 2020a: 19–22. While sentences are less ontologically controversial than, say, propositions, they do involve a further complication. If a sentence could have meant something other than what it does mean, the full account of the truthmaker for the *sentence* (but not the proposition it expresses) will require an accounting of what makes it true that the sentence means what it does. I shall set aside that further complication in what follows; the topic of what makes sentences mean what they do will arise again in Section 6.1.

exists and "There are sharks" is true. But it's possible (though incredibly unlikely) that sharks could go extinct during Opal's lifetime. If they did, Opal would still exist, but "There are sharks" would be false. This possibility undermines the idea that Opal makes true "There are sharks," since her existence is compatible with the sentence being false. Opal's being in the world offers no guarantee that "There are sharks" is true. Something else, then, would seem to be responsible for the truth of the sentence (cf. Armstrong 2004: 6–7). By contrast, so long as Opal exists, "There are orcas" will be true. If we presume that being an orca is *essential* to Opal (such that she couldn't have been born an iguana, say), then it's impossible for Opal to exist without "There are orcas" being true.

The takeaway from these observations is that truthmaking involves *necessitation*. A truthmaker is an alethic guarantor: a truthmaker guarantees the truth of any sentence it makes true. Formally put, an object φ is a truthmaker for a sentence S only if it's necessary that if φ exists, S is true. This condition states that necessitation is a *necessary* condition on truthmaking; it must be in place if there is to be any truthmaking. Whether it is a *sufficient* condition on truthmaking is a further question I broach in Section 2.2.2.

Taking necessitation to be a necessary condition for truthmaking is incredibly common; it's been referred to as truthmaking "orthodoxy" (e.g., Merricks 2007: 5). But not everyone agrees (e.g., Briggs 2012). Oftentimes the dispute depends on how some particularly thorny cases should be handled. Suppose that Bobo was the very last dodo. Shortly before he died, "There is exactly one dodo" was true. Bobo doesn't necessitate this sentence because it was false when he was born, as there were still other dodos around (such as his mother). The question is whether Bobo, near the end of his species, is nonetheless the truthmaker for "There is exactly one dodo." If he is, then his status as its truthmaker is contingent on the fact that no other dodos are around.[4] That is, Bobo is a truthmaker for "There is exactly one dodo" only if "There are no dodos besides Bobo" is true. Bobo, presumably, isn't a truthmaker for that latter claim – he's not responsible for the near demise of his species. In response, the orthodox view maintains that the real truthmaker for "There is exactly one dodo" is Bobo *plus* whatever makes true "There are no dodos besides Bobo."

2.2.2 Explanation

The language of truthmakers being "responsible" for their truths suggests that there is more to truthmaking than just necessitation. I have said that sentences

---

[4] I argue (Asay 2016a) that this fact is problematic for the view, as it raises further truthmaking questions that the orthodox view doesn't face.

are true *because of*, or because they *depend on*, their truthmakers. Oftentimes the point is made that truths are true *in virtue of* their truthmakers (e.g., Rodriguez-Pereyra 2005). Many truthmaker theorists have argued that underlying this language is the idea that truthmaking is *explanatory*: what it is to make something true is to explain why it is true (e.g., Griffith 2013: 305).

Necessitation doesn't appear to be sufficient for explanation. Here are two classic kinds of cases.[5] Is it possible that you could have existed without your parents ever having existed? Many think not: if your parents hadn't existed, then neither would have the particular gametes essential to *you*. Perhaps a person very similar could have existed, but if they had a different genetic origin than you, that person wouldn't be you. If so, then you necessitate the truth of "Your parents exist(ed)": your existence guarantees that your parents existed. But *you* don't explain the truths about your parents' existence. *They* do. If you necessitate truths about your parents without making them true, then necessitation by itself is insufficient for truthmaking.

The other common example involves necessary truths. It's necessary that if Mount Vesuvius exists, then the Pythagorean theorem is true. That's another way of saying that it's impossible for Mount Vesuvius to exist and the Pythagorean theorem to be false. Because it's necessary, it's impossible for the Pythagorean theorem to be false, and so it's impossible for the Pythagorean theorem to be false *and* for Mount Vesuvius to exist. Trivially, then, any existing object necessitates the truth of any necessary truth. But the existence of Italian volcanoes doesn't explain Euclidean geometry, and the truth of "2 + 2 = 4" doesn't depend upon the existence of my favorite whiteboard marker. These sorts of cases, then, also suggest that necessitation is not sufficient for truthmaking.

These examples aim to show that there is more to the truthmaking relationship than just necessitation. Even if some sentence must be true if a certain object exists, that doesn't mean that the object is a truthmaker for that sentence. Philosophers, therefore, often describe truthmaking as being a *hyperintensional* relationship (e.g., Schaffer 2008). This means that there is more to an object making something true than just that object guaranteeing, with necessity, the truth in question. The idea is that although two things might necessarily occur together, that doesn't suffice to show that they are relevant to each other, or that one explains or causes the other. A world with Koko the gorilla is a world where "Either there are pangolins or there aren't any pangolins" is true, but that doesn't reveal that Koko has any relevance to the question of why that disjunction is true.

---

[5] See Smith 1999 and Restall 1996, respectively.

To say that necessitation is not enough for truthmaking is not to say what is. Thus, the notion of explanation is frequently invoked to bridge the gap between necessitation and truthmaking. Koko doesn't explain why "Either there are pangolins or there aren't any pangolins" is true, but she does explain the truth of "Koko exists." Similarly, my existence doesn't account for why "My parents exist" is true, though it perfectly accounts for why "I exist" is true. The notion of *aboutness* is often appealed to here (e.g., Merricks 2007 and Schipper 2020). "My parents exist" isn't about me, so I can serve no role in explaining its truth. "I exist," by contrast, is, so I am a suitable truthmaker for it. Though the notions of aboutness and explanation are philosophically fraught, and are themselves the subject of enormous theoretical controversy, they both appear to be hyperintensional notions. (For example, the sentences "Triangles have three sides" and "2 is prime" are necessarily equivalent in that it's impossible for one of them to be true and the other false, yet they are about different things.) If they are part of the truthmaking relation, they can be used to explain why necessitation is not sufficient for truthmaking.[6]

Putting together necessitation and explanation, we arrive at a dominant perspective in truthmaker theory:

For any object φ and sentence S, φ is a truthmaker for S if and only if it's necessary that if φ exists, S is true, and the truth of S is explained by φ.

This account can be used to maintain that Koko is a truthmaker for "There are gorillas" but not "There are sharks" or "$2 + 2 = 4$."

Another reason to include a hyperintensional dimension to truthmaking is to account for that basic slogan of truthmaker theory: truth depends on being, but not vice versa. Sometimes necessitation runs in both directions. The existence of Koko guarantees that "Koko exists" is true, and the truth of "Koko exists" guarantees the existence of Koko. If the truthmaking relation itself is to account for the asymmetry between truth and being, then necessitation alone is inadequate. Explanation, however, is an asymmetric relation. If α explains β, then β doesn't explain α. So an explanatory account of the truthmaking relation is better positioned for capturing the dependency between truth and being.

The main impetus for believing that there is a hyperintensional dimension to the truthmaking relation is dealing with the counterexamples considered above, and accounting for how truth depends on being. The main challenge for such accounts is spelling out the relevant notion of explanation (or any other hyperintensional notion deployed). For instance, Jonathan Tallant (2018) wields the

---

[6] A related hyperintensional notion is *grounding*, which has also been employed to show what separates truthmaking from necessitation (e.g., Schaffer 2008 and Jago 2018).

notion of explanation *against* truthmaking. He agrees with the view that the purpose of providing truthmakers is to provide explanations of truth. But, Tallant claims, providing explanations of truth is very easy. The reason why "Sichuan peppercorns are numbing" is true is that Sichuan peppercorns are numbing. In general, any true sentence "*S*" is true because *S*. Because providing explanations for truth is ridiculously easy (one need only "disquote" the sentence in question), there is no point to exploring the sorts of challenging ontological questions like those pursued in this Element.

I agree with Tallant that an explanation-focused approach to truthmaking leads to trouble, precisely because of the teeming availability of explanations (see Asay 2018).[7] I disagree with Tallant that truthmaking is first and foremost an exercise in explanation. Moreover, as I've argued elsewhere, truthmaking needn't incorporate *any* hyperintensional notion at all: necessitation is necessary *and sufficient* for truthmaking (Asay 2020a: chapter 3). This means that I accept, for example, that I am a truthmaker for both "My parents exist" and "7 + 3 = 10." It might *sound* strange to say that I make it true that my parents exist, and that 7 and 3 are 10; but remember that "truthmaking" is a term of art, employed for a certain theoretical purpose within metaphysics. And the purpose of truthmaking, as I've articulated it, is developing a proper harmony between one's "ontology department" and "truth department." Admitting that I make true certain truths involving my parents doesn't show that my parents won't end up in my ontology; there are at least some truths involving them for which they, but not I, will be required (e.g., "My parents were married in 1972"). Whether it's tolerable to admit that everything in the universe, trivially, is a truthmaker for every necessary truth may well depend on one's background views about how substantive or trivial necessary truths themselves are, and one's view about the ontological status of things like numbers (see Asay 2020a: chapter 11). Even Restall, who initiated the concern about truthmaking and necessary truth, writes that "There is something quite touching in the view that every particle in the universe (and everything else besides!) is witness to all necessary truths" (Restall 1996: 333).

Ultimately, how one understands the purported counterexamples – and thus whether one regards truthmaking to be hyperintensional or not – turns on some big-picture questions about the fundamental theoretical motivations behind truthmaking. Truthmaking understood as "ontological accounting," as the project of maintaining a proper balance between what one takes to exist and what one takes to be true, is not obviously beholden to any hyperintensional notion.

---

[7] Others, meanwhile, deny that "'*S*' is true because *S*" is any sort of explanation at all (e.g., Lewis 2001b: 611–612 and Rodriguez-Pereyra 2022).

If there is more to truthmaking than necessitation, if it needs to capture an important explanatory relationship between a truth and its truthmaker, then truthmaking includes some kind of hyperintensional component, to be spelled out in terms of explanation, grounding, aboutness, or something similar. By going beyond the goal of ontological accountability, this perspective takes the truth of a sentence to itself be something in need of explanation.[8]

2.3 Truthmaking at Work

Having considered some central theoretical questions for the notion of truth-making, it will be useful to consider some classic examples of how truthmaking has implications for ontology. So far I have relied on some very basic examples, like Opal is a truthmaker for "There are orcas." Even this case is not entirely straightforward. Some might dispute it if they require truthmakers to be funda-mental objects, and don't think that Opal is such a thing. Furthermore, those who require truthmaking to be hyperintensional need to explain in what sense the sentence is about *Opal*, or explained by her. The sentence, after all, isn't about Opal in particular. But supposing Opal really is a truthmaker for "There are orcas," we can learn a few more things about truthmaking. For one, although the existence of truthmakers are *sufficient* conditions for the truth of the sentences they make true, they are not *necessary* conditions. Opal's existence guarantees that the sentence is true. But the sentence being true doesn't guaran-tee that *Opal* exists: it only ensures that some orca or other exists.[9] So although Opal is a truthmaker for "There are orcas," her existence is not required for it to be true. Second, the example reveals that truthmaking is not a "one–one" relation. That means that there is not a unique truthmaker for each truth. A truth like "There are orcas" can have many truthmakers: each individual orca, for example. And any individual object can be a truthmaker for many truths. Opal makes true both "Opal exists" and "Orcas exist," among (infinitely) many others.

Most everyone can agree that orcas, great white sharks, oceans, and glaciers exist.[10] Where truthmaking becomes theoretically interesting is with more

---

[8] I've argued elsewhere against relying on the notion of explanation in explicating truthmaker theory. See Asay 2016b, 2018, and 2020a: chapters 2, 3, and 6. But see also Griffith 2022, Kitamura 2022, and Rodriguez-Pereyra 2022 for the opposing view.

[9] By contrast, Smith and Simon (2007: 93) argue that truthmakers are both necessary and sufficient for their truths, and so they reject Opal as a candidate truthmaker for "There are orcas."

[10] But not everyone – this is metaphysics after all. Mereological nihilists (e.g., Merricks 2001) argue that no compound object – no object with parts – exists. (Some, like Merricks, make exceptions for living organisms.) So they deny that oceans and glaciers exist, since, if they do, they are composite objects built out of billions upon billions of H_2O molecules. Because these philosophers argue that "Oceans exist" and "Glaciers exist" are false, they don't need to provide them with a truthmaker.

contentious cases. Opal is a truthmaker for "Orcas exist" only because being an orca is *essential* to Opal. If she could have been a chimpanzee, her existence wouldn't guarantee the truth of "Orcas exist." But not all of our properties are essential to us. Kierkegaard was Danish, yet that fact isn't essential to him: it's an "accidental" or contingent feature. Kierkegaard's parents could have immigrated to the United States, say, while he was still in the womb, and acquired citizenship there. So it's possible for Kierkegaard to have existed and not had the property of being Danish. Kierkegaard himself, then, was not a necessitator for "Kierkegaard was Danish." Nor is Kierkegaard *plus* the property *being Danish*. For those two things could exist without "Kierkegaard was Danish" being true: just imagine that Kierkegaard ended up American, but somebody else was Danish. So while Kierkegaard is a truthmaker for many truths involving him, he's not a truthmaker for all of them.

Reflection on cases like these – what are called *contingent* or *accidental predications* – leads to what is perhaps the most famous ontological argument in truthmaker theory, and it's due to David Armstrong (1997: 115). First some terminology. A compound object – an object with parts – is *mereologically* composed by those parts when there is nothing more to the whole than the existence of its parts. A *mereological sum*, then, is just the sum of its parts and nothing more. It exists so long as the parts do. A compound object is *non-mereologically* composed by its parts when there is more to it than just the parts. Suppose you've just received a Lego space shuttle set as a gift, and have yet to put it together. The collection of Lego bricks – the *set* – exists already; it's just the mereological sum combining each of the individual bricks. But the *model* doesn't exist yet, even though all its parts do. The model, once put together, is a non-mereological composite of the bricks – the bricks *plus* their being properly arranged. So the set and the model have all the same parts, but there is more to the model (but not the set) than just the existence of the parts. That's why the set endures, but not the model, when it takes a tumble to the ground and the pieces fly everywhere.[11]

Armstrong's argument is that when an object possesses a property nonessentially, neither the object nor the property is a necessitator for the truth that the object possesses that property. Nor is the mereological sum composed by the object and the property, since that sum could exist even if the object in question doesn't have the property (but some other object does). So there must be another object, a compound object composed by the object and property, but in a non-mereological way: an object that consists in the "coming together" of object and property. This sort of entity – what Armstrong calls a "state of affairs" – exists if

---

[11] Everything I've said in this paragraph is controversial. For overviews of some of the issues involved, see Hudson 2007, McDaniel 2010, and Paul 2010.

and only if a property is instantiated by an object. So in any case where an object instantiates a property, there are two distinct objects that have that object and property as parts. First, there is a mereological sum, such as that composed by Kierkegaard and the property *being Danish* (which I'll denote by "Kierkegaard + *being Danish*"). This object exists just so long as Kierkegaard exists and someone or other (but not necessarily Kierkegaard) is Danish.[12] Second, there is a state of affairs non-mereologically composed by Kierkegaard and *being Danish* (which I'll denote by "{*being Danish* (Kierkegaard)}"). This object exists only if Kierkegaard instantiates *being Danish*. Only the non-mereological sum necessitates the truth of "Kierkegaard is Danish," and so only it is fit to be a truthmaker for it. Had Kierkegaard been American, that state of affairs wouldn't have existed; instead, there would have been the state of affairs {*being American* (Kierkegaard)}. States of affairs exist only when objects and properties come together, and so are appropriate truthmakers for truths about which properties objects possess.

In this way, Armstrong uses the idea of truthmaking to defend an ontological conclusion: in addition to ordinary objects and properties, there are also states of affairs. An alternative view respects the spirit of Armstrong's argument, but derives a different ontological conclusion. It agrees with Armstrong that con-tingent predications need truthmakers. But that doesn't settle the case for states of affairs. Armstrong thinks of properties as *universals*: objects that can exist multiply instantiated, across a diverse set of objects. But a competing perspec-tive treats properties as nonrepeated individuals, sometimes called *tropes*. Suppose Opal and Opie are both Icelandic: they share the property of being Icelandic. The defender of universals takes this claim literally: there is an entity, the property *being Icelandic*, that is shared by the distinct objects Opal and Opie. The trope theorist interprets the claim differently. There isn't one thing that Opal and Opie share by being Icelandic. Instead, they possess individual tropes of being Icelandic. These tropes are similar to one another in all relevant respects, and account for one way in which Opal and Opie are the same. But they are nonetheless distinct individuals: Opal's being-Icelandic trope is a separate entity from Opie's being-Icelandic trope. Moreover, these tropes couldn't have belonged to anyone else. Opal's being-Icelandic trope couldn't

---

[12] This sentence makes two major presuppositions. First, it assumes that properties exist whenever they are instantiated, and that they are distinct from the objects that possess them. See Armstrong 1989 and Maurin 2022 for introductions to the metaphysical debate over the existence of properties. Second, it assumes that if any objects x and y exist, then there is automatically a mereological sum composed by them: $x + y$. This is the doctrine known as *mereological universalism* or *unrestricted composition*, and it is highly controversial. See Lewis 1991 for a defense, and van Inwagen 1990 for the case against.

have been Opie's. As a result, the existence of Opal's being-Icelandic trope guarantees that "Opal is Icelandic" is true. So tropes, too, can be offered as truthmakers for contingent predications.

Being a truthmaker theorist, then, does not by itself settle the dispute between defenders of states of affairs and defenders of tropes.[13] The role of truthmaking arguments is not to settle ontological disputes once and for all, but rather to recognize their importance and offer a framework for formulating and defending ontological positions. They are a call for ontological accountability – of making sure our ontologies and beliefs are properly aligned.

3 Maximalism

Let's return to the plans you've drawn up for your universe. After careful reflection, you've decided against including any unicorns. You've informed the ontology department not to include any unicorns, and told the truth department to add "Unicorns don't exist" to their manuscript. Your accounting appears to be in order. Given the absence of any unicorns from your universe, "Unicorns don't exist" is true. And given that "Unicorns don't exist" is true, no unicorn belongs in your ontological inventory. Is everything settled vis-à-vis truthmaking?

The answers to this question turn out to reflect the most fundamental theoretical divide between truthmaker theorists. Suppose that necessitation is required for truthmaking. (Whether it's also sufficient doesn't matter for the current discussion.) If "Unicorns don't exist" has a truthmaker, then some combination of things from your ontological inventory must necessitate its truth. Furthermore, whatever those things are, you need to remove them should you change your mind and want to add a unicorn after all. It's not enough simply to add the unicorn; you also need to subtract something else. If there is a truthmaker for "Unicorns don't exist" – let's call it "Abby" – then the existence of Abby guarantees that "Unicorns don't exist" is true. So if you decide to add a unicorn, it can't coexist with Abby. The unicorn guarantees that "Unicorns exist" is true, and Abby guarantees that "Unicorns don't exist" is true. If they both existed, a contradiction would be true. That's impossible, so your universe can have Abby, or a unicorn, but not both.

Hence, if there is a truthmaker for "Unicorns don't exist," it can't be any of the other things in your universe that can coexist with unicorns, such as horses, elephants, echidnas, blocks of gold, creeks, cumulus clouds, and whatever else is in your universe. It can't even be the sum total of all those things.

---

[13] See Armstrong 1989 for an introduction to the issue of tropes and universals (and other nearby views). For an alternative truthmaking account for contingent predications, see Lewis 2003.

Imagine a tiny toy universe with just two horses, say. In that universe, it's true that unicorns don't exist, but the existence of those two horses doesn't guarantee that: if you added a unicorn to the universe, the horses would still exist although "Unicorns don't exist" would now be false. If things like Abby exist, they are not the familiar sorts of things we normally encounter.

Truthmaker *maximalism* is the thesis that all truths have truthmakers. It entails that the accounting I described in the opening paragraph of this section is incomplete. If you want "Unicorns don't exist" to be true, it's not enough for the ontology department to do *nothing*. They need to have something on hand like Abby, something that guarantees the truth of "Unicorns don't exist." *Non-maximalism*, by contrast, is the thesis that not all truths have truthmakers. Some sentences are true, but nothing exists that necessitates their truth. Such sentences, if there are any, I call *truthmaker gaps*.

Much of the debate between maximalism and non-maximalism involves whether truths like negative existentials (i.e., truths about what doesn't exist) have truthmakers. If they don't, non-maximalism is correct. If they do, one has to defend a view as to what they are. In this section, I cover the central motivations both for and against maximalism, and show how this debate aligns with the previous debate from Section 2.2.2 regarding whether truthmaking has an ontological or explanatory focus.

3.1 Arguments for Maximalism

Maximalism is a bold ontological thesis. It maintains that in addition to horses, United Nations member states, and Atlanta, there are also excluders for unicorns, the Illuminati, and Atlantis. Infamously, the philosopher most responsible for developing and popularizing the idea of truthmaking – David Armstrong – admits that he does "not have any direct argument" for maximalism, and hopes that "philosophers of realist inclinations will be immediately attracted to the idea that a truth, any truth, should depend for its truth [on] something 'outside' it, in virtue of which it is true" (Armstrong 2004: 7). Nevertheless, some arguments for maximalism have surfaced over the years; I consider two here.[14]

3.1.1 The Unity of Truth

One argument for maximalism turns on the claim that those who reject it are thereby saddled with a disunified account of truth. What it is for some sentences to be true is that they have a truthmaker; what it is for some other sentences to be true is something else. A theory of truth that posits truthmakers for some, but not

---

[14] For others, see Asay 2020a: 71–79 and Jago 2020.

for others, is unfortunate. It turns truth itself into a disjointed, heterogeneous phenomenon. Put another way, it posits two different properties of truth. One is *being made true*, and the other is *something else*. Other things being equal, a unified account of truth is preferable (especially when one of the options is *something else*), and so maximalism bears a significant advantage over non-maximalism.[15]

For this argument to succeed, one must presuppose that by offering a theory of truthmakers one is also offering a theory of truth. On this view, what it is for the sentence "There are orcas" to have the property of truth is for it to have a truthmaker. Truth is defined in terms of truthmaking. Many philosophers, however, have argued that this perspective is backward. If anything, truthmaking should be defined in terms of truth. Hence, any attempt to define truth in terms of truthmaking is circular.[16] Note, for example, how the necessitation and explanation conditions on truthmaking discussed in Section 2 are both defined in terms of truth. To be a truthmaker is to be a guarantor (and perhaps also) explainer of *truth*.

Furthermore, there are many dualities among the *truths*. There are those that are known, and those that are unknown. There are those favored by Frank, and those not favored by Frank. There are those found in this book, and those found elsewhere. None of these suggests a duality within the nature of *truth* itself. Similarly, the class of truths may be divided into those with truthmakers, and those without, and this needn't have any implications for what one says about the property of truth. As on deflationary accounts (e.g., Horwich 1998), it may be that all there is to the property of truth is that it is the property that a sentence "p" has if and only if p. The question nevertheless remains: Given that "p" is in the truth department's manuscript, what does the ontology department need to add or subtract from its logs?

The unity argument, therefore, depends upon the claim that truthmaking must be put to use in the service of defining truth. That task may be impossible – if indeed truthmaking must already be defined in terms of truth – and is optional at best. Nothing about truthmaking's ontological aims is furthered by coupling it with the project of defining truth.

3.1.2 Jago's Dilemma

Another argument for maximalism has been offered by Mark Jago (2012, 2018). As we have seen, negative truths (such as those about what doesn't exist) have

---

[15] See, for example, Armstrong 2005: 272, Barker and Jago 2012: 136, Griffith 2015b, Jago 2018: 89, and Saenz 2020.

[16] See Merricks 2007: 15, David 2009: 144, Schulte 2011: 420, and Asay 2020a: 111–122.

been offered as counterexamples to truthmaker maximalism. A natural thought, then, is to divide the truths into the positive and the negative. Positive truths are about the way the world is, and so are true in virtue of that existing world. Negative truths, by contrast, are about the way the world isn't, and so aren't fit to be made true by the way the world is. If only positive truths need truthmakers, then there appears to be no need for an ontology with unfamiliar entities such as excluders like Abby.

Jago offers a dilemma against this sort of view. If the non-maximalist divides the truths into the positive and the negative, they will find that some of those positive truths require exactly the same truthmaking treatment that maximalists give to negative truths. If non-maximalists offer excluding entities like Abby as truthmakers for these positive claims, then they are no better off, ontologically speaking, than the maximalist, and may as well posit excluders for negative truths as well. If non-maximalists claim that the positive truths in question have more straightforward truthmakers that don't involve exotic excluders like Abby, then maximalists can claim the same for negative truths: they don't require strange entities after all. Either way, the non-maximalist has earned no onto-logical advantage over the maximalist.

The truths Jago has in mind involve knowledge of negative truths. George R. R. Martin knows that White Walkers don't exist. This would seem to be a positive truth, a truth about the way the world (specifically, Martin's epistemic state) is. Because of the necessitation requirement on truthmaking, any truth-maker it has must guarantee that "George R. R. Martin knows that White Walkers don't exist" is true. But then any such truthmaker will also guarantee the truth of "White Walkers don't exist," since anything known must be true. Any truthmaker for the knowledge claim must therefore be an excluder of White Walkers: its existence is incompatible with the existence of any White Walker. Non-maximalists now face the same dialectical situation faced by the maximal-ists: either accept these excluding entities into your ontology, or show how they're not necessary after all.

Jago's argument, in my view, effectively shuts down the kind of non-maximalism he envisions.[17] But it doesn't put a stop to non-maximalism across the board. Rather, it counters attempts to cleanly divide the truths with truth-makers from the truthmaker gaps. Dividing truths into positive and negative is fraught terrain. Just consider the fact that any (seemingly positive) universal generalization – that all ravens are black – is logically equivalent to a negative existential: there are no nonblack ravens. Furthermore, any claim about the way

---

[17] For less concessive responses, see Simpson 2014 and Skiles 2014.

the world *isn't* is still a claim about the way the world *is*. Reality is such that there aren't unicorns.

Jago's dilemma, then, shows how *not* to be a non-maximalist. Perhaps the best argument for maximalism itself begins here. Anyone who thinks that some, but not all, truths have truthmakers has some explaining to do. What accounts for the difference? This question is not an easy one to address, and Jago's argument shows how unsatisfactory a straightforward answer to it is.[18] Maximalism enjoys a theoretical advantage precisely because it doesn't have to answer this question. I turn to how one should be a non-maximalist in Section 3.3. But before I do, let's consider the options maximalists have explored when it comes to identifying the excluders needed to make negative existentials true.

3.2 Truthmakers for Negative Existentials

The predominant challenge for non-maximalists is answering the question why some but not all truths have truthmakers. The predominant challenge for maximalists is answering the question concerning what makes true negative truths such as negative existentials. In this section I canvass some of the familiar attempts to offer truthmakers for negatives.[19]

3.2.1 Totalities

At the start of this section, I asked you to imagine a toy universe with just two horses. But if maximalism is true, that wasn't really possible. In that universe, "Whales don't exist" is true, but neither of the horses necessitate its truth. It's possible for a horse to exist and "Whales don't exist" to be false (i.e., it's possible for horses and whales to coexist, as the actual world demonstrates), and so no horse is a candidate truthmaker for the claim that whales don't exist. So something else must exist in that universe, something that is an excluder of whales (and perhaps everything else that doesn't exist in the universe).

One view about what that thing is, long defended by David Armstrong (e.g., Armstrong 1997: chapter 13, 2004: chapter 6), is that there is a totality

---

[18] For some attempts to answer it, see Saenz 2014 and Schipper 2018.

[19] For more on these and other attempts see, for example, Rodriguez-Pereyra 2006b: 194–198, Asay 2014, section 3, Jago 2018, chapter 5, and MacBride 2020, section 2.1. One salient view I do not discuss here is the "incompatibility" view that maintains that truthmakers for truths about the various properties objects have also serve as truthmakers for truths about the various properties objects don't have (because those properties are incompatible with the object's actual properties). Discussion of this sort of account commences with Demos 1917; it has more recently been defended by Veber 2008.

state of affairs that makes true negative truths (and, moreover, all other truths at the same time). We saw in Section 2.3 how Armstrong understands states of affairs. They are entities non-mereologically composed by objects and properties. Because states of affairs are themselves objects, they can partially compose *higher-order* states of affairs: states of affairs that bring together lower-order states of affairs with properties. Higher-order states of affairs can, in turn, be posited to serve as truthmakers for negative truths.

Return to our two horses; let's call them "Thelma" and "Louise." Suppose they're both brown, and nonessentially so. So "All horses are brown" is true in this universe, as is the logically equivalent negative existential: "There are no nonbrown horses." Thelma and Louise don't make this claim true. They can coexist with a black horse, and so they are not excluders of nonbrown horses. Furthermore, neither Thelma nor Louise are truthmakers for "Thelma is brown" and "Louise is brown," since they might have been some other color. So in addition to Thelma, Louise, and *being brown*, this universe also contains the states of affairs {*being brown* (Thelma)} and {*being brown* (Louise)}. These states of affairs make true the claims about the horses' color, but they don't make the general and negative existential claims true. The issue is that Thelma and Louise themselves, alongside the states of affairs that involve them, don't guarantee that they are *all* the horses. But they *are* all the horses: this looks to be a property that they possess in this universe. That is to say, the mereological sum Thelma + Louise enjoys the property of *being all the horses*. This is a contingent fact about this small universe; Thelma + Louise wouldn't have the property if a third horse, Brad, entered the scene. But they do have the property in this universe, and Armstrong harnesses this fact to find a truthmaker for general and negative truths.

Armstrong's totality states of affairs take the following form. They involve a special relation, which I'll call *exhausts*. (Armstrong uses "totals.") Relations are like properties, but are instantiated by multiple objects, not just a single one. (*Being prime* is a property of 7, while *being greater than* is a relation that 7 stands in with respect to 6 and others.) The idea is that *exhausts* is a two-place relation that is inhabited by (1) the sum of everything that instantiates a certain property, and (2) that property. Thus, in the toy universe the mereological sum Thelma + Louise stands in the *exhausts* relation to the property *being a horse*. They don't stand in this relation to *being a horse* in the universe with Brad; in that case, Thelma + Louise + Brad is what exhausts *being a horse*. In the two-horse universe, there is the state of affairs {*exhausts* (Thelma + Louise, *being a horse*)}. The existence of this state of affairs guarantees that Thelma and Louise are all the horses.

The last two paragraphs identify three states of affairs. One guarantees that Thelma is brown, one guarantees that Louise is brown, and one guarantees that

Thelma and Louise are all the horses. Together, then, these three states of affairs guarantee that all horses are brown. Now consider the fact that there are no whales. Within Armstrong's metaphysics, there are no uninstantiated properties; if nothing is a whale, then *being a whale* doesn't exist. So there cannot be an *exhausts*-based state of affairs that involves *being a whale*. But notice that if none of the first-order states of affairs involve *being a whale*, then there aren't any whales. (If there were a whale, then there would be a state of affairs composed of the whale and *being a whale*.) Hence, we need a state of affairs that establishes that all the first-order states of affairs (none of which involves *being a whale*) are all the first-order states of affairs. This state of affairs has the mereological sum of all the first-order states of affairs *exhausting* the property *being a first-order state of affairs*. This second-order *totality* state of affairs guarantees that none of the first-order states of affairs involves *being a whale*, and so guarantees that "There are no whales" is true. Moreover, this totality state of affairs would seem to make *everything* true. For example, one part of the totality state of affairs is {*being brown* (Thelma)}, which makes true "Thelma is brown." The totality state of affairs "inherits" all the truthmaking abilities from its parts, and its parts exhaust all there is.[20] So the totality state of affairs that is composed by all the first-order states of affairs exhausting *being a first-order state of affairs* is, in Armstrong's turn of phrase, the "least discerning" and "most promiscuous" truthmaker of all (Armstrong 2004: 19; see Schaffer 2010 for a novel take on this feature).

Armstrong needs just the one totality state of affairs to provide a truthmaker for all negative truths (and, moreover, all positive truths). This would seem to be a striking case of ontological economy: by positing merely *one* entity, he vindicates truthmaker maximalism. Yet totality states of affairs have come in for abundant criticism.

One prominent critic is David Lewis. Lewis adopts a strict Humean metaphysics that rejects the existence of necessary connections between completely distinct objects. From this perspective, anything can coexist with anything else. Hence, excluders are problematic for the Humean metaphysician; the totality state of affairs, Lewis (2001b: 611) writes, "would be objectionable because its

---

[20] This sentence presupposes that if some object φ is a truthmaker for S, then any entity that includes φ as a part will also be a truthmaker for S. For example, Koko + Luxembourg is a truthmaker for "There are gorillas" because Koko by herself is. This principle (that truthmaking is, in effect, *monotonic*) has been disputed (e.g., Rodriguez-Pereyra 2006c). It's indisputable that if some object φ is a *necessitator* for S, then any entity that includes φ as a part will be a necessitator for S as well. But one might think that the truth in question isn't true in virtue of the larger object, only the smaller one. "There are gorillas" isn't made true by Koko + Luxembourg; *that* entity has nothing to do with it. I've argued (Asay 2020a: 34–36) that this perspective falsely presupposes the idea that truthmaking is fundamentally an exercise in the explanation of truth, rather than ontological accountability.

raison d'être would require it to be involved in mysterious necessary connections." In the actual world, because the totality state of affairs exists, other things like unicorns and hobbits and wookies can't exist. (Likewise, had there been unicorns or hobbits or wookies, then the actual totality state of affairs couldn't have existed.) Lewis finds this metaphysically suspicious: How can one entity somehow constrain the existence of something else?[21]

Another objection to totality states of affairs also derives from a certain set of antecedent metaphysical scruples. In his framing of the problem of negative truths, George Molnar (2000: 84–85) advances the following (conditionally) inconsistent tetrad:

(i)   The world is everything that exists.
(ii)   Everything that exists is positive.
(iii) Some negative claims about the world are true.
(iv) Every true claim about the world is made true by something that exists.

These four theses are inconsistent if "positive" entities cannot be truthmakers for negative truths, as Molnar believed. The first and third theses seem beyond reproach.[22] The fourth is maximalism, and so rejected by many, as we have seen. Totality states of affairs violate (ii): they are in some sense a "negative" entity: they dictate what there can't be by establishing that what there is is *all* there is (see Armstrong 2004: 81–82).[23]

Philosophers suspicious of necessary connections between distinct existences and negative entities will therefore be wary of positing a totality state of affairs. Jago (2018: 148–149) offers a different kind of argument that directly argues against the existence of totality states. The *exhausts* relation holds between a property on the one hand, and the sum of all the individuals instantiating that property on the other. The totality state of affairs is a higher-order state of affairs because it brings together all the *first-order* states of affairs. There can't be a state of affairs that exhausts all the states of affairs (of every order), since in that case the totality state of affairs would have to include *itself* as a part, and that's impossible.[24] Thus, there can be no state of affairs that exhausts the property *being a state of affairs*. But, by definition, the *exhausts* relation *just is* the relation that holds between a property and everything that instantiates it.

---

[21] Lewis offers an account of maximalist truthmaking consistent with his own metaphysics in Lewis and Rosen 2003.

[22] But see Mumford 2007, which rejects (iii).

[23] Gale (1976: 43) thus calls it a "Porky the Pig" fact: that's all folks! See also Cheyne and Pigden 2006.

[24] By contrast, Kukso (2006: 27) detects an infinite regress lurking here.

Thus, there is no such property. But if there is no *exhausts* relation, there are no totality states of affairs.

3.2.2 Negative States of Affairs

Armstrong's hope is that by positing the existence of a single totality state of affairs, he does minimal damage to the idea that reality is predominantly "positive" in nature. Indeed, the desire to avoid any "negative" ontology drives much of the debate over maximalism. Over a century ago, Bertrand Russell (1919a: 4) wrote: "There is implanted in the human breast an almost unquenchable desire to find some way of avoiding the admission that negative facts are as ultimate as those that are positive." Russell, nevertheless, found a way to vanquish his desire, and ultimately defended the existence of negative states of affairs. This in turn "nearly produced a riot" when he shared his findings during a lecture to some (apparently quite metaphysically uppity) students (Russell 1919b: 42).

Following Russell's lead, Barker and Jago (2012) have developed an account of the nature of negative states of affairs, and argue that they are just as palatable as positive states of affairs. They build on Armstrong's account of states of affairs, according to which they are complex objects non-mereologically composed by particular objects and the properties and relations they instantiate. Barker and Jago's idea is that there are *two* kinds of non-mereological composition. Thelma is brown, but not blue. On Armstrong's account, what makes "Thelma is brown" true is the state of affairs {*being brown* (Thelma)}. But there is no property of not being blue,[25] so Armstrong employs his totality state of affairs to make true "Thelma is not blue." By contrast, Barker and Jago argue that first-order states of affairs are sufficient in both cases. The state of affairs {*being brown* (Thelma)} is bound by a certain kind of non-mereological composition; I'll indicate that by referring to it by "{*being brown* (Thelma)}[+]." This kind of composition is a form of *instantiation*; it exists when Thelma instantiates *being brown*. But there is another kind of non-mereological composition: *anti-instantiation*. This is the kind of composition that brings together Thelma and *being blue*, because Thelma *doesn't* instantiate *being blue*. So there is another state of affairs – {*being blue* (Thelma)}⁻ – that makes "Thelma is not blue" true, since this state of affairs guarantees that Thelma does not instantiate blueness.[26]

---

[25] This is due to Armstrong's defending a *sparse* account of universals. See, for example, Armstrong 1997: 44.

[26] See Beall 2000 for a similar view. Compare also Martin 1996 and Kukso 2006 on absences.

Negative states of affairs can serve as truthmakers for negative existentials such as "There are no unicorns." According to Barker and Jago, in addition to there being an instantiation-based form of composition, there is also a property of *being instantiated*. This property is possessed by other properties when they have instances. Negative existentials concern properties that aren't instantiated. So *being a unicorn*, for instance, anti-instantiates *being instantiated*. Hence, there is a state of affairs {*being instantiated (being a unicorn)*}⁻. This state of affairs guarantees that nothing instantiates the property of being a unicorn, and hence makes true "There are no unicorns."

Those (like Armstrong) who embrace positive states of affairs manifest their willingness to accept non-mereological composition into their worldview. So why not, argue Barker and Jago, embrace a second form of it, and thereby obviate the need for totality states of affairs and the problems they incur?[27] One reply is that the costs of negative states of affairs are not limited to just the second type of non-mereological composition. According to Armstrong's "modest" form of realism about properties, they exist only when instantiated. Thus, while there are properties such as *being blue* and *being a horse*, properties like *being a unicorn* and *being a vampire* don't exist. But Barker and Jago need such properties, for their not being instantiated is necessary to make true their corresponding negative existentials. The stock of extra properties required to build all the needed negative states of affairs is, then, far less modest than Armstrong's positing of just the *exhausts* relation. (But recall Jago's argument that there is no such relation.)[28]

3.2.3 The World

Here is one final account of what makes negative existentials true. Recall that Armstrong's totality state of affairs is the "most promiscuous and least discerning" truthmaker in that it is a truthmaker for every last truth, including negative existentials. Other truthmaker theorists have similarly argued that in some sense, the entire world can serve as a truthmaker for negative existentials. But – crucially – not in a way that is committed to Armstrong's totalities.

Ross Cameron (2008a) develops this idea, arguing that the world can serve as a truthmaker for negative existentials, provided that it has all of its features essentially.[29] Opal is essentially an orca, but Icelandic only accidentally.

---

[27] Jago (2018: 154–160) argues that some but not all accounts of positive facts can be extended to negative facts.

[28] Tallant (2018: 74–81) offers a thoroughgoing critique of negative facts.

[29] Other views that in some way or other put the whole world to work as a truthmaker for negative existentials include Lewis and Rosen 2003, Cheyne and Pigden 2006, Schaffer 2010, and Griffith 2015a. I am inclined to include Armstrong's totality view here as well, since he may as well

Thus, she can be a truthmaker for "Opal is an orca" but not "Opal is Icelandic." The World (I capitalize it to emphasize that we are thinking of it as a single, unified entity – the biggest entity there is) is such that there are no unicorns. If this were an essential feature of the World, then it would be impossible for it to exist and "There are no unicorns" to be false, just as it's impossible for Opal to exist and "Opal is an orca" to be false. It doesn't follow that "There are no unicorns" is necessarily true. Rather, had there been unicorns, then the World would not have existed. Something very similar to the World – something that includes all its parts plus a unicorn, say – might have existed instead.

The salient benefit of Cameron's account is supposed to be that its truthmaker is something we already believe in: the World. (For this reason Jago [2013] calls it a "parsimonious" solution to the problem of negative existentials.) We just need to update one of our beliefs about it – that in all its respects it is the way it is essentially so. However, it seems to me that the World is no more familiar an entity than totality or negative states of affairs (cf. Saenz 2014: 87). In fact, I now argue that the World is best understood as just being a totality state of affairs.

Consider again the Thelma and Louise universe with just two brown horses. Here, "There are no kinkajous" is true. On Cameron's view, the truthmaker for this claim is not the World – it exists only in the actual world – but a parallel entity I'll christen "Cosmo." From the perspective of the toy universe, Cosmo is the world. It's part of the essence of Cosmo that if it exists, there are no kinkajous. So what is Cosmo? Cameron (2008a: 417) tells us that "The world is the biggest thing. It is a world because there is nothing bigger than it that it is a proper part of." Cosmo, then, is the biggest thing in the universe. What Cosmo cannot be is the mereological sum of all the parts we've identified in the universe. For example, Cosmo cannot be Thelma + Louise + *being brown* + *being a horse*. That complex can coexist alongside kinkajous. If there are (first-order) states of affairs, we can add those to the mix, but we still won't end up with a sum that necessitates the absence of kinkajous. So Cosmo must be something above and beyond all the parts of the universe.

Cosmo needs to be the largest object in our tiny universe, something that guarantees an absence of kinkajous, and something that cannot exist in any other possible universe. Cosmo cannot be any mereological sum of the various parts of the universe. What Cosmo *can* be is a totality state of affairs. A totality state of affairs is composed by all the first-order states of affairs, which are in turn composed by all the particular objects and properties that exist in the

---

identify the world with the totality state of affairs (see Armstrong 1997: 197). See Griffith 2013, Jago 2013, and Saenz 2014 for objections to some of these views.

universe. So it has claim to being the largest object, since everything else that exists is part of it. By design, totalities exclude the existence of all the objects that don't figure in their first-order states of affairs. Finally, no totality state of affairs can exist in any other possible universe. Suppose there are four first-order states of affairs – A, B, C, and D – that establish that Thelma and Louise are both brown horses. A + B + C + D exhausts *being a first-order state of affairs*, giving rise to the existence of the totality state of affairs I'll dub "Kosmo." Kosmo can't exist anywhere else, because in no other universe does A + B + C + D exhaust all the first-order states of affairs,[30] and Kosmo just is the state of affairs composed by A + B + C + D exhausting all the first-order states of affairs. I submit that, given the kind of thing that Cosmo needs to be, Cosmo is Kosmo. If so, Cameron's advocacy of the World is no advance beyond Armstrong's totality account. The World, if it exists, just is Armstrong's totality state of affairs.

3.3 Non-Maximalism

A chief advantage for non-maximalism is that it need not engage in the defense of or fight between the views surveyed in Section 3.2. Non-maximalists can maintain that negative existentials are truthmaker gaps: truths without a truthmaker. But that advantage would amount to nothing if non-maximalism is, as many have held, a nonstarter for truthmaker theory.

There are two basic views regarding non-maximalism, only one of which finds it to be at all tenable. One maintains that in some sense maximalism is the default position in truthmaker theory, such that adopting non-maximalism amounts to "ontological frivolity" (Molnar 2000: 85) or giving up "as soon as the going gets hard" (Armstrong 2004: 70). This perspective is defensible only if something about the nature of truth itself requires that truths have truth-makers. Cameron (2008a: 412), for instance, writes: "Truthmaker theory is a theory about *what it is* for a proposition to be true; it's just not the kind of theory that can apply only in a restricted domain. What possible reason could one have for thinking of some propositions that they need to be grounded in what there is that doesn't apply to all propositions?" A straightforward reply to Cameron's question is that because truths are grounded by what they're about, and negative existentials are not about the things that exist, they are not fit to be made true by what there is. Hence, they're not fit to be made true at all.[31] Furthermore, Cameron claims that truthmaker theory is also a theory of the

---

[30] I'm bracketing the issue of indiscernible universes here – two universes that are qualitatively exactly similar but nevertheless distinct. Their existence is relevant only in the context of concrete modal realism (e.g., Lewis 1986) that takes nonactual universes to be real.

[31] Schipper (2018) provides a systematic development of this idea.

nature of truth, but we have already seen that this claim is both optional and contentious – it risks adopting a circular theory of truth.[32]

The other perspective on non-maximalism promotes the attitude that it can be independently motivated, and so is in no way just a metaphysical fallback position. Here is Peter Simons (2005: 255): "Maximalism is a theoretical position extrapolating from a fundamental insight, it is not itself a fundamental insight." To say that some truths owe their truth to the things that exist in the world is about as incontrovertible as anything in philosophy. To say that *all* truths owe their truth to existing objects is a further and substantive metaphysical claim, one with dramatic ontological implications, as we have seen. And, of course, one that flies in the face of the non-maximalist's position that truths concerning what *doesn't* exist aren't fit to be made true by what *does*. Look again at the first paragraph of this section. If truthmaking is an exercise in ontological accounting, then the right response to the truth of a negative existential is to ensure that the relevant things are *excluded* from one's ontology, not to ensure that some other thing is included.

One theoretically appealing feature of maximalism is its simplicity: all truths, without exception, possess truthmakers. Non-maximalism, by nature, must be more complicated. At best, it can offer a restricted kind of maximalism: maximalism with respect to contingent truths (Armstrong 1989: 88), synthetic truths,[33] atomic truths (Mulligan, Simons, and Smith 1984), or positive truths (but see Jago 2012). For my own part, I agree with Rodriguez-Pereyra's (2005: 18) assertion that truthmakers are to be found for "the members of an important class of synthetic true propositions," but only because it's so open-ended. On my view (see Asay 2020a), there is no simple, straightforward way of dividing up the truths with truthmakers from those without. One must approach the question of which truths have truthmakers on a case-by-case basis.

Negative existentials are the most commonly cited candidate truthmaker gaps, but there are other potential cases. Analytic truths, such as "All bachelors are unmarried," have been offered as truthmaker gaps.[34] If analyticities are "true solely in virtue of meaning," then giving them an *ontological* grounding would be inappropriate. For to say that analyticities are ontologically grounded by their meanings is to say that their truth depends upon the existence of those meanings. And that entails, falsely, that had the meanings of the words "bachelor" and "unmarried" never come about (or just been different), bachelors wouldn't have been unmarried.[35] Another example (which might also be a case of both an

---

[32] See the references in note 16.

[33] Rodriguez-Pereyra (2005: 31) comes close to endorsing synthetic maximalism.

[34] See, for example, Rodriguez-Pereyra 2005, Schulte 2011: 428, and Asay 2020b.

[35] Boghossian (1996) uses this observation to undermine all "metaphysical" forms of analyticity. I use it to motivate a better form of metaphysical analyticity (Asay 2020b).

analyticity and a negative existential) is "This sentence has no truthmaker."[36] If this sentence were false, it would have a truthmaker, and therefore be true. That's inconsistent, so it must be true. And since it's true, it has no truthmaker. Therefore, "This sentence has no truthmaker" is provably a truthmaker gap.[37]

Regardless of what the truthmaker gaps are, it is vital to recognize that admitting their existence need not be an exercise in ontological frivolity, or nothing more than an ad hoc commitment to maintain one's metaphysical scruples. One final way to appreciate this fact is to consider a perspective that, while being non-maximalist about truthmakers, is still in some sense maximalist about the relationship between truth and ontology. This perspective finds its articulation in the work of John Bigelow (1988: 121–127). For Bigelow, everything that is true must (at least) *supervene* on what exists.[38] That is, *all* truths are such that their failing to be true would have resulted in some difference in the world's ontology, even if all truths are not necessitated by something in that ontology. Negative existentials clearly satisfy this principle, even if they don't satisfy maximalism. For had "There are no unicorns" failed to be true, the world's ontology would have been different: it would have included unicorns. Hence, Bigelow's supervenience principle can be seen as an alternative to maximalism when it comes to articulating the basic insight that truthmaker theory intends to capture.

A familiar rebuttal to this proposal is that the supervenience of truth on being is insufficient to capture the idea of truthmaking because ontology also supervenes on truth (had the world's ontology been different, so too would the world's stock of truths), and truthmaking is intended to be an asymmetrical notion.[39] Answering this objection takes us back to the differing overall perspectives on truthmaking explored in Section 2, and whether or not the truthmaking relation itself needs to be analyzed in terms of an asymmetric, explanatory relation.

4 The Past

The previous sections have explored some fundamental questions about what truthmaking is, why we should care about it, and how wide its scope is. My focus now changes: how can we put truthmaking to work in metaphysics? This section tackles one of truthmaker theory's most expansive

---

[36] See Khlentzos 2000: 122–123 and Milne 2005.

[37] Rodriguez-Pereyra (2006a) argues that this sentence doesn't pose a problem for maximalism since maximalists will treat the sentence as paradoxical, akin to the liar sentence "This sentence is not true." And however one handles that paradox, one can handle the truthmaking case in parallel fashion.

[38] See also Armstrong 1969: 23. Lewis (2001b) considers an even weaker supervenience claim.

[39] See, for example, Armstrong 2004: 8 and Rodriguez-Pereyra 2005: 19. Merricks (2007, chapter 4) offers a sustained critique of supervenience-based theories of truthmaking.

topics: the implications that truths about the past have for the debate between presentism and eternalism.

There are three basic positions in the ontology of time. *Presentism* is the view that only present things exist. *Eternalism* is the view that past and future things exist alongside present things. *Growing Blockism* is the view that only past and present things exist, such that the universe grows larger each moment as the present merges into the past. Presentism has long faced a truthmaking-based objection. Uncontroversially, there are truths that concern the past.[40] Dinosaurs existed. Caesar crossed the Rubicon. Geraldo didn't find anything in Capone's vault.[41] But dinosaurs, Caesar, and Geraldo's live television broadcast don't exist anymore. If what is true depends on what exists, then it appears that presentism is false: it doesn't provide any ontology to ground truths about the past.[42]

There are two straightforward presentist responses to this objection. First, the presentist can identify presently existing objects that serve as ontological grounds for truths about the past. Second, the presentist can argue that truths about the past don't need such grounds (but that this fact doesn't involve a wholesale rejection of the impetus behind truthmaking). After considering the options and challenges for these two perspectives, I offer an objection against both routes.

4.1 The Upstanding Easy Road

The first response to the truthmaking objection to presentism is to identify objects that exist in the present that can serve as truthmakers for truths concerning the past. Such responses have been variously labeled as "upstanding" approaches to the objection (e.g., Tallant and Ingram 2015) or as the "easy road" to presentism (Asay and Baron 2014). In many ways, these views resemble the defenses of maximalism when it comes to negative existentials. The entities that are posited in the name of maximalism (totality states of affairs, negative facts, absences) are defended by way of their theoretical merits – their ability to satisfy maximalism – not their antecedent, independent plausibility. Similarly, the entities that presentists have offered to solve the truthmaking objection earn their keep mostly by way of their ability to answer the objection,

---

[40] But see Dawson 2021, which denies this. I'm not sure how to dialectically engage a view that is committed to denying that it was ever formulated.

[41] More controversially: there are contingent truths that concern the future. Because the status of future contingent claims (e.g., "Humans will walk on Mars by 2050") is of greater dispute, whether there is a parallel challenge for growing blockism is likewise more contentious.

[42] There are many presentations of the objection and surveys of the possible responses. See, for example, Armstrong 2004: chapter 11, Caplan and Sanson 2011, Tallant 2013: 369–372, and Griffith 2021.

which raises the concern that they are posited on a strictly ad hoc basis. Here it is important to keep in mind the dialectical significance of the objection. The point is not to show that presentists *can't* commit to entities that satisfy their truth-making commitments; no objection could demonstrate that. Rather, the objection shows that eternalists have the upper hand as compared to easy road presentists concerning their shared goal of providing truthmakers for truths about the past.

Still, consider some of the options that have been explored. John Bigelow (1996), taking his cue from the ancient Roman Epicurean Lucretius, advocates the existence of *tensed world properties*, temporally imbued properties that are possessed by the totality of things that exist.[43] Consider "Einstein used to be a German citizen." This sentence became true in March 1933 when Einstein surrendered his German passport and renounced his citizenship. At that moment, the world gained a new property, the property *being such that Einstein used to be a German citizen*, and it has continued to carry this property ever since. This property (or perhaps the state of affairs that joins it to the world) makes it true that Einstein used to be a German citizen. (An eternalist, by contrast, might instead cite the event of the renunciation as the truthmaker, since they remain committed to its existence.)

There are some familiar worries about these kinds of properties. One is that they are intrinsically problematic due to their "hypothetical" nature, which is to say that they are not possessed by objects solely in virtue of the way those things are (e.g., Sider 2001: 41). If the world has tensed properties, that is because of what used to exist, not because of how it is today.[44] Another objection is that they fail to be properly relevant to the truths in question, or fail to be properly explanatory (e.g., Merricks 2007: 137; Rhoda 2009: 48–49; Sanson and Caplan 2010: 30–31). A sentence about Einstein's past citizenship is about *Einstein*, not the totality of the world (which, for presentists, doesn't even include Einstein) having a certain property. So, tensed world properties can't provide the right kind of explanation for the sentence's truth.

Other paths along the easy road to presentism create a similar dialectic. Certain present-tense entities are proposed to be past-truth truthmakers, and are then charged with being nonexplanatory, irrelevant, ad hoc, or all of the above.[45] Eternalists, meanwhile, contend that their proposed truthmakers face none of these challenges, and so are preferable overall. If we start out neutral on presentism versus eternalism, the latter appears to have the upper hand when it

---

[43] See Tallant and Ingram 2020 for a recent defense.

[44] Kierland and Monton (2007: 494) dismiss this objection as "sheer metaphysical prejudice."

[45] Other easy road views include Kierland and Monton 2007, Rhoda 2009, and Cameron 2011. Critics include Sanson and Caplan 2010, Baron 2013a, 2013b, and Tallant and Ingram 2015.

comes to truthmaking for the past. But there remains a third camp in the debate, which retains presentism but posits none of easy road presentism's ontological suggestions. Simultaneously, it claims to do complete justice to the ontological accounting pursued by truthmaker theory. Is such a path really available?

4.2 The Nefarious Hard Road

The basic position of this third view – variously labeled "nefarious presentism" (Tallant and Ingram 2015), "hard road presentism" (Asay and Baron 2014), and "ostrich presentism" (Torrengo 2014) – is that truths about the past are truthmaker gaps. They are not made true, and are in no need of being made true. There is, thus, no reason to accept the eternalist's inflated ontology (or the easy road presentist's, for that matter). The nefarious presentist still offers *explanations* for truths about the past, but insists that these accompany no ontological implications.

"Nefarious presentists," claim Tallant and Ingram (2015: 370), "argue that truths about the past are true because of how things were, where no analysis of this primitive, past-tensed claim is given." For example, "Socrates existed" is true. Although there is nothing in the world to make this true, the world *used to be* such that Socrates existed. And "Socrates existed" is true because Socrates existed. The nefarious presentist, then, maintains that truths about the past are grounded in how the world used to be, where how the world used to be is an ontologically empty commitment: one can have infinitely many beliefs about what the past was like and what existed without incurring a single ontological commitment.[46]

One objection against nefarious presentism is that it fails to accomplish its own explanatory ambitions. Notice that it makes use of explanations of the form "'*p*' is true because *p*."[47] Such explanations posit an explanatory relationship between a "semantically ascended" truth – an ascription of truth to a truth-bearer – and the truth from which the former ascends. Hence, the truth of "'Socrates existed' is true" is explained by the truth of "Socrates existed." But this just pushes back the main question: What is the explanation for the truth of "Socrates existed"? Answering this question by citing the fact that Socrates existed is to offer the smallest possible explanatory circle.

Another problem for nefarious presentism is that its acceptance of the "because" explanations above undermine what is distinctive about presentism. The presentist's main idea is that the present is ontologically privileged: present things, and only present things, make up the world. Yet at the same time,

---

[46] See Sanson and Caplan 2010 for a similar view.

[47] Recall the discussion of these purported explanations in Section 2.2.2.

nefarious presentists accept that the "because" explanations are sufficient to address the ontological concerns raised by truthmaker theorists. As a result, nefarious presentists should also accept that such explanations are perfectly adequate ontological explanations when it comes to truths concerning the present as well. "If I were to heat this water to 373 Kelvin it would boil" is true because if I were to heat this water to 373 Kelvin it would boil. If this is all one needs to say when thinking about the truthmakers for counterfactuals, then truthmaker theory is moot across the board, not just for truths about the past. Nefarious attitudes about truthmaking for presentism instantly seep into a nefarious attitude about truthmaking full stop.[48]

Baia (2012) advocates a similar form of presentism. On his view, truths about the past don't require truthmakers. What is required instead is that they *used* to have truthmakers. Though nothing currently grounds "Socrates existed," there used to be something that grounded the truth "Socrates exists," namely, Socrates. Baia's presentist might therefore claim to be upholding the idea of ontological accounting that underwrites truthmaking; it's just that truths about the past need to be accounted for by *past* ontology, which doesn't exist anymore.

Baia's presentism requires an unstable understanding of ontology. What is the significance of ontology for this kind of presentism? How does it understand what it is to be ontologically committed to something? The truthmaking idea is that our ontological commitments are guided by our ontological accounting. If Baia stresses that presentists are not ontologically committed to the entities of the past, then they have literally nothing to appeal to when doing their accounting. One can't settle the books with assets one doesn't have. Alternatively, Baia could stress that his view does provide ontological accounting. It does take seriously the ontology of the past in some sense; it just recognizes that it doesn't presently exist. But if presentists appeal to the past to account for past truth, they are, for all intents and purposes, ontologically committing themselves to past ontology. Put another way: to maintain their accounting (for they don't want to deny that "Socrates exists" at least used to have a truthmaker), they need to take past ontology to be just as relevant to ontological accounting as present ontology. In effect, the nefarious form of presentism wants things both ways. It wants to ontologically account for past and present truth in parallel fashion (thereby *not* treating present ontology as ontologically special), but also insist that present and past ontology are not similar at all: only the former exists! In this way, the nefarious presentist divorces ontology from ontological accounting. As a result, it's left unclear what the philosophical significance is for the project of

---

[48] For other criticisms of this presentist tactic, see Asay 2020a: 209–212, Asay and Baron 2020, and Rodriguez-Pereyra 2022.

ontology in the eyes of the nefarious presentist. Like the eternalist, they seem committed to the task of using past existents (like dinosaurs) for ontological accounting, and agree that dinosaurs don't exist in the present. (Eternalists agree that dinosaurs went extinct.) Hence, there is no clear *ontological* disagreement between the eternalist and nefarious presentist; at best there appears to be a disagreement about how to use the words "ontology" and "ontological commitment." Perhaps present ontology is still metaphysically special in some way. But denying the reality of the past is not the only way of securing what's special about the present (see, for instance, Cameron's [2015] version of the "moving spotlight" theory).

4.3 History and Fiction

In the last section I noted that while the nefarious presentist denies that truths about the past require truthmakers, they typically accept that such claims *used* to have truthmakers (back when they weren't truths about the past). After all, they believe there are facts about the way the world used to be. Dinosaurs used to exist. Someone who thought the opposite would be wrong, though this disagreement would have no ontological implications for nefarious presentists. Neither the claim that dinosaurs existed, nor the claim that dinosaurs never existed, has any immediate ontological implications for nefarious presentists. That is to say, they think that they could change their minds about which of these claims is true without having to revise their ontologies with respect to it.

But this disagreement about the truth of "Dinosaurs used to exist" *should* reflect an ontological disagreement about dinosaurs. After all, it is a straightforward claim about the existence of dinosaurs. One way to probe this objection is to consider the difference between history and fiction. From the perspective of presentism, history and fiction are ontologically indiscriminate. Creatures of fiction don't exist; but neither do creatures of history. Chinese hopping vampires are no less real than the emperors of the Qing dynasty. All presentists agree to this. Nefarious presentists who disagreed about which of these things belonged to history and which to myth need not have any ontological disagreement with one another. By placing the fictional and the historical on an ontological par, presentists offer an impoverished perspective on what ontology as a philosophical enterprise accomplishes. In terms of ontological accounting, it gives you nothing beyond the present moment. But ontology ought to have more comprehensive ambitions; we want a total ontological accounting for the whole universe, in all its spatiotemporal glory. We care about what's over there, not just what's here. So too with time: ontology should be concerned with what was, just as it is concerned with what is. But taking on board a comprehensive ontological accounting that covers the past, present, and future is to concede eternalism, the thesis that no special moment of time is exclusively real.

Consider again the metaphor of the accounting departments. The ontology department will act differently when it learns that "In 2023, it is true that dinosaurs used to exist" is in the truth department's records, compared to if it had learned that "Dinosaurs are fictional" is there instead. The ontology department needs to *act* in the former case on dinosaurs, and that means that dinosaurs *are* relevant to ontology, even after they've gone extinct. It may need to act in the latter case as well (see Asay 2020a: chapter 12, on truthmaking and fiction), but it won't be adding any dinosaurs. (Maybe it will need to add a story about dinosaurs.) An ontology department that doesn't add dinosaurs to its rosters for a world where dinosaurs are extinct, not made-up, is failing at its job.

5 The Possible

Some truths are about what is possible, about how things might have been. Some truths are about what would have been the case, had things been different. I might have been a chemist, or perhaps a journalist. If I had remembered to fill the ice cube tray last night, there would have been ice cubes this morning. In one sense, these claims concern ways that the world *isn't*. I'm not a chemist, I'm not a journalist, and I didn't remember to fill the ice cube tray last night. In another sense, they do concern the way the world is. The actual world really is the kind of place where I could have been a chemist or a journalist. (The actual world is not such that I could have been a platypus.) And while it's true that my freezer would have frozen the water in the trays overnight, this too is due to the actual features of the world. Had the world been very different – with different laws of physics, say – then maybe the freezer wouldn't have frozen the ice.

Truths about possibilities and ways the world could have been provide an interesting case study for truthmaker theory. (I will sometimes refer to them as "modal truths," since they explicitly evoke concerns with the metaphysics of modality.) Many modal claims involve how the actual world isn't, but still seem to be true in virtue of the way the actual world is. The truthmaking question for metaphysicians is what kinds of ontological commitments these truths press upon us.

In this section I explore two broad outlooks on this question. First, I consider the "expansionist" strategy of *possibilists*, those philosophers who look beyond the actual world to find truthmakers for the truths about what might have been. Then I look to the "repurposing" strategy of *actualists* who argue that truths about possibilities can be handled by the same sorts of actual-world things that make true truths about actualities. I finish with some brief remarks about the truthmakers for counterfactual conditionals.[49]

5.1 Expansion

The expansion strategy is perhaps best exemplified by David Lewis. Lewis (1986) defends "concrete modal realism," the infamous ontological thesis that there are infinitely many concrete possible worlds, each as real as our own. These worlds are causally and spatiotemporally isolated from our own; each way that our world could be literally is a way that one of those other worlds is. Lewis puts his modal realism to work in order to offer, among other things, a reduction of modality, an analysis of the truth-conditions for counterfactuals, and accounts of what properties and propositions are. It would be anachronistic to say that Lewis develops his view in order to provide an account of the truthmakers for truths about possibilities. Lewis's development of modal realism predates the recent resurgence of truthmaking, and his own contributions to the truthmaking literature (Lewis 1992, 1998, 2001a, 2001b) are intentionally neutral regarding his own controversial metaphysical stance. (The exception is Lewis 2003, in which he shows how incorporating at least some amount of counterpart theory can solve certain outstanding problems for truthmaking.) Nevertheless, by committing himself to a plurality of concrete possible worlds, Lewis does provide himself with an answer to many questions about the ontological grounds for truths about possibilities.

Start with Lewis's (1986) own first example: "*On the Plurality of Worlds* might have been finished on schedule." According to the modal realist, in another possible world resides a philosopher quite similar to David Lewis, and who in fact is more similar to David Lewis than is anything else in that world. This Lewis counterpart is the author of *On the Plurality of Worlds* (or a counterpart of the book), but submits the manuscript on time to his publisher. In that world, "*On the Plurality of Worlds* was finished on schedule" is true; its truthmaker, presuming it has one, is also the truthmaker for the true modal claim in our world, that *On the Plurality of Worlds* might have been finished on schedule. In general, for any claim "It is possible that p" that is true in the actual world, any truthmaker for "p" in some possible world also serves as a truthmaker for "It is possible that p" in the actual world. As a result, the Lewisian can grant that the truths of one world are made true by the objects of another; but this is no shocking consequence for the Lewisian, as the modal realist happily ontologically commits to the objects of all possible worlds.

---

[49] For a pessimistic take on truthmaking and modal truth that aims to avoid all the strategies considered here, see Thomasson 2020.

The overall merits of Lewis's view are remarkable, and the criticisms that have been brought against it are familiar. My focus concerns its merits and flaws specifically as a theory of modal truthmakers. When it comes to this issue, Lewis's view is far from appealing. Perhaps it is ultimately worth its many theoretical costs on other grounds, but not solely on the basis of its utility for the theory of ontological grounds.

The most salient concern with the view is its extreme ontological price tag. In order to account for the modal truths of the actual world, infinitely more worlds are brought into the fold. Lewis is quick to note that while his possible worlds involve infinitely many new ontological commitments, at least they only involve *more of the same*. Lewis isn't positing new *kinds* of entities, just more of the same sorts of entities we find in the actual world. Nevertheless, Lewis's view is still chock-full of ontological commitments, and there is no doubt that accepting it comes with a great loss of parsimony. As Armstrong (2004: 83) puts the point, Lewis is "bringing in giants to do a boy's work."

A second objection is epistemological in nature. On Lewis's view, the truthmakers for statements of possibility turn out to be, at least in some cases, the concrete entities of other possible worlds. But these are entities with which, *ex hypothesi*, we have no causal interaction. Supposing that knowledge of truths typically involves some sort of relation to what makes those truths true, one wonders how we can have any modal knowledge at all.[50] It's true that *On the Plurality of Worlds* could have been submitted on time only if Lewis's counterpart does submit it on time. What epistemic access do we have to such an event taking place? I seem to have no better evidence as to what's going on in some other possible world than I do as to what's going on at some distant planet. Hence, if I don't have justification for asserting that in some distant galaxy there's a philosopher who looks a lot like David Lewis and is punctually turning in a manuscript that looks a lot like *On the Plurality of Worlds* (and I don't), then I don't have justification for asserting that in some other possible world there's a philosopher who looks a lot like David Lewis and is punctually turning in a manuscript that looks a lot like *On the Plurality of Worlds*. Modal realism leads to modal skepticism.

Lewis (1986: 108–115) brings up this style of objection himself and deals with it at length. One of his strategies is to stage a "partners in crime" defense with mathematical truth. Mathematics, too, is a field in which we seem to have knowledge in spite of having no causal access to the things that that knowledge concerns, that is, numbers. The strength of this response turns on the strength of

---

[50] For more on the relationship between truthmaking and epistemology, see, for example, Sorensen 2001: chapter 11 and Heathcote 2006.

the analogy between modal and mathematical truth. And part of Lewis's own view undermines the analogy – his possible objects in other possible worlds are supposed to be just like their counterparts in the actual world, not more like abstract entities such as numbers (that, admittedly, raise genuine epistemic concerns).

Lewis also challenges the idea that knowledge of otherworldly entities is just like knowledge of actual-worldly entities. Lewis believes that there is a crucial difference. That the actual world contains a tardy author of *On the Plurality of Worlds* is a contingent matter; that some world or other contains a timely author of *On the Plurality of Worlds* is not contingent. Causal acquaintance is required for knowledge only of contingent matters, according to Lewis. I find this response puzzling. On what grounds, given the modal realist perspective, can we say that it is not contingent that some world or other contains a timely author of *On the Plurality of Worlds*? If one world contains the timely author, then it's possible that the manuscript is turned in on time. If no world contains the timely author, then it's not possible, our suspicions to the contrary notwithstanding. For all I know, there is no world out there where the manuscript is submitted on time; I have no more guarantee that it's out there than I have a guarantee that in this world, in some galaxy far, far away, some Lewis-like creature is submitting a defense of modal realism to his publisher on time.

Lewis's view requires that the space of what we take to be the possibilities is completely filled in; but the epistemological objection wonders how we could ever know that. For example, it's supposedly possible that I could have been a chemist. For Lewis, for that to be true there must be a world out there where I have a counterpart who is a chemist. But perhaps there just isn't one of those worlds. If so, then it turns out I couldn't have been a chemist. One way to think about the objection is that the contingent/noncontingent distinction to which Lewis appeals does not help. For his noncontingent modal truths are still deeply *synthetic*: true in virtue of what's going on in the worlds themselves. And given that possible worlds are just things that happen to exist, like our world, there is no a priori guarantee as to which ones do.

The final objection to modal realism of particular interest to truthmaker theory is a variant of Kripke's (1972: 344–345, footnote 13) famous "Humphrey" objection. It's possible that I might have been a chemist. Since I'm not a chemist, this claim must be true in virtue of the career pursuits of one of my counterparts. But none of those counterparts is identical to me – they're no more identical to me than they are to any actual chemist. The fact that lots of people other than me are chemists seems to be irrelevant to *my* possibly being a chemist. The objection is the familiar one of irrelevance. My counterparts are not identical to me – the modal realist rejects the idea of "trans-world identity" – and so facts about them do not make true facts about me. That some other person is a chemist is irrelevant to whether or not I could have been a chemist. Objects must be relevant to the truths they make true; by inserting counterparts into the picture, modal realism inaccurately pairs actual modal truths with otherworldly truth-makers that the modal truths are in no way about and do not concern.

5.2 Repurposing

Lewis's concrete modal realism hopes to offer an elegant account of truth-makers for the truths about possibilities that runs fully parallel to accounts of truthmakers for truths about actualities. (In this way, the account is similar to how eternalists, but not presentists, posit the same kinds of truthmakers for truths, regardless of their temporal status; see Dyke 2007.) But the ontological and theoretical costs are severe. Hence, it will be worthwhile to consider the options for a nonexpanding ontology to provide ontological coverage for modal truths.

David Armstrong's approach to modal truthmakers fits the current mold.[51] His basic strategy is to argue that "truthmakers for a contingent truth . . . are also truthmakers for the unactualized possibility of the contradictory of that truth" (Armstrong 2006: 247). It's false that I am a chemist. But I might have been. Suppose that what makes it true that I'm not a chemist is some object T. T contingently exists. After all, "I am not a chemist" is contingently true, so if T were a necessary being "I am not a chemist" would be a necessary truth. Now, T's existence isn't tied to anything else in the world. In a "lonely" world with just T, it's true that I'm not a chemist. But it's also true of the lonely world that *it's contingent that* I am not a chemist, and nothing else but T is around to make that true. And since "It's contingently true that I am not a chemist" entails "It's possible that I am a chemist," then, by the entailment principle (the principle that if *p* entails *q*, then any truthmaker for *p* is a truthmaker for *q*), T is a truthmaker for the latter.[52] The truthmakers for "I am not a chemist" and "I might have been a chemist" are one and the same.

I applaud Armstrong's argument for its aim to maximize ontological econ-omy. It suggests that we don't need to reach beyond the actual world to ground modal truth. Objects and their properties together ground not only what is, but what could have been. Armstrong's argument, however, does face criticism.

---

[51] See Armstrong 2000: 154–159, 2003, 2004: 83–111, 2005: 271–272, 2006: 247, and 2007. For criticism, see Simons 2005, Keller 2007, Cameron 2008b, Kalhat 2008, and Pawl 2010. Armstrong's argument for his view evolves, but his basic stance remains consistent. See Pawl 2010 for discussion of how Armstrong's view develops.

[52] This principle is controversial within truthmaker theory. See Restall 1996, Armstrong 2004: 10–12, and Rodriguez-Pereyra 2006c.

Timothy Pawl (2010: 423–426) raises two central objections. First, he thinks it relies on the false generalization that for any object x, if x is contingent then x is a truthmaker for "x is contingent." Take the state of affairs {*being composed by N atoms* (Armstrong)}, where the number in question is in the billions. This state of affairs makes true "Something is composed by more than fifty atoms," a contingent truth. Therefore, by Armstrong's reasoning, it also makes true "It's possible that nothing is composed by more than fifty atoms." In reaction to this consequence, Pawl writes:

> But this is false! Armstrong's being composed of ten billion atoms has nothing to do with whether or not it could be the case that nothing is composed of more than fifty atoms. At the very least, it is not clear that Armstrong's being composed of ten billion atoms is a truthmaker for that claim; we need an argument for this. (Pawl 2010: 424).

Second, Pawl points out that Armstrong's argument entails that in a "lonely" world with just one object lying around, it must be the truthmaker for all modal truths. Armstrong claimed that in a world with just T – that is, the truthmaker for "I am not a chemist" – T must also be a truthmaker for "T is contingent," since nothing else is around. But so too must T be a truthmaker for other modal truths, such as "Chemists might never have existed at all" or "Al Gore might have won the US presidency in 2000." These truths, by Armstrong's lights, are necessary truths, and so are true in the world with just T. So T must make them true. As a result, Armstrong's account "sins" against the relevance requirement that Armstrong himself and others impose upon truthmaker theory.

The second problem, it seems to me, is more serious than the first. The first is also a relevance problem, and the problem with relevance objections is that it's unclear how to argue for them. Pawl no more offers an argument for his judgments about relevance than does Armstrong. Adjudicating these kinds of standoffs is no straightforward matter.[53] But the second objection goes beyond relevance and lands on triviality. Essentially, every object ends up being a truthmaker for all modal truths. This is a consequence with which Armstrong (2004: 8) should not be content, as it is out of sync with his own goal of defending nontrivial truthmaker maximalism.

Beyond Armstrong's view, there is another repurposing view currently being defended. This account grounds modal truth in the actual properties of actual objects. In Jacobs's (2010: 234) telling of the view, "the properties-based view grounds all of modality in properties and their inter-connections, however

---

[53] On my view, they are best handled by adopting the ontology-first approach, as I discussed in Section 2.2.2.

properties are conceived." It's true that I could have been a chemist. Why? Presumably because I'm human, know how to read and write, could have chosen to major in chemistry, etc. By possessing these properties, I gained the ability to be a chemist, and so they make true the fact that I could have been a chemist. Modal claims involve the way the world could have been, and the properties objects possess account for not just the way things are, but how they could be. Given the properties I have (such as being essentially human), I couldn't have been a banjo-playing puppet frog, but I could have been a bluegrass legend.

The properties view is plausible enough. It need not disagree with Armstrong's own account in many cases, given Armstrong's own commitment to universals and their substantive role as truthmakers in his philosophy. Furthermore, it need not invoke any kind of ontological addition, supposing anyway that one is already ontologically committed to properties for other reasons (such as grounding nonmodal truths). I would be suspicious of a view that posited properties *only* because of modal truths, but I don't know that anyone takes that particular approach (nor would it then qualify as a repurposing view).[54]

In fact, the properties view (broadly speaking, and perhaps in conjunction with elements of Armstrong's view) is the most appropriate view for handling *contingent* modal truths. The modal status of modal claims is not uncontroversial, but it will make a difference in one's overall truthmaking view. To get a handle on the relevant kind of cases, consider this line of reasoning from David Lewis:

> An ape can't speak a human language – say, Finnish – but I can. Facts about the anatomy and operation of the ape's larynx and nervous system are not compossible with his speaking Finnish. The corresponding facts about my larynx and nervous system are compossible with my speaking Finnish. But don't take me along to Helsinki as your interpreter: I can't speak Finnish. My speaking Finnish is compossible with the facts considered so far, but not with further facts about my lack of training. What I can do, relative to one set of facts, I cannot do, relative to another, more inclusive, set. (Lewis 1976: 150)

Here, Lewis is addressing the context-sensitivity of modal claims, in the efforts of deconstructing the appearance of contradiction between apparently conflicting modal claims. There are a whole host of modal claims to be found – and sometimes expressed with the very same language – and they may well differ on their modal status.

---

[54] Another option to consider is that there are *dispositional* properties in addition to categorical ones, and that the former are needed for various truthmaking purposes. See Austin 2015 for discussion and criticism of this view.

On the one hand, I could not have been a chemist: I chose to go to graduate school in philosophy. So "I could have been a chemist," while false, might have been true had I chosen a different academic path. Hence, it is a contingent falsehood that I could have been a chemist. On the other hand, I could have been a chemist. There's no incoherence in the very idea of my being in that line of work; the world would have had to have gone differently for me to have ended up that way, but the world going that way is entirely consistent with the basic laws of the universe, however understood. Understood in this light, it's unclear how it might have failed to be the case that I could have been a chemist. Perhaps it wouldn't be true that I could have been a chemist had I failed to exist. But as long as I'm around, it seems little else, if anything, also needs to be around in order to ground the possibility of my being a chemist.

The lesson I draw from these considerations is that we use our modal language to communicate various nuanced claims about the world, and our views about the ontological grounds for those claims need to be similarly nuanced. As a first pass, what makes it true that I couldn't have been a chemist is whatever makes it true that I lack the training to be one. This might be best ontologically cashed out as an absence (of any relevant credential, say) or totality (of actual chemists, a set to which I do not belong). What matters is that my modal claim here does make an ontological difference to the world – I'm trying to communicate something whose truth depends on contingently existing reality, something that could have turned out otherwise had different things existed. The sense in which "I could have been a chemist" is true requires less, ontologically speaking. Again as a first pass, what makes this true is my essence, as there's no incoherence in the idea of my being a chemist. I'm the sort of thing that can do the kind of activity that is constitutive of being a chemist. I take away from this observation the idea that what makes it true is mainly me and my features. It's consistent with my essence that I could have ended up a chemist.

Hence, truthmaking for contingent modal claims is not really that different from truthmaking for contingent nonmodal claims. How much ontology is required for our modal claims depends on what we are trying to communicate with our modal language. Getting clearer on the truthmakers for these modal claims can help us get clearer on what modal claim it is that we're trying to express, and vice versa. Hence, I see myself in broad agreement with repurposing modal truthmaker theorists, at least when it comes to modal truths of a contingent variety. I would hesitate to make a general claim, such as Jacobs's, that it's always *properties* that are modal truthmakers. Truthmakers, even in the modal realm, will belong to various ontological categories. After all, everything is a truthmaker for some truth or other. And every truth entails a modal truth (e.g., "*p*" entails "Possibly, *p*"). So everything is a truthmaker for some modal truth or other.

5.3 Counterfactuals

Counterfactual conditionals take the form "If it were the case that *p*, then it would be the case that *q*," where "*p*" is something contrary to fact. Counterfactuals, from the beginning, have played a critical role in motivating the broader truthmaking project. As Armstrong (2004: 1-3) tells the tale, ontologically averse philosophers of an earlier age took refuge in counterfactual analyses of notions that threatened their desert landscapes. Phenomenalism, the view that there are only presently existing sense perceptions, provides a tidy ontological inventory. But how can truths about unperceived objects be explained? No empirically respectable theory can deny that there might be planets deep in the universe with flourishing ecosystems that no one has yet perceived. But such possibilities appear to be incoherent by phenomenalist standards: a planet full of unperceived perceptions! To make sense of such claims, phenomenalists might take up the retreat to counterfactuals: it's not that there are unperceived ecosystems, it's that if one were to travel to such-and-such corner of the universe, one would have an ecosystem-like experience. That may be true, of course, but it leaves unanswered the question of what ontologically grounds that counterfactual. Lacking, at least, the relevant idea in the mind of a supernatural being (à la Berkeley 1999), it seems that the counterfactual must be accepted as a brute truth, a fundamental fact of the universe that in no way depends upon what does or doesn't exist. Better to leave the phenomenalist desert altogether than fill it with brute facts.

Truthmaker theorists do not rest content with accepting the truth of counterfactual conditionals: they instead offer accounts of what makes them true. That said, it seems to me that a systematic account of truthmaking for counterfactuals is ill-conceived. In other words, there is no reason to expect a special account of truthmakers that applies uniquely to counterfactuals. Hence, the truthmakers for, say, ethical counterfactuals are probably more similar to the truthmakers for ethical noncounterfactuals than they are to, say, counterfactuals about political states of affairs. For this reason, investigating the truthmakers for counterfactuals is not like taking up Nelson Goodman's "problem of counterfactual conditionals." In *Fact, Fiction, and Forecast*, Goodman (1983: 8) explores the difficulties in giving an account of "what sentences are meant to be taken in conjunction with an antecedent as a basis for inferring the consequent," and then accounting for the nature of the connection between them, since it's usually not a logical one. This project is fundamentally one of giving something in the neighborhood of truth-conditions for counterfactuals – an attempt to say what counterfactuals say, but not in a counterfactual way. So Goodman's project is not the ontological one in which I am interested. Perhaps it would be a useful addition, if the resulting analysis of Goodman's project yielded truths whose truthmakers were more perspicuous. In any event, even if a uniform semantics for counterfactuals is forthcoming, that is no reason to expect a uniform theory of truthmaking for them.[55]

To see why, consider the great variety of counterfactuals. If someone were to utter a never-before-expressed truth, then he or she would have spoken truly. That's a true counterfactual, but a trivially true one. It's also true that if Obama had lost the 2012 US presidential election, then Romney would have won. Spelling out a truthmaker for this claim would be a dizzyingly complex affair, incorporating Obama and Romney themselves, what makes true the facts about Romney's candidacy and eligibility, the dispositions in the minds of voters, and perhaps, among many other things, the truthmakers for other relevant facts about the US electoral system. It's true that if I were to kick a dog for fun, my doing so would be wrong. This truth is presumably due to the various mental states of the dog (that dispose it to feel pain when kicked), plus states of my physical body (which make me able to cause pain in the dog). Finally, it's true that if I were to place a glass of water into the freezer, the water would turn to ice within a few hours. What makes this true will involve the water, my freezer, and perhaps – importantly – various laws of nature.

The point is that we shouldn't expect a straightforwardly uniform account of the truthmakers for counterfactuals, since the class of counterfactuals does not constitute, metaphysically speaking, a straightforwardly uniform class. Counterfactual truths can arise in any intellectual domain, can be contingent or necessary, and are as subject to context as any other kind of truth. So, in general, I do not think that counterfactuals qua counterfactuals introduce any particularly distinctive element to truthmaker theory.

6 The Socially Constructed

Truthmaker theorists study the relationship between what is true and what exists. One topic where this relationship is particularly fraught is social construction. On the one hand, ideas about some domain being socially constructed can conjure up thoughts that truth is irrelevant in the domain, or that it concerns that which isn't real.[56] On the other hand, the idea that something is socially

---

[55] I detect something like the view I'm resisting in Jacobs 2011.

[56] Here is Thomasson (2009: 545): "The fact that social entities depend on human beliefs and intentions for their existence raises metaphysical questions about them that do not arise for mere natural objects. If we in some sense just make these things up, should we consider them to be

constructed implies that *something* has indeed been *constructed*. If this is the case, then social constructions do involve real (albeit constructed) things, and so, presumably, lots of truths concerning them. It will be productive, therefore, to approach the topic of social construction with the theory of truthmaking in mind.[57] This, I maintain, will help us to think more critically about the onto-logical and alethic implications of social constructions.

6.1 Preliminaries

In Plato's dialogue *Cratylus*, Socrates joins a conversation between Hermogenes and Cratylus, who represent, respectively, "conventionalist" and "naturalist" accounts of language. Here is Hermogenes describing his oppon-ent's view: "There is a correctness of name for each thing, one that belongs to it by nature. A thing's name isn't whatever people agree to call it – some bit of their native language that applies to it – but there is a natural correctness of names, which is the same for everyone, Greek or foreigner" (Plato 1997: 102; 383a–b). Hermogenes's view, by contrast, rejects this perspective: "No one is able to persuade me that the correctness of names is determined by anything besides convention and agreement. I believe that any name you give a thing is its correct name. If you change its name and give it another, the new one is as correct as the old" (Plato 1997: 103; 384 c–d).

Hermogenes and Cratylus disagree over whether or not language is a socially constructed (as opposed to a natural) phenomenon. The claim that some phe-nomenon is a social construction can be controversial, but I think there are plenty of mundane examples, language being among them.[58] The concern is a distinctly *metaphysical* one: What is it that *determines* the correctness of names? Because of its metaphysical nature, the claim that some phenomenon is a social construction can be understood from the perspective of truthmaker theory: What are the ontological grounds for the truths related to social constructions?

Consider some elated new parents who decide to name their baby daughter "Sophia." It's now true that the baby's name is Sophia. What is the truthmaker for "The baby's name is 'Sophia'"? The straightforward answer begins (and may well end) with the parents' intentions, decisions, and behaviors. In short, the baby's name is "Sophia" because that's what the parents have chosen, and

---

genuine parts of our world at all – or should we consider them just as illusory as the creatures in the stories we make up?"

[57] For work connecting social constructions and the metaphysical topic of grounding, see Griffith 2018a, 2018b, and 2020b.

[58] See Hacking 1999: 1 for a laundry list of phenomena that have been claimed to be socially constructed.

it's *up to them* what the baby's name is.[59] The parents didn't need to *discover* what the baby's name is; they needed to *decide* what it was. And that decision, more or less, provides the ontological grounds for the facts about the baby's name.

This example centers on a *semantic* truth: that "Sophia" is the name of a particular individual. Other semantic truths – such as that "dogs" refers to dogs, and that "snow" (in English) and "Schnee" (in German) mean the same thing – are, historically speaking, harder to pin down. But ultimately the grounds for these truths will settle on the decisions, intentions, and practices of the people who use these words. There may not have been a definitive linguistic "baptism" for the English "snow," similar to the way that "Sophia" came to refer to the new baby.[60] Yet it remains the case that what makes it true that "snow" means snow is the set of practices, conventions, and intentions of those who speak English. Getting clear on which of those practices and conventions matter, and what, precisely, those things come to, ontologically speaking, is the task for thoroughgoing investigation into the truthmakers for semantic facts.

If the semantic facts that ultimately constitute a language (e.g., that "water" in English means the stuff out in the ocean and that "smoke" in English refers to the gaseous product of fires) are made true by the linguistic conventions of English speakers, then we have a plausible case for the claim that language is a social convention. The community of English speakers is a social group,[61] and they "construct" and sustain the English language and all the facts about it. The markings "snow" wouldn't mean anything if people didn't confer meaning on it, just like how "shnuzzybuggle" is meaningless. The markings and sounds that constitute our languages have no meaning prior to the social practices that give rise to and sustain them.

The claim that a particular phenomenon is a social construction, then, can be supported by way of identifying the truthmakers for the truths associated with that phenomenon. It is because a certain set of truths are made true by a distinctively social ontology that those truths constitute a socially constructed phenomenon.[62] Those who disagree about the social nature of that phenomenon

---

[59] The answer might be more elaborate if names are thought of in a way that requires institutional approval, such that acts like the filing of particular kinds of paperwork, satisfying institutionally approved lists of names, etc., are also part of the process.

[60] But presumably there was a more definitive baptism for "neĝo," the word for snow in the planned language Esperanto.

[61] See Epstein 2015 for a thorough investigation into the ontology of social groups.

[62] This claim shouldn't be taken as an analysis of what it is to be socially constructed, as it at best offers a necessary condition on being a social construction. The idea is that a phenomenon, such as the naming of people, is a social construction because the truths concerning that phenomenon are made true by social conventions. But not all truths made true by social conventions are

will, in turn, identify a very different account of truthmaking for those truths; the truthmakers they identify will, presumably, turn to "natural" things as opposed to "social" things.[63] So a debate over whether or not some phenomenon is a social construct will reflect differing views about the ontological grounds for the truths about that phenomenon. But notice just how much may be held in common by the interlocutors in such a debate. They can agree that there are truths (i.e., facts of the matter) about the phenomenon, and that they are made true by perfectly *real* things (even if those things are "social" in nature). These truths (as well as their truthmakers) might even be highly "objective," even if they are socially constructed.

In Sections 6.2 and 6.3, I take up the examples of race and gender, and show how the debates over their nature have implications for how we think about truthmaking for the truths about race and gender. My goal is not to defend any particular view about the nature of race and gender, but rather to demonstrate how the metaphysical questions that concern them fit perfectly within the framework of truthmaking.

6.2 Race

The use of racial classifications is widespread across contemporary societies, and their implications can have profound and ubiquitous effects on nearly every aspect of a person's life. A person's race – in conjunction with others' perceptions of their race – has consequences for their educational and employment opportunities, susceptibility to violence, access to important social and political goods (such as voting), and countless others matters.

Metaphysical interest in the topic of race begins with the question of whether or not race is real.[64] Do people actually have racial properties, and thereby belong to racial groups? Or is race an illusion, such that there are no racial

---

socially constructed. For example, "The baby's name is Sophia" is a socially constructed fact because it's made true by a decision of the parents, and a disposition within the community to recognize that decision. But those things also make true "The parents made a decision" and "The community is disposed to accept the parents' decision," and *those* claims, presumably, aren't socially constructed facts.

[63] The word "natural" is extremely slippery in these contexts. Consider: "Hermogenes defends the view that language is a social (as opposed to natural) phenomenon. That is to say, while it is perfectly natural that humans go about inventing languages, the choices they settle on (e.g., that those animals over there are to be called "zebras") are ultimately metaphysically arbitrary: there's no right or wrong to what a thing is to be called prior to some decision (however collective) being made. This is equally true of both natural languages like English and Cantonese and artificially constructed languages like Quenya and Esperanto." Note how "natural" means something different in each instance, evoking a distinct contrast class in each case.

[64] Barnes (2014, 2016) argues that some approaches in contemporary metaphysics are unable to recognize the value in studying the ontology of socially constructed phenomena. See Mikkola 2015, 2017, Schaffer 2017, and Taylor (in press) for further discussion.

groups, and no one belongs to any racial category whatsoever? Regardless of how one answers these questions, they are tangled up with issues concerning truthmaking. If races don't exist, and sentences like "Martin Luther King, Jr. is Black" aren't true, why not? What is "missing" from the world that would be needed for there to be such truths? But if races do exist, and there are truths about what races people belong to, what is it in the world that is responsible for such truths? Getting clearer on these answers enables us to better understand the notion of race, and whether or not it is an inevitable element of human societies.

First consider "anti-realist" views about race that deny that race is real. On these views, racial groups don't exist.[65] No one is Black, White, American Indian, Asian, or Pacific Islander (to use the five categories currently employed by the US Census Bureau). It's important to note that anti-realism about race doesn't deny that *racialization* is a very real phenomenon. People identify (or don't) with various racial categories and make judgments about others' races as well. Governmental institutions collect data on racial identification and produce legislation that depends upon it. In short, people have plenty of beliefs about what races people belong to (beliefs that go on to inform their behavior in explicit and implicit ways), but anti-realists maintain that these beliefs are for the most part false.[66]

Given that race at least seems to play a hugely dramatic and consequential role in people's lives, what is the basis for denying its reality? Naomi Zack (1998: 10) provides a succinct presentation of the basic argument: "To say that race in the physical sense has no foundation in science is to say that race in the physical sense is not real. Since by race, most Americans mean something physical, the lack of a foundation in science means that race is not real. Period." The argument begins with a claim about what sorts of presuppositions are built into people's concept of race (the concept that is then expressed by the word "race"). The claim is that the concept of race is inextricably caught up with "biologically essentialist" ideas. Ron Mallon (2006: 528–529) provides a helpful summary of such theses: "Races were believed to share *biobehavioral* essences: underlying natural (and perhaps genetic) properties that (1) are heritable, biological features, (2) are shared by all and only the members of a race,

---

[65] Note that Mills (1998: 49), a social constructionist about race, identifies his view as a form of anti-realism. Haslanger (2019: 8, footnote 4) and Jeffers (2019) reserve "anti-realism" for views that deny that races exist. This point is merely terminological. (On my view, it's ultimately up to the partisans in a debate about realism to decide which views are best labeled "realist" or not; see Asay 2020a: 159–160.) Mills's choice reflects his interest in distancing himself from mind-independent accounts of race, whereas Haslanger's and Jeffers's choice reflects their emphasis that race does indeed exist.

[66] And where race-based beliefs are true, they are often true for unsuspecting reasons. Someone's belief that Martin Luther King, Jr. isn't Asian is true. But according to anti-realism, that belief is true because *no one* is (racially) Asian, not because King belongs to a different race.

and (3) explain behavioral, characterological, and cultural predispositions of individual persons and racial groups." Hence, what it is to be a member of a race is to possess one of those biobehavioral essences that are distinctive of the different racial groups. But, as we have discovered, those sets of traits do not exist: there is no biological basis for thinking that the groups of people classified together on the basis of race share any such essence. Thus, there are no races for anyone to belong to. As Kwame Anthony Appiah (1992: 45) puts the point, "there is nothing in the world that can do all we ask race to do for us." We conceive of race in biologically essentialist terms, and because those biological essences don't exist, neither do races.[67]

What underlies this anti-realist perspective on race is a view about the ontological grounds, or truthmakers, for claims about race: for a sentence like "S belongs to racial group R" to be true, there must, in the world, be a set of identifiable biological features shared by the members of the supposed racial group. Realists about race, therefore, must disagree with the anti-realist either about the nonexistence of those biobehavioral essences, or their view as to what the truthmakers need to be for there to be genuine facts about race. Either way, the dispute turns on competing views concerning the truthmakers for claims about race.

Support for the first kind of realism – that agrees with the anti-realist about what is needed to ground claims about race, but believes that such grounds do exist – is hard to come by these days, and is unsupported by contemporary biology.[68] The second kind of realism, by contrast, challenges the truthmaking account offered by the anti-realists. For these realists, the world *does* provide the needed material for there to be truths about race. Some of these realists still opt for a nonsocial understanding of race, albeit one that rejects the biologically essentialist account.[69] But my remaining focus will be on those who advance a social constructionist perspective on race, which we can now understand as the view that the ontological grounds for the truths about race are found in the distinctively social corners of ontology.

A key question facing social constructionists is what it is about social reality in virtue of which the facts about race obtain. One prominent view is Sally Haslanger's (2000, 2012, 2019) sociopolitical account.[70] According to

---

[67] For more on racial anti-realism (sometimes called "error theory") see, for example, Zack 1993, Blum 2002, and Glasgow 2009.

[68] See Mallon 2006: 529 and the sources cited within.

[69] See, for example, Andreasen's (2000) "cladism," Glasgow and Woodward's (2015) "basic racial realism," Hardimon's (2017) "deflationary realism," and Spencer's (2019a) "ancestralism". Note also Spencer's (2019b) pluralist approach that takes there to be multiple notions at work in racial discourse, and Outlaw's (1996) view that understands race to be a "cluster" concept that combines biological, geographical, and social elements.

[70] See also Mills 1997, 1998 and Taylor 2013.

Haslanger, a person's race is a function of the systematic subordination or privilege they are dealt in virtue of their belonging to a group that is singled out on the basis of its perceived ancestry. More formally, she presents the view as follows:

> A group G is *racialized* relative to context C iff$_{df}$ members of G are (all and only) those:
>
> (i) who are observed or imagined to have certain bodily features presumed in C to be evidence of ancestral links to a certain geographical region (or regions);
>
> (ii) whose having (or being imagined to have) these features marks them within the context of the background ideology in C as appropriately occupying certain kinds of social position that are in fact either subordinate or privileged (and so motivates and justifies their occupying such a position); and
>
> (iii) whose satisfying (i) and (ii) plays (or would play) a role in their systematic subordination or privilege in C, i.e., who are *along some dimension* systematically subordinated or privileged when in C, and satisfying (i) and (ii) plays (or would play) a role in that dimension of privilege or subordination.
>
> (Haslanger 2000: 44)

Haslanger is pointing to the existence of efficacious social hierarchies based on perceived ancestry as what constitutes a person's race. The basic idea is that groups of people are imagined (correctly or incorrectly) to share a particular ancestry on the basis of their bodily traits, and those groups are then positioned within a social hierarchy such that people enjoy particular privileges or are subject to forms of oppression in virtue of their place in that hierarchy. So what it is to be of a particular race is to be subject to some form of privilege or oppression in virtue of your perceived ancestry.

In short, then, according to sociopolitical constructionists like Haslanger, social hierarchies predicated upon perceived ancestry are the ontological grounds for the facts about race. The ontology of such hierarchies is a difficult question on its own.[71] But that they exist, and provide the grounds for facts about race, are central commitments for social constructionists about race. Racial anti-realists might agree that the social hierarchies exist, and provide the grounds for facts about *racialization*. (For example, the hierarchies make it true that people [falsely] identified as of a particular race are subject to certain forms of privilege or oppression.) But they would deny that they make it true that people, in fact, belong to racial categories.

One way to critically engage the social constructionist view is to consider the implications of its commitments when it comes to race and truthmaking.

---

[71] See, for example, Thomasson 2003, 2009 and Haslanger 2012, 2016.

First, consider the contextual nature of Haslanger's account. People don't have races simpliciter. They have races relative to contexts. Having a race is belonging to a group racialized in a particular way, and groups can be racialized (or not) in different ways at different times in different parts of the world. There are multiple social hierarchies in the world, and they confer oppression and privilege in different ways, and onto different divisions of people. Thus people can have multiple races. Is that correct?

Consider an example. Take a person, Alpha, who is racialized in a particular way in a particular sociopolitical context, C_1, alongside Beta and Gamma. These three form a racialized group G_1, and as a result all belong to the race R_1 relative to C_1. Now suppose that in a different sociopolitical context, C_2, these three are not racialized in the same way. Perhaps in C_1 all three are ethnic minorities, but in C_2 Gamma is not an ethnic minority. Consequently, there is no racialized group in C_2 that includes Alpha, Beta, and Gamma, and so these three do not share the same race in C_2, though they do in C_1.

As a result, Haslanger's view entails that many, if not all, people belong to multiple races, and that you can share your race with a person in some contexts, but not others. Is this consequence a feature or a flaw? The social constructionist sees an advantage here. People *are* racialized in different ways in different contexts, and this account captures that fact. Opponents, however, will argue that while racialization is context-sensitive, race isn't. Thus, being racialized (i.e., being treated differentially on the basis of one's perceived ancestry) is not the same thing as belonging to a race.

A second consequence of Haslanger's kind of view pertains to the subjunctive conditionals that it entails. Because social hierarchies are the truthmakers for the facts about race (and, presumably, nothing else in the world is), their disappearance would entail the disappearance of race. Hence, if all race-based social hierarchies were razed, then no one would belong to any race. "Racial equality," then, is a contradiction in terms for sociopolitical social constructionists.[72] The existence of race implies the existence of inequality, so those who fight against racial inequality are, at the same time, fighting against the very existence of race.

Again we can ask: Is this an acceptable consequence of Haslanger's view? She believes that it is. One point that Haslanger stresses is that her view has a normative dimension. Although she recognizes that she is "asking us to use an old term in a new way," she stresses that her goal is to ask "us to understand ourselves and those around us as deeply molded by injustice and to draw the appropriate prescriptive inference" (Haslanger 2000: 48). By beginning to think

---

[72] See Glasgow 2009: 120, 2019: 131–134 and Jeffers 2013: 421.

about race in a way that treats it as inherently unjust, we are better able to pay attention to and fight that injustice. Opposing views (e.g., Outlaw 1996: 36) will again stress that one can fight against unjust racialization without at the same time fighting against the very existence of race.

Other social constructionist accounts take issue with Haslanger on this point as well. On these views, while race is socially constructed, what does the constructing is not, fundamentally, unjust social hierarchies. Taking his inspiration from W. E. B. Du Bois (1897), Chike Jeffers defends a *cultural* form of social constructionism: "In speaking of the impact of race on our lives, we necessarily speak of the shaping of our lives by our socialization into particular ways of life where being this or that race is among the modes of identification that influence how we think and act. Race must therefore also be understood as a cultural phenomenon" (Jeffers 2013: 420). If there are cultural underpinnings to race (in place of or in addition to the political underpinnings), then race could continue to exist even in the absence of racism.

On Jeffers's view, race has political and cultural foundations. The question that I want to probe – and that is better appreciated by approaching the view from the perspective of truthmaker theory – is whether or not one of these dimensions takes metaphysical priority. Jeffers inclines toward a view that respects both, but doesn't put an inherent priority on either dimension. He writes:

> Race is fundamentally social, in my view, but I do not take either politics or culture to be more fundamental in the sense of being what is essential for the social reality of race. Culture cannot be essential in this way if, as I hold, race is political at its origin. Politics cannot be essential if, as I believe, a future in which race is merely cultural is possible. (Jeffers 2019: 58)

Central to Jeffers's view is an important asymmetry when it comes to race and its relation to politics and culture. He agrees with political constructionists that race needs a political *origin*. However, he disagrees with political constructionists that race must be *sustained* by those political forces from which it came to be. Racism breathes life into race, but culture carries it along.

If neither politics nor culture takes priority when it comes to the ontological grounds of race, there are two possibilities. First, race could be a metaphysically *disjunctive* notion, such that all it takes for there to be races is for there to be either the political or cultural forces that constructionists identify. (Or both: there's no problem with there being more than enough truthmakers for a given set of truths.) Second, race could be *conjunctive*, in the sense that the truths about race need to be made true by political and cultural factors working in tandem. Either way, politics and culture are on the same footing. They're either both necessary for race, or both able to handle race on their own.

However, it seems to me that neither account will work for Jeffers: contrary to his intentions, Jeffers is committed to political forces being ontologically required for race in a way that cultural forces aren't. For Jeffers, the "racial timeline" of the actual world runs as follows. At some point, an ancestry-based social hierarchy came to be, and consequently established the existence of races. Over time, that hierarchy, which has continued to exist, has given rise to various new cultural phenomena that have attached themselves to the hierarchy's racial categories, and has had effects on preexisting cultures as well. That brings us to today, where the hierarchy is still in full force.

What reveals Jeffers's commitments vis-à-vis truthmaking are his commitments to some crucial subjunctive conditionals. Most important is his claim that if the hierarchy were to disappear, race wouldn't disappear with it because of the cultural forces still in play.[73] This suggests the above "disjunctive" view that you need either the political or the cultural forces to have race, but not necessarily both. But this can't be correct, given the aforementioned asymmetry that Jeffers introduces. Suppose that humanity achieves racial equality by 2123, such that the social hierarchies that have fueled racism for centuries have finally broken down. Jeffers's view is that the cultural practices in place in 2123, that is, the "participation in distinctive ways of life" that constitute cultural diversity (Jeffers 2019: 50), are enough to continue making it true that race still exists. But now imagine a very different timeline for our world, a "utopian" one. In this timeline, the social hierarchies never existed in the first place, but we ended up, culturally speaking, much the same. The world is full of cultural diversity, in a way similar to the post-racist cultural landscape of our hoped-for 2123, but is one in which these different ways of life are not systematically arranged into hierarchies of privilege and oppression. I gather that Jeffers is committed to saying that in this timeline, race *doesn't* exist. This is the force of his claim that he agrees with political constructionists that hierarchies are necessary for the establishment of race (Jeffers 2019: 57). Race and racism are like children and their parents. One can survive the other, but never would have come to be without it. So the people in the utopian timeline don't belong to any race, even though the same cultural phenomena that sustain race in our hoped-for 2123 exist there as well. This implies that for it to be true that a person belongs to a race, a racializing social hierarchy must have existed at some point, even if it exists no longer.

By contrast, consider a "dull" timeline in which an ancestry-based social hierarchy is established, but cultural diversity never flourishes. The world is

---

[73] I refer to this as a subjunctive conditional rather than a counterfactual because I hold out hope that its antecedent is true! (Counterfactuals are subjunctive conditionals with false antecedents.)

a monocultural place, though one that doles out oppression and privilege as a function of perceived ancestral heritage. I take it that Jeffers would say this *is* a world with race, given his stress on its political origins. Culture's role in the story of race comes later, and can continue after the politics dissolves away. If so, then the cultural phenomena that can keep race going after the collapse of racist social hierarchies are not themselves necessary for race, as race can exist independently of them. Furthermore, if, on the dull timeline, the social hierarchy were to disappear, so too would race, as there isn't any cultural diversity around to sustain it.

What emerges, then, is a view where even a cultural constructionist like Jeffers is committed to a kind of metaphysical priority for the political grounds of race. For it to be true that a person belongs to a race, there *must* be (or have been) an ancestry-based social hierarchy that systematically subjects that person to a network of privilege and oppression. Sometimes cultural phenomena have no truthmaking role to play in race, but are required in certain cases. In those cases where they are required, they will work in conjunction with the social hierarchy (even if it is now relegated to the past) in order to be racial truthmakers.

Hence, Jeffers's view ends up very similar to the political constructionists' in terms of what is most important for the existence of race. Both views maintain that sociopolitical hierarchies are *always* necessary for there to be truths about race; what separates them is that the cultural constructionist adds on an additional claim that cultural phenomena can take on a race-bearing load should those hierarchies collapse. The advantage for Jeffers is that he can maintain the possible existence of racial harmony, and the preservation of facts about people's races in the face of the hierarchies' demise. The disadvantage is the more complicated metaphysical story required; perhaps the political constructionist will see the proffered truthmaking role for cultural phenomena as being ad hoc. Why are cultural phenomena able to sustain the existence of race, but not originate it? In response, Jeffers could reply that since race is a social construction, it's ultimately up to us what sort of concept we end up constructing, and there's no reason we couldn't have constructed one with a somewhat complicated metaphysical structure.

This brief tour into truthmaking and race isn't intended to settle the questions about the metaphysics of race, but my hope is that it does bring into relief some of the dimensions of the ontological debates concerning race. A fully developed metaphysical account of race needs to properly align a defensible ontology with what it takes to be true with respect to race. Oftentimes, the focus of truthmaking arguments is on disagreements over the correct ontology for a mutually agreed upon set of truths. Interestingly, the case is different here. Many of the opposing metaphysical views agree on much of the ontology – the absence of biobehavioral essences, the existence of racializing social hierarchies – but disagree on what these things make true, such that there are severe disagreements about what is true in the realm of race.[74] Regardless, though, of whether one "starts" with a set of truths or a set of truthmakers, the duty to keep them aligned that is the fundamental duty of truthmaker theory is fully intact when it comes to the metaphysics of race.

6.3 Gender

The metaphysics of gender is frequently thought to share a structural similarity with the metaphysics of race. From a social constructionist point of view, race is the product of socially significant patterns of privilege and oppression founded upon perceived ancestral status: the "social meaning of color" as Haslanger (2000: 43) puts it. Analogously, gender is the product of socially significant patterns of privilege and oppression founded on perceived reproductive role: the "social meaning of sex." For Haslanger, to be a *man* (where this term is taken strictly to express gender alone) is to reap certain privileges in virtue of being perceived to play the *male* (where this term is taken strictly to express biological sex alone) role in reproduction. To be a *woman* is to face certain forms of oppression in virtue of being perceived to play the *female* role in reproduction.

Because of these similarities, the same sorts of objections and replies that arose in the section on race arise here as well.[75] Is gender equality conceptually impossible? Should the goal of feminism be the elimination of women? Would people have multiple genders if there happens to be a very different reproduction-based social hierarchy (a true matriarchal society, say) somewhere in the world?[76]

---

[74] Of course, the views disagree on the ontology of race itself, given their competing accounts of what grounds the facts about race.

[75] But there may also be potent dissimilarities between the two cases. The social constructionist thinks race is a social construct, but not, presumably, the things that race is founded upon: ancestry, skin color, etc. And while some social constructionists may think that gender is likewise a social construct based upon something not socially constructed (biological sex), others argue that biological sex is itself socially constructed (e.g., Butler 1990 and Ásta 2018).

[76] It's not clear to me how Haslanger would understand a matriarchal society where individuals receive privilege in virtue of being perceived to be playing the female reproductive role (and perhaps, in addition, are subject to oppression in virtue of being perceived to be playing the male reproductive role, as depicted in, say, Eléonore Pourriat's short film *Majorité Opprimée*). Such people are *gendered* (in that they receive privileges in virtue of their perceived reproductive role), but they aren't *women* (since for Haslanger women are those who are oppressed in virtue of being perceived to play the female reproductive role specifically) or *men* (since men are those who are privileged in virtue of being perceived to play the male reproductive role). Another concern for Haslanger's view involves whether it can classify transwomen as women; see Jenkins 2016.

Instead of revisiting these structurally similar questions, in this section I consider a different approach to social construction, the *conferralist* account defended by Ásta (2018).[77] The main idea behind Ásta's approach is that gender is a communal property conferred onto individuals by others with appropriate standing in a given context on the basis of their perception of the individual's possessing certain relevant properties. A person has the gender properties they do in various contexts in virtue of others' perceptions of certain of their socially relevant traits. The account is "radically context dependent" in that a person's gender is sensitive to context, where the contexts can be particularly fine-grained (Ásta 2018: 73). Ásta offers this example:

> Consider this scenario: you work as a coder in San Francisco. You go into your office where you are one of the guys. After work, you tag along with some friends at work to a bar. It is a very heteronormative space, and you are neither a guy nor a gal. You are an other. You walk up the street to another bar where you are a butch and expected to buy drinks for the femmes. Then you head home to your grandmother's eightieth birthday party, where you help out in the kitchen with the other women while the men smoke cigars. (Ásta 2018: 73)

The example provides four different contexts that a person might be in during some given day, and where that person's gender is distinct in each context. In each context, there are individuals who carry *standing*, a status that enables them to be "in charge" of how gender functions in that context (much like how an umpire in baseball has the standing to confer the properties of *being a strike* and *being a ball* onto pitches). A person's gender is determined by the perception of those with standing as to whether a given person possesses a certain *base property*, where the relevant base property can itself change from context to context. As Ásta emphasizes, the relevant base property for gender is highly variable. It could be one's "role in biological reproduction" or a "person's role in societal organization of various kinds, sexual engagement, bodily presentation, preparation of food at family gatherings, self-identification, and so on" (Ásta 2018: 75). Hence, in a given context, gender is conferred onto a person by those with standing on the basis of whether they perceive that person to possess the relevant base property for gender for that context.

Ásta's account naturally fits into the truthmaking framework. She writes: "Acts of conferral always result in a new feature being bestowed on something, and new facts come into being as a result" (Ásta 2018: 13). Conferrals, therefore, make new truths about social categories.[78] Absent any conferring, no statement of the form "In context C person P is gender G" is true. When such

---

[77] Other social constructionist views on gender include Alcoff 2006 and Witt 2011.

[78] At least when supplemented by the truthmakers for facts about standing, as detailed below.

claims are true, they are made true by conferrals. Which conferrals are the relevant truthmakers depends on the context. I might be able to confer certain properties onto a baseball pitch (some aesthetical properties, perhaps), but I can't confer *being a strike* onto it because I'm not the umpire. The conferrals that serve as truthmakers for the facts about gender must be made by those with the relevant standing, and concerning the base properties that are relevant in the context. If no such conferrals take place, then no sentence of the form "In context C person P is gender G" is true, which is precisely what the social constructionist maintains. There is no gender in the world if there is no social reality creating it.

The basic thesis of Ásta's account, that the facts about gender are made true by conferrals, is straightforward. The details, less so. Notice, for instance, how Ásta's account has an extra layer of variability as compared to, say, Haslanger's account. On both views, gender is relative, and dependent on context. But for Haslanger, gender is always the social meaning of *sex*; it's just that the social meaning can vary from context to context. For Ásta, gender is the social meaning of *something*, where that something can vary widely: reproductive role here, washing up role there. One question for Ásta, then, is what, if anything, constrains the range of base properties that are relevant to gender. Not all socially meaningful base properties are relevant to gender. For example, when it comes to institutional racial properties (such as those employed by government bodies), Ásta (2018: 99) holds that the relevant base property is "supposed actual geographic ancestry." Conferrals made by those with standing on the basis of their perceptions of someone's geographic ancestry do not create any facts about *gender*; they create facts about *race*. Since multiple base properties can be the basis for gender properties, what is it that makes them gender-relevant properties?

Framed in terms of truthmaking, the question for Ásta is this: Why is a given conferral a truthmaker for a fact about gender, rather than a fact about some other socially constructed property? Let's examine the account in detail, drawing on Ásta's example of the coder, whom I'll name "Cody." In C_{HB} – the context of the heteronormative bar – it's not the case that Cody is a woman. In C_{GK} – the context of the grandmother's kitchen – it is the case that Cody is a woman. To further simplify things, let's suppose that in each context there is one person who has standing (Stan in C_{HB} and Stanley in C_{GK}), and one relevant base property: having traditionally feminine bodily appearance in the former, and doing the dishes in the latter. The conferral that matters in the bar is Stan's perception that Cody lacks traditional feminine bodily appearance.[79] This mental state – call it M_{HB} – does not,

---

[79] Note, then, that what matters is that Cody is perceived to have the base property, not that Cody has it. Ásta argues against competing accounts – "constitutive accounts" such as Searle's (1995) – that require the person in question to possess the base property.

by itself, necessitate that Cody is not a woman in C_{HB}, because it's possible that Stan could have had this perception but failed to have standing. So the full truth-maker for the fact that Cody is not a woman in C_{HB} is M_{HB} taken together with whatever makes it true that Stan has standing with respect to gender in C_{HB}. Stan has other perceptions, and Cody has other socially meaningful properties, but they are irrelevant to the facts concerning Cody's gender. Meanwhile, Stanley has M_{GK}, a perception that Cody is doing the dishes. M_{GK}, taken together with whatever makes it true that Stanley has standing regarding gender in C_{GK}, makes it true that Cody is a woman in C_{GK}.

What is it about M_{HB} and M_{GK} that makes them truthmakers for the facts about gender? These mental states create women (or nonwomen) – not prime ministers, Catholics, or ombudspeople. Furthermore, they can create other things, too. Suppose that in Grandma's kitchen, doing the dishes is also a base property for the social property *being a mensch* (and that Stanley has standing with respect to this, too). So Stanley's perception that Cody is doing the dishes – M_{GK} again – is a (partial) truthmaker for "In C_{GK}, Cody is a mensch." But this is not a fact about Cody's gender; it's a fact about the social recognition of Cody's character. What's the difference, then, between being a woman and being a mensch in this context? Looking to the metaphysics involved can't answer that question, since in certain contexts the metaphysics may be exactly the same.

A prominent feature of Ásta's account, then, is that it is flexible enough to account for the fact that anything can be socially meaningful in any particular way. The social significance of having red hair can vary widely across different contexts. In some contexts it may have multiple meanings, and in others no social meaning at all. Moreover, Ásta can maintain that what makes someone a woman is highly dependent on context. The metaphysics of gender can be highly variable. But this flexibility is a double-edged sword, as it may foreclose on the ability to find some kind of unity behind the variability. A person's gender may differ in different contexts, and what perceptions make someone a particular gender can differ across contexts as well. But presumably the gender itself is something stable. There is something significant in common between women in C_{HB} and women in C_{GK}. These aren't *two* distinct genders; there are just two distinct metaphysical pathways to acquiring that one gender. Hence, what *makes* one a woman in a given context is distinct from what it is to *be* a woman. What it is to be a mensch is distinct from what it is to be a woman, even if others' perceptions of you doing the dishes is what makes you both in a given context.

Ásta's metaphysical account of gender, then, seems to leave an important question open. What is it to be *gendered*, given that one can be gendered in radically disjunctive ways? For someone like Haslanger, the metaphysics seems to answer this question. What it is to be gendered is to have one's perceived role in reproduction be socially meaningful. The hierarchies that provide that social meaning are what make it true that someone is or isn't a woman. For Ásta, one can be gendered even in contexts where reproductive role is not socially meaningful, and the same property that is the basis for gender in one context can be the basis for a nongendered property in another. So what distinguishes gender from other socially meaningful categories?[80]

Ásta does observe that on her view, a social property (like *being a woman*) "is fleshed out in terms of the constraints and enablements, institutional or communal, on a person's behavior and action. To have the status in question *just is* to have the constraints and enablements in question" (Ásta 2018: 29). But if being a woman is identical with being subject to various institutional and communal constraints and enablements, then it's unclear why *those* things – which sound very much like the forms of privilege and oppression central to Haslanger's view – aren't the truthmakers for the facts about gender (or at least an important component of the full truthmaking account).

Approaching Ásta's views with a focus on truthmakers also makes salient some other implications of her view. Cody's being a woman in the context of her grandmother's kitchen depends upon Stanley's perception of her doing the dishes. What happens if Stanley leaves the room, or turns his attention to something else? Does Cody stop being a woman, simply because Stanley is focused on something else? The concern, then, is that conferrals may not be enough to *sustain* the facts about gender, even if they manage to bring them about.[81]

Ásta might reply by pointing out that in the example, none of the features that are socially significant vis-à-vis gender are of any significance, since those with standing are paying no attention to the base properties. So it's appropriate that there isn't any gender in the scenario. After all, on any social constructionist view, if some feature stops being socially significant, the socially constructed property goes away. (Similarly, when umpires go on strike, there are no more strikes.) Given how significant gender is in the actual world, it's hard to imagine genuine contexts in which gender-related conferrals really don't exist at all. (On Witt's [2011: 10–11] view, for instance, gender is *uniessential*: "the numerous social positions that we occupy are systematically unified by our gender.") Of course, the case where Stanley stops paying attention isn't a case where his *disposition* to attach social significance to doing the dishes goes away. And one might think that so long as the dispositions to attach significance are there, so

---

[80] I see a similar line of thought in Roth (2021). For Ásta's response see her 2021.

[81] See also Griffith's (2020a) concerns about Ásta's individualistic methodology.

too is the social significance. And that is to shift the metaphysical burden away from the conferrals themselves and onto something else: a disposition to confer in certain ways in certain contexts. In any event, the project of articulating what we take to be true when it comes to gender, and what sustains it, must accompany our attention to what's needed in our ontology to make these claims true.

7 Conclusion

Theorizing about truthmaking isn't the only way to explore metaphysical and ontological questions. Lewis's modal realism, Haslanger's social constructionism, and Ásta's conferralism are all metaphysical views formulated without explicit attention to truthmaking as such. But this doesn't mean, of course, that their views have no implications for truthmaking. What truthmaker theory provides is a systematic and uniform perspective from which to interrogate ontological questions, wherever they may arise. Importantly, this perspective allows us to explore the metaphysical dimensions of the social side of reality in exactly the same way as we can explore the metaphysical dimensions of the nonsocial side of reality. As a result, truthmaker theory avoids Barnes's (2014) charge against other metaphysical programs that they cannot regard social metaphysics as a substantive source of inquiry. Within any domain where we can find truth – realist or not, social or not – there are important questions concerning what the ontological grounds are for those truths. Metaphysics and ontology aren't limited to the realm of the fundamental, and neither is truthmaking.

My goal in this Element has been to introduce the fundamental questions that all truthmaker theorists must engage, and then highlight how truthmaking arguments can be put to work in various domains. I explored three – time, modality, and social construction – but truthmaker theory can tackle ontological questions in any arena. Recent work on truthmaking has explored, for example, mathematics (Donaldson 2020), causality (Anjum and Mumford 2014), metaethics (Akhlaghi 2022), and emergence (Morris 2018). What ties each of these inquiries together is a commitment to the idea that by probing the thesis that truth depends on reality, we can arrive at a more perspicuous perspective on ontology and how it connects to what we take to be true.

References

Akhlaghi, Farbod. 2022. Non-realist cognitivism, truthmaking, and ontological cheating. *Ethics* 132: 291–321. https://doi.org/10.1086/716872.

Alcoff, Linda Martín. 2006. *Visible Identities: Race, Gender, and the Self*. Oxford: Oxford University Press. https://doi.org/10.1093/0195137345.001.0001.

Andreasen, Robin O. 2000. Race: biological reality or social construct? *Philosophy of Science* 67 (Supplement): S653–S666. https://doi.org/10.1086/392853.

Anjum, Rani Lill, and Stephen Mumford. 2014. Powers as causal truthmakers. *Disputatio* 4: 5–31.

Appiah, Kwame Anthony. 1992. *In My Father's House: Africa in the Philosophy of Culture*. New York: Oxford University Press.

Aristotle. 1984. *Categories*, trans. J. L. Ackrill. In *The Complete Works of Aristotle, Volume One*, ed. Jonathan Barnes, 3–24. Princeton, NJ: Princeton University Press. https://doi.org/10.1515/9781400835843.

Armstrong, David M. 1969. Dispositions are causes. *Analysis* 30: 23–26. https://doi.org/10.1093/analys/30.1.23.

1989. *Universals: An Opinionated Introduction*. Boulder, CO: Westview Press. https://doi.org/10.4324/9780429492617.

1997. *A World of States of Affairs*. Cambridge: Cambridge University Press. https://doi.org/10.1017/CBO9780511583308.

2000. Difficult cases in the theory of truthmaking. *The Monist* 83: 150–160. https://doi.org/10.5840/monist200083112.

2003. Truthmakers for modal truths. In *Real Metaphysics: Essays in Honour of D. H. Mellor*, eds. Hallvard Lillehammer and Gonzalo Rodriguez-Pereyra, 12–24. London: Routledge. https://doi.org/10.4324/9780203164297.

2004. *Truth and Truthmakers*. Cambridge: Cambridge University Press. https://doi.org/10.1017/CBO9780511487552.

2005. Reply to Simons and Mumford. *Australasian Journal of Philosophy* 83: 271–276. https://doi.org/10.1080/00048400500111196.

2006. Reply to Heil. *Australasian Journal of Philosophy* 84: 245–247. https://doi.org/10.1080/00048400600759084.

2007. Truthmakers for negative truths, and for truths of mere possibility. In *Metaphysics and Truthmakers*, ed. Jean-Maurice Monnoyer, 99–104. Frankfurt: Ontos Verlag. https://doi.org/10.1515/9783110326918.99.

Asay, Jamin. 2014. Truthmaker theory. In *Internet Encyclopedia of Philosophy*, eds. James Fieser and Bradley Dowden. www.iep.utm.edu/truth-ma.

2016a. The facts about truthmaking: an argument for truthmaking necessitarianism. *Ergo* 3: 493–500. https://doi.org/10.3998/ergo.1240 5314.0003.018.

2016b. Logic and/of truthmaking. In *Structural Analysis of Non-Classical Logics: The Proceedings of the Second Taiwan Philosophical Logic Colloquium*, eds. Syraya Chin-Mu Yang, Duen-Min Deng, and Hanti Lin, 37–55. Heidelberg: Springer. https://doi.org/10.1007/978-3-662-48357-2_3.

2018. We don't need no explanation. *Philosophical Studies* 175: 903–921. https://doi.org/10.1007/s11098-017-0898-1.

2020a. *A Theory of Truthmaking: Metaphysics, Ontology, and Reality.* Cambridge: Cambridge University Press. https://doi.org/10.1017/9781108 759465.

2020b. Truth(making) by convention. *American Philosophical Quarterly* 57: 117–127. www.jstor.org/stable/48570842.

Asay, Jamin, and Sam Baron. 2014. The hard road to presentism. *Pacific Philosophical Quarterly* 95: 314–335. https://doi.org/10.1111/papq .12029.

2020. Deflating deflationary truthmaking. *Philosophical Quarterly* 70: 1–21. https://doi.org/10.1093/pq/pqz036.

Ásta. 2018. *Categories We Live By: The Construction of Sex, Gender, Race, and Other Social Categories.* Oxford: Oxford University Press. https://doi.org/ 10.1093/oso/9780190256791.001.0001.

2021. *Categories We Live By*: reply to Alcoff, Butler, and Roth. *European Journal of Philosophy.* https://doi.org/10.1111/ejop.12744.

Austin, Christopher J. 2015. The truthmaking argument against dispositionalism. *Ratio* 28: 271–285. https://doi.org/10.1111/rati.12071.

Baia, Alex. 2012. Presentism and the grounding of truth. *Philosophical Studies* 159: 341–356. https://doi.org/10.1007/s11098-011-9711-8.

Barker, Stephen, and Mark Jago. 2012. Being positive about negative facts. *Philosophy and Phenomenological Research* 85: 117–138. https://doi.org/ 10.1111/j.1933-1592.2010.00479.x.

Barnes, Elizabeth. 2014. Going beyond the fundamental: feminism in contemporary metaphysics. *Proceedings of the Aristotelian Society* 114: 335–351. https://doi.org/10.1111/j.1467-9264.2014.00376.x.

2016. Realism and social structure. *Philosophical Studies* 174: 2417–2433. https://doi.org/10.1007/s11098-016-0743-y.

Baron, Sam. 2013a. Presentism, truth and supervenience. *Ratio* 26: 3–18. https://doi.org/10.1111/j.1467-9329.2011.00523.x.

2013b. Talking about the past. *Erkenntnis* 78: 547–560. https://doi.org/10 .1007/s10670-013-9434-7.

Beall, JC. 2000. On truthmakers for negative truths. *Australasian Journal of Philosophy* 78: 264–268. https://doi.org/10.1080/00048400012349551.

Berkeley, George. 1999. *Principles of Human Knowledge and Three Dialogues*. Ed. Howard Robinson. Oxford: Oxford University Press.

Bernstein, Sara. 2021. Could a middle level be the most fundamental? *Philosophical Studies* 178: 1065–1078. https://doi.org/10.1007/s11098-020-01484-1.

Bigelow, John. 1988. *The Reality of Numbers: A Physicalist's Philosophy of Mathematics*. Oxford: Clarendon Press.

    1996. Presentism and properties. *Philosophical Perspectives* 10: 35–52. https://doi.org/10.2307/2216235.

Blum, Lawrence. 2002. *"I'm Not a Racist, But . . . ": The Moral Quandary of Race*. Ithaca, NY: Cornell University Press. https://doi.org/10.7591/9781501701962.

Boghossian, Paul Artin. 1996. Analyticity reconsidered. *Noûs* 30: 360–391. https://doi.org/10.2307/2216275.

Briggs, R. A. 2012. Truthmaking without necessitation. *Synthese* 189: 11–28. https://doi.org/10.1007/s11229-012-0093-z.

Butler, Judith. 1990. *Gender Trouble: Feminism and the Subversion of Identity*. New York: Routledge. https://doi.org/10.4324/9780203824979.

Cameron, Ross Paul. 2008a. How to be a truthmaker maximalist. *Noûs* 42: 410–421. https://doi.org/10.1111/j.1468-0068.2008.00687.x.

    2008b. Truthmakers and modality. *Synthese* 164: 261–280. https://doi.org/10.1007/s11229-007-9225-2.

    2008c. Truthmakers and ontological commitment: or how to deal with complex objects and mathematical ontology without getting into trouble. *Philosophical Studies* 140: 1–18. https://doi.org/10.1007/s11098-008-9223-3.

    2011. Truthmaking for presentists. In *Oxford Studies in Metaphysics, Volume 6*, eds. Karen Bennett and Dean W. Zimmerman, 55–100. Oxford: Oxford University Press. https://doi.org/10.1093/acprof:oso/9780199603039.003.0002.

    2015. *The Moving Spotlight: An Essay on Time and Ontology*. Oxford: Oxford University Press. https://doi.org/10.1093/acprof:oso/9780198713296.001.0001.

Caplan, Ben, and David Sanson. 2011. Presentism and truthmaking. *Philosophy Compass* 6: 196–208. https://doi.org/10.1111/j.1747-9991.2010.00380.x.

Cheyne, Colin, and Charles Pigden. 2006. Negative truths from positive facts. *Australasian Journal of Philosophy* 84: 249–265. http://dx.doi.org/10.1080/00048400600759092.

David, Marian. 2009. Truth-making and correspondence. In *Truth and Truth-Making*, eds. E. J. Lowe and A. Rami, 137–157. Stocksfield: Acumen. https://doi.org/10.4324/9781315711683.

Dawson, Patrick. 2021. Hard presentism. *Synthese* 198: 8433–8461. https://doi.org/10.1007/s11229-020-02580-9.

Demos, Raphael. 1917. A discussion of a certain type of negative proposition. *Mind* 26: 188–196. https://doi.org/10.1093/mind/XXVI.1.188.

Donaldson, Thomas M. E. 2020. David Armstrong on the metaphysics of mathematics. *Dialectica* 74: 113–136. https://doi.org/10.48106/dial.v74.i4.05.

Du Bois, William Edward Burghardt. 1897. *The Conservation of Races*. Washington, DC: The American Negro Academy.

Dyke, Heather. 2007. Tenseless/non-modal truthmakers for tensed/modal truths. *Logique et Analyse* 50: 269–287. www.jstor.org/stable/44084866.

Epstein, Brian. 2015. *The Ant Trap: Rebuilding the Foundations of the Social Sciences*. Oxford: Oxford University Press. https://doi.org/10.1093/acprof:oso/9780199381104.001.0001.

Gale, Richard M. 1976. *Negation and Non-Being*. Oxford: Blackwell.

Glasgow, Joshua. 2009. *A Theory of Race*. New York: Routledge. https://doi.org/10.4324/9780203880951.

——— 2019. Is race an illusion or a (very) basic reality? In *What Is Race? Four Philosophical Perspectives*, by Joshua Glasgow, Sally Haslanger, Chike Jeffers, and Quayshawn Spencer, 111–149. Oxford: Oxford University Press. https://doi.org/10.1093/oso/9780190610173.003.0005.

Glasgow, Joshua, and Jonathan M. Woodward. 2015. Basic racial realism. *Journal of the American Philosophical Association* 1: 449–466. https://doi.org/10.1017/apa.2015.7.

Goodman, Nelson. 1983. *Fact, Fiction, and Forecast*. Fourth edition. Cambridge, MA: Harvard University Press.

Griffith, Aaron M. 2013. On some alleged truthmakers for negatives. *Thought* 1: 301–308. https://doi.org/10.1002/tht3.52.

——— 2015a. How negative truths are made true. *Synthese* 192: 317–335. https://doi.org/10.1007/s11229-014-0570-7.

——— 2015b. Towards a pluralist theory of truthmaking. *Erkenntnis* 80: 1157–1173. https://doi.org/10.1007/s10670-014-9717-7.

——— 2018a. Social construction: big-G grounding, small-g realization. *Philosophical Studies* 175: 241–260. https://doi.org/10.1007/s11098-017-0865-x.

2018b. Social construction and grounding. *Philosophy and Phenomenological Research* 97: 393–409. https://doi.org/10.1111/phpr.12376.

2020a. Individualistic and structural explanations in Ásta's *Categories We Live By. Journal of Social Ontology* 5: 251–260. https://doi.org/10.1515/jso-2020-2003.

2020b. Realizing race. *Philosophical Studies* 177: 1919–1934. https://doi.org/10.1007/s11098-019-01291-3.

2021. Presentism, truthmaking, and the nature of truth. *Analytic Philosophy*. https://doi.org/10.1111/phib.12226.

2022. The dependence of truth on being in Asay's *A Theory of Truthmaking. Asian Journal of Philosophy* 1(2): 1–6. https://doi.org/10.1007/s44204-021-00007-x.

Hacking, Ian. 1999. *The Social Construction of What?* Cambridge, MA: Harvard University Press.

Hardimon, Michael O. 2017. *Rethinking Race: The Case for Deflationary Realism*. Cambridge, MA: Harvard University Press.

Haslanger, Sally. 2000. Gender and race: (What) are they? (What) do we want them to be? *Noûs* 34: 31–55. https://doi.org/10.1111/0029-4624.00201.

2012. *Resisting Reality: Social Construction and Social Critique*. Oxford: Oxford University Press. https://doi.org/10.1093/acprof:oso/97801998 92631.001.0001.

2016. What is a (social) structural explanation? *Philosophical Studies* 173: 113–130. https://doi.org/10.1007/s11098-014-0434-5.

2019. Tracing the sociopolitical reality of race. In *What Is Race? Four Philosophical Perspectives*, by Joshua Glasgow, Sally Haslanger, Chike Jeffers, and Quayshawn Spencer, 4–37. Oxford: Oxford University Press. https://doi.org/10.1093/oso/9780190610173.003.0002.

Heathcote, Adrian. 2006. Truthmaking and the Gettier problem. In *Aspects of Knowing: Epistemological Essays*, ed. Stephen Hetherington, 151–167. Amsterdam: Elsevier.

Horwich, Paul. 1998. *Truth*. Second edition. Oxford: Clarendon Press. https://doi.org/10.1093/0198752237.001.0001

Hudson, Hud. 2007. Simples and gunk. *Philosophy Compass* 2: 291–302. https://doi.org/10.1111/j.1747-9991.2007.00068.x.

Inman, Ross D. 2017. *Substance and the Fundamentality of the Familiar: A Neo-Aristotelian Mereology*. New York: Routledge.

Jacobs, Jonathan D. 2010. A powers theory of modality: or, how I learned to stop worrying and reject possible worlds. *Philosophical Studies* 151: 227–248. https://doi.org/10.1007/s11098-009-9427-1.

2011. Powerful qualities, not pure powers. *The Monist* 94: 81–102. https://doi.org/10.5840/monist20119415.

Jago, Mark. 2012. The truthmaker non-maximalist's dilemma. *Mind* 121: 903–918. https://doi.org/10.1093/mind/fzs124.

2013. The cost of truthmaker maximalism. *Canadian Journal of Philosophy* 43: 460–474. https://doi.org/10.1080/00455091.2013.849059.

2018. *What Truth Is*. Oxford: Oxford University Press. https://doi.org/10.1093/oso/9780198823810.001.0001.

2020. A short argument for truthmaker maximalism. *Analysis* 80: 40–44. https://doi.org/10.1093/analys/anz064.

Jeffers, Chike. 2013. The cultural theory of race: yet another look at Du Bois's "The Conservation of Races." *Ethics* 123: 403–426. https://doi.org/10.1086/669566.

2019. Cultural constructionism. In *What Is Race? Four Philosophical Perspectives*, by Joshua Glasgow, Sally Haslanger, Chike Jeffers, and Quayshawn Spencer, 38–72. Oxford: Oxford University Press. https://doi.org/10.1093/oso/9780190610173.003.0003.

Jenkins, Katharine. 2016. Amelioration and inclusion: gender identity and the concept of *woman. Ethics* 126: 394–421. https://doi.org/10.1086/683535.

Kalhat, Javier. 2008. A critique of Armstrong's truthmaking account of possibility. *Acta Analytica* 23: 161–176. https://doi.org/10.1007/s12136-008-0027-z.

Keller, Phillipp. 2007. A world of truthmakers. In *Metaphysics and Truthmakers*, ed. J. Monnoyer, 105–156. Frankfurt: Ontos Verlag. https://doi.org/10.1515/9783110326918.

Khlentzos, Drew. 2000. "What in the world could correspond to truth?" *Logique et Analyse* 43: 109–144. www.jstor.org/stable/44074521.

Kierland, Brian, and Bradley Monton. 2007. Presentism and the objection from being-supervenience. *Australasian Journal of Philosophy* 85: 485–497. https://doi.org/10.1080/00048400701572279.

Kitamura, Naoaki. 2022. In defense of explanation-first truthmaking. *Asian Journal of Philosophy* 1(23): 1–9. https://doi.org/10.1007/s44204-022-00026-2.

Kripke, Saul A. 1972. Naming and necessity. In *Semantics of Natural Language*, eds. Donald Davidson and Gilbert Harman, 253–355. Dordrecht: D. Reidel.

Kukso, Boris. 2006. The reality of absences. *Australasian Journal of Philosophy* 84: 21–37. https://doi.org/10.1080/00048400600571679.

Lewis, David. 1976. The paradoxes of time travel. *American Philosophical Quarterly* 13: 145–152. www.jstor.org/stable/20009616.

1986. *On the Plurality of Worlds*. Oxford: Basil Blackwell.

1991. *Parts of Classes*. Oxford: Basil Blackwell.

1992. Critical notice [of D. M. Armstrong, *A Combinatorial Theory of Possibility*]. *Australasian Journal of Philosophy* 70: 211–224. https://doi.org/10.1080/00048409212345101.

1998. The truthmakers. *Times Literary Supplement* 4950: 30–33.

2001a. Forget about the "correspondence theory of truth." *Analysis* 61: 275–280. https://doi.org/10.1111/1467-8284.00305.

2001b. Truthmaking and difference-making. *Noûs* 35: 602–615. https://doi.org/10.1111/0029-4624.00354.

2003. Things qua truthmakers. In *Real Metaphysics: Essays in Honour of D. H. Mellor*, eds. Hallvard Lillehammer and Gonzalo Rodriguez-Pereyra, 25–42. London: Routledge. https://doi.org/10.4324/9780203164297

Lewis, David, and Gideon Rosen. 2003. Postscript to "Things qua truthmakers": negative existentials. In *Real Metaphysics: Essays in Honour of D. H. Mellor*, eds. Hallvard Lillehammer and Gonzalo Rodriguez-Pereyra, 39–42. London: Routledge. https://doi.org/10.4324/9780203164297

MacBride, Fraser. 2020. Truthmakers. In *The Stanford Encyclopedia of Philosophy* (Spring 2020 Edition), ed. Edward N. Zalta. https://plato.stanford.edu/archives/spr2020/entries/truthmakers.

Mallon, Ron. 2006. 'Race': normative, not metaphysical or semantic. *Ethics* 116: 525–551. https://doi.org/10.1086/500495.

Martin, C. B. 1996. How it is: entities, absences and voids. *Australasian Journal of Philosophy* 74: 57–65. https://doi.org/10.1080/00048409612347061.

Maurin, Anna-Sofia. 2022. *Properties* (Elements in Metaphysics). Cambridge: Cambridge University Press. https://doi.org/10.1017/9781009008938.

McDaniel, Kris. 2010. Parts and wholes. *Philosophy Compass* 5: 412–425. https://doi.org/10.1111/j.1747-9991.2009.00238.x.

Merricks, Trenton. 2001. *Objects and Persons*. Oxford: Clarendon Press. https://doi.org/10.1093/0199245363.001.0001.

2007. *Truth and Ontology*. Oxford: Clarendon Press. https://doi.org/10.1093/acprof:oso/9780199205233.001.0001.

Mikkola, Mari. 2015. Doing ontology and doing justice: what feminist philosophy can teach us about meta-metaphysics. *Inquiry* 58: 780–805. https://doi.org/10.1080/0020174X.2015.1083469.

2017. On the apparent antagonism between feminist and mainstream metaphysics. *Philosophical Studies* 174: 2435–2448. https://doi.org/10.1007/s11098-016-0732-1.

Mills, Charles W. 1997. *The Racial Contract*. Ithaca, NY: Cornell University Press.

1998. *Blackness Visible: Essays on Philosophy and Race*. Ithaca, NY: Cornell University Press. https://doi.org/10.7591/9781501702952.

Milne, Peter. 2005. Not every truth has a truthmaker. *Analysis* 65: 221–224. https://doi.org/10.1093/analys/65.3.221.

Molnar, George. 2000. Truthmakers for negative truths. *Australasian Journal of Philosophy* 78: 72–86. http://dx.doi.org/10.1080/00048400012349361.

Morris, Kevin. 2018. Truthmaking and the mysteries of emergence. In *Brute Facts*, eds. Elly Vintiadis and Constantinos Mekios, 113–129. Oxford: Oxford University Press. https://doi.org/10.1093/oso/9780198758600.003.0007.

Mulligan, Kevin, Peter Simons, and Barry Smith. 1984. Truth-makers. *Philosophy and Phenomenological Research* 44: 287–321. https://doi.org/10.2307/2107686.

Mumford, Stephen. 2007. Negative truth and falsehood. *Proceedings of the Aristotelian Society* 107 (Part 1): 45–71. https://doi.org/10.1111/j.1467-9264.2007.00211.x.

Outlaw, Lucius. 1996. "Conserve" races? In defense of W. E. B. Du Bois. In *W. E. B. Du Bois on Race and Culture: Philosophy, Politics, and Poetics*, eds. Bernard W. Bell, Emily Grosholz, and James B. Stewart, 15–37. New York: Routledge. https://doi.org/10.4324/9780203379509.

Paul, L. A. 2010. The puzzles of material constitution. *Philosophy Compass* 5: 579–590. https://doi.org/10.1111/j.1747-9991.2010.00302.x.

Pawl, Timothy. 2010. The possibility principle and the truthmakers for modal truths. *Australasian Journal of Philosophy* 88: 417–428. https://doi.org/10.1080/00048400903193353.

Plato. 1997. Cratylus. In *Complete Works*, trans. C. D. C. Reeve, ed. John M. Cooper, associate ed. D. S. Hutchinson, 101–156. Indianapolis, IN: Hackett Publishing Company.

Restall, Greg. 1996. Truthmakers, entailment and necessity. *Australasian Journal of Philosophy* 74: 331–340. https://doi.org/10.1080/00048409612347331.

Rettler, Bradley. 2016. The General Truthmaker View of ontological commitment. *Philosophical Studies* 173: 1405–1425. https://doi.org/10.1007/s11098-015-0526-x.

Rhoda, Alan R. 2009. Presentism, truthmakers, and God. *Pacific Philosophical Quarterly* 90: 41–62. https://doi.org/10.1111/j.1468-0114.2009.01328.x.

Rodriguez-Pereyra, Gonzalo. 2005. Why truthmakers. In *Truthmakers: The Contemporary Debate*, eds. Helen Beebee and Julian Dodd, 17–31. Oxford: Clarendon Press. https://doi.org/10.1093/acprof:oso/9780199283569.003.0002.

  2006a. Truthmaker Maximalism defended. *Analysis* 66: 260–264. https://doi.org/10.1093/analys/66.3.260.

  2006b. Truthmakers. *Philosophy Compass* 1: 186–200. https://doi.org/10.1111/j.1747-9991.2006.00018.x.

2006c. Truthmaking, entailment, and the conjunction thesis. *Mind* 115: 957–982. https://doi.org/10.1093/mind/fzl957.

2022. A defense of explanation-first truthmaking: some thoughts on Jamin Asay's *A Theory of Truthmaking. Asian Journal of Philosophy* 1(4): 1–6. https://doi.org/10.1007/s44204-022-00008-4.

Roth, Abraham Sesshu. 2021. The stability of social categories. *European Journal of Philosophy*. https://doi.org/10.1111/ejop.12746.

Russell, Bertrand. 1919a. On propositions: what they are and how they mean. *Proceedings of the Aristotelian Society Supplementary Volume* 2(1): 1–43. https://doi.org/10.1093/aristoteliansupp/2.1.1.

1919b. The philosophy of logical atomism [lectures 3–4]. *The Monist* 29: 32–63. https://doi.org/10.5840/monist191929120.

Saenz, Noël Blas. 2014. The world and truth about what is not. *Philosophical Quarterly* 64: 82–98. https://doi.org/10.1093/pq/pqt015.

2020. An account of truthmaking. *Synthese* 197: 3413–3435. https://doi.org/10.1007/s11229-018-1894-5.

Sanson, David, and Ben Caplan. 2010. The way things were. *Philosophy and Phenomenological Research* 81: 24–39. https://doi.org/10.1111/j.1933-1592.2010.00357.x.

Schaffer, Jonathan. 2008. Truthmaker commitments. *Philosophical Studies* 141: 7-19. https://doi.org/10.1007/s11098-008-9260-y.

2010. The least discerning and most promiscuous truthmaker. *Philosophical Quarterly* 60: 307–324. https://doi.org/10.1111/j.1467-9213.2009.612.x.

2017. Social construction as grounding; or: fundamentality for feminists, a reply to Barnes and Mikkola. *Philosophical Studies* 174: 2449–2465. https://doi.org/10.1007/s11098-016-0738-8.

Schipper, Arthur. 2018. Aboutness and negative truths: a modest strategy for truthmaker theorists. *Synthese* 195: 3685–3722. https://doi.org/10.1007/s11229-017-1396-x.

2020. Aboutness and ontology: a modest approach to truthmakers. *Philosophical Studies* 177: 505–533. https://doi.org/10.1007/s11098-018-1192-6.

2021. Fundamental truthmakers and non-fundamental truths. *Synthese* 198: 3073–3098. https://doi.org/10.1007/s11229-019-02266-x.

Schulte, Peter. 2011. Truthmakers: a tale of two explanatory projects. *Synthese* 181: 413–431. https://doi.org/10.1007/s11229-010-9716-4.

Searle, John R. 1995. *The Construction of Social Reality.* New York: Free Press.

Sider, Theodore. 2001. *Four-Dimensionalism: An Ontology of Persistence and Time.* Oxford: Clarendon Press. https://doi.org/10.1093/01992444 3X.001.0001.

Simons, Peter. 2005. Negatives, numbers, and necessity: some worries about Armstrong's version of truthmaking. *Australasian Journal of Philosophy* 83: 253–261. https://doi.org/10.1080/00048400500111162.

Simpson, Matthew. 2014. Defending truthmaker non-maximalism. *Thought* 3: 288–291. https://doi.org/10.1002/tht3.144.

Skiles, Alexander. 2014. Is there a dilemma for the truthmaker non-maximalist? *Synthese* 191: 3649–3659. https://doi.org/10.1007/s11229-014-0485-3.

Smith, Barry. 1999. Truthmaker realism. *Australasian Journal of Philosophy* 77: 274–291. https://doi.org/10.1080/00048409912349041.

Smith, Barry, and Jonathan Simon. 2007. Truthmaker explanations. In *Metaphysics and Truthmakers*, ed. Jean-Maurice Monnoyer, 79–98. Frankfurt: Ontos Verlag. https://doi.org/10.1515/9783110326918.

Sorensen, Roy. 2001. *Vagueness and Contradiction*. Oxford: Clarendon Press.

Spencer, Quayshawn. 2019a. How to be a biological racial realist. In *What Is Race? Four Philosophical Perspectives*, by Joshua Glasgow, Sally Haslanger, Chike Jeffers, and Quayshawn Spencer, 73–110. Oxford: Oxford University Press. https://doi.org/10.1093/oso/9780190610173.003.0004.

2019b. Spencer's reply to Glasgow, Haslanger, and Jeffers. In *What Is Race? Four Philosophical Perspectives*, by Joshua Glasgow, Sally Haslanger, Chike Jeffers, and Quayshawn Spencer, 203–244. Oxford: Oxford University Press. https://doi.org/10.1093/oso/9780190610173.003.0008.

Tahko, Tuomas E. 2021. *Unity of Science* (Elements in the Philosophy of Science). Cambridge: Cambridge University Press. https://doi.org/10.1017/9781108581417.

Tallant, Jonathan. 2013. Time. *Analysis* 73: 369–379. https://doi.org/10.1093/analys/ant022.

2018. *Truth and the World: An Explanationist Theory*. London: Routledge. https://doi.org/10.4324/9781315143491.

Tallant, Jonathan, and David Ingram. 2015. Nefarious presentism. *Philosophical Quarterly* 65: 355–371. https://doi.org/10.1093/pq/pqu095.

2020. A defence of Lucretian presentism. *Australasian Journal of Philosophy* 98: 675–690. https://doi.org/10.1080/00048402.2019.1697709.

Taylor, Elanor. In press. Substantive social metaphysics. *Philosophers' Imprint*. https://doi.org/10.3998/phimp.1972.

Taylor, Paul C. 2013. *Race: A Philosophical Introduction*. Second edition. Cambridge: Polity.

Thomasson, Amie L. 2003. Foundations for a social ontology. *ProtoSociology* 18/19: 269–290. https://doi.org/10.5840/protosociology200318/199.

2009. Social entities. In *The Routledge Companion to Metaphysics*, eds. Robin Le Poidevin, Peter Simons, Andrew McGonigal, and Ross

P. Cameron, 545–554. London: Routledge. https://doi.org/10.4324/9780203879306.

2020. *Norms and Necessity.* Oxford: Oxford University Press. https://doi.org/10.1093/oso/9780190098193.001.0001.

Torrengo, Giuliano. 2014. Ostrich presentism. *Philosophical Studies* 170: 255–276. https://doi.org/10.1007/s11098-013-0211-x.

van Inwagen, Peter. 1990. *Material Beings*. Ithaca, NY: Cornell University Press. https://doi.org/10.7591/9781501713033.

Veber, Michael. 2008. How to derive a "not" from an "is": a defense of the incompatibility view of negative truths. *Metaphysica* 9: 79–91. https://doi.org/10.1007/s12133-008-0024-0.

Witt, Charlotte. 2011. *The Metaphysics of Gender.* Oxford: Oxford University Press. https://doi.org/10.1093/acprof:oso/9780199740413.001.0001.

Zack, Naomi. 1993. *Race and Mixed Race*. Philadelphia, PA: Temple University Press.

1998. *Thinking about Race*. Belmont, CA: Wadsworth.

Acknowledgments

I dedicate this book to my parents, Fred and Jo Marie Asay. My family as always could not have been more supportive: thank you to Emily, Charlie, and Sid for all of your love and encouragement. My thanks also go to Tuomas Tahko, who edits the series, for his support on the project, and to the production team at Cambridge. My thinking about truthmaking is the product of fifteen years of engagement with many wonderful interlocutors, and there are simply too many of you to name at this point. But I am still incredibly grateful for the contributions you have made. The research presented here was partially supported by a grant from the Research Grants Council of the Hong Kong Special Administrative Region (project number HKU 17618420), and funding from the University of Hong Kong's Outstanding Young Researcher Award.

Cambridge Elements

Metaphysics

Tuomas E. Tahko
University of Bristol

Tuomas E. Tahko is Professor of Metaphysics of Science at the University of Bristol, UK. Tahko specializes in contemporary analytic metaphysics, with an emphasis on methodological and epistemic issues: 'meta-metaphysics'. He also works at the interface of metaphysics and philosophy of science: 'metaphysics of science'. Tahko is the author of *Unity of Science* (Cambridge University Press, 2021, *Elements in Philosophy of Science*), *An Introduction to Metametaphysics* (Cambridge University Press, 2015) and editor of *Contemporary Aristotelian Metaphysics* (Cambridge University Press, 2012).

About the series

This highly accessible series of Elements provides brief but comprehensive introductions to the most central topics in metaphysics. Many of the Elements also go into considerable depth, so the series will appeal to both students and academics. Some Elements bridge the gaps between metaphysics, philosophy of science, and epistemology.

Cambridge Elements ≡

Metaphysics

A full series listing is available at: www.cambridge.org/EMPH